Caribbean Renewal
Tackling Fiscal and Debt Challenges

EDITORS
Charles Amo-Yartey and Therese Turner-Jones

INTERNATIONAL MONETARY FUND

Cover design: IMF Multimedia Services Division

Cataloging-in-Publication Data
Joint Bank-Fund Library

Caribbean renewal : tackling fiscal and debt challenges / edited by Charles, Amo-Yartey and Therese Turner-Jones. – Washington, D.C. : International Monetary Fund, c2014.
p. ; cm.

Includes bibliographical references and index.
ISBN: 978-1-48436-914-2

1. Fiscal policy—Caribbean Area. 2. Debts, Public—Caribbean Area. I. Yartey, Charles Amo. II. Turner-Jones, Therese. III. International Monetary Fund.

HJ844.3.C37 2014

Please send orders to:
International Monetary Fund, Publication Services
P.O. Box 92780, Washington, DC 20090, U.S.A.
Tel.: (202) 623-7430 Fax: (202) 623-7201
E-mail: publications@imf.org
Internet: www.elibrary.imf.org
www.imfbookstore.org

Contents

Acronyms

BAICO	British American Insurance Company
CANEC-DMAS	Canada Eastern Caribbean Debt Management Advisory Service
CAPB	cyclically adjusted primary balance
CCMF	Caribbean Center for Money and Finance
CEMAC	Central African Economic and Monetary Community
CIDA	Canadian International Development Agency
CLICO	Colonial Life Insurance Company
FDI	foreign direct investment
ECCB	Eastern Caribbean Central Bank
ECCU	Eastern Caribbean Currency Union
EMU	European Monetary Union
EU	European Union
HIPC	Heavily Indebted Poor Countries Initiative
MDG	Millennium Development Goal
NPV	net present value
OECD	Organization for Economic Co-operation and Development
MDRI	Multilateral Debt Relief Initiative
SACU	Southern African Customs Union
SOE	state-owned enterprises
VAT	value-added tax
WAEMU	West African Economic and Monetary Union

Foreword

It is indeed a pleasure and honor to be a part of this effort to produce an important analysis of such quality on the fiscal and debt challenges of the Caribbean. This book culminates more than a year's collaboration and preparation by teams in the Caribbean II Division of the IMF's Western Hemisphere Department. It also comes at an important time for the IMF, where work on small states is receiving more attention. The IMF is working to promote deeper understanding of small countries' economic concerns and ways their economic problems can be addressed in a manner that suits their idiosyncratic nature.

This book also follows a series of regional conferences the IMF has been hosting around the world to tackle small states' issues. In Port of Spain, Trinidad and Tobago in September 2012, close to one hundred high-level officials from around the CARICOM region came together to discuss their economic concerns with the IMF and other development partner participants. This was the first time in many years that prime ministers, central bank governors, and other key policymakers in the Caribbean gathered in one space to deal with some of the most pressing issues facing the region. It is no surprise that urgency for more action was underscored at the event, given the impact of the 2008 global crisis on the Caribbean. The region was by far one of the worst hit by the crisis, given its openness and its dependence for growth on international tourism and trade. It was in this context that the IMF presentation on fiscal issues garnered attention.

This book synthesizes the issues discussed in Trinidad and Tobago in 2012 and elaborates on the theoretical underpinnings supporting the IMF recommendations for the Caribbean at this juncture. The chapters draw on a broad and relevant swath of academic literature as well as experiences from around the world. The real challenge for the Caribbean is to not just read this book and admire its analytics but to find the willingness to adopt a new policy framework, one that will help sustain public finances in such a manner that transparency, predictability of fiscal policy, and debt sustainability can all be achieved. This is a tall order, but I have every expectation that the region will rise to the challenge and reach its goals in this important area of economic management. There has never been a more urgent time to address this challenge than now.

Min Zhu
Deputy Managing Director
International Monetary Fund

Acknowledgments

The authors would like to acknowledge the valuable comments and suggestions provided on earlier versions of the chapters in this book by the Caribbean authorities during the 2012 high-level forum in Port of Spain, Trinidad and Tobago. We also thank the Caribbean academics and policymakers who attended conferences and seminars held in the Caribbean (the 2011 Caribbean Centre for Money and Finance [CCMF] Annual Monetary Studies Conference and the 2013 Sir Arthur Lewis Institute for Social and Economic Studies [SALISES] conferences in Barbados) for comments and suggestions.

We are extremely grateful to our external peer reviewers, Dr. Winston Moore of the University of the West Indies, Cave Hill, Barbados; and Prof. Olajide Oladipo of York College of the City University of New York. We are also indebted to current and former colleagues at the IMF—particularly Gilbert Terrier, Luis Breuer, Marcelo Estevao, Charles Kramer, and Adrienne Cheasty—for comments and guidance on previous versions of the chapters of this book. Thanks are also due to Genevieve Lindow for excellent research assistance. The authors would like to thank Marc DeFrancis for his skillful editing of the book and Sean Culhane, Joanne Johnson, and Patricia Loo of the Communications Department of the IMF for coordinating the book's production.

The views expressed in the book, as well as any errors, are the sole responsibility of the authors and do not necessarily reflect the views of the Caribbean authorities, the Executive Directors of the IMF, or other members of the IMF staff.

About the Authors

Charles Amo-Yartey is a senior economist in the Caribbean II Division of the Western Hemisphere Department of the IMF. He holds a Ph.D. in economics from the University of Cambridge, which he attended as a Gates Scholar. He is the author of the book, *Stock Market Development in Africa,* published by VDM Verlag, and has published in leading journals including *Applied Economics, Applied Financial Economics,* and *the Journal of International Trade and Economic Development.*

Yehenew Endegnanew is a Ph.D. candidate in economics in the International Doctorate of Economic Analysis (IDEA) program at the Universitat Autonoma de Barcelona (UAB). His research interests include fiscal policy, time series analysis, monetary policy, and macroeconomics.

Machiko Narita is an economist (as part of the IMF's Economist Program) in the Asian Division at the IMF Institute for Capacity Development. She has worked in the Caribbean II Division of the Western Hemisphere Department. She holds a Ph.D. in economics from the University of Minnesota. Her research interest includes consumption, housing, resource reallocation, aggregate productivity, fiscal policy, and macroeconomics.

Garth Peron Nicholls is a senior economist in the South America II Division of the Western Hemisphere Department of the IMF. He holds a Ph.D. in economics from the University of the West Indies (UWI). He is the coauthor of the book, *The Regulation of Non-bank Financial Institutions in the Eastern Caribbean Currency Union,* published by the UWI. Before joining the IMF, he was Senior Director of Research at the Eastern Caribbean Central Bank. His research interests include monetary policy, financial regulation, economic growth, fiscal policy and pension reform.

Joel Chiedu Okwuokei is an economist in the Caribbean II Division of the Western Hemisphere Department of the IMF. He holds a Ph.D. in economics from the University of Benin, Nigeria. Before joining the IMF, he worked with the federal government of Nigeria for several years. His research interests include economic growth, fiscal policy, monetary policy, and environmental policy.

Alexandra Peter is an economist (as part of the IMF's Economist Program) in the Financial Supervision and Regulation Division of the Monetary and Capital Markets Department of the IMF. She worked in the Caribbean II Division of the Western Hemisphere Department prior to her current assignment. She holds a Ph.D. in economics from the University of Bonn. Her research interests include fiscal and monetary policy, financial regulation, and financial stability.

Therese Turner-Jones is a former deputy division chief in the Caribbean II Division of the Western Hemisphere Department of the IMF. She holds a master's degree in economics from the University of East Anglia (United Kingdom). She worked at the IMF for more than 20 years (1993–2013) in various positions and departments, including at the Executive Board. In May 2013, she assumed the position as Country Representative for the Inter-American Development Bank in Jamaica.

CHAPTER 1

Fiscal Consolidation and Debt Reduction in the Caribbean: An Overview

CHARLES AMO-YARTEY AND THERESE TURNER-JONES

Caribbean economies face high and rising debt-to-GDP ratios that jeopardize prospects for medium-term debt sustainability and growth. In 2011, the region's overall public sector debt was estimated at about 70 percent of regional GDP (Figure 1.1). Interest payments on the existing debt stock in the most highly indebted countries with rising debt ratios are already in the range of 16 percent to 42 percent of total revenues. In addition, high amortization exposes some countries to considerable roll-over risk that could trigger a fiscal crisis.

Structural fiscal problems have resulted in a sizable accumulation of debt. Between 1997 and 2004, the average debt-to-GDP ratio in the region increased from 54 percent to 84 percent, driven mainly by deteriorating primary balances. Successive years of fiscal deficit, public enterprise borrowing, and off-balance-sheet spending, including financial sector bailouts, all contributed to high debt levels. Prior to the onset of the global crisis, moderate growth rates helped some countries to broadly stabilize and reduce their debt ratios, albeit at high levels.

The global financial crisis worsened the already high debt burdens in the Caribbean. The crisis and the subsequent slow recovery in advanced countries had a significant adverse effect on the Caribbean, undermining growth in the largely tourism-dependent economies and exposing balance sheet vulnerabilities built up over many years. These vulnerabilities originated from a strategy of increasing public spending to counteract declining trade performance, partly due to the erosion of trade preferences, and rebuilding costs after frequent natural disasters. As a result, the ratio of public debt to GDP increased by about 15 percentage points between 2008 and 2010 in tourism-dependent economies. By contrast, Caribbean commodity exporters rebounded rapidly after the crisis, buoyed by high commodity prices, and their debt ratios have stabilized at relatively low levels.

Past attempts at tackling high debt in the region have not yielded lasting gains. Several countries have made attempts at reducing debt, mainly through ad hoc restructuring or fiscal consolidation. Since most countries have not adopted comprehensive economic reforms to complement these adjustment efforts, the initial gains have not been sustained. Further, because of their middle-income status, the

Figure 1.1 The Caribbean: Total Government Debt, 1997–2011 *(weighted average; percent of GDP)*

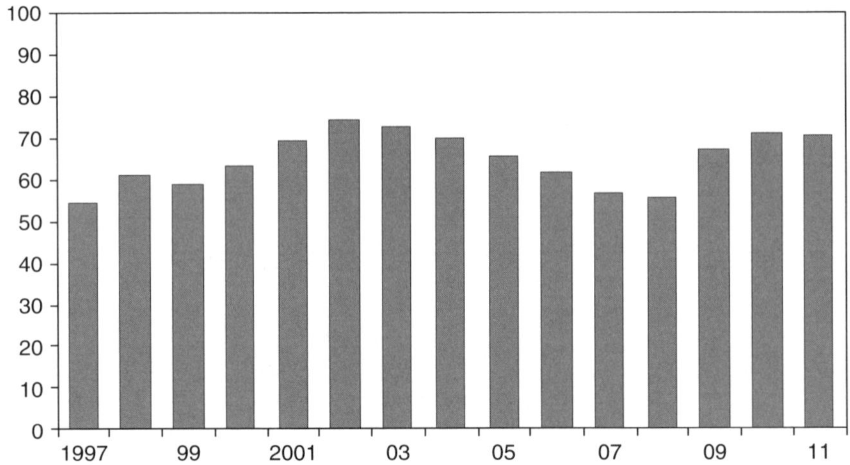

Source: Author's calculations.

majority of the region's nations have not been able to benefit from international debt relief. Moreover, only a few Caribbean countries still qualify for concessional borrowing at the World Bank. At the same time, their small size and geographical location makes them highly vulnerable to a host of frequent shocks, against which it is costly to insure. As a result, Caribbean economies have had a silent debt crisis for the past two decades, contributing to a high debt–low growth trap.

This book examines the challenges of fiscal consolidation and debt reduction in the Caribbean. It looks at the problem of high debt in the region, examines the reasons for this debt, and discusses policy options for improving debt sustainability, including fiscal consolidation. The book examines empirically the factors underlying global large debt reduction episodes to draw important policy lessons for the Caribbean. It also reviews the literature on successful fiscal consolidation experiences and provides an overview of past and current consolidation efforts in the Caribbean region.

More specifically, the book attempts to address the following questions:

- What are the impacts of the global financial crisis on fiscal performance and debt levels in the Caribbean?
- How large are fiscal multipliers in the region?
- Has there been fiscal consolidation?
- What policies are the region's countries currently pursuing to reduce debt?
- What are the challenges to fiscal consolidation?
- Is there an optimal level of debt for the region?
- What is the impact of fiscal consolidation on the current account in the region?

- What lessons can these countries draw from successful fiscal consolidation and large debt reduction experiences around the world?
- What is the impact of fiscal policy rules on fiscal performance in the region?
- Is fiscal consolidation enough to significantly reduce the debt levels? What other policy options may be available?

In an environment where the level of public debt remains high, reducing public debt is crucial to reduce vulnerabilities. How then can the Caribbean countries lower their debt-to-GDP ratio? What factors explain the success of public debt reduction, and why are some countries able to reduce public debt to prudent levels faster than others? To answer these questions, this book analyzes past global large debt reduction episodes in order to yield relevant policy lessons for the Caribbean. The analyses show that major debt reductions are mainly driven by decisive and lasting fiscal consolidation efforts focused on reducing government expenditure. In addition, robust real GDP growth increases the likelihood of a major debt reduction because it helps countries grow their way out of indebtedness.

Since growth in the current environment is virtually nonexistent, significant fiscal consolidation is inevitable. Based on a survey of country experiences, fiscal consolidation based on expenditure reductions tends to be more effective than tax-based consolidations. However, for countries with large adjustment needs, fiscal consolidation may need to be a balanced combination of spending cuts and revenue increases (Baldacci, Gupta, Mulas-Granados, 2010). Given the already sizable public sector in Caribbean countries, most of the fiscal consolidation would have to be done by restraining spending while implementing measures to boost revenues. Fiscal consolidation needs to be complemented by a comprehensive strategy to reduce public debt, including tax policy reforms, improvements in the efficiency of government spending, containment of contingent liabilities, rationalization of the public sector, active debt management and debt restructuring, and growth-enhancing structural reforms.

THE SOCIAL, ECONOMIC, AND POLITICAL CONTEXT

This section briefly discusses the social, economic, and political setting of the Caribbean to identify the main constraints to macroeconomic policy making in the region. Knowledge of the setting within which macroeconomic policies will take place is essential in order to design and implement successful fiscal consolidation and debt reduction strategies.

The Caribbean enjoys a relatively high GDP per capita, well-developed social indicators, and a long history of political stability (see Table 1.1). The region performs relatively well on most social development indicators, even though unemployment and poverty levels are rising. Life expectancy, for instance, averages more than 75 years, higher than the average for middle-income countries. Significant progress has been made in reaching the objectives of the millennium

TABLE 1.1

The Caribbean: Selected Social and Economic Indicators, 2012

	GDP (US$, billions)	Population (millions)	GDP per Capita (US$)	Real GDP Growth (percent)	Trade Openness (X+M, % of GDP)	Poverty Rate[a] (percent)	Unemployment Rate[a] (percent)	Sovereign Credit Rating[b]
The Caribbean[c]	**67.6**	**7.0**	**9,666**	**1.0**	**165.5**	**...**	**...**	**...**
The Bahamas	8.0	0.4	22,833	2.5	102.4	9.3	14.2	BBB+
Barbados	4.5	0.3	16,152	0.0	91.9	18.3	11.2	BBB–
Belize	1.6	0.3	4,536	5.3	130.2	43.0	16.1	C
Guyana	2.8	0.8	3,596	3.3	145.6	...	...	...
Jamaica	15.2	2.8	5,541	0.1	79.7	9.9	13.7	B–
Suriname	4.7	0.5	8,686	4.5	110.0	...	7.6	BB–
Trinidad and Tobago	25.3	1.3	19,018	0.4	97.7	17.0	5.3	A–
Eastern Caribbean Currency Union[d]	5.6	0.6	8,945	0.0	94.7	...	...	...
Anguilla	0.3	0.0	16,891	–2.2	898.3	...	...	...
Antigua and Barbuda	1.2	0.1	13,429	1.6	104.5	18.3	16.2	...
Dominica	0.5	0.1	7,022	0.4	92.8	28.8	14.0	...
Grenada	0.8	0.1	7,496	–0.8	77.0	37.7	24.9	B–
Montserrat	0.1	0.0	11,861	1.1	272.8	...	...	...
St. Kitts and Nevis	0.7	0.1	12,804	–0.9	84.9	21.8	5.1	...
St. Lucia	1.2	0.2	7,276	–0.4	111.0	28.8	21.2	...
St. Vincent and the Grenadines	0.7	0.1	6,489	0.5	82.9	30.2	18.8	B+

Sources: Bloomberg, L.P.; Caribbean Development Bank Country Poverty Assessments; IMF, World Economic Outlook database; International Labour Organization; World Bank, World Development Indicators; and authors' calculations.

[a]Latest available data.

[b]Median ratings published by Moody's, Standard and Poor's, and Fitch Ratings.

[c]The Caribbean includes The Bahamas, Barbados, Belize, Guyana, Jamaica, Suriname, Trinidad and Tobago, and the Eastern Caribbean Currency Union (ECCU). GDP and population are sums of individual countries. Real GDP growth and trade openness are simple averages.

[d]ECCU includes Anguilla, Antigua and Barbuda, Dominica, Grenada, Montserrat, St. Kitts and Nevis, St. Lucia, and St. Vincent and the Grenadines.

development goals. Primary school enrollment is close to 100 percent, and the average tuberculosis detection rate has increased to close to 99 percent in the Eastern Caribbean Currency Union (ECCU). Additionally, the proportion of seats held by women in national parliaments in the Caribbean has increased significantly (Jack and Wendell, 2013).

Despite this progress, poverty levels and unemployment, which are likely to have been exacerbated by the global financial crisis, remain stubbornly high. Country poverty assessment studies conducted by the Caribbean Development Bank show that the collapse of the sugar and banana industries has worsened poverty levels in rural communities even though the levels are not as high as in some urban communities (Jack and Wendell, 2013). Labor force survey data are limited in the Caribbean, but anecdotal evidence suggests that the unemployment rates increased during the global financial crisis.

Policy decision making in most Caribbean countries is guided by social partnership arrangements, under which the government, the private sector, and labor unions meet to discuss and agree on policies of national concern. As a result, the implementation of macroeconomic programs needs the support of all the major stakeholders in the economy. There are also other elements of the social fabric of the Caribbean that could help improve economic performance. Generally, greater social homogeneity and cohesion in a country lead to greater flexibility and decision-making efficiency and greater openness to change, resulting in greater gains for the country as a whole (Streeten, 1993). For instance, greater social homogeneity should enable adjustment to shocks to be more promptly handled because the shifting of adjustment onto other social groups is less feasible (Alesina and Drazen, 1991).

On the economic front, domestic markets in the Caribbean are small, so the level of domestic demand lies below the minimum efficient scale of output (Armstrong and others, 1993). Due to their small size, these countries are usually disadvantageous as locations for extensive industrial activities, especially those that could substantially raise growth. The small domestic market is less conducive for the development of indigenous technologies, limiting the growth of research and development, technical progress, and technology acquisition. In addition, a small domestic market does not allow competitive firms to emerge within the Caribbean because of the limited number of participants involved in any economic activity. As a result, prices of goods are generally higher in the Caribbean than in other regions (Armstrong and others, 1993). The relatively small population tends to make labor very scarce in the Caribbean. As a result, output in the region is usually enhanced through the accumulation of human or physical capital rather than through employment (Bhaduri, Mukherji, and Sengupta, 1982). The small size of domestic markets and the scarcity of labor tend to narrow the structure of domestic output, making these countries dependent on a small number of activities and hampering the potential to implement import substitution industrialization strategies. This leaves them exposed to exogenous shocks.

Exports and export markets are also narrow, due in part to the narrowness of their domestic production structures. The need for specialization tends to limit export-oriented domestic output to just a few products. Tourism and financial services are the main service sectors, normally complemented by an uncompetitive agricultural sector. Offshore financial services have become an important sector in the Caribbean due to their strategic location and enabling local laws. Highly liberalized financial systems based on lax regulatory standards or strong supervisory frameworks have been a major attraction in the emergence of the Caribbean as an offshore financial center. The export specialization of Caribbean countries renders them vulnerable to external shocks, and this vulnerability is worsened by the fact that reliance is on export markets in just a few countries (Armstrong and others, 1998).

The Caribbean continues to gain from its proximity to the U.S. market and historical ties to the United Kingdom in the areas of tourism and financial services. At the same time, this trade openness and these strong ties imply that global economic crises are easily transmitted to the Caribbean. The importance of tradable goods to these economies necessitates their pursuit of highly open trading regimes. Consequently, import barriers are less important in the Caribbean than in other regions (Selwyn, 1975). There is a substantial asymmetry between domestic production patterns and consumption in the Caribbean, making the proportion of imports in domestic consumption very high. This feature has led some researchers (see Worrel, 2012) to argue that currency devaluation may not be beneficial to the Caribbean.[1]

The small size of domestic economies, the negligible nontradable sector, and the fact that the development of nontraditional exports is hampered by domestic constraints rather than external obstacles have led many of these countries to adopt a fixed exchange rate regime (either soft or hard pegs). The bigger economies of the region have moved over time from soft to hard pegs. Barbados, The Bahamas, and Belize have hard pegs, while Guyana, Suriname and Trinidad and Tobago have opted for soft pegs. Jamaica, in principle, currently has a flexible exchange rate regime (ECLAC, 2003). Within the hard peg category, some countries have explicitly opted for a currency union. This is the case of the small economies of the Eastern Caribbean (Anguilla, Antigua and Barbuda, Dominica, Montserrat, St. Kitts and Nevis, St. Lucia, and St. Vincent and the Grenadines), following the formation of the Eastern Caribbean Currency Union (ECCU) and the parallel creation of the Eastern Caribbean Central Bank in 1983.

The choice of exchange rate regime was also a direct consequence of the development model adopted by Caribbean economies following their political independence. The main features of the development model include the attraction of capital flows, fiscal incentives, protectionism, and the development of exports to the industrialized world. In most of the Caribbean, the exchange rate is a nominal anchor and thus an avenue to control costs and prices and import credibility (ECLAC, 2003). The fixed exchange rate regime combined with the hard foreign currency constraints makes fiscal policy the main tool of macroeconomic management.

Labor markets in the Caribbean are very rigid. Typically, the indigenous labor force tends to be highly protected, or custom makes it socially difficult for private

[1]Assessing the impact of devaluation on Caribbean economies is beyond the scope of this book.

sector managers to fire them. This creates an inflexible indigenous labor force, which tends to be employed mainly in central government, parastatals, or other relatively secure jobs (Imam, 2010). As a result, a large chunk of the indigenous population in the region is not employable by market standards, and there is high unemployment or underemployment. The public sector often then acts as the employer of last resort and the bureaucracy becomes overstaffed with poorly trained individuals (see also Rodrik, 1998).

The institutional framework governing industrial relations in the region varies from a model of statutory intervention, as observed in Trinidad and Tobago, to a voluntaristic model, as followed in Barbados (Downes, Mamingi, and Antoine, 2000). Across the region, there exist strong labor unions with significant membership in strategic sectors of the economy (Rama, 1995). Strong labor unions have emerged from the culture of trade unionism and the need to maintain labor and economic stability in order to propel economic development. Nevertheless, there are differences among the institutional frameworks within the region. For example, Jamaica and Trinidad and Tobago are known to have much more militant trade union movements than Barbados and Belize (Downes, Mamingi, and Antoine, 2000). In The Bahamas, Guyana, and Trinidad and Tobago, there are statutory provisions making all collective agreements legally enforceable, while in Barbados there is no such provision. There are no legal provisions for the recognition of trade unions in Barbados, Belize, and Guyana.

The political system in most of the Caribbean was inherited from the United Kingdom, a consequence of the region's colonial history. This colonial legacy has served the Caribbean well, delivering stable democracies with relatively smooth transitions and high participation rates in national political affairs. However, concerns remain in many countries about the impact of this system on economic policy making and development, since the current system appears to worsen economic cycles and has resulted in a persistent increase in public debt levels in many countries (Jack and Samuel, 2013). Empirical evidence shows that good economic performance ahead of elections tends to increase the probability of success of the incumbent (Paldam, 1997). Jack and Samuel (2013) argue that most Caribbean governments tend to focus on short-term policy solutions, paying little attention to long-term planning that would promote sustained economic growth. Even though some recent attempts have been made to reform the political system, foster domestic electoral reform, and move toward greater regional political integration, these efforts have been largely unsuccessful.

THE DANGERS OF HIGH DEBT LEVELS

High public debt raises the risk of a fiscal crisis and also imposes costs on the economy by keeping borrowing costs high, discouraging private investment, and constraining fiscal flexibility. Theoretically, high public debt is expected to reduce long-term economic growth through a number of channels:

- Higher public debt crowds out private sector investment and lowers economic growth. It requires higher taxes to service the debt, which reduces investment and growth. Further increases in government expenditure financed by higher debt from already elevated levels are likely to be self-defeating, leading to lower long-term growth, as public sector debt crowds out private investment.

- Higher debt can also increase roll-over risks. It is likely to increase the public sector borrowing requirement, because a higher debt ratio would require a larger share of GDP to service the debt and investors are likely both to demand higher interest rates and to switch to shorter maturities as the debt level increases. This directly increases the roll-over risk with the size and frequency with which the government needs to tap the debt market.
- A higher public-debt-to-GDP ratio increases a country's vulnerability to shocks. For example, higher interest rates and lower growth would have a larger impact on countries with higher debt ratios. An increasing interest rate raises the debt service burden and may hasten debt distress.
- A high debt ratio reduces the space for policy flexibility, including the ability to respond to shocks. Countries that had a high debt ratio at the time of the global financial crisis were unable to respond with countercyclical fiscal policies due to the lack of fiscal space. Instead, many countries had to tighten their fiscal stance to stave off a financing crisis, thus pursuing procyclical policies.

Several empirical papers have documented a nonlinear relationship between public debt and growth, suggesting that public debt beyond certain levels can have negative effects on economic activity. A simple way of thinking about the relationship between public debt and growth is that once the debt-to-GDP ratio crosses a country-specific threshold, it increases the chances of a crisis and enhances volatility, thereby lowering growth (Gill and Pinto, 2005). Reinhart and Rogoff (2010) examine the relationship between public debt and GDP growth in advanced economies between 1946 and 2009. They find that whereas the link between growth and debt seems relatively weak at normal debt levels, the average growth rates for countries with public debt of over 90 percent of GDP are negative and substantially lower than countries with lower debt levels (see Figure 1.2). They highlight the existence of a nonlinear relationship between GDP growth and public debt with effects appearing at debt levels higher than 90 percent of GDP.

Herndon, Ash, and Pollin (2013) replicate Reinhart and Rogoff (2010) and find that the latter's coding errors, selective exclusion of available data, and unconventional weighting of summary statistics lead to serious errors that inaccurately represent the relationship between public debt and GDP growth in 20 advanced economies in the postwar period. They find that when properly calculated, the average real GDP growth rate for countries carrying public-debt-to-GDP ratios over 90 percent is actually 2.2 percent and not the –0.1 percent found by Reinhart and Rogoff. Overall, they provide evidence to contradict Reinhart and Rogoff's claim that public debt of more than 90 percent of GDP consistently reduces GDP growth.

Figure 1.2 Median Real GDP Growth Associated With Various Public Debt Levels, 1790–2009 *(20 advanced economies)*

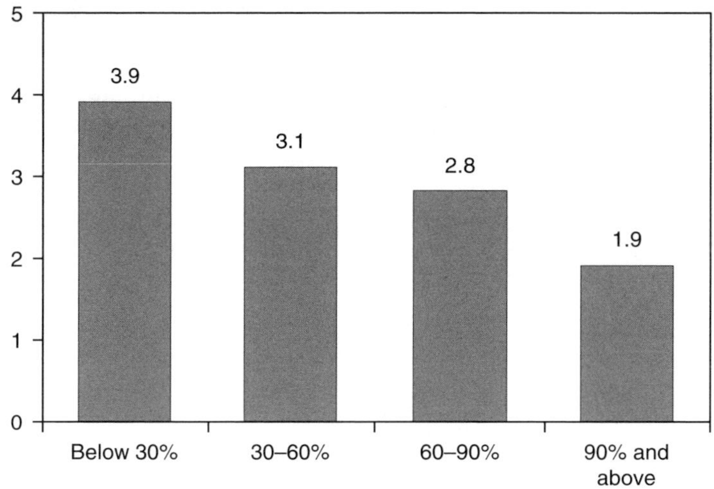

Source: Reinhart and Rogoff (2010).

Using a novel empirical approach and an extensive dataset developed by the Fiscal Affairs Department of the IMF, Pescatori, Damiano, and John (forthcoming) document that countries with high levels of public debt do not systematically experience lower growth. In particular, they find no evidence of any particular debt threshold above which medium-term growth prospects are dramatically compromised. In addition, their results show that the debt trajectory can be as important as the debt level in explaining future growth, since countries with high but declining debt appear to grow equally as fast as countries with lower debt. While higher debt does not seem to unequivocally lower growth in their analysis, the authors find some evidence that higher debt may induce a higher degree of output volatility.

Boamah and Moore (2009) analyze the relationship between external debt, economic policies, and growth using data on 12 Caribbean countries over the period 1970 to 2000. Their results suggest that in the initial stages, as countries seek external resources to support domestic savings, external debt could have a positive impact on growth, particularly in countries with good policy environment. However, above a certain threshold, persistent high levels of debt can have a negative impact on growth, even when the policy environment is good. They argue that debt-to-GDP ratios above 63 percent for the group of countries studied would tend to have a negative influence on growth. They argue further that the estimated benchmark of 63 percent of GDP should be considered an upper bound as applied to countries with macroeconomic environments characterized by stable inflation, manageable fiscal deficits, and open trade regimes.

Greenidge and others (2012) address the use of threshold effects between public debt and economic growth in the Caribbean. Their results show that, at debt levels lower than 30 percent of GDP, increases in the debt-to-GDP ratio are associated with *faster* economic growth. However, the effect on growth diminishes rapidly as debt rises beyond 30 percent of GDP, and when it exceeds 55 percent of GDP debt becomes a drag on growth.

The conclusion from the literature is that the debt trajectory is equally important as the debt level in influencing economic growth. Even though there is no consensus on the impact of high debt on growth, there is some evidence that high debt levels may induce greater volatility of output.

THE IMPACT OF THE GLOBAL FINANCIAL CRISIS ON PUBLIC DEBT

The Caribbean has a track record of high fiscal deficits, partly reflecting procyclical fiscal policies in good times. This has resulted in elevated levels of public-debt-to-GDP ratios since 1990. The predominant source of the budget imbalance is the central government, even though public enterprises have also contributed significantly to the debt buildup. The debt accumulation stems from countercyclical fiscal policy in bad times and procyclical fiscal policy during periods of economic boom. The net result is that debt accumulated during periods of weak growth is not offset in good times, resulting in higher levels of debt in the medium term (Egert, 2011).

The global financial crisis severely affected Caribbean countries, as spillovers from the United States and Europe led to a collapse of GDP growth and soaring debt levels. Debt rose from already elevated levels, and the crisis exposed balance sheet vulnerabilities that had built up over many years. These vulnerabilities originated from a strategy of increasing public spending to counteract declining trade performance, partly due to the erosion of trade preferences, and rebuilding costs after frequent natural disasters.

Chapter 2 of this book examines the impact of the global financial crisis on fiscal outcomes in the Caribbean. It analyzes fiscal performance in the region over the last 15 years to determine the nature of underlying fiscal problems and the extent of the impact that crisis has had on fiscal outcomes. Specifically, it examines whether the reaction of fiscal indicators during the crisis was different from what it was during previous downturns. The chapter also analyzes the factors that contributed to the debt accumulation during the financial crisis.

Fiscal performance in the region is analyzed by dividing the 15-year period into three distinctive sub-periods. The first period (1997–2002) was characterized by rising debt levels as the average debt-to-GDP ratio increased from 54 percent to 74 percent by the end of 2002. During the second period (2003–2007), debt declined by around 18 percentage points of GDP, while the third period (2008–2011) saw more debt accumulation, with the average rising to 70 percent of GDP. The debt buildup in the first period occurred in a relatively benign growth environment, with growth averaging 3.4 percent and the primary surplus close to 2½ percent.

The analyses show that Caribbean countries were severely affected by the global economic crisis due to negative spillovers from the United States and

Europe. Tourism declined sharply, accompanied by declines in offshore activity and other services. Real GDP declined by 2.2 percentage points between 2008 and 2010. The global financial crisis impacted commodity exporting and tourism-intensive countries differently. On average, commodity exporters had higher growth during the last 15 years than countries more dependent on tourism (4 versus 2½ percent) and a better primary balance (3½ versus 2 percent of GDP). Many countries responded to the economic crisis by loosening fiscal policy, thereby increasing the debt-to-GDP ratio. In particular, governments generally raised spending in an effort to curb job losses and to stimulate the economy. Since buffers in the form of public sector savings were limited or nonexistent, they borrowed more to finance higher current spending.

Chapter 2 also analyzes the accumulation of public debt during the period of the financial crisis (2008–11) using an approach that decomposes the accumulation of government debt into different factors, including interest payments, the primary balance, inflation and exchange rate effects, and other exogenous events modifying public debt. The results show that the debt accumulation during the financial crisis period can be attributed to high interest payments and slow growth. On average, the debt-to-GDP ratio increased by 12.7 percentage points during 2008–11. This was driven mainly by high interest payments, which were responsible for about 90 percent of the debt buildup. The high contribution of interest payments was not due to higher interest rates, however, as these decreased on average from 5.2 percent (2004–07) to 4.6 percent (2008–11). Instead, this shows how the already high debt level elevates the debt burden even more. Low GDP growth and primary deficits also contributed to the debt accumulation. Residual encompassing factors, such as inflation, exchange rate changes, and other events changing public debt (e.g., debt restructuring), had a negative effect on the debt ratio.

THE CURRENT PROFILE OF PUBLIC DEBT IN THE REGION

The public debt characteristics are heterogeneous, and in some cases they have increased macroeconomic vulnerabilities. While in general there has been a shift to domestic debt, there are important holdings of foreign currency debt, which leaves some countries exposed to exchange rate adjustments. In addition, some countries have increased their exposure to the local financial system and, with this, strengthened the link between fiscal sustainability and financial stability. Additional concerns arise from the exposure of some countries to floating rate debt and lower borrowing on concessional terms as well as, for some countries, shorter maturity profiles. These vulnerabilities increase the risk of a major fiscal crisis, given the high and increasing unsustainable debt ratios.

Chapter 3 reviews the region's recent public debt profile and debt management practices. In particular, it assesses whether the structure of public debt offsets the high public-debt-to-GDP ratios and briefly discusses estimates of selected contingent fiscal liabilities and the institutional framework for debt management.

The largest component of Caribbean public debt is domestic debt, representing about 60 percent of the total, an increase from 39 percent in 2001 (see Figure 1.3). It is held mainly by the domestic financial systems in the form of medium- to long-term instruments. Social security schemes in some countries, including Barbados, are also important holders of government debt. Bonds remain the instrument of choice for most countries, but there are important differences. Domestic bonds represent about 52 percent of total public debt in the Caribbean and are more prevalent in The Bahamas, Barbados, Jamaica, and Trinidad and Tobago, representing over 50 percent of total debt. On the other hand, foreign bonds are more important in Belize and Grenada. In terms of currency composition, about 62 percent of total public debt is held in domestic currency. While large holdings of domestic debt may indicate that the so-called "original sin" problem may not exist, the experience in the Caribbean for some countries suggests that in some ways this large debt has actually increased the long-term vulnerability of the economy and has reduced the degree of policy freedom where it has not been effectively managed.

Of the foreign currency debt, over 70 percent, on average, is held in U.S. dollars. For some countries, such as Belize and Grenada, the proportion is over 90 percent. Foreign currency debt also remains substantial in countries with high domestic debt, making them still vulnerable to exchange rate movements. The trend on concessionality of external debt appears to be mixed for the region as a whole. In particular, while the proportion of external concessional debt to total external debt has risen for most countries, the average grant element of new debt

Figure 1.3 Composition of Public Debt, Caribbean Nations, 2011 *(percent of GDP)*

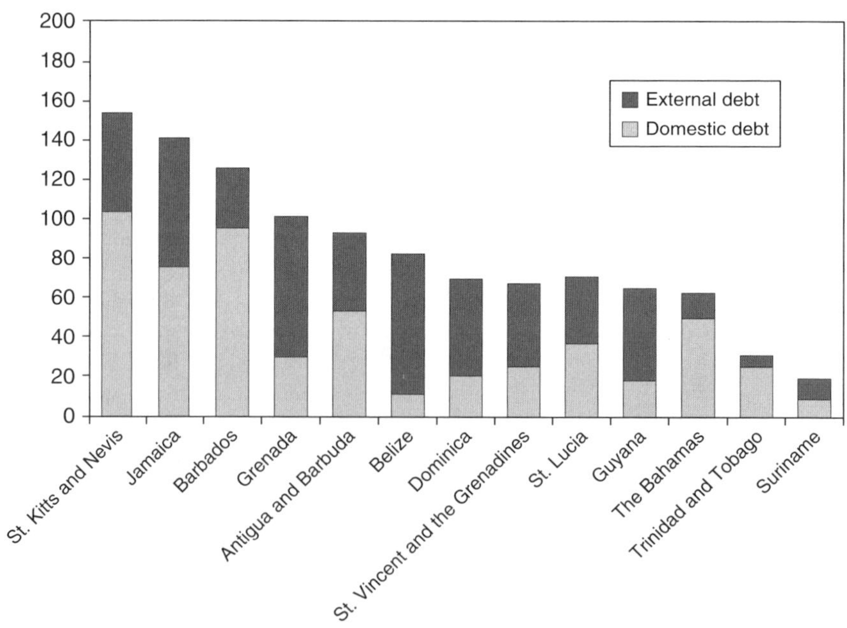

Sources: National authorities; and authors' calculations.

has risen for some and fallen for others, while the average grace period for new external debt commitments has declined for most countries.

Debt management in Caribbean economies is currently undergoing a slow transition from a relatively weak framework and practices to more internationally recognized standards. Using the World Bank's Debt Management Performance Assessment (DeMPA) framework, the region on average does not rank very well. Regarding the institutional frameworks, the legal framework for issuing and managing debt is very fragmented, apart from Jamaica and Suriname, which have a single debt management law. Debt is issued using several pieces of legislation, often targeted at a specific purpose. In addition, in many countries the coordination mechanism between debt management and the requirements for sustainability of fiscal and monetary policies is either limited or very weak.

The region lags behind on other debt management indicators as well. In particular, the government debt markets are fragmented and very inefficient, which prevents effective price discovery. Further, most borrowing activities are generally not supported by appropriate loan evaluation, which impacts negatively on fiscal and debt sustainability.

HOW CAN THE REGION'S HIGH PUBLIC DEBT BE REDUCED?

How can the Caribbean countries lower their debt-to-GDP ratios? What factors explain the success of public debt reduction, and why are some countries able to reduce public debt to prudent levels faster than others? Chapter 4 of this book examines these important policy questions. It examines the factors explaining the success of global public debt reduction and draws lessons for the Caribbean.

Throughout this book, a "large" debt reduction episode is defined as one in which the debt-to-GDP ratio declines by at least 15 percentage points. Using this definition, about 206 episodes of large debt reductions around the world were recorded between 1970 and 2009.

- About 100 of the debt reduction episodes (48 percent) were achieved through debt restructuring or default.
- About 107 of the debt reduction episodes (52 percent) were achieved through higher GDP growth, higher inflation, or fiscal consolidation.
- Of the debt reduction episodes achieved through fiscal consolidation, about 25 percent were preceded or accompanied by the existence of fiscal rules.
- Most of the large debt reduction episodes lasted over a relatively long period, ranging from 4 years in Panama to 18 years in Australia. The average duration of large debt reduction episodes achieved through fiscal consolidation was about 7 years.

To examine the determinant of large debt reduction, the chapter uses a dataset spanning more than three decades for a large sample of developed and developing economies. The analysis uses a panel data set of about 160 countries to estimate the probability that a large debt reduction will be initiated using the logit regression approach. The dependent variable is the probability of a large debt reduction. The explanatory variables are measures of fiscal consolidation, macroeconomic variables, and political and institutional variables, and fiscal rules. Simple comparative analysis shows that countries that experienced a large debt reduction were on average able to achieve a higher GDP growth and larger primary surpluses and were more likely to have fiscal rules than countries that did not experience a large debt reduction.

The result of the econometric analysis shows that global large debt reductions are associated with robust economic growth, decisive and lasting fiscal consolidation, and a favorable external environment characterized by strong global growth. Fiscal rules are positively associated with a higher probability of debt reduction because they increase fiscal discipline and the credibility of fiscal policy and they help secure the gains of fiscal consolidation. The initial level of debt and debt servicing cost appears to play a disciplinary role by enhancing the incentives of governments to consolidate aggressively. The results are robust to alternative estimation methodologies and alternative thresholds for identifying large debt reduction episodes. The chapter concludes that future large debt reduction programs in the Caribbean need to be based on credible fiscal plans to increase primary balances, fiscal rules to enhance fiscal credibility, and structural reforms to promote growth.

WHAT CARIBBEAN COUNTRIES CAN LEARN FROM SUCCESSFUL FISCAL CONSOLIDATION ELSEWHERE

Governments facing high debt levels and seeking to undertake fiscal consolidation often confront a number of interrelated questions. What promotes a successful fiscal consolidation? How large should the adjustment be, and how quickly should it occur? Should one adjust now or later, and what are the consequences of postponing adjustment? Should one cut expenditures, raise revenues. or do both? Which components of expenditures or revenues should one adjust, and does the composition of adjustment really matter? Would the adjustment be self-defeating? Is there a political price for fiscal adjustment?

Chapter 5 attempts to answer many of these questions that policymakers may have in their quest for prudent fiscal consolidation strategies. The chapter uses two main approaches. First, it undertakes a comprehensive survey of a large body of mostly empirical literature on fiscal consolidation, covering industrial, emerging markets, and developing economies. Second, it explores specific country experiences with fiscal consolidation dating back to the 1990s, examining 25 cases studies, consisting of 14 advanced economies, 8 emerging markets, and 3 developing economies, including Barbados and Jamaica. It focuses on the prevailing economic and political conditions preceding fiscal consolidation, the various measures adopted, the composition of the adjustments, and the resulting achievements. The goal of the analysis is to draw useful lessons on the determinants of a successful fiscal consolidation.

The findings from this analysis indicate that fiscal consolidation is generally associated with low economic growth although that there are few cases where fiscal consolidation can be expansionary in the short term. Expansionary fiscal consolidation operates through wealth effects on consumption and credibility effects on the interest rate. An alternative channel of expansionary adjustment emphasizes supply-side considerations through effects on labor cost and competitiveness. Fiscal consolidation must be understood as part of a credible plan designed to permanently reduce government deficit and therefore future tax liabilities.

The main lessons for Caribbean countries from both country experiences and the empirical literature may be summed up as follows:

- It is easier to build a broad consensus about the need for fiscal consolidation in difficult times. Fiscal consolidations were initiated during periods of economic recession, or at early stages of a recovery, which are often characterized by macroeconomic imbalances in the form of worsening fiscal deficits, high debt levels, current account deficits, high unemployment, and high inflation.
- Significant fiscal consolidations were initiated by new governments. In particular, about three-quarters of the episodes in advanced countries were started by new governments, many with an explicit mandate for fiscal consolidation.
- Fiscal consolidation based on expenditure reductions have tended to be more effective than tax-based consolidations. A probable reason is that expenditure measures reflect greater commitment, make substantial consolidation more feasible, and can lead to efficiency gains.
- The composition of the adjustments as mixtures of revenue and expenditure measures varied, with many countries leaning toward expenditure-based reductions. Expenditure measures accounted for an 85 percent improvement in fiscal balances in Canada and Finland and a 75 percent improvement in the Netherlands, Sweden, and the United Kingdom.
- In several successful episodes, spending cuts adopted to reduce deficits were associated with economic expansions rather than recessions. The more successful expenditure-based consolidations focused on cuts in transfers and wages, the so-called politically sensitive budget items.
- The empirical literature also finds that cuts in transfer programs and government wage expenditures are more effective than capital expenditure cuts. Adjustments that lasted longer were driven by reductions in wages and transfers. and cuts in wages, transfers and subsidies contributed about 86 percent on average to successful cases.
- Frontloaded adjustments emphasized revenue measures, while gradual adjustments relied on cuts in primary current spending. In advanced countries, gradual adjustments were more successful and sometimes extended up to a decade, for example in Finland, Sweden, and Spain. This reflects efforts to anchor policy objectives within a medium-term framework with a credible commitment to adopted strategies.
- Successful revenue measures focused on broadening the tax base and making reforms to simplify tax administration and reduce the tax burden. Base

broadening measures were common in countries with more developed revenue administrations and longer period of implementation. In some cases, tax reforms resulted in tax buoyancy and higher revenues over the medium term. Revenue-based adjustment was sustained when the revenue-to-GDP ratio was low.

- Adjustment efforts were also enhanced by broad political consensus and public support. The presence of an external political or economic anchor influenced fiscal adjustment, especially in Europe in the 1990s, where the need to achieve membership in the European Monetary Union was the motivating factor. In that context, the introduction of a broad medium-term strategy was important in mobilizing public support.

FISCAL SUSTAINABILITY AND NATURAL DEBT LIMITS IN THE REGION

The high debt levels in the region impose a high cost on Caribbean economies and put at risk the social and development gains made over the last 50 years. Consequently, many of the countries are implementing measures to consolidate government finances and reduce public debt. The question then is what public-debt-to-GDP ratio should these economies adjust to, taking into consideration their stage of development and vulnerability to shocks, and what is the appropriate speed of adjustment to that targeted debt-to-GDP ratio?

While theory offers little or no guidance on these matters, before the global crisis some Caribbean countries adopted a 60 percent ratio, and most considered a 60 percent ratio as a safe medium-term public debt target. Yet many countries have encountered fiscal and debt distress and are unlikely to meet these medium-term targets without ambitious adjustments. Against this background, it would appear that a total rethinking of fiscal sustainability and safe debt limits for all Caribbean economies is required.

Chapter 6 reviews different concepts of debt sustainability and seeks to determine the optimal debt levels for the region's economies. In particular, it addresses three important policy-related issues. First, it delineates the key aspects of the different approaches to measure fiscal sustainability and public debt limits. Second, it measures the sustainability of fiscal policy and the extent of over- or under-borrowing by the public sector over the last two decades. And third, the chapter derives, through illustrative scenarios, debt benchmarks using reasonable assumptions about growth and interest rate shocks for Caribbean economies.

Overall, the results suggest that most of these economies are pursuing unsustainable fiscal policies and have over-borrowed relative to their calibrated debt limits. Several sensitivity analyses have shown their high vulnerability to negative shocks from interest rates and contingent liabilities, but they have also shown that higher growth and fiscal consolidation could lead the way back to sustainable paths. Consequently, these countries will need to adopt ambitious fiscal adjustment or other debt reduction strategies over the medium term to reduce the drag of high public debt on economic activity.

Several important implications for policy follow from these insights. In particular, policy needs to refocus on reducing public debt to sustainable levels. Moreover, those sustainable levels are likely to be different for each country, given countries' differing growth prospects and volatility of revenues and spending. Further, public debt policy needs to target a debt ratio in normal times that would not create financing difficulties in the presence of negative economic shocks. Finally, Caribbean governments need to develop a comprehensive framework to fully account for all public debt obligations, including contingent fiscal liabilities. This is important to fully determine debt sustainability.

FISCAL CONSOLIDATION EXPERIENCES

Countries in the Caribbean have undertaken fiscal consolidation at various times with the primary objective of putting the debt-to-GDP ratio on a sustainable downward trajectory. Yet public debt levels in most of the countries remain high today, suggesting that past and ongoing fiscal consolidation efforts have not yielded durable benefits. A question that immediately comes to mind is why are public debts levels not falling as one would expect? Would it be connected with the Caribbean approach to fiscal consolidation, country–specific circumstances, or some challenges unique to the region? What are the characteristics of fiscal consolidation in the region, and how different are they from other nations' experiences around the world?

Chapter 7 takes a broad look at the Caribbean experience with fiscal consolidation, covering a sample of 14 countries, including 6 that have been part of a currency union, over three decades (1980–2011). The chapter's aim is to provide useful insights into the nature of fiscal consolidation across the region and the possible implications for policy. In addition, it assesses current fiscal consolidation efforts in case studies of Barbados, Jamaica, and St. Kitts and Nevis. Further, it identifies a number of challenges to successful fiscal consolidation.

The analysis in this chapter finds that fiscal consolidation efforts in the Caribbean have been slow but steady. A number of countries have embarked on fiscal consolidation to put their debt-to-GDP ratio on a sustainable downward path and improve external stability. Recently, the emphasis has been on maintaining social stability and mitigating the impact of the global financial crisis. Since 2008, they have adopted various tax and expenditure measures to reduce the fiscal deficit. In most of the region, the emphasis has been on raising revenues as opposed to spending cuts. However, in countries with IMF-supported programs, expenditure controls by the central government have been an important aspect of the fiscal consolidation strategy, in addition to reducing losses in public enterprises. In a small number of countries where spending has been restrained, countries have preferred to reduce capital spending rather than current spending. In some countries, including Antigua and Barbuda, Jamaica, and St. Kitts and Nevis, fiscal consolidation has also been accompanied by debt restructuring.

Despite these ongoing fiscal consolidation efforts, countries in the region are generating much lower primary fiscal surpluses than is needed to reduce the debt-to-GDP ratios. Debt sustainability analysis suggests that stabilizing these ratios at 2011 levels would require adjustments of about 1 percent of GDP for the average Caribbean country. If those adjustments were to come mainly from spending cuts, this would translate into large real spending cuts for a number of countries.

As mentioned earlier, common challenges to fiscal consolidation in the region include high levels of public debt, fiscal rigidity, high exposures to global economic conditions, and natural disasters. The high levels of public debt that many countries have has put pressure on expenditure by increasing the interest payment burden, and this could limit their ability to access additional financing. In many countries, fiscal expenditures are mostly committed to wages, interest payments, and social security, limiting the flexibility of fiscal adjustment. The region is highly exposed to global economic conditions through tourism and commodity prices, which pose risks to continuous implementation of a sustainable fiscal program. The Caribbean region is also prone to frequent natural disasters, such as hurricanes, tropical storms, and floods, whose social and economic impacts can be catastrophic.

Despite these challenges, there is a need to reorient fiscal policy in the region, given that debt levels are high. There is currently no fiscal space that can be used, as in the past, to boost economic growth. Rather, the countries need to adjust to lower their debt ratios. Fiscal multipliers in the Caribbean are quite low (see Chapter 8), suggesting that any negative impact fiscal consolidation might have on growth would be smaller than in countries outside the region. Caribbean countries can learn from successful fiscal consolidation in other regions to guide their current efforts.

THE SIZE OF FISCAL MULTIPLIERS IN THE REGION

The recent global financial crisis has drawn renewed attention to the effectiveness of fiscal policy, as many countries implemented fiscal stimulus measures to boost economic activity. The effectiveness of fiscal policy is often assessed by the size of fiscal multipliers, which measure a change in output caused by an exogenous change in government spending or tax revenue. Chapter 8 of this book estimates fiscal multipliers for the Caribbean using quarterly data for 14 countries in the region and investigates key determinants of the size of the multipliers.

Different multipliers are used in the literature, depending on the timeframe considered. The most frequently used measure is the impact multiplier, which is defined as $\Delta Y_t / \Delta G_t$, where ΔY_t is a change in output and ΔG_t is a change in government expenditure in period t. It measures the increase in output generated by each additional dollar in government spending in period t. Another frequently used notion is the cumulative multiplier, which is defined as $\sum_{j=0}^{N} \Delta Y_{t+j} / \sum_{j=0}^{N} \Delta G_{t+j}$. Since fiscal stimulus packages can only be implemented over time and there may be lags in the economy's response, the cumulative multiplier may be more accurate in capturing the impact of fiscal policy.

The analysis shows that the estimated fiscal multipliers in the Caribbean are modest, consistent with evidence from existing empirical studies (for example, Guy and Belgrave, 2012). The impact multiplier of government spending is 0.13 and the cumulative multiplier is 0.53 after 24 quarters. The tax multiplier is 0.51 on impact and is 0.62 after 24 quarters. The modest size of fiscal multipliers can be attributed to the high levels of trade openness and public debt in the Caribbean. The authors of this chapter find that the "leakages" through imports are actually positive and statistically significant in the region. In addition, they find that the cumulative spending multiplier is essentially zero in the subgroup of high-public-debt countries, while it is 0.77 and statistically significant in the subgroup of low-public-debt countries.

Interpreting these fiscal multipliers requires caution, because they do not constitute a deep structural parameter. Instead, they consist of policy reactions and structural parameters. That is, the fiscal multipliers depend on various factors that can differ case by case, such as the fiscal policy instrument, its duration, its associated fiscal adjustments, the stance of monetary policy, and country-specific circumstances. Therefore, fiscal multipliers are best interpreted as empirical summaries of average reactions of output following exogenous changes in government spending or tax revenue.

DEBT RESTRUCTURING EXPERIENCES

Many academics and policymakers in the Caribbean are of the view that fiscal consolidation might not be enough to reduce public debt in the region, since high primary surpluses need to be run over a long period of time. Chapter 9 reviews selected Caribbean restructuring cases and explores the scope for debt restructuring in the region. In particular, the chapter examines three interrelated policy questions. First, the chapter delineates the case for public debt restructuring, and outlines the history of resolving debt overhang in emerging-market and low-income economies. Second, it reviews the experience of selected past debt restructuring cases in the Caribbean and draws lessons from them. And third, it assesses the scope for additional traditional debt restructuring in Caribbean economies.

Overall, the results suggest that, while a number of Caribbean countries have pursued debt restructuring over the past 25 years, the relief secured has not been sufficient, by itself, to restore long-term fiscal and debt sustainability. Moreover, the changing structure of public debt in the Caribbean necessitates more innovative debt restructuring strategies to reduce public debt without instigating a financial crisis. Finally, credible macroeconomic frameworks are needed to lock in the fiscal space achieved through debt restructuring.

The recent experience with debt restructurings in the Caribbean provides helpful guidance as to what can be done. It confirms the importance of close coordination with creditors to design a menu of options carefully calibrated to deliver optimal results given the policy constraints in each country. It also underscores the importance of effectively communicating the government's economic policy and strategy. However, the structure of the Caribbean debt, a large share of which is held by the domestic financial system, imposes limitations on the scope for traditional debt restructuring.

The author of chapter 9 takes the view that the IMF could help to catalyze additional external resources to assist the region in its adjustment efforts. Greater reliance on external rather than domestic financing would reduce borrowing costs and free up resources from the domestic banking system to lend to the private sector, which would help finance growth.[2] These strategies would have to be buttressed with carefully calibrated policies to raise production and productivity in key export sectors.

Several policy implications can be drawn from these insights. First, there is a need for a holistic economic strategy over the medium term, one that is anchored in debt sustainability. Second, nontraditional debt reduction and restructuring strategies are likely to have a key role in restoring fiscal sustainability, given the structure of the region's debt. Third, policy reforms, which lock in the gains of debt relief for future generations, would be essential to avoid a repeat of unsustainable fiscal policies.

FISCAL POLICY AND THE CURRENT ACCOUNT

The extent to which fiscal adjustment can lead to predictable development in the current account remains controversial. There are two competing views. The traditional view argues that changes in fiscal policy are associated with changes in the current account through a number of channels. This view is challenged by the Ricardian equivalence principle, which states that an increase in budget deficit (through reduced taxes) will be offset by increases in private saving, insofar as the private sector fully discounts the future tax liabilities associated with financing the fiscal deficit, and therefore it does not affect the current account balance.

Chapter 10 examines the empirical link between fiscal policy and the current account, focusing on *microstates,* which are defined as countries with populations of less than 2 million between 1970 and 2009. The chapter employs panel regression and panel vector autoregression (VAR) to estimate the impact of fiscal policy on the current account. The main challenge in the empirical literature is how to measure fiscal policy in a way that reflects deliberate policy decisions and not simply the impact of business cycle fluctuations. The conventional approach to addressing this problem is to use the cyclically adjusted fiscal data to identify deliberate changes in fiscal policy. The presumption is that cyclically adjusted changes in the fiscal balance reflect decisions by policymakers to adjust tax rates and expenditure levels. The IMF (2010) uses an alternative approach, based on identifying changes in fiscal policy directly from historical records. While that approach could be superior to the conventional approach, this book follows the

---

[2]This, of course, would also need to be managed within a fully articulated debt management strategy that takes into account the cost-risk trade-off. An important risk from foreign borrowing that must be managed is the foreign exchange risk.

conventional approach because of the difficulties in constructing exogenous fiscal policy measures from historical records in microstates.

Panel regression results show that a percentage-point improvement in the fiscal balance improves the current account balance by 0.4 percentage points of GDP (similar to the coefficient of 0.34 found for the global sample). The real effective exchange rate has no significant impact on the current account in microstates, but in the global sample the coefficient is significant. Panel VAR results show that an increase in government consumption results in real exchange appreciation, but the effect on the current account after an initial deterioration dies out quicker in microstates in contrast to the global sample, where the deterioration remains for extended periods. The results imply that fiscal policy has little effect on the current account in microstates beyond its direct impact on imports. Overall, the results suggest that the weak relative price effect makes fiscal adjustment much more difficult in microstates.

FISCAL POLICY RULES AND FISCAL PERFORMANCE

Several governments across the world have adopted fiscal policy rules, especially against the backdrop of worsening fiscal performance and rising debt levels. Recently, following the global financial crisis, fiscal rules have been advocated to support fiscal consolidation efforts and to ensure long-term sustainability of government finances. Chapter 11 of this book analyzes empirically the impacts of fiscal rules on fiscal performance in microstates, with a focus on the Caribbean, where fiscal consolidation has been a major challenge. Broadly, the chapter addresses three questions. Are there fiscal rules in microstates in general and the Caribbean in particular? If the answer is yes, what types of rules exist and what are their characteristics? And finally, is the existence of fiscal rules in microstates associated with improved fiscal performance?

The author of this chapter finds ample evidence of the existence of fiscal rules in microstates. In total, 17 countries—equivalent to 40 percent of the sample—have fiscal rules. The rules are relatively new, about two decades old. Although the institutional coverage slightly favors the central government, the rules in place aim to address fiscal and debt sustainability concerns. Budget balance and debt rules constitute 90 percent of all the fiscal rules. Most debt rules constrain the public-debt-to-GDP ratio to 70 percent or less.

The author estimates a fiscal policy reaction function for a panel of 40 microstates using annual data for 1970–2009. Similar to Debrun and Kumar (2007), and Debrun and others (2008), he characterizes fiscal policy as a response of the cyclically adjusted primary balance (CAPB) to fiscal rules, controlling for other determinants of fiscal policy, including measures of institutional quality and temporary events such as natural disaster. Empirical results show that the presence of fiscal rules in microstates significantly influences fiscal performance. Chapter 11 suggests that by increasing the discipline and credibility of fiscal policy, fiscal rules tend to bolster fiscal consolidation efforts and lower high debt levels in microstates, including the Caribbean countries.

REDUCING PUBLIC DEBT IN THE CARIBBEAN: A NEW AGENDA

Chapter 12 concludes the analysis in this book with an agenda for moving the region forward, drawing on the previous discussion of preceding chapters and the accompanying empirical analyses. While a survey of current policies through the Caribbean suggests that there is plenty of work yet to do on the fiscal sustainability agenda, the fact of a lack of economic recovery in the presence of high debt for many countries has called attention to a time for action. While each country will need to tailor its specific strategy, the chapter outlines some key elements that should be part of any medium term framework that countries in the region may consider adopting. Already, some countries are responding by selecting some elements and putting them in place to meet their debt reduction targets (including difficult and complex new institutional arrangements, for example Jamaica and its proposals for a new fiscal rule).

The chapter argues that robust growth and fiscal consolidation are needed to reduce the high debt in the region. However, since growth in the region is virtually nonexistent, significant fiscal consolidation is inevitable. Views differ regarding the most appropriate route to follow in the current environment given that the need to reduce debt comes in a difficult environment of fragile growth. Based on a survey of country experiences, fiscal consolidation based on expenditure reductions tend to be more effective than tax-based consolidations. However, for countries with large adjustment needs, fiscal consolidation may need to be a balanced combination of spending cuts and revenue increases (Baldacci, Gupta, and Mulas-Granados, 2010). Given the already sizable public sector, most of the fiscal consolidation would have to be done by restraining spending while implementing measures to boost revenues. Better control of the public wage bill, an increase in public sector efficiency, and transfer spending are obvious targets to reduce spending. On the revenue side there is significant potential for reducing tax expenditure, eliminating distortions, and broadening the tax base.

Fiscal consolidation in the Caribbean needs to be credible in order to anchor market expectations about fiscal sustainability (Baldacci, Gupta, and Mulas-Granados, 2010). It is essential to strengthen the fiscal framework by adopting fiscal rules and establishing independent fiscal agencies to guide the budget process and improve fiscal transparency. In the adjustment process, it is imperative to protect the poor. To that effect, social safety nets and well-targeted programs need to be enhanced while reducing or eliminating general subsidies. Targeting subsidies and transfers would also help improve the overall efficiency of nonproductive spending.

The chapter argues that fiscal consolidation is necessary, but may not be sufficient to bring down debt levels, as high primary surpluses would have to be maintained over a relatively long period to have a lasting impact on debt. The very highly indebted Caribbean countries would also need to reduce the net present value of the outstanding debt stock to levels that provide fiscal space and room for countries to resume their growth. The region needs a broad and sustained package of reforms to reduce debt ratios to more manageable levels and strengthen economic resilience. Reforms should signal a new commitment to credible and sound macroeconomic policies. These should include tax policy reforms, public sector rationalization, measures to improve fiscal discipline and credibility, active debt management, containment of contingent liabilities, active privatization programs, and structural reforms to boost growth and improve competitiveness.

In conclusion, this books shows that there is a new agenda waiting to be adopted and implemented. Policymakers and policy advisors in the Caribbean countries, which will face complex challenges in the years ahead, can benefit by learning from successful fiscal strategies around the world, which this book intends to illuminate.

REFERENCES

Alesina, Alberto, and Allan Drazen 1991, "Why Are Stabilizations Delayed? *American Economic Review,* Vol. 81, pp. 1170–80.

Alesina, Alberto, and Roberto Perotti, 1997, "Fiscal Adjustments in OECD: Composition and Macroeconomic Effects," *IMF Staff Papers*, Vol. 44, No. 2, pp. 210–248 (Washington: International Monetary Fund).

Armstrong, H., R. J. De Kervenoael, X. Li, and R. Read, 1998, "A Comparison of the Economic Performance of Different Micro-States, and between Micro-States and Larger Countries," *World Development,* Vol. 26, pp. 639–56.

Armstrong, H. W., G. Johnes, J. Johnes, and A. I. Macbean, 1993, "The Role of Transport Costs as a Determinant of Price-Level Differentials Between the Isle of Man and the United Kingdom, 1989," *World Development,* Vol. 21, pp. 311–18.

Baldacci, Emanuele, Sanjeev Gupta, and Carlos Mulas-Granados, 2010, "Getting Debt Under Control," *Finance and Development,* Vol. 47, No. 4 (December) (Washington: International Monetary Fund).

Bhaduri, Amit, Anjan Mukherji, and Ramprasad Sengupta, 1982, "Problems of Long-Term Growth in Small Economies: A Theoretical Analysis," in *Problems and Policies in Small Economies: 1982,* ed. by B. Jalan (London and Canberra: Croom Helm).

Boamah, Daniel, and Winston Moore, 2009, "External Debt and Growth in the Caribbean," *Money Affairs*, Vol. 22, No. 2, pp. 139–57.

Debrun, Xavier, and Manmohan Kumar, 2007, "Fiscal Rules, Fiscal Councils and All That: Commitment Devices, Signaling Tools or Smokescreens?" Proceedings of the 9th Banca d' Italia Workshop on Public Finance, Perugia, March.

Debrun, Xavier, Laurent Moulin, Alessandro Turrini, Joaquim Ayuso-i-Casals, and Manmohan S. Kumar, 2008, "Tied to the Mast? National Fiscal Rules in the European Union," *Economic Policy*, Vol. 23, Issue 54, pp. 297–362, April.

Downes, Andrew S., Nalandu Mamingi, and Rose-Marie Belle Antoine, 2000, "Labor Market Regulation and Employment in the Caribbean," Research Network Working Paper R-388 (Washington: Inter-America Development Bank).

Economic Commission for Latin America and the Caribbean (ECLAC), 2003, "Exchange Rate Regimes in the Caribbean," ECLAC Series LC/CAR/G.715 (Santiago: Economic Commission for Latin America and the Caribbean).

Egert, Balazs, 2011, "Bring French Public Debt Down: The Options for Fiscal Consolidation," OECD Economics Department Working Paper No. 858 (Paris: Organization for Economic Cooperation and Development).

Gill, Indermit, and Brian Pinto, 2005, "Public Debt in Developing Countries: Has the Market Based Model Worked?" World Bank Policy Research Working Paper No. 3674 (Washington: World Bank).

Greenidge, Kelvin, Roland Craigwell, Chrystol Thomas, and Lisa Drakes, 2012, "Threshold Effects of Sovereign Debt: Evidence from the Caribbean," IMF Working Paper No. 12/157 (Washington: International Monetary Fund).

Guy, Kester, and Anton Belgrave, 2012, "Fiscal Multipliers in Microstates: Evidence from the Caribbean," *International Advances in Economic Research*, Vol. 18, No. 1, pp. 74–86.

Herndon, Thomas, Michael Ash, and Robert Pollin, 2013, "Does High Public Debt Consistently Stifle Economic Growth? A Critique of Reinhart and Rogoff," PERI Working Paper No. 322, April (Amherst: University of Massachussets).

Imam, Patrick, 2010, "Exchange Rate Choices of Microstates," IMF Working Paper No. 10/12 (Washington: International Monetary Fund).

International Monetary Fund, 2010, *World Economic Outlook: Recovery, Risk, and Rebalancing*, World Economic and Financial Surveys (October, Washington).

Jack, Jehann, and Wendell Samuel, 2013, "The Economic, Social, and Political Setting," in *The Eastern Caribbean Economic and Currency Union: Macroeconomics and Financial Systems,* ed. by Alfred Schipke, Aliona Cebotari, and Nita Thacker (Washington: International Monetary Fund).

Kumar, Manmohan S., and Jaejoon Woo, 2010, "Public Debt and Growth," IMF Working Paper No. 10/174 (Washington: International Monetary Fund).

Paldam, Martin, 1997, "Political Business Cycles," in *Perspectives on Public Choice: A Handbook*, ed. by Dennis C. Mueller (Cambridge: Cambridge University Press).

Pescatori, Andrea, Sandri Damiano, and Simon John, forthcoming, "Debt and Growth: Is There a Magic Threshold?" IMF Working Paper (Washington: International Monetary Fund).

Price, Robert, 2010, "The Political Economy of Fiscal Consolidation," OECD Economics Department Working Paper No. 776 (Paris: OECD Publishing).

Rama, Martin, 1995, "Do Labour Market Policies and Institutions Matter? The Adjustment Experience in Latin America and the Caribbean," *Labour* (Special Issue), pp. S243–68.

Reinhart, Carmen, and Kenneth Rogoff, 2010, "Growth in a Time of Debt," *American Economic Review*, Vol. 100, No. 2, May, pp. 573–78.

Rodrik, Dani, 1998, "Why Do More Open Economies Have Bigger Governments?" *Journal of Political Economy*, Vol. 106, pp. 997–1032.

Selwyn, Percy, 1975, *Development Policy in Small Countries* (London: Croom Helm).

Streeten, Paul, 1993, "The Special Problems of Small Countries," *World Development,* Vol. 21, pp. 197–202.

Von Hagen, Jurgen, Andre Hughes Hallet, and Rolf Strauch, 2002, "Budgetary Consolidation in Europe: Quality, Economic Conditions, and Persistence," *Journal of the Japanese and International Economies,* Vol. 16, pp. 512–35.

Worrel, Delisle, 2012, "Policies for Stabilization and Growth in Small Very Open Economies," Occasional Paper No. 85 (Washington: Group of Thirty).

CHAPTER 2

Fiscal Performance in the Caribbean Before and After the Global Financial Crisis

ALEXANDRA PETER

The Caribbean has a track record of high fiscal deficits, partly reflecting procyclical fiscal policies in good times. This has resulted in elevated levels of public-debt-to-GDP ratios since 1990. The predominant source of the budget imbalance is the central governments, even though public enterprises have also contributed significantly to the debt buildup. The debt accumulation stems from countercyclical fiscal policy in bad times and procyclical fiscal policy during periods of economic boom. The net result is that debt which has accumulated during periods of weak growth is not offset in good times, resulting in higher levels of debt in the medium term (Egert, 2011).

The global financial crisis severely affected the region's countries as spillovers from the United States and Europe led to a collapse of GDP growth and soaring debt levels. Debt rose from already elevated levels, and the crisis exposed balance sheet vulnerabilities that had built up over many years. These vulnerabilities originated from a strategy of increasing public spending to counteract declining trade performance, partly due to the erosion of trade preferences, and rebuilding costs incurred after frequent natural disasters.

Prior to the onset of the global financial crisis, moderate growth rates helped some countries broadly stabilize and reduce their debt ratios, albeit at high levels. As the Caribbean countries entered the global crisis with low fiscal buffers, fiscal risks were exacerbated and materialized. This chapter sets out to assess how these countries ended up in this serious situation and what role fiscal policy played in this regard. In particular, it analyzes fiscal performance in the region over the last 15 years to determine the nature of underlying fiscal problems and the extent of the impact of the global financial crisis on fiscal outcomes. It complements that by examining whether the reaction of fiscal indicators during the crisis was different from previous downturns.

Not all Caribbean countries were affected the same way by the crisis. While tourism-dependent economies were hit hard by the deep slump and slow recovery in advanced economies, commodity exporters rebounded rapidly after the crisis, buoyed by high commodity prices. The chapter takes a look at these differences, comparing fiscal outcomes for commodity exporters and tourism-intensive countries.

Lastly, since debt ratios increased substantially during the global financial crisis, the chapter closes with an analysis of the factors that contributed to this debt accumulation.

FISCAL PERFORMANCE DURING THE PAST TWO DECADES

This part analyzes the fiscal performance in the Caribbean over the last 15 years by dividing the period into three distinct sub-periods. The first sub-period (1997–2002) was characterized by rising debt levels, as the average debt-to-GDP ratio increased from 54 percent to 74 percent by the end of 2002. During the second sub-period (2003–07) debt declined by around 18 percentage points of GDP, while the third sub-period (2008–11) saw more debt accumulation, with the average reaching 70 percent of GDP (see Figure 2.1).[1]

The debt buildup in the first sub-period occurred in a relatively benign growth environment. We calculated averages over the three sub-periods for GDP growth and the primary balance together with the end-of-period debt stock (see Figure 2.2). The analysis shows that during the first sub-period, GDP grew at an average rate of 3.4 percent, while the primary surplus was close to 2.4 percent of GDP. In the second sub-period, the primary surplus increased by 1.7 percentage

Figure 2.1 Real GDP Growth and Government Debt, Regional Average, 1997–2011

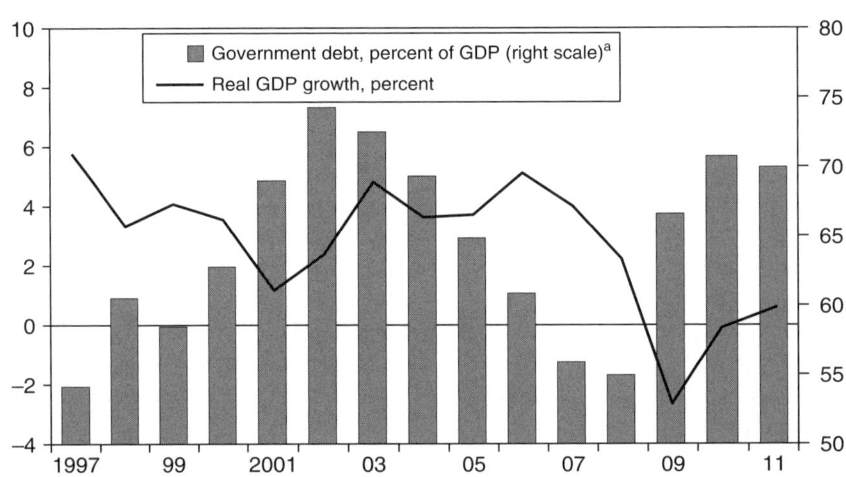

Source: Author's calculations.
[a]Weighted average.

[1]All figures including weighted averages use GDP as weights to calculate Caribbean averages.

Figure 2.2 GDP Growth, Primary Balance, and Debt, Regional Average, 1997–2011

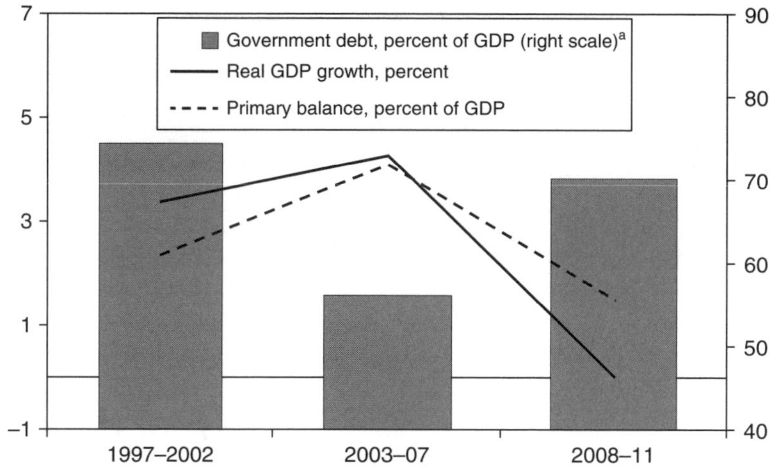

Source: Author's calculations.

[a]Government debt is measured as end of period, growth and primary balance represent average over period. Government debt and primary balance represent weighted Caribbean averages.

points of GDP accompanied by average growth rates of 4.3 percent. During the recent financial crisis, primary balances deteriorated to about 1.5 percent of GDP, while GDP was stagnant.

Individual country experiences show that most countries had the highest debt buildup during the first sub-period (see Figure 2.3). Exceptions are Guyana and Trinidad and Tobago, where debt declined from 1997 to 2011. Aided by the Heavily Indebted Poor Countries Initiative (HIPC) and the Multilateral Debt Relief Initiative (MDRI), Guyana's debt was more than halved between 1997 and 2011. Debt in Trinidad and Tobago started to increase during the financial crisis after having declined strongly in earlier years, so that in sum debt in 2011 was still lower than in 1997. Suriname's debt fell in the second sub-period by as much as it had increased in the first and the last sub-period. Thus, overall, Suriname's debt level in 2011 was as high as in 1997. On the other hand, in The Bahamas and Barbados debt levels rose over the entire period and increased particularly sharply during the latest sub-period.

The behavior of cyclically adjusted primary balances varied across countries (see Figure 2.4). In about half of the countries, primary balances improved between 2003 and 2007, before deteriorating again during the financial crisis in 2008–11. In other countries, primary balances deteriorated in 2003–07 with some improvement in the last sub-period. In Belize and St. Kitts and Nevis, primary balances have continously improved. In The Bahamas and Barbados, primary balances mirror the debt behavior and have continously deteriorated. Taking this together with the debt development shows that in some countries high primary balances have contributed to falling debt levels, while in others

Figure 2.3 Change in Government Debt by Country, 1997–2011 *(percent of GDP)*

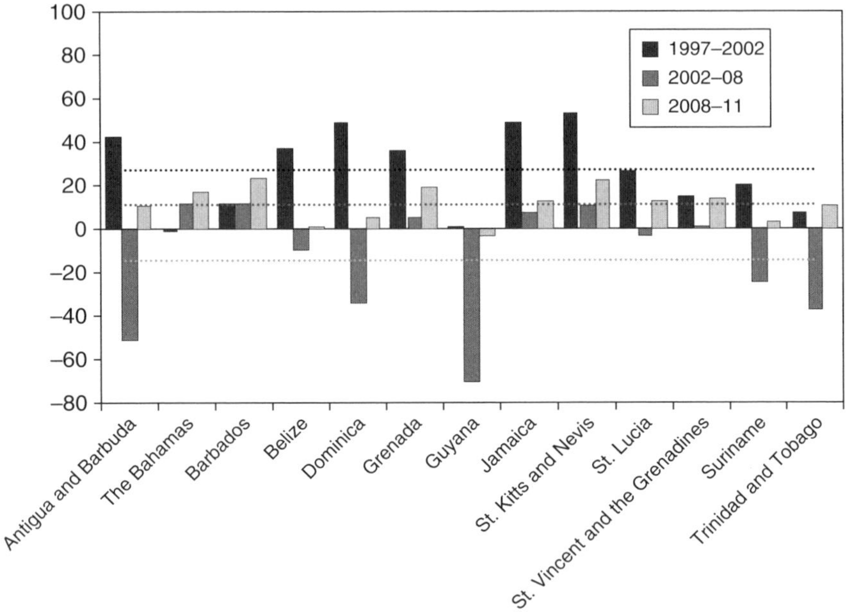

Source: Author's calculations.

Figure 2.4 Cyclically Adjusted Primary Balance by Country, 1997–2011 *(percent of GDP)*

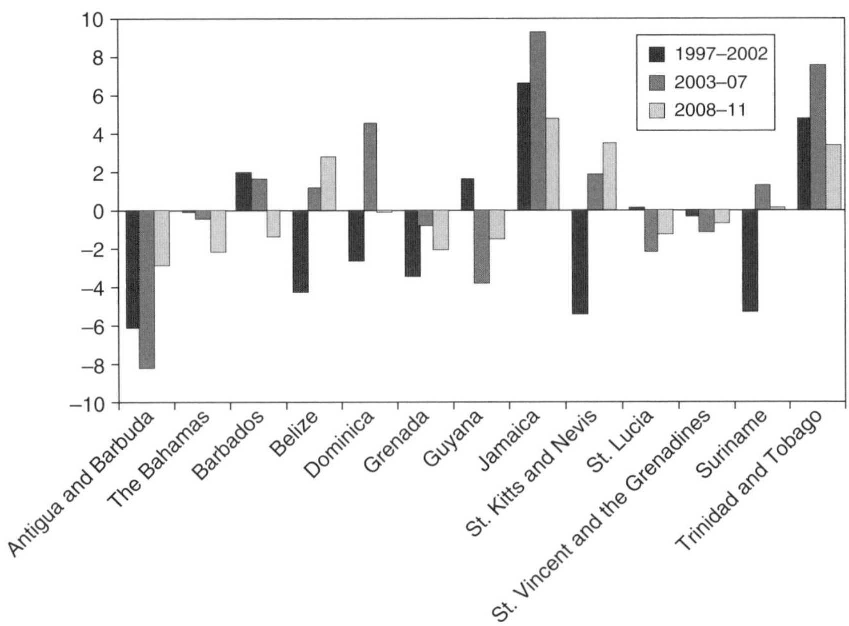

Source: Author's calculations.

falling debt levels were achieved despite primary deficits due to exogenous forces (e.g., Guyana getting debt relief).

Over the years, revenue performance has improved significantly in the Caribbean, while at the same time primary spending has strongly increased. During the first five years of the sample period, revenues in percent of GDP averaged around 23 percent before increasing to around 29 percent by 2008 (see Figure 2.5). In 2009, revenues dipped briefly to 26 percent of GDP before increasing again to around 28 percent. This was due to revenue measures adopted by some countries (e.g., VAT introductions or VAT and excise rate increases). Primary spending hovered around 21 percent of GDP until 2005 before it started to increase strongly to above 26 percent of GDP in 2011. Real primary expenditure and revenue growth have tended to move together (see Figure 2.6) except during the growth slowdown in 2001–02 and the 2008–09 recession. In both cases, expenditures grew strongly, while revenue growth was subdued.

Turning to the composition of total expenditures, we find that on average public wages and salaries make up the biggest component of total expenditure in the Caribbean. Decomposing total expenditures in the region into five subcomponents (wages and salaries, interest payments, goods and services, transfers, and capital expenditures) reveals that public wages and salaries account for an average 8.1 percent of GDP (see Figure 2.7). Their share of GDP has been very stable over the last 15 years, falling only slightly to 7 percent by 2007 before increasing again to around 8 percent in the last three years.

Public wage growth outstripped real GDP growth over the last 15 years. Analyzing the real growth of expenditures on public wages and salaries together with real GDP growth shows that overall, the growth of real expenditures on public wages has been higher than real GDP growth during the last 15 years, excluding

Figure 2.5 Primary Expenditure and Revenue, Regional Average, 1997–2011[a] *(percent of GDP)*

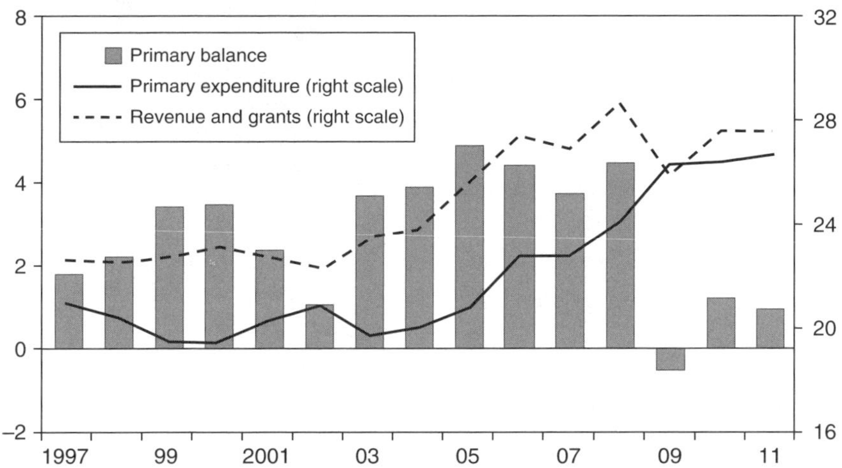

Source: Author's calculations.
[a]Weighted average.

Figure 2.6 Primary Expenditure and Revenues, Regional Average, 1997–2011 *(percentage change)*

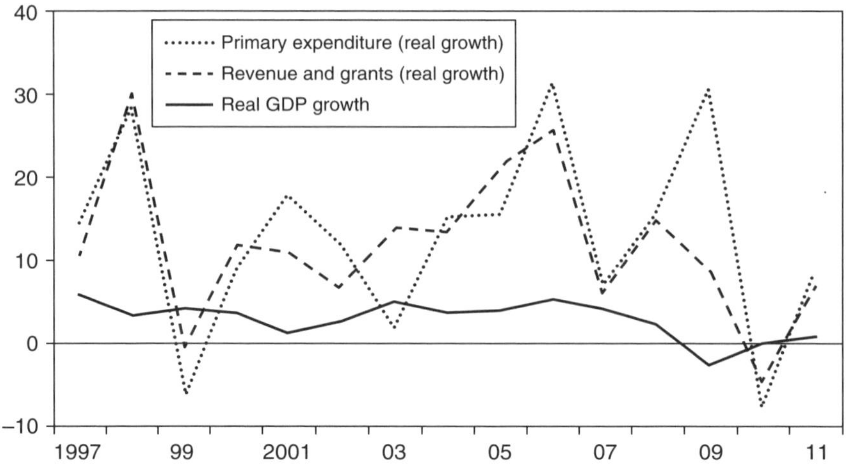

Source: Author's calculations.

Figure 2.7 Decomposition of Total Expenditure, Regional Average, 1997–2011[a] *(percent of GDP)*

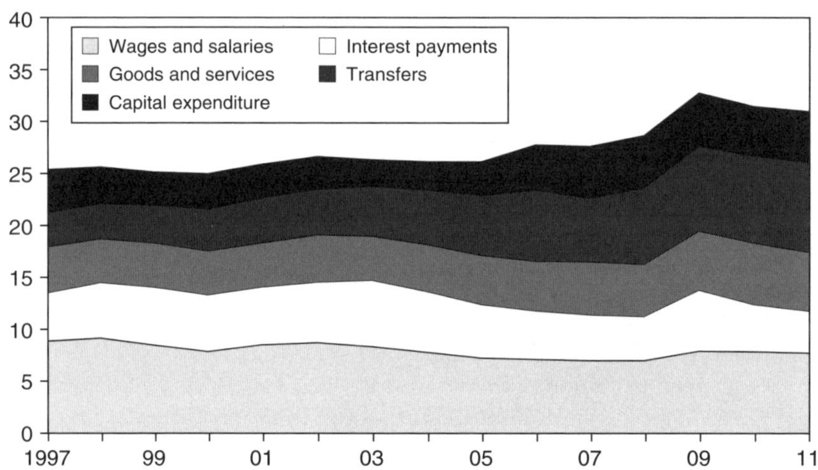

Source: Author's calculations.
[a]Weighted average.

1999 and 2010 (see Figure 2.8). The wage growth was particularly high in times of low GDP growth (e.g., 2001 and 2009). However, in years immediately after wage hikes, wage growth decelerated. For example, in 2010 public wage growth fell significantly and was below the growth rate of GDP.

Higher total expenditure during the financial crisis was mainly driven by increased spending on goods and services and transfers. The average spending on

Figure 2.8 GDP Growth and Public Wages, Regional Average, 1997–2011 *(percentage change)*

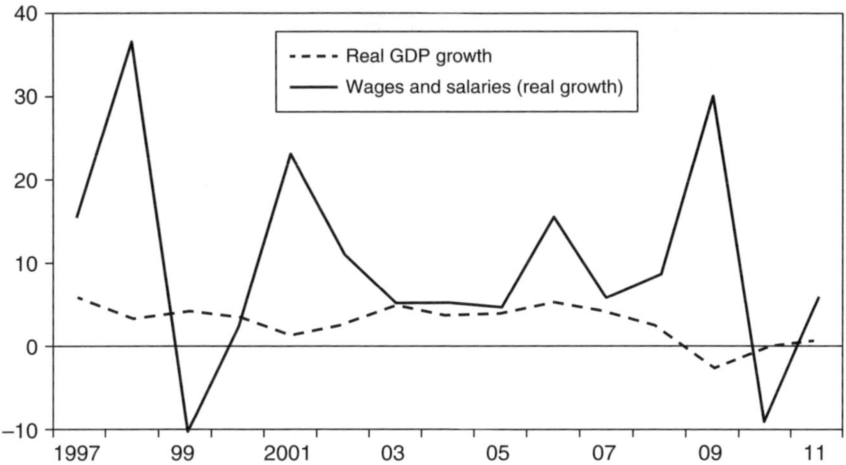

Source: Author's calculations.

goods and services rose from 5 percent of GDP to 6 percent, while transfers climbed from 6 percent of GDP to more than 8 percent. Transfers are also the category that saw the biggest increase over the last 15 years. While they made up a mere 3.3 percent of GDP (being the lowest spending category) in 1997, they have increased strongly to 8.7 percent of GDP in 2011, becoming the largest spending category. Capital outlays fluctuated between 2.5 and 5 percent over the last 15 years. Interest payments increased from about 4.5 percent of GDP to over 6 percent by the mid 2000s before decreasing again to 4 percent in 2011.

PUBLIC DEBT AND FISCAL BALANCES DURING THE FINANCIAL CRISIS

This section takes a closer look at the effects of the financial crisis on the fiscal performance comparing the impacts to earlier downturns, while also analyzing how tourism-intensive and commodity-exporting countries differed.

Caribbean countries were severely affected by the global economic crisis due to negative spillovers from the United States and Europe. Tourism declined sharply, accompanied by declines in offshore activity and other services. Real GDP declined by 2.2 percentage points between 2008 and 2010, with tourism-intensive economies more strongly affected than commodity-exporting economies (see Figure 2.11).[2] On the fiscal side, the region entered the recession with

[2]The tourism-intensive economies are Antigua and Barbuda, The Bahamas, Barbados, Belize, Dominica, Grenada, Jamaica, St. Kitts and Nevis, St. Lucia, and St. Vincent and the Grenadines, while commodity-exporting countries include Guyana, Suriname, and Trinidad and Tobago.

few fiscal buffers. Although government debt declined during the boom period of the mid-2000s, on average it was still around 55 percent of GDP in 2008.

Many countries responded to the economic crisis by loosening fiscal policy, thereby increasing the debt-to-GDP ratio. In particular, governments generally raised spending in an effort to curb job losses and to stimulate the economy. Since buffers in the form of public sector savings were limited or non-existent, governments borrowed more to finance higher current spending. As a result, public debt, on average, increased to around 70 percent of GDP in 2011 (though still below the nadir during the early 2000s). Further, the collapse of the financial conglomerate Colonial Life Insurance Company (CLICO) affected several budgets in the region, as countries financed measures to resolve the insurance crisis and to support the financial system.

Primary balances deteriorated in many countries, contributing to the buildup of public debt. The average primary balance declined from a surplus of 4.4 percent of GDP in 2008 to a deficit of 0.5 percent of GDP in 2009 (see Figure 2.9). During the growth slowdown in 2001–02 the drop of primary balances was about half that amount, as they decreased by around 2.5 percentage points of GDP over two years. The strong deterioration of the average primary balance in 2009 was driven almost equally by an increase in primary spending and a decline in revenue income (see Figure 2.10). The subsequent improvement of the primary balance was driven by higher revenue collection in 2010 before a primary spending increase led to a renewed, albeit small, deterioration in 2011. In 2001–02, the deterioration of the primary balance was mostly driven by expenditure increases and to a smaller extent by revenue decreases, while the recovery period in 2003 was due to both a revenue pick-up and an expenditure restraint. However, these

Figure 2.9 Primary Expenditure and Revenue, Regional Average, 1997–2011[a] *(percent of GDP)*

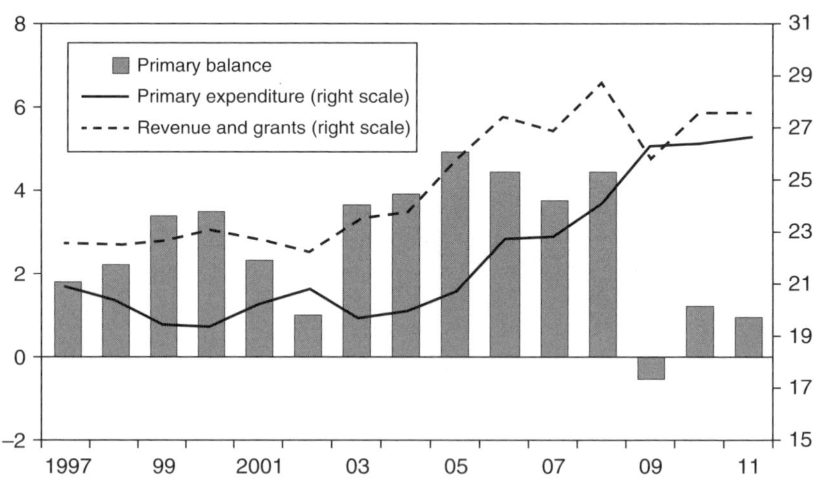

Source: Author's calculations.
[a]Weighted average.

Figure 2.10 Contributions to Primary Balance Changes, Regional Average, 1997–2011[a]
(percent of GDP)

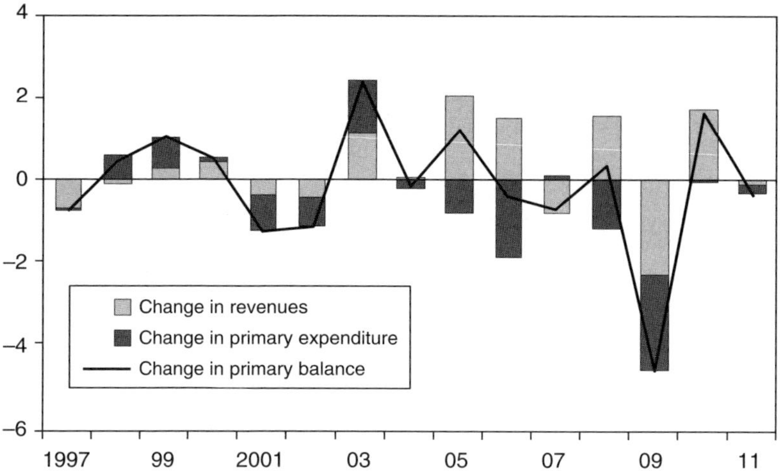

Source: Author's calculations.
[a]A decrease in primary expenditure is depicted as a positive contribution to an improvement of the primary balance. Weighted average.

developments for the entire region mask some differences between tourism-intensive and commodity-exporting economies, which will be explored next.

The global financial crisis impacted commodity-exporting and tourism-intensive countries differently. On average, commodity exporters had higher growth during the last 15 years (3.9 vs. 2.4 percent) and a better primary balance (3.5 vs. 2.1 percent of GDP). Particularly during the recent financial crisis, growth in commodity exporters was less impacted than growth in tourism-intensive countries. Growth in the former group fell by 2 percentage points to around 1 percent before recovering quickly to almost 3 percent; while the latter group went into a deep recession in 2009 with average growth barely hitting zero in 2011 (see Figure 2.11). Reflecting the commodity boom at the onset of the financial crisis, commodity-exporting countries had strong primary surpluses of around 8 percent of GDP in 2008. As commodity prices plunged in 2009, primary balances of commodity exporters went into deficit (see Figure 2.12). However, a year later primary balances had improved again, to 1.6 percent of GDP. On the other hand, in tourism-intensive countries primary balances halved from 2007 to 2008 and continued to decrease slowly thereafter being at 0.4 percent of GDP in 2011.

The somewhat different reaction of primary balances for the two country groups was rooted in different contributions of revenue and expenditure changes (see Figures 2.14 and 2.15). In commodity-exporting countries, the strong decline in primary balances was driven by both a revenue fall-off and an expenditure increase, whereas the smaller decline in primary balances in tourism-intensive economies was mainly driven by revenue decreases. However, the strong decline

Figure 2.11 Real GDP Growth, Regional Average, 1997–2011 *(percentage change)*

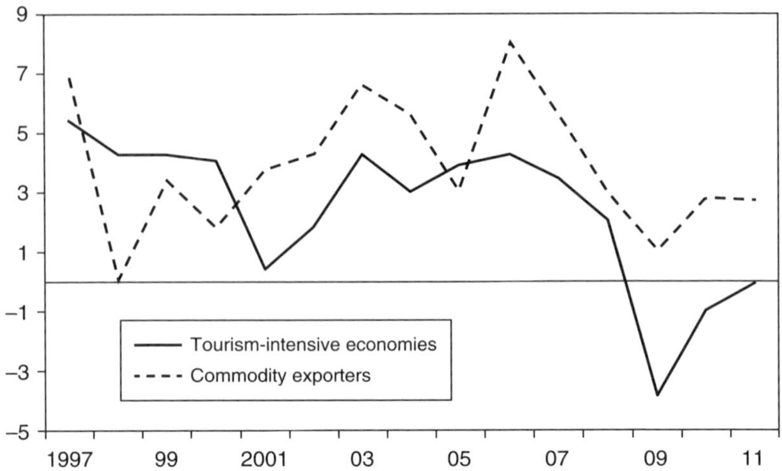

Source: Author's calculations.

Figure 2.12 Primary Balance, Regional Average, 1997–2011[a] *(percent of GDP)*

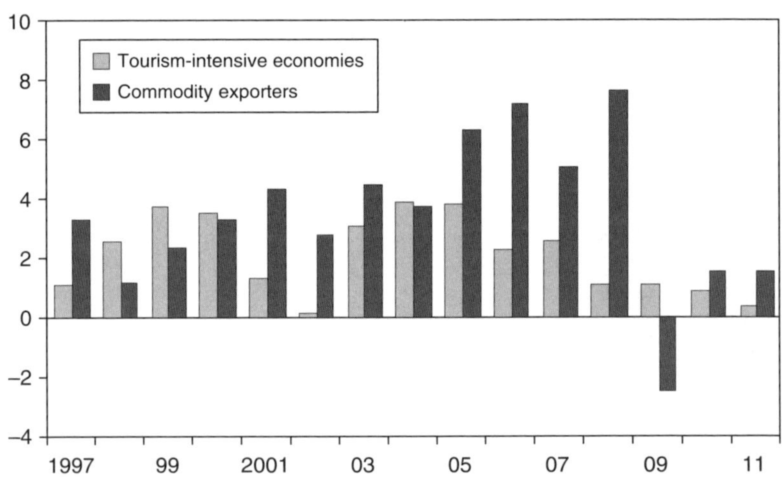

Source: Author's calculations.
[a]Weighted average.

of primary balances in tourism-intensive economies in 2008 was due to expenditure hikes, which could be linked to high fuel and food prices that year. The subsequent recovery in commodity exporters was due to a strong increase in revenue and slightly falling expenditures. In tourism-intensive countries, primary balances deteriorated further as expenditures increased, while revenues increased only slightly.

Figure 2.13 Government Debt, Regional Average, 1997–2011[a] *(percent of GDP)*

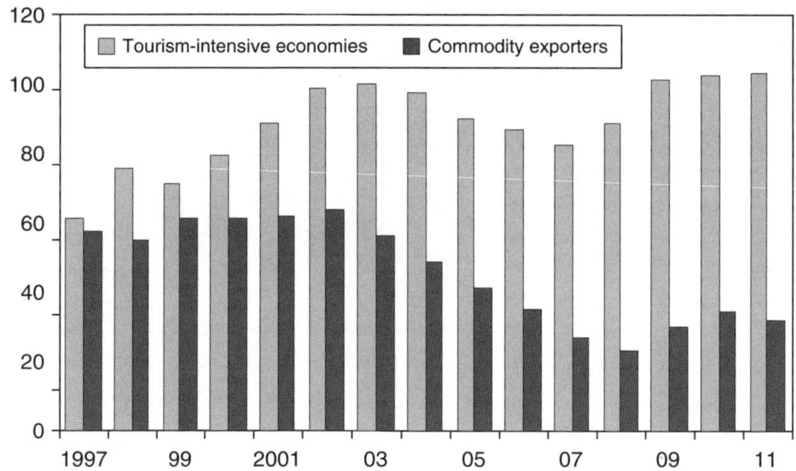

Source: Author's calculations.
[a]Weighted average.

Figure 2.14 Contributions to Primary Balance Changes: Tourism-Intensive Economies, Regional Average, 1997–2011[a] *(percent of GDP)*

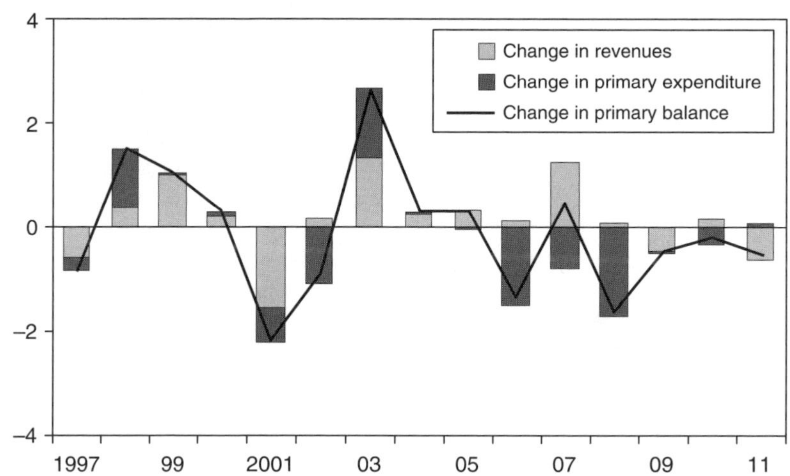

Source: Author's calculations.
[a]A decrease in primary expenditure is depicted as a positive contribution to an improvement of the primary balance. Weighted average.

Comparing the recent crisis with earlier episodes of growth slowdowns (1998 for commodity exporters and 2001 for tourism-intensive economies), one finds that experiences were quite similar. In 1998, both revenue decreases and expenditure increases contributed to the deterioration of primary balances in commodity exporters, while in 2001 the primary balance in tourism-intensive economies

Figure 2.15 Contributions to Primary Balance Changes: Commodity-Exporting Economies, Regional Average, 1997–2011[a] *(percent of GDP)*

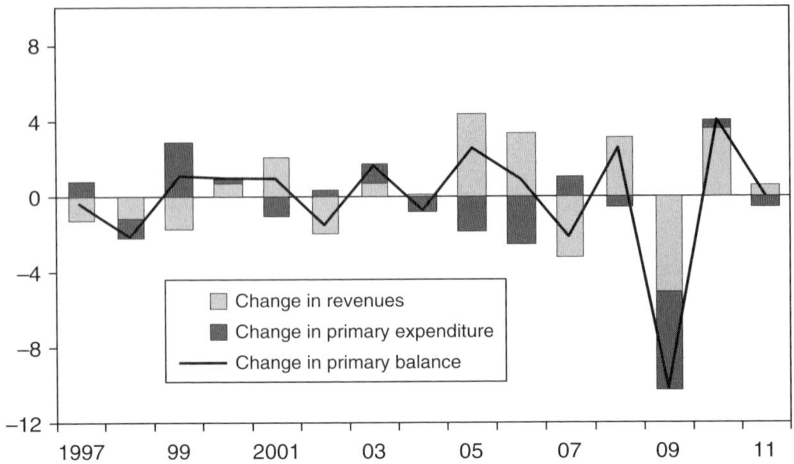

Source: Author's calculations.

[a]A decrease in primary expenditure is depicted as a positive contribution to an improvement of the primary balance. Weighted average.

deteriorated mainly due to revenue shortfalls. The analysis also shows that primary balances were more volatile over the last 15 years in commodity-exporting countries than in tourism-intensive countries.

There are also noticeable differences in the behavior of government debt between tourism-intensive and commodity-exporting countries. On average, commodity-exporting countries' debt ratios were similar to those of the tourism-intensive countries in 1997, both averaging around 60 percent of GDP (see Figure 2.13). However, subsequently commodity-exporting countries halved their debt from 64 percent of GDP in 2002 to 32 percent of GDP in 2011. The decline reflects the debt relief Guyana received under the HIPC initiative and Suriname's clearance of foreign arrears, which included partial debt write-offs. During the same period, tourism-intensive countries almost doubled their debt-to-GDP ratio from around 62 percent in 1997 to 104 percent in 2011.

ACCOUNTING FOR PUBLIC DEBT ACCUMULATION DURING THE CRISIS

In this section, we analyze what factors contributed to the accumulation of public debt during the financial crisis period 2008–11. In order to do this we follow the debt accounting methodology in Sahay (2005).[3] This approach decomposes the accumulation of government debt into different factors, including interest

[3]For a detailed discussion of the debt accounting exercise also see Helbling, Mody, and Sahay (2004).

payments, the primary balance, inflation and exchange rate effects, and other exogenous events modifying public debt.

The debt accounting exercise starts with the equation showing the evolution of government debt (equation 1). Total government debt in the next period B_{t+1}, decomposed into domestic (D_{t+1}) and foreign (F_{t+1}) debt, is equal to the current government debt stock B_t plus interest payments (i_tD_t and r_tF_t), the primary balance PB_t, and other events that modify public debt but do not necessarily appear in the fiscal accounts, RES_t.[4] Variables in foreign currency are converted to domestic currency with the nominal exchange rate S_{t+1}, which is measured in units of foreign currency per unit of domestic currency.

$$D_{t+1} + F_{t+1}\frac{1}{S_{t+1}} = (1+i_t)D_t + (1+r_t)F_t\frac{1}{S_{t+1}} - PB_t + RES_t. \qquad (2.1)$$

For the analysis, it is useful to express all variables as ratios to GDP. In this case, we also have to take into account that changes to the denominator have an impact on debt accumulation. Dividing both sides of equation (2.1) by GDP (P_tY_t) and rearranging gives equation (2.2):

$$b_{t+1} - b_t = \overline{r}_t - \overline{g}_t^r - pb_t + res_t. \qquad (2.2)$$

The left-hand side shows the evolution of the debt-to-GDP ratio, where

$$b_{t+1} = \frac{D_{t+1} + F_{t+1}\frac{1}{S_{t+1}}}{Y_tP_t}.$$

The right-hand side shows the different factors' contribution to the debt accumulation. Interest payments, represented by $\overline{r}_t$, have a positive effect on debt accumulation. Interest payments can be higher due to higher interest rates or due to higher debt levels. The effect of GDP growth, represented by

$$\overline{g}_t^r = \frac{g_t^r}{(1+g_t^n)}b_t,$$

on debt accumulation is negative. A higher real GDP growth can help contain the growth of the debt-to-GDP ratio. Similarly, the primary balance in percent of GDP, pb_t, contributes negatively to debt accumulation. A primary surplus will help reduce the debt burden, whereas a primary deficit elevates it. Lastly, the residual res_t includes exogenous debt-changing events and also captures inflation and exchange rate effects.

[4]These events could either increase government debt, for example, the recognition of contingent liabilities, or decrease government debt, for example, debt restructurings. If the fiscal accounts only include the central government, changes of debt by public enterprises would also fall under this category.

The results of applying Equation (2.2) to the Caribbean countries for the period 2008–11 are shown in Figures 2.16 and 2.17. They depict the cumulative debt buildup between 2008 and 2011 for the entire region, the two country groups, and individual countries.

The debt accumulation during the financial crisis period 2008–11 can be attributed to high interest payments and slow growth. On average, the debt-to-GDP ratio increased by 12.7 percentage points during 2008–11. This was driven mainly by high interest payments, which were responsible for about 90 percent of the debt buildup. The high contribution of interest payments was not due to higher interest rates, since these decreased on average from 5.2 percent (2004–07) to 4.6 percent (2008–11). Instead, this shows how the already high debt level elevates the debt burden even more.

Low GDP growth and primary deficits also contributed to debt accumulation. Several factors contributed to low or negative GDP growth during the financial crisis. Tourist arrivals dropped sharply as the major tourist markets (the United States and Europe) underwent deep recessions, which also affected offshore activity and other services negatively. In addition, traditional export sectors, including banana and sugar, faced competitiveness issues due to the loss of preferential trade agreements. In addition, some countries were hit by hurricanes that caused significant damage, creating a further drag on growth (examples include Dominica and St. Kitts and Nevis in 2008 and St. Lucia and St. Vincent and the Grenadines in 2010).

The residual, encompassing factors, such as inflation, exchange rate changes and other events changing public debt (e.g. debt restructuring), had a negative effect on the debt ratio. In tourism-intensive countries, the most important factor was the interest bill, while subdued growth also contributed to the debt increase of almost 16 percentage points. By contrast, the relatively higher real GDP growth rates in commodity exporters helped them to contain their debt accumulation to less than 3 percentage points.

Individual country experiences show varying levels of debt accumulation, but in the majority of countries the interest bill was the most important factor. Debt-to-GDP ratios increased in all countries with the exception of Guyana, and the magnitude ranged from as low as 3 percentage points of GDP (Suriname) to over 20 percentage points (Barbados and St. Kitts and Nevis). Interest payments were the most important contributor to debt accumulation in all countries but Antigua and Barbuda, The Bahamas, and Guyana.

For Antigua and Barbuda, the high negative residual can be explained by restructuring activities, while negative GDP growth contributed strongly to debt accumulation. In The Bahamas, the primary deficit was the most important contributor to the debt increase, as interest payments were comparatively low due to a relatively low initial debt level. In Guyana, the debt decrease was strongly facilitated by high GDP growth rates. Jamaica has a particularly high interest bill (on average over 10 percent of GDP), which more than overcompensated a high primary surplus. Similarly, in St. Kitts and Nevis and in Belize a primary surplus was overcompensated by other factors. In St. Kitts and Nevis, subdued GDP growth elevated the effect of interest payments. Belize's debt increase was relatively small, as both a primary surplus and relatively robust GDP growth counteracted the effect of the interest bill.

Figure 2.16 Debt Accumulation Decomposition, 2008–11 *(percent of GDP)*

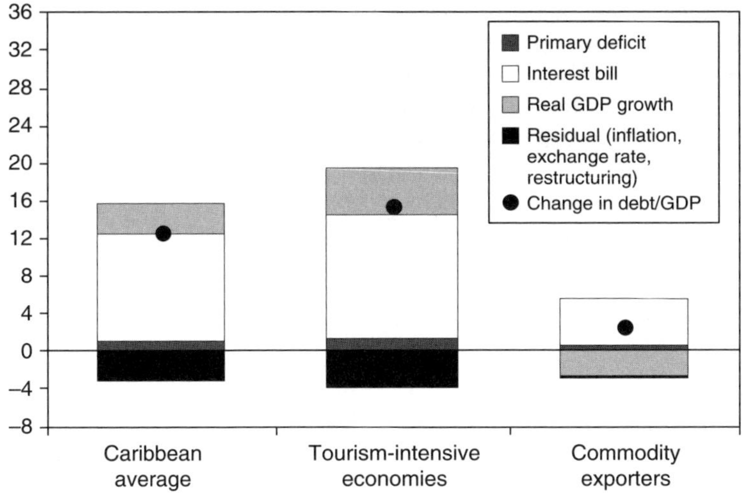

Source: Author's calculations.

Figure 2.17 Decomposition of Accumulations by Country, 2008–11 *(percent of GDP)*

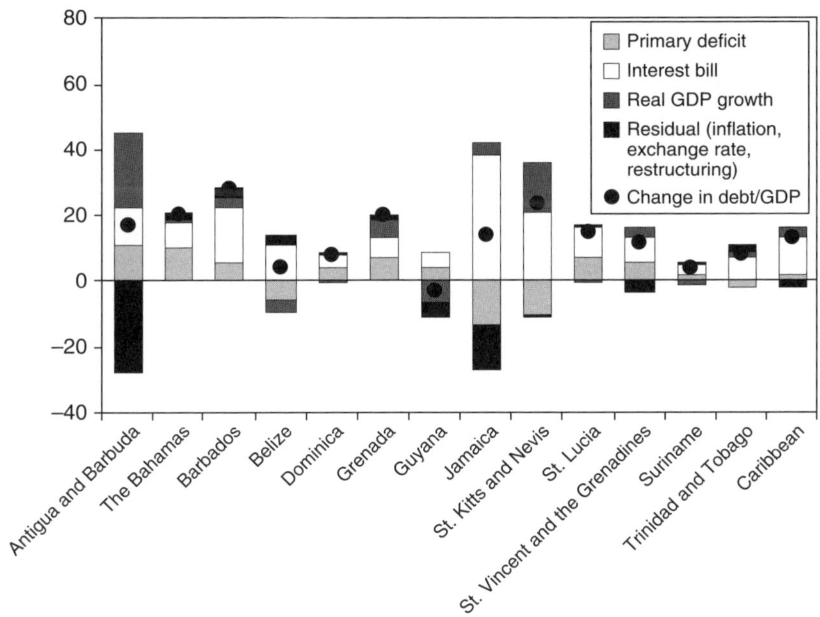

Source: Author's calculations.

SUMMARY AND CONCLUSION

This chapter has given an overview of the fiscal performance in the Caribbean over the last 15 years, focusing on the recent financial crisis period. Although there has been a period of debt reduction, the Caribbean countries entered the crisis with few fiscal buffers, which were fast depleted during the deep recession. Specifically, the high debt burden through high interest payments contributed to a further debt accumulation, which in some countries has been exacerbated by low growth rates and primary deficits. The differences between tourism-intensive and commodity-exporting countries are striking as well.

REFERENCES

Egert, Balazs, 2011, “Bring French Public Debt Down: The Options for Fiscal Consolidation,” OECD Economics Department Working Paper No. 858 (Paris: Organization for Economic Cooperation and Development).

Helbling, Thomas, Ashoka Mody, and Ratna Sahay, 2004, “Debt Accumulation in the CIS-7 Countries: Bad Luck, Bad Policies, or Bad Advice?” IMF Working Paper 04/93 (Washington: International Monetary Fund).

Sahay, Ratna, 2005, “Stabilization, Debt, and Fiscal Policy in the Caribbean,” IMF Working Paper 05/26 (Washington: International Monetary Fund).

CHAPTER 3

Public Debt Profile and Public Debt Management in the Caribbean

GARTH PERON NICHOLLS

This chapter reviews the current public debt and debt management characteristics of Caribbean economies. In particular, it reviews the debt profile in the region and assesses whether the structure of public debt offsets the risks emanating from the high public debt ratios. It also briefly discusses estimates of selected contingent fiscal liabilities and reviews the institutional framework for debt management.

Caribbean economies face high and rising debt-to-GDP ratios, which put at risk their prospects for medium-term sustainability and growth. In 2011, overall public sector debt was estimated at about 84 percent of regional GDP (see Table 3.1 and Appendix Table 3.1), and it has increased further since then. Interest payments on the existing debt stock in the most highly indebted countries with rising debt ratios are already in the range of 16 percent to 42 percent of total revenues. In addition, high amortization exposes some countries to considerable roll-over risk, which could help instigate a financial crisis.

Meanwhile, the institutional framework for debt management is not fully developed. Some countries have a full set of debt management functions, while for others the functions are accorded low priority. The ensuing weak debt management framework and practices constitute a major hidden risk and in some countries have been a key contributor to the rapid accumulation of public debt. Moreover, only in some countries is the public debt market viewed as a tool that creates the infrastructure for the future development of vibrant private capital markets.

A MIXED PROFILE OF RISING PUBLIC DEBT

The public debt characteristics are heterogeneous among these countries, and in some cases have contributed to macroeconomic vulnerabilities. While in general there has been a shift to domestic debt, there are important holdings of foreign currency debt that leave some countries exposed to risks from exchange rate adjustments. In addition, some countries have increased their reliance on the local

This chapter has benefited from some very useful suggestions and comments from Mervyn Anthony.

TABLE 3.1

Selected Debt Indicators, 2001–11

	2001	2002	2003	2004	2005	2006	2007	2008	2009	2010	2011
Public-Debt-to-GDP Ratios											
Countries with debt-to-GDP ratios above 90 percent	94.3	104.7	108.3	112.3	106.7	103.7	99.6	101.6	118.2	122.8	123.0
Countries with debt-to-GDP ratios of 60 to 90 percent	75.1	78.2	78.2	77.5	76.9	71.1	62.2	60.7	65.7	68.9	70.0
Countries with debt-to-GDP ratios below 60 percent	48.2	49.6	43.5	38.3	32.9	28.3	21.8	18.6	23.0	27.0	26.2
All Caribbean	**78.3**	**84.0**	**84.4**	**84.9**	**81.6**	**77.1**	**70.4**	**69.9**	**79.3**	**83.2**	**83.7**
Debt-Service-to-Total-Revenue Ratios											
Countries with debt-to-GDP ratios above 90 percent	53.5	50.5	51.9	54.7	45.2	45.9	34.0	36.9	56.7	41.9	37.6
Countries with debt-to-GDP ratios of 60 to 90 percent	19.0	25.9	25.1	28.5	28.7	21.1	18.6	15.7	20.9	19.1	19.1
Countries with debt-to-GDP ratios below 60 percent	26.2	23.1	24.0	15.7	16.8	13.4	15.5	4.6	12.7	8.5	6.0
All Caribbean	**33.4**	**34.9**	**35.2**	**36.6**	**33.3**	**29.5**	**24.0**	**22.2**	**33.4**	**26.3**	**24.2**

Source: Debt sustainability analysis for countries from IMF staff reports.

financial system and with this the link between fiscal sustainability and financial stability. Additional concerns arise from the exposure of some countries to floating rate debt, lower concessional borrowing terms, and shorter maturity profiles. These vulnerabilities increase the risk of a major fiscal crisis given the high and increasingly unsustainable debt ratios.

Rising Public Debt and Its Originators

Public debt is trending higher, and the proportion held by domestic agents has risen for some countries. High debt burdens and fiscal deficits, in most Caribbean economies, were worsened by the onset of the global financial and economic crisis. Prior to the crisis, moderate growth rates helped some countries to broadly stabilize their debt ratios, albeit at high levels (Table 3.1 and Appendix Table 3.1).

The major portion of the public debt has been accumulated by the central government. This pattern remains whether the debt is broken down into domestic or external debt. Trinidad and Tobago, The Bahamas, and St. Kitts and Nevis stand out as countries where public enterprises contribute more than 20 percent to the total public debt (see Table 3.2).

The largest component of Caribbean public debt is domestic, representing about 60 percent of the total, an increase from 39 percent in 2001 (see Figure 3.1). It is held mainly by commercial banks and non-bank financial institutions, in the form of medium- to long-term instruments. Social security schemes in some countries are also important holders of government debt. However, there are important differences among countries. In some—Belize, Dominica, Grenada, Guyana, St. Vincent and the Grenadines, and Suriname—the public debt portfolio comprises mainly external debt averaging about 69 percent of total debt. In the remaining five countries, domestic debt averages about 70 percent of total public

TABLE 3.2

Government and Government-Guaranteed Debt by Country, 2011

	Antigua and Barbuda	The Bahamas	Barbados	Belize	Dominica	Grenada	Guyana	Jamaica	St. Kitts and Nevis	St. Lucia	St. Vincent and the Grenadines	Suriname[a]	Trinidad and Tobago	Total Caribbean
Total public debt (US$ millions)	1,043.2	4,901.0	5,469.7	1,228.6	341.6	831.5	1,679.0	19,768.0	1,103.2	862.0	468.8	868.9	7,119.6	45,684.5
Central government (percent of debt)	85.3	77.6	82.3	97.1	83.5	86.5	97.4	86.0	78.5	90.5	84.3	99.1	51.5	78.6
Public sector enterprises (percent of debt)[b]	14.7	22.4	17.7	2.9	16.5	13.5	2.6	14.0	21.5	9.5	15.7	0.9	48.5	21.4
External debt (US$ millions)	440.7	1,003.5	1,333.6	1,062.3	244.1	584.5	1,204.0	9,150.7	361.6	420.2	295.3	460.9	1,491.0	18,052.5
Central government (percent of external debt)	88.6	79.8	90.0	93.6	83.3	86.3	98.1	91.6	84.0	91.7	87.9	100.0	98.8	86.1
Other public sector (percent of external debt)	11.4	20.2	10.0	6.4	16.7	13.7	1.9	8.4	16.0	8.3	12.1	0.0	1.2	13.9
Domestic debt (US$ millions)	602.5	3,897.5	4,136.1	166.3	97.5	246.9	475.0	10,617.3	741.6	441.9	173.4	408.0	5,628.6	27,632.6
Central government (percent of domestic debt)	83.0	77.0	79.8	99.7	84.1	86.9	95.3	81.2	77.7	89.3	78.2	98.0	38.9	74.0
Other public sector (percent of domestic debt)	17.0	23.0	20.2	0.3	15.9	13.1	4.7	18.8	22.3	10.7	21.8	2.0	61.1	26.0

Sources: Country authorities; and author's calculations.

[a]For Suriname, breakdown into central government and public sector enterprises is not available.

[b]This includes government-guaranteed debt.

Figure 3.1 Public Debt Composition, Regional Totals, 2011

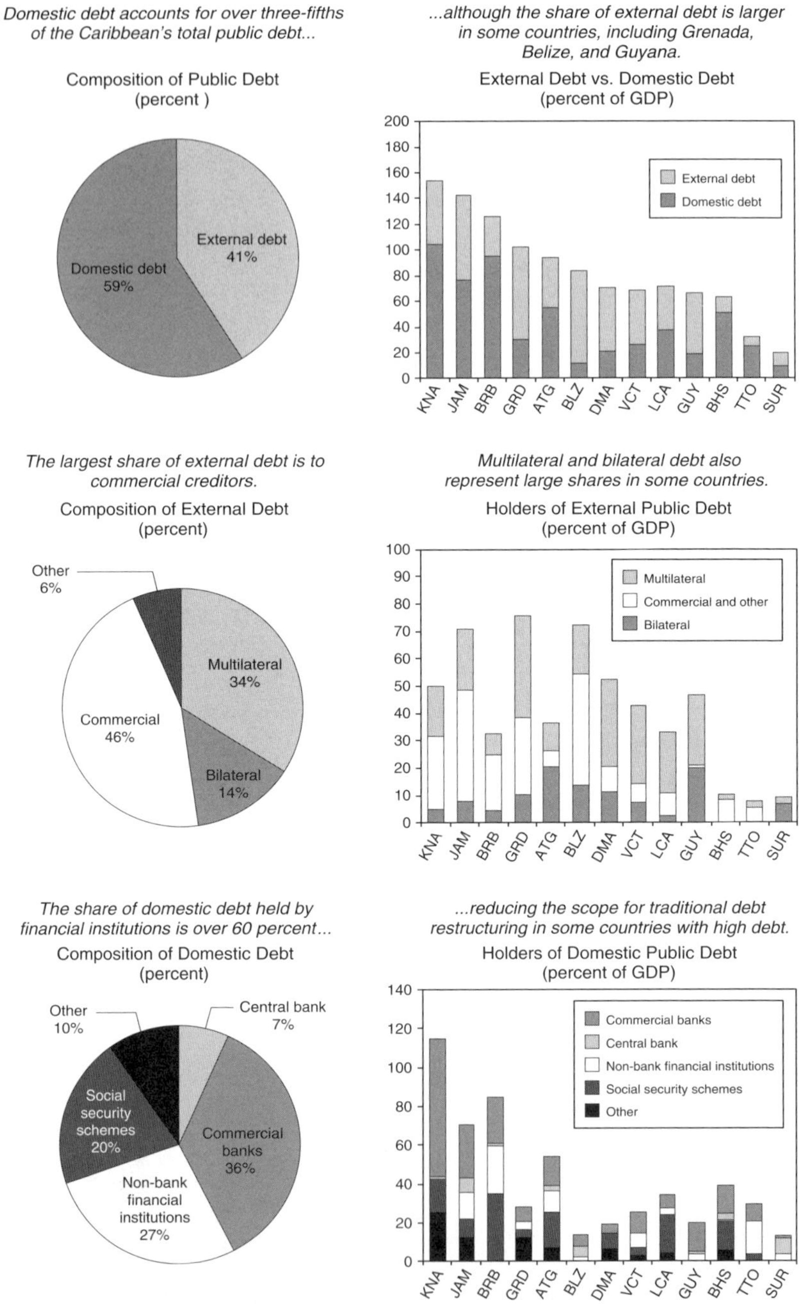

Sources: National authorities; and author's calculations.

Note: ATG=Antigua and Barbuda; BHS=The Bahamas; BRB=Barbados; BLZ=Belize; DMA=Dominica; GRD=Grenada; GUY=Guyana; JAM=Jamaica; KNA=St. Kitts and Nevis; LCA=St. Lucia; VCT=St. Vincent and the Grenadines; SUR=Suriname; TTO=Trinidad and Tobago.

debt. Foreign debt is held mainly by commercial and private lenders, representing about 52 percent of the external debt (21 percent of total), while multilateral holders represent about 34 percent (14 percent of total). Of the multilaterals, the Caribbean Development Bank holds over 10 percent of the external debt.

Bonds remain the instrument of choice for most countries, but there are important differences.

Debt by Instruments

Domestic bonds represent about 52 percent of total public debt in the Caribbean. Other instruments represent the following proportions: Foreign loans 20 percent, foreign bonds 14.5 percent, treasury bills 3.6 percent, domestic overdrafts 5 percent, and others, including suppliers' credit, over 4 percent of total debt. However, the holdings of different instruments differ by country (see Figure 3.2). Domestic bonds are more prevalent in The Bahamas, Barbados, Jamaica, and Trinidad and Tobago, where they represent over 50 percent of total debt.

On the other hand, foreign bonds represent the most important instrument in Belize at about 48 percent of total debt. They also represent a significant portion of total debt in Grenada and Jamaica. Treasury bills are important in Guyana, St. Kitts and Nevis, and Suriname at over 10 percent of total public debt. Foreign loans represent over 40 percent of total public debt in Dominica, Grenada, Guyana, St. Vincent and the Grenadines, and Suriname.

Have these different debt structures helped to mitigate or offset the risks associated with higher debt levels? No, to the contrary, several factors suggest that the elevated debt levels are accompanied by increased risks emanating from the existing debt structures and, through this, in some countries overall vulnerability is increased.

Figure 3.2 Public Debt by Instruments and Country, 2011 *(share of individual country debt)*

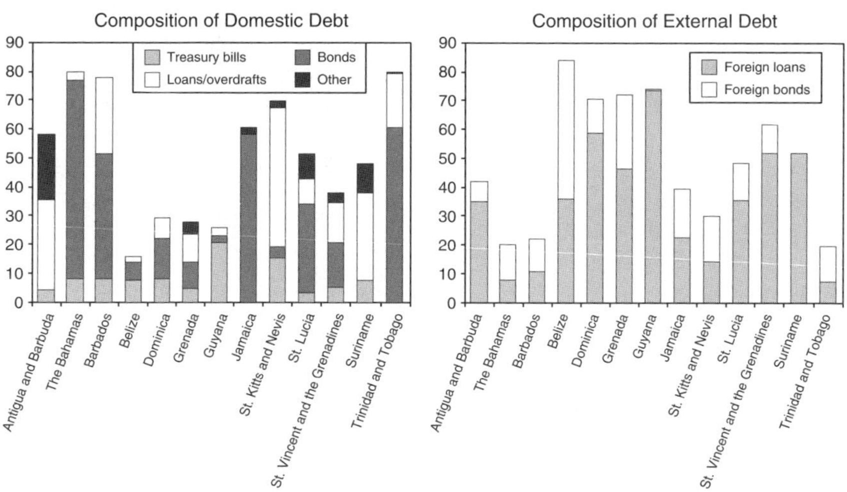

Sources: National authorities; and author's calculations.

Risks from Domestic Debt

Although large holdings of domestic debt may help shield the economy from external debt market impulses and provide some degrees of policy freedom, the experience of some countries in the Caribbean is that it has increased their long-term macroeconomic vulnerability and reduced policy space when it has not been effectively managed. There are several channels through which this works. First, with narrow domestic debt markets, government debt holdings are concentrated in the domestic banking system. This has made the banking system's stability dependent on the fiscal solvency of the sovereign. Second, in countries where the monetary authorities are concerned with defending the exchange rate, they would have to adjust interest rates more aggressively in periods of stress. However, such interest rate adjustments are likely to impact the value of government debt and through this the capital positions of the banks, at times adversely.[1]

Third, where the return on domestic public debt is higher than the return on funding productive private sector projects, the banking system is likely to become a mere funnel for resources to meet public sector borrowing requirement at the expense of funding private investment. Over time, this directly lowers private investment, GDP growth and employment, and exacerbates the country's debt overhang. And fourth, with a concentration of public debt in the banking system, the scope for debt relief is considerably reduced should the sovereign need to restructure its debts. Ordinary domestic debt restructuring operations would have a direct impact on the capital and income position of the financial sector, which may call into question the financial probity of these institutions and may cause the public to lose confidence in the system's capacity to keep its promises.

Debt by Currency

While domestic currency debt represents about 51 percent of total public debt for the region as a whole, foreign currency debt remains substantial for some countries, making them still vulnerable to exchange rate movements.[2] The Bahamas, Barbados, St. Kitts and Nevis, St. Lucia, Suriname, and Trinidad and Tobago have over 50 percent of their public debt in domestic currency. For foreign currency debt, on average over 70 percent is held in U.S. dollars. For some countries, such as Belize and Grenada, the proportion of foreign currency debt is over 90 percent. In general, since 2003 the share of U.S. dollar debt has increased. This general trend for external debt helps to contain risks from intra-currency movements.

Roll-Over Risk

Roll-over risk is an emerging potential problem for some countries. Roll-over risks are clearly evident in respect of external debt.[3] Some countries are borrowing increasing

---

[1]This holds where banks mark-to-market the value of their holding of government debt.

[2]For those countries that have a dollar peg, the large share of U.S. dollar debt means that in practice this vulnerability is reduced, provided that the peg remains sustainable. For those countries with floating exchange rate against the dollar, a large share of U.S. dollar debt increases debt vulnerability through the exchange rate fluctuations.

[3]While it is important to manage total roll-over risks, in some cases in the Caribbean an important distinction may need to be made between domestic and external roll-over risk. Domestic rollover risk

amounts of short-term external debt, aggravating a potential roll-over problem (see Appendix Table 3.2). Available data suggests that roll-over risks have risen in both Guyana and St. Lucia, as both have an increasing share of short-term external debt in total external debt. On the other hand, the share of short-term external debt in total external debt has declined in Dominica, suggesting that roll-over risks may have somewhat declined, other things equal. Regarding domestic debt, St. Kitts and Nevis, with treasury bills representing about 20 percent of total domestic debt, is clearly exposed to roll-over risks.

Gross Financing Needs

Gross financing needs, another indicator of potential roll-over risks, are relatively high for some countries (see Appendix Table 3.3 and Appendix Table 3.4).[4] In 2011, gross financing needs averaged about 20 percent of GDP for those countries with a debt ratio over 90 percent of GDP. St. Kitts and Nevis and Barbados were highest within this group, with gross financing needs of about 25 percent and 48 percent of GDP, respectively. Countries with debt ratios between 60 and 90 percent of GDP (including Guyana and St. Lucia) on average had gross financing needs of about 11 percent of GDP. Suriname and Trinidad and Tobago, both of which have debt ratios below 60 percent of GDP, had gross financing needs below 5 percent of GDP.

Over the medium term—2013 to 2016—gross financing needs on average for all Caribbean countries are projected to decline while still remaining at a relatively high level (about 10 percent of GDP). A number of countries, including Barbados, Guyana, St. Kitts and Nevis, and St. Lucia, are projected to maintain high gross financing needs of between 10 and 26 percent of GDP. These high annual gross financing needs increase the macroeconomic vulnerability of Caribbean economies to shocks.

Floating Interest Rate Risks

Some countries are highly exposed to floating interest rate debt. The public sector's exposure to floating interest rates is mainly on external debt, which has been increasing as a share of total external debt (see Figure 3.3 and Appendix Table 3.5). In this context, three country groups can be identified. The first group includes countries (Belize, Grenada, and Jamaica) that have over 30 percent of their external debt exposed to floating interest rates. In the case of Belize and Jamaica, this exposure has been increasing over time, but it has been decreasing for Grenada (since 2006). The second group includes those countries (St. Kitts and Nevis, St. Lucia, St. Vincent and the Grenadines, and Suriname) where between 10 and 20 percent of external debt is exposed to a floating interest rate. The final group includes countries (The Bahamas, Dominica, and Guyana) where the exposure to floating interest rates is less than 10 percent.

---

may be less serious given the near-captive nature of domestic holders of government debt and the dearth of alternative financial investment instruments.

[4]For some countries increasing gross external financing needs over the medium term—partly due to the precarious fiscal situation and debt rollover needs—would make them highly vulnerable to external shocks. Reducing gross external financing needs and vulnerability would require robust and sustained fiscal consolidation.

On the domestic front, except for Antigua and Barbuda, The Bahamas, and Jamaica, all countries have only fixed-rate debt. For The Bahamas, interest rates on government domestic securities are tied to the Bahamian prime rate, which exposes over 90 percent of domestic debt to floating interest rates.[5]

Interest Rate Resetting Risks

Interest rate resetting risks are concentrated mainly on domestic debt—for treasury bills—and other instruments that mature within one year. In the Caribbean as a whole, about 8 percent of total debt is exposed to interest rate resetting risks. There are, however, important differences across the region, as some countries had an exposure of up to 20 percent of total debt in 2011 (see Figure 3.4).

The total debt service burden has risen for most countries, partly reflecting the higher cost of domestic debt.

Debt Service Burdens

Debt service (interest and amortization) averaged 24 percent of central government revenues and grants at end-2011, down from 37 percent in 2004 (see Table 3.1). The average ratio for the high-debt countries was 38 percent of

Figure 3.3 Interest Rate Structure of Public Debt by Country, 2011 *(percent of total public debt)*

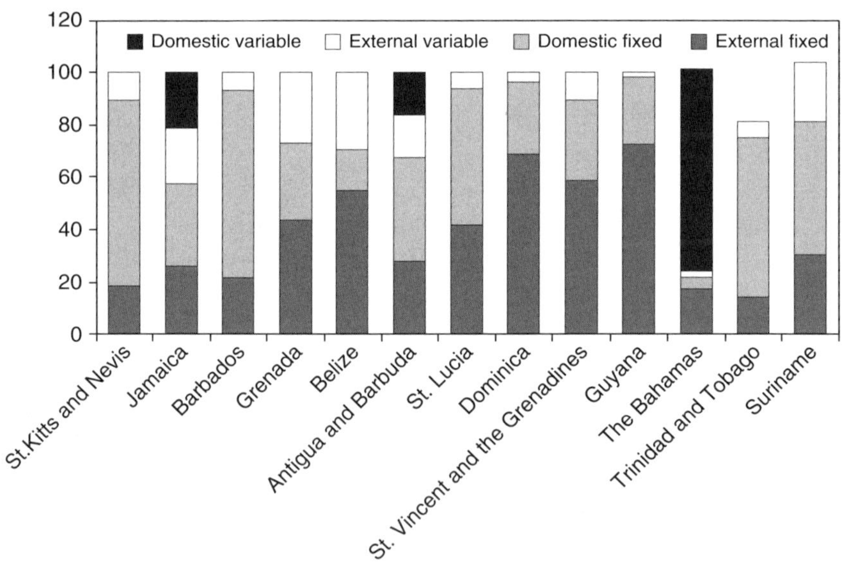

Sources: World Bank, Global Development Finance; and author's calculations.

[5]However, from a practical standpoint, to the extent that the prime rate has remained stable for decades the risk from this may be low.

Figure 3.4 Public Debt Exposed to Interest Rate Resetting Risks by Country, 2011[a]
(percent of total public debt)

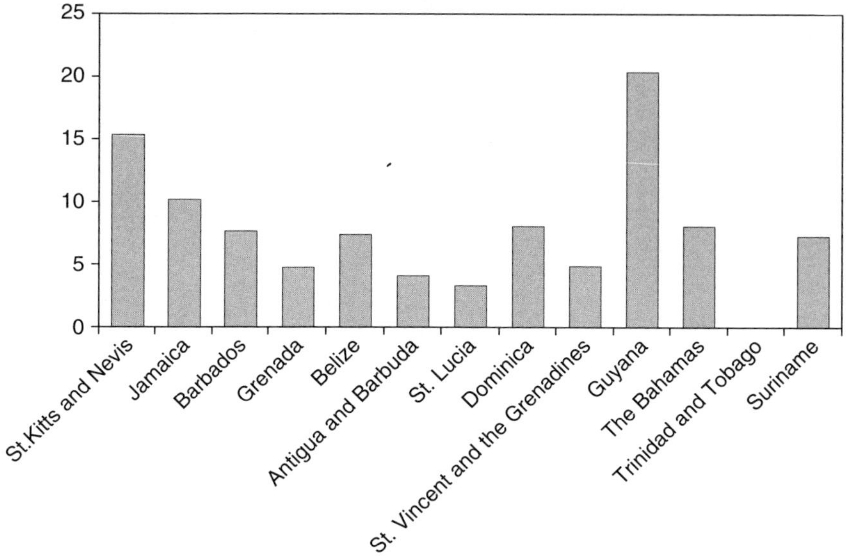

Source: Author's calculations.
[a]Public debt exposed to interest rate resetting is measured for most countries as the share of treasury bills in total debt.

revenues, led by Jamaica (77 percent). The average for the medium-debt countries was 19 percent, led by The Bahamas (27 percent). In the low-debt countries, debt service averaged 6 percent, led by Trinidad and Tobago (6.6 percent). The vulnerability of a number of countries is also revealed by the external debt service ratios shown in Appendix Table 3.6. This ratio averaged about 21 percent of exports of goods and services for high-debt countries, 10 percent for medium-debt countries, and less than 2 percent for low-debt countries (Suriname and Trinidad and Tobago). Over the medium term, external debt service ratios are projected to rise to about 14 percent for the medium-debt countries, but fall to about 13 percent of exports of goods and services for the high-debt countries (as some benefit from debt restructuring operations). In this mix a number of countries, including Dominica, Grenada, Jamaica, and St. Lucia, are projected to have high external debt service ratios over 20 percent of exports of goods and services.

Interest Costs

The average nominal interest cost fell marginally since the onset of the global financial crisis to about 6.5 percent, down from 6.7 percent in the period prior to the crisis, while the real cost rose in all countries, except for Antigua and Barbuda, Belize, Grenada, and Jamaica. On average, domestic debt was more expensive than external debt during the 2001–11 period. In the case of new external debt commitments, interest rates have risen in 2011 for four countries: Belize, Dominica,

TABLE 3.3

Concessionality of External Debt by Country, 2003-11[a] *(In percent of total public and publicly guaranteed external debt)*

	2003	2004	2005	2006	2007	2008	2009	2010	2011
Antigua and Barbuda	...	...	...	...	...	...	...	...	...
The Bahamas	...	...	...	...	...	...	...	...	...
Barbados	...	...	...	...	...	...	...	...	...
Belize	9.1	12.6	14.5	15.8	17.3	15.8	17.1	17.5	18.4
Dominica	43.8	47.4	50.7	54.1	47.4	43.9	48.8	54.6	58.4
Grenada	28.4	26.3	35.5	36.0	37.8	41.7	43.5	42.9	43.3
Guyana	75.0	77.1	80.0	75.2	70.9	72.6	61.4	54.7	52.5
Jamaica	17.6	14.8	13.1	11.9	10.8	10.8	10.2	8.6	7.2
St. Kitts and Nevis	36.4	36.3	38.5	42.3	45.3	47.8	49.4	54.2	...
St. Lucia	28.8	28.9	25.0	32.7	29.1	23.2	46.8	38.4	51.1
St. Vincent and the Grenadines	48.1	43.4	37.7	38.7	48.5	46.6	47.9	62.8	66.4
Suriname	...	...	...	...	...	...	...	...	...
Trinidad and Tobago	...	...	...	...	...	...	...	...	...

Source: World Bank, Global Development Finance.

[a]Concessional debt to total external debt stocks. Concessional debt is defined as loans with an original grant element of 25 percent or more.

Jamaica, and St. Kitts and Nevis. On the other hand, average interest rates have fallen for four other countries: Grenada, Guyana, St. Lucia, and St. Vincent and the Grenadines.

Debt by Concessionality

The story on concessionality of external debt is mixed. Since 2003, except for Guyana and Jamaica, the proportion of concessional debt to total external debt has almost steadily risen (see Table 3.3 and Appendix Table 3.7).[6] In the case of Jamaica, concessional debt in 2011 was about 7 percent of total public and publicly guaranteed external debt, down from 17 percent in 2003. In Guyana, while the proportion of concessional external debt has fallen, the country still maintains over 50 percent of external debt as concessional.

Average Grant Element

Based on available data, the average grant element of recent new external commitments remains generally favorable.[7] Most countries maintained a grant element

[6]St. Vincent and the Grenadines had a temporary fall in concessional debt during 2004 and 2007. St Lucia also experienced a temporary fall in concessional debt during 2005 and 2008.

[7]It must be noted that the average grant element for some countries in some years has been quite volatile. For example in 2006, Dominica and St. Vincent and the Grenadines had a grant element of zero on new external commitments. Since then the average element on new commitments has risen to about 50 percent for St. Vincent and the Grenadines. For Dominica the average grant element has declined to about 47 percent in 2011 from 78.4 percent in 2007.

in the range of 40 to 60 percent on new external debt commitments. In fact, in 2011 only Jamaica experienced a sharp fall in its grant element to about 24 percent from 58 percent in 2010 (see Appendix Table 3.7).

Average Grace Period

Since 2007 the average grace period on new external commitments has declined for most countries. The sharpest fall was for St. Lucia, which declined to less than one year in 2011 from 10 years in 2007. For St. Vincent and the Grenadines, the average grace period for new external commitments is just under two years. This means that the governments in St. Vincent and St. Lucia are borrowing on terms that require them to start repaying almost immediately (see Appendix Table 3.7).

Average Interest Rates on New Debt

The average interest rate on new external commitments generally fell for most countries during the period under consideration. Two broad patterns can be identified. First, there are those countries (Dominica, Jamaica, St. Lucia, St. Vincent and the Grenadines, and Grenada) for which average interest rates first rose, relative to 2007, but then started to decline from 2010 onwards. The second pattern can be observed in those countries (Belize and St. Kitts and Nevis) where the average interest rate first declined up until 2009 and then started rising in 2010. In 2011, except for Belize and Dominica, the average interest rates on new external debt declined relative to those obtained in 2010 (see Appendix Table 3.7).

Debt Payment Arrears

Repayment arrears on public debt, both on principal and on interest payments, remain a key challenge for many countries. Concerning principal repayments, Grenada and Guyana stand out with the highest proportion of arrears to total external debt since 2003 (see Appendix Table 3.8).[8] For Antigua and Barbuda (not shown in the table), it is estimated that arrears on external debt in 2011 were about 20 percent of total external debt. For St. Kitts & Nevis external arrears were estimated at about 10.7 percent of total external debt.[9] Concerning official interest payments, Grenada, Guyana, and Jamaica had the highest arrears among countries reporting interest payment arrears. For Guyana and Jamaica (due to the debt exchange in 2010 in the case of Jamaica) the share of interest payment arrears to GDP has declined since 2010 (see Appendix Table 3.8).

---

[8]For Guyana these are arrears on non-Paris Club debt that should get debt relief terms similar to the Heavily Indebted Poor Countries Initiative relief on Paris Club debt, and therefore they are not paid.

[9]In 2011 total arrears (domestic and external) were about 15.1 percent of total debt for Antigua and Barbuda, and 3.5 percent for St. Kitts and Nevis (see Government of Antigua and Barbuda, 2011, and for St. Kitts and Nevis, IMF, 2011c). In the case of Suriname, total arrears in 2011 were about 1.3 percent of total public debt stock.

ESTIMATES OF CONTINGENT FISCAL LIABILITIES

A key factor in the rising public sector debt levels for Caribbean economies has been the realization of contingent liabilities. In this section, we provide a general estimate of contingent liabilities for all countries. Contingent liabilities consist of both explicit liabilities, which the government is obligated to satisfy once an event occur, and implicit liabilities, which the government may satisfy once an event takes place. Total explicit contingent liabilities in the Caribbean are conservatively estimated to average 19 percent of GDP. This estimate is derived from published IMF staff reports and other publicly available information (see Appendix Table 3.9).

However, the estimate of explicit fiscal contingent liabilities varies among countries. It consists primarily of the Petro-Caribe debt, pending payments for nationalized companies, government debt guarantees for state-owned enterprises (SOEs), and estimated annual spending related to hurricane damage mitigation. Meanwhile, implicit contingent liabilities have been estimated to average 9 percent of GDP, which reflects exposure to the failure of the CLICO/BAICO insurance conglomerate.[10]

It must be noted that not all countries fully record contingent liabilities in their public debt statistics. As the case of Belize has shown, realization of contingent fiscal liabilities can precipitate a fiscal crisis. In 2007, the obligations of the state-owned Development Finance Corporation had to be assumed by the central government as part of an overall restructuring of government's external debt obligations. The government also had to pay debt obligations of domestic private enterprises when guarantees were called. In 2013, the government negotiated a second debt restructuring on the obligations originating from the 2007 debt exchange operations. At the same time, new contingent fiscal liabilities, arising mainly from the combination of adverse court rulings against the state and pending compensation payments for nationalized assets, amounted to about 17 percent of GDP. These were not addressed by the 2013 debt exchange operation.

A FRAGMENTED INSTITUTIONAL FRAMEWORK FOR PUBLIC DEBT MANAGEMENT[11]

Debt management in Caribbean economies is currently weak, and most countries do not have an explicit debt management strategy. Using the World Bank's Debt Management Performance Assessment (DeMPA) framework, the region does not rank very well on average (see Table 3.4 and Appendix Table 3.10).[12] The

[10]The Colonial Life Insurance Company (CLICO) and the British American Insurance Company (BAICO) were part of the CL financial group, which suffered adverse clearings and collapsed during the 2009 global financial crisis. CLICO and BAICO operated in most of the Caribbean countries, but some countries were impacted more severely depending more or less on the rigor of their regulatory framework and enforcement.

[11]This section draws partly on Robinson (2010).

[12]DeMPA evaluates strengths and weaknesses in public debt management, through a comprehensive set of 15 performance indicators covering six core areas of public debt management: (1) governance and strategy development; (2) coordination with macroeconomic policies; (3) borrowing and related financing activities; (4) cash flow forecasting and cash balance management; (5) operational risk management; and (6) debt records and reporting.

TABLE 3.4

Debt Management Practices in the Caribbean

	Factor	Findings	Progress Indicators
1	Institutional framework	In most countries the legal framework is fragmented; fragmented organizational framework, low staff capacity (limited application of training and high staff turnover).	Modernized debt legislation in the form of a single debt management act (in Suriname); Draft legislation for modernized single debt management act (Jamaica). In the ECCU the issues of staff capacity and institutional strengthening are being addressed through an ongoing training and technical support program coordinated by the ECCB with technical support and funding from CIDA.
2	Coordination	In some countries there is very limited coordination with monetary and fiscal policies; irregular information exchange.	Some debt management committees have been formed (Barbados, Grenada, and Jamaica). In the ECCU more generally the activities of the RGSM are overseen by a Regional Debt Coordinating Committee comprising the financial secretaries from each participating country. They receive reports on market activity and projections on the likely future demand and supply of government securities. In addition, they also make decisions on the future development of the market.
3	Debt management strategy	There are no explicit or comprehensive debt management strategies in most countries based on cost/risk analysis, and no formal risk management strategy.	Jamaica has published a medium-term debt strategy. Barbados has published a medium-term fiscal strategy paper. Countries in the ECCU have adopted a medium-term debt target of 60 percent debt-to-GDP ratio by 2020. They have also committed to providing annual progress reports on these efforts.
4	Borrowing activities	Government securities are market inefficient; there are few documented loan evaluations or public borrowing plans; limited involvement of government legal advisors.	Growing use of the RGSM (which involves auctions and dematerialized securities) is helping to improve price discovery and overall efficiency of the Government Securities Market in the ECCU; Barbados and Jamaica have also moved to dematerialization; and competitive auctions (Jamaica and Trinidad and Tobago); primary dealers (Jamaica, Trinidad and Tobago, and the ECCU). In the ECCU an annual issuance calendar is prepared based on the government's borrowing plan; this information is disseminated on the ECCB's website and is updated monthly.
5	Operational risk management	Most countries do not have well-documented operational risk management procedures. There is little, if any, compliance monitoring with existing policies and procedures.	Some progress is being made in this area, including clearly articulated/documented job descriptions for debt management (Jamaica, Guyana, Suriname, the ECCU) and for debt recording and reporting procedures (Guyana).
6	Debt recording and reporting	Few countries have validated data; few countries disseminate comprehensive debt statistics at regular intervals during the calendar year.	Comprehensive debt statistics available on website (Jamaica); Antigua and Barbuda and St. Kitts and Nevis recently restructured their public debt, and part of the preparations involved validating and updating the database. More generally the ECCU is working together to improve the debt recording, reporting, and analysis of the debt units with the help of CIDA.

Sources: Robinson (2010); Government of Antigua and Barbuda (2011); and www.eccb-centralbank.org.

Note: CIDA = the Canadian International Development Agency; ECCB = the Eastern Caribbean Central Bank; ECCU = the Eastern Caribbean Currency Union; RGSM = Regional Government Securities Market.

institutional framework is fragmented, facilitating only limited coordination with macroeconomic policies. Borrowing plans are not fully articulated, and there is only limited practice of comprehensive debt recording and reporting to parliament. The following debt management features are generally observed in the Caribbean.

Fragmented Legal Framework

Apart from Jamaica and Suriname, which have a single debt management law, the legal framework for issuing and managing debt is very fragmented (see Appendix Table 3.10). Debt is issued using several pieces of legislation, often targeted at a specific purpose, and while these laws generally provide the minister of finance with the sole authority to borrow, they may or may not prescribe specific borrowing limits.

Weak Coordination between Debt Management and Fiscal and Monetary Policy

In many countries, the coordination mechanism between debt management and the requirements for sustainability of fiscal and monetary policies is either limited or very weak. Even though some countries, including Barbados and Jamaica, have recently created debt management committees to address issues in this area, there is still some way to go to improve coordination. At the ECCU level, there is an explicit limit on direct access to central bank credit, and there is a regional debt coordinating committee for the Regional Government Securities Market (RGSM—See Box 3.1). At the domestic level, however, the mechanism remains underdeveloped.

Weak Debt Management Frameworks

Debt management frameworks are weak, as only a few countries have explicit debt management strategies.[13] Even where these strategies exist, they are generally not comprehensive and not focused on or informed by a cost/risk analysis. In addition, in some countries, while parliament provides the ultimate authority on borrowing, there are no explicit requirements for reporting to parliament or for the conduct of audits.

Fragmented and Inefficient Debt Markets

Government debt markets remain underdeveloped, particularly the secondary markets, which are limited and inefficient, preventing effective price discovery. Further, most borrowing activities are generally not supported by evaluation of their impact on the fiscal and debt sustainability of a government's fiscal strategy. For example, debt sustainability analysis is infrequently done and therefore does not sufficiently influence policy.

---

[13]In some countries the legal framework does not contemplate the development of debt management strategies or the use of debt management objectives to guide borrowing.

Inadequate Risk Management and Debt Recording

Operational risk management procedures are not generally well documented, and even where they exist, they are often not observed. Concerning debt recording and reporting, most countries do not regularly disseminate comprehensive debt statistics, due in part to staffing constraints and the relatively low priority that has been given to debt management and, in particular, measuring accurately and comprehensively the total liabilities of the public sector in some countries. It must be noted that in the case of the ECCU, at one time the central bank facilitated the publication of external debt statistics for its membership. This publication has since been discontinued.

Current Efforts to Improve Debt Management

Against this background, however, deliberate efforts are being made to improve the framework for debt management in the Caribbean, including in the ECCU, Jamaica, and Trinidad and Tobago.

BOX 3.1

Recent Developments in Public Debt Management in the Eastern Caribbean Currency Union

At the core of the ECCU's debt management modernization plan is the Regional Government Securities Market (RGSM).[a] This market is modernizing the way governments issue and manage public debt. Supporting components of this initiative include, among others, technical support to the individual debt units in ECCU member countries. This component builds on a previous Commonwealth debt management debt recording and management system and is being supported by the Canadian International Development Agency (CIDA).[b] According to the Eastern Caribbean Central Bank (ECCB), during 2013 the focus under this initiative would be training and technical support in negotiation techniques for sources of finance; a review of the current debt legislation in the ECCU; and assistance utilizing policy tools, such as debt management strategies. Thus far, this project has facilitated the preparation of debt sustainability analyses to inform policy discussions; conducted training in the evaluation of sources of finance; increased usage of the RGSM; and enhanced debt data quality and security.[c]

---

[a] Not all governments in the ECCU have issued debt on the RGSM, or otherwise use it fully to meet their borrowing requirements.

[b] The Canada Eastern Caribbean Debt Management Advisory Service (CANEC-DMAS) Project is a CIDA-funded debt management project, which commenced operations at the ECCB in 2009. The main objective of the project is to provide capacity building to the ECCU member countries to effectively manage their debt portfolios. This is being done in close collaboration with the ministries of finance in the ECCU member states. The Project Steering Committee, which comprises the governor of the ECCB as chairman, the financial secretaries in the ECCU, and a representative of CIDA, is responsible for providing oversight to the project.

[c] See Eastern Caribbean Central Bank (2013).

A number of countries are making concerted efforts to strengthen their framework for public debt management with the help of technical assistance, in some cases from international agencies. In particular, the new CIDA-funded technical assistance project for Barbados, Belize, the ECCU, and Jamaica, which, along with efforts of other technical assistance providers, including the Commonwealth Secretariat, Inter-American Development Bank, and the World Bank, will support capacity building in the Caribbean over the coming years.

A key issue that all countries in the region, particularly ECCU countries, need to tackle is how to retain highly trained and skilled persons in the management of public debt portfolios. Part of the solution may rest with the authorities' utilizing more fully the considerable potential of the existing debt systems and personnel. Further, an accompanying initiative would be the sharing of skills, know-how, technology, and perhaps eventually some back-office functions. Additionally, an appropriate salary structure could be used to retain skilled debt managers, as is done in other countries.

CONCLUSION

This chapter contains several insights about the key characteristics of public debt and debt management practices in the Caribbean. Of particular note is that, although in aggregate about 60 percent of total public debt is held domestically, for some countries a sizeable proportion remains as foreign debt, especially with multilateral institutions. For most countries, the current structure of their public debt is not mitigating but exacerbating the macroeconomic vulnerabilities attendant to their high debt-to-GDP ratio. Indeed, the high level of domestic debt held by the banking system in some countries has reduced the degrees of freedom for public policy. In addition, contingent fiscal liabilities appear to be a growing problem for most countries, and recent events such as the CLICO/BAICO debacle have increased the risk exposure for most countries. At the same time, the debt management framework and practices in the Caribbean have not kept in step with international best practices. That said, some countries have recognized this problem and are now actively working to close this gap in the midst of the public debt overhang.

A number of policy implications flow from these insights. First, while an increase in domestic debt holdings reduces exchange rate risks, care must be taken that an increase in domestic debt does not dominate the financial system and take resources away from private productive activity. Second, to protect the financial system from excessive exposure to public debt, regulators may consider imposing risk weights (or concentration limits) on the banking system's holdings of government debt.[14] This would help to appropriately budget the risk that banks face when investing in government securities. Third, specific measures must be taken

[14]Banks in Trinidad and Tobago already have concentration limits on holding government debt.

to properly develop the domestic government bond market, which could be a benchmark for developing private capital markets. Fourth, governments should adopt appropriate guidelines for issuing government guarantees, including limiting the scope and duration of contingent liabilities through time and terminating clauses for contingent claims. Further, these should be recorded and reported regularly to parliament. Fifth, international best practices in debt management should be adopted in a systematic and sustainable program. This should involve legal reform to create a single debt law, adoption of explicit debt management strategies, and ongoing capacity building in management techniques and analysis.

APPENDIX TABLE 3.1

Selected Debt Indicators by Country, 2001–11

	2001	2002	2003	2004	2005	2006	2007	2008	2009	2010	2011
Public-Debt-to-GDP Ratios											
Countries with Debt-to-GDP Ratios above 90 percent											
St. Kitts and Nevis	105.8	120.5	143.2	156.0	159.9	145.3	134.0	131.0	148.5	163.9	153.6
Jamaica	133.3	126.3	123.1	119.9	119.3	117.1	114.6	125.6	139.4	140.8	141.5
Barbados	66.8	70.6	70.0	69.4	71.9	73.2	81.8	90.9	104.1	118.3	125.5
Grenada	44.4	78.5	78.8	94.2	88.0	92.6	88.9	83.7	97.1	100.2	101.2
Antigua and Barbuda	121.3	127.5	126.1	122.1	94.6	90.4	78.8	76.9	102.0	90.6	93.3
Average	**94.3**	**104.7**	**108.3**	**112.3**	**106.7**	**103.7**	**99.6**	**101.6**	**118.2**	**122.8**	**123.0**
Countries with Debt-to-GDP Ratios of 60 to 90 percent											
St. Vincent and the Grenadines	56.5	56.5	59.0	62.3	64.8	65.2	55.6	57.3	64.6	66.2	67.8
St. Lucia	47.9	59.8	56.5	61.2	63.3	59.4	57.5	57.1	61.3	66.0	71.1
The Bahamas	31.8	33.8	36.8	37.8	36.8	38.9	40.4	44.1	55.0	61.4	63.0
Guyana	129.7	131.3	119.5	118.2	115.7	93.1	59.9	61.6	64.8	65.3	65.2
Dominica	100.8	99.2	95.3	86.5	82.6	77.9	71.9	64.3	63.3	68.9	70.2
Belize	83.8	89.0	102.3	99.2	98.1	92.3	87.9	79.6	84.9	85.3	83.0
Average	**75.1**	**78.2**	**78.2**	**77.5**	**76.9**	**71.1**	**62.2**	**60.7**	**65.7**	**68.9**	**70.0**
Countries with Debt-to-GDP Ratios Below 60 percent											
Suriname	39.8	40.1	33.7	31.4	28.9	24.0	17.5	15.6	15.5	18.5	19.1
Trinidad and Tobago	56.5	59.1	53.2	45.2	36.8	32.6	26.1	21.5	30.6	35.5	33.4
Average	**48.2**	**49.6**	**43.5**	**38.3**	**32.9**	**28.3**	**21.8**	**18.6**	**23.0**	**27.0**	**26.2**
All Caribbean	**78.3**	**84.0**	**84.4**	**84.9**	**81.6**	**77.1**	**70.4**	**69.9**	**79.3**	**83.2**	**83.7**
Debt Service to Total Revenue Ratios											
Countries with Debt-to-GDP Ratios above 90 percent											
St. Kitts and Nevis	45.2	40.5	46.0	45.8	36.9	38.3	40.4	39.1	37.6	47.2	48.3
Jamaica	138.8	129.6	126.1	133.5	125.5	126.0	77.3	86.0	119.3	73.5	77.2
Barbados	12.4	15.4	15.1	13.9	14.5	16.5	16.2	15.4	18.4	30.1	22.1
Grenada	8.9	17.4	19.3	20.1	7.0	6.5	7.7	7.5	9.8	14.1	14.4
Antigua and Barbuda	62.3	49.5	53.2	60.3	42.3	42.1	28.2	36.5	98.7	44.7	25.7
Average	**53.5**	**50.5**	**51.9**	**54.7**	**45.2**	**45.9**	**34.0**	**36.9**	**56.7**	**41.9**	**37.6**

(Continued)

APPENDIX TABLE 3.1 ***(continued)***

Selected Debt Indicators by Country, 2001–11

	2001	2002	2003	2004	2005	2006	2007	2008	2009	2010	2011
	Countries with Debt-to-GDP Ratios of 60 to 90 percent										
St. Vincent and the Grenadines	12.5	25.7	16.7	17.4	23.1	22.0	19.7	18.6	21.7	23.7	20.6
St. Lucia	11.9	18.8	15.0	19.2	19.9	20.2	21.2	15.4	24.7	27.5	17.4
The Bahamas	19.2	25.8	38.6	18.7	16.9	17.1	17.3	16.5	36.1	23.5	27.9
Guyana	29.0	28.2	25.4	20.5	16.4	9.5	7.2	7.1	5.8	8.1	9.3
Dominica	12.3	12.3	9.1	12.3	12.7	14.5	12.1	9.5	11.7	10.6	16.3
Belize	28.9	44.9	45.7	83.1	83.5	43.4	34.2	27.3	25.1	21.3	23.0
Average	**19.0**	**25.9**	**25.1**	**28.5**	**28.7**	**21.1**	**18.6**	**15.7**	**20.9**	**19.1**	**19.1**
	Countries with Debt-to-GDP Ratios Below 60 percent										
Suriname	20.7	19.7	16.9	12.4	14.3	14.7	21.9	4.1	16.5	5.4	5.3
Trinidad and Tobago	31.8	26.5	31.0	18.9	19.3	12.2	9.0	5.2	9.0	11.6	6.6
Average	**26.2**	**23.1**	**24.0**	**15.7**	**16.8**	**13.4**	**15.5**	**4.6**	**12.7**	**8.5**	**6.0**
All Caribbean	**33.4**	**34.9**	**35.2**	**36.6**	**33.3**	**29.5**	**24.0**	**22.2**	**33.4**	**26.3**	**24.2**

Source: Countries' debt sustainability analyses from IMF staff reports.

APPENDIX TABLE 3.2

Short-Term External Debt by Country, 2003–11[a] *(In percent of total external debt)*

	2003	2004	2005	2006	2007	2008	2009	2010	2011
Antigua and Barbuda	...	...	...	...	...	...	...	...	...
The Bahamas	...	...	...	...	...	...	...	...	...
Barbados	...	...	...	...	...	...	...	...	...
Belize	7.6	0.1	0.7	0.7	0.7	0.6	0.7	0.5	0.6
Dominica	24.0	22.8	14.6	8.6	21.6	27.3	13.9	11.5	9.7
Grenada	19.1	17.6	1.5	7.0	9.1	10.9	6.4	6.7	6.0
Guyana	8.1	9.5	6.6	13.9	12.3	11.3	16.7	27.6	33.0
Jamaica	17.4	16.8	9.3	13.6	14.6	12.1	6.8	7.7	7.0
St. Kitts and Nevis	0.6	1.0	0.9	1.4	0.8	0.5	0.4	0.6	...
St. Lucia	32.6	30.7	42.3	31.7	36.5	61.8	19.5	38.9	21.6
St. Vincent and the Grenadines	1.6	1.6	1.7	0.2	0.8	0.1	0.2	0.0	0.0
Suriname	...	...	...	...	...	...	...	...	...
Trinidad and Tobago	...	...	...	...	...	...	...	...	...

Source: World Bank, Global Development Finance.

[a]Short-term debt includes all debt having an original maturity of one year or less and interest in arrears on long-term debt. Total external debt is debt owed to nonresidents repayable in foreign currency, goods, or services. Total external debt is the sum of public, publicly guaranteed, and private nonguaranteed long-term debt, use of IMF credit, and short-term debt.

APPENDIX TABLE 3.3

Gross Financing Needs by Country, 2002–16 *(In percent of GDP)*

												Projections			
	2002	2003	2004	2005	2006	2007	2008	2009	2010	2011	2012	2013	2014	2015	2016
St. Kitts and Nevis	60.8	60.8	60.8	73.3	67.1	55.5	54.3	51.1	52.2	47.7	40.9	21.2	22.7	25.1	24.8
Jamaica	26.9	24.2	28.2	23.9	27.2	14.5	17.6	26.3	14.8	16.5	11.5	7.5	3.9	8.2	1.8
Barbados	3.2	8.1	13.5	17.4	15.5	19.0	20.3	22.4	30.5	24.9	22.5	21.6	20.5	21.1	19.1
Antigua and Barbuda	21.0	20.0	15.8	16.3	10.6	4.8	7.9	22.2	6.1	4.8	11.8	−0.7	−0.7	5.8	12.5
Grenada	13.4	6.5	2.2	−0.3	4.9	6.3	4.2	5.4	5.0	6.0	6.5	8.3	8.6	9.0	9.5
Average	**25.1**	**23.9**	**24.1**	**26.1**	**25.1**	**20.0**	**20.9**	**25.5**	**21.7**	**20.0**	**18.6**	**11.6**	**11.0**	**13.9**	**13.5**
The Bahamas	3.8	6.5	3.7	3.0	2.5	3.8	3.3	9.4	6.2	7.9	6.4	6.4	5.9	5.4	5.8
Belize	13.8	15.7	18.2	18.4	6.7	5.7	2.5	5.9	3.9	4.2	4.1	3.4	4.1	3.9	6.6
Dominica	2.7	−1.5	0.8	−1.2	0.1	0.9	2.0	3.5	8.9	9.2	9.0	7.9	8.5	7.9	7.9
Guyana	20.3	22.8	23.8	32.6	28.9	23.0	21.7	20.7	21.3	22.3	31.1	21.4	16.5	12.9	12.9
St. Lucia	7.3	8.9	7.1	12.0	11.2	6.7	3.4	9.4	12.6	14.0	18.1	20.6	20.9	23.2	21.9
St. Vincent and the Grenadines	6.7	4.3	6.4	10.2	...	9.6	5.6	9.4	12.3	7.6	9.4	13.7	10.9	9.0	8.2
Average	**9.1**	**9.4**	**10.0**	**12.5**	**9.9**	**8.3**	**6.4**	**9.7**	**10.9**	**10.9**	**13.0**	**12.2**	**11.1**	**10.4**	**10.6**
Suriname	11.5	9.8	9.9	10.1	7.8	8.2	2.5	7.8	9.0	3.6	4.3	2.7	0.5	−1.8	−2.8
Trinidad and Tobago	7.8	4.6	2.1	0.8	−2.5	−1.7	−7.0	10.2	6.3	1.4	1.5	2.4	2.6	3.1	3.7
Average	**9.6**	**7.2**	**6.0**	**5.4**	**2.7**	**3.3**	**−2.3**	**9.0**	**7.7**	**2.5**	**2.9**	**2.6**	**1.6**	**0.7**	**0.4**
Caribbean mean	**15.5**	**15.3**	**15.9**	**18.1**	**15.9**	**12.5**	**11.2**	**16.5**	**15.4**	**13.7**	**14.2**	**10.7**	**9.7**	**10.3**	**10.2**
Caribbean median	**9.6**	**9.3**	**11.7**	**14.2**	**10.6**	**7.5**	**4.5**	**9.8**	**10.7**	**8.6**	**10.5**	**7.7**	**7.2**	**8.1**	**8.1**

Source: Countries' debt sustainability analyses from IMF staff reports.

APPENDIX TABLE 3.4

Gross External Financing Needs by Country, 2002–16 *(In percent of GDP)*

												Projections			
	2002	2003	2004	2005	2006	2007	2008	2009	2010	2011	2012	2013	2014	2015	2016
St. Kitts and Nevis	36.6	37.8	28.6	26.4	24.3	27.0	34.5	35.2	30.9	24.7	33.4	23.4	24.3	25.3	23.0
Jamaica	19.4	11.4	12.8	15.4	18.9	21.5	22.6	10.2	11.0	19.0	16.2	13.0	14.8	12.7	11.5
Barbados	6.4	5.2	9.1	8.9	6.4	4.0	10.9	6.8	12.9	11.9	7.7	7.6	6.8	7.0	6.2
Antigua and Barbuda	13.1	14.7	19.5	34.6	28.7	31.4	30.7	20.6	15.9	11.2	12.2	14.0	17.2	18.6	19.5
Grenada	17.0	18.3	7.1	23.3	27.7	29.2	27.2	26.2	27.7	25.8	25.7	28.4	32.5	28.3	23.4
Average	**18.5**	**17.5**	**15.4**	**21.7**	**21.2**	**22.6**	**25.2**	**19.8**	**19.7**	**18.5**	**19.0**	**17.3**	**19.1**	**18.4**	**16.7**
The Bahamas	6.8	6.8	2.8	8.6	17.8	11.9	10.8	11.2	11.5	14.2	14.3	14.1	12.8	11.0	9.7
Belize	...	30.2	27.8	28.4	7.9	52.1	16.6	9.3	5.4	4.9	4.9	5.0	5.5	5.9	6.8
Dominica	14.2	15.0	16.2	20.3	15.1	22.2	28.3	23.6	18.2	15.3	16.1	15.9	17.0	16.6	22.1
Guyana	10.6	9.0	10.2	12.9	14.1	11.6	13.7	9.5	10.7	14.6	23.9	18.3	23.9	23.3	20.8
St. Lucia	18.8	21.4	14.7	18.0	35.5	37.7	33.5	16.4	25.2	24.1	26.4	26.0	25.4	27.3	25.3
St. Vincent and the Grenadines	10.6	18.3	22.4	21.2	22.5	30.6	35.6	32.1	34.0	32.0	31.0	30.0	28.3	25.5	23.4
Average	**12.2**	**16.8**	**15.7**	**18.2**	**18.8**	**27.7**	**23.1**	**17.0**	**17.5**	**17.5**	**19.4**	**18.2**	**18.8**	**18.3**	**18.0**
Suriname	12.0	9.0	4.6	12.1	−6.6	−6.7	−8.8	2.7	−6.0	−5.4	−5.9	−0.5	1.0	−0.4	−7.3
Trinidad & Tobago	−0.1	−8.1	−11.7	−20.9	−39.1	−23.0	−30.3	−8.3	−18.8	−11.8	−9.7	−8.3	−7.9	−6.8	−6.2
Average	**5.9**	**0.5**	**−3.6**	**−4.4**	**−22.8**	**−14.8**	**−19.5**	**−2.8**	**−12.4**	**−8.6**	**−7.8**	**−4.4**	**−3.4**	**−3.6**	**−6.8**
Caribbean mean	**13.5**	**14.2**	**13.1**	**15.5**	**12.1**	**18.4**	**16.5**	**14.1**	**12.6**	**12.9**	**14.2**	**13.2**	**14.1**	**13.8**	**12.9**
Caribbean median	**12.0**	**13.1**	**13.8**	**16.7**	**16.5**	**21.9**	**19.6**	**10.7**	**12.2**	**14.4**	**15.2**	**14.0**	**15.9**	**14.6**	**15.5**

Source: Countries' debt sustainability analyses from IMF staff reports.

APPENDIX TABLE 3.5

Proportion of External Debt Stock with Variable Interest Rate by Country, 2003–11[a] *(In percent of total external debt)*

	2003	2004	2005	2006	2007	2008	2009	2010	2011
Antigua and Barbuda	...	...	...	...	...	...	...	...	...
The Bahamas	...	...	...	...	...	...	...	...	...
Barbados	...	...	...	...	...	...	...	...	...
Belize	10.7	13.3	15.0	16.3	17.9	32.0	32.4	34.9	34.4
Dominica	4.9	5.4	5.3	5.7	4.5	3.7	3.9	4.3	5.4
Grenada	2.3	2.2	54.1	50.1	47.1	40.5	39.0	38.4	38.5
Guyana	5.7	1.1	1.2	1.1	1.7	2.4	2.0	2.0	2.2
Jamaica	20.0	18.5	24.2	24.5	31.1	32.0	40.9	45.6	46.4
St. Kitts and Nevis	...	...	...	...	...	...	...	...	...
St. Lucia	8.0	12.6	10.7	11.7	10.6	8.0	15.2	11.2	13.0
St. Vincent and the Grenadines	31.8	26.3	22.3	22.2	13.7	14.1	17.3	17.5	17.1
Suriname	...	...	...	...	...	...	...	...	...
Trinidad and Tobago	...	...	...	...	...	...	...	...	...

Source: World Bank, Global Development Finance.

[a]Variable interest rate is long-term external debt with interest rates that float with movements in a key market rate; for example, the London interbank offered rate (LIBOR) or the U.S. prime rate.

APPENDIX TABLE 3.6

External Debt Service by Country, 2002–16 *(As a ratio of exports of goods and services)*

												Projections			
	2002	2003	2004	2005	2006	2007	2008	2009	2010	2011	2012	2013	2014	2015	2016
St. Kitts and Nevis	36.1	41.8	42.9	37.0	36.9	35.3	31.9	39.2	38.2	44.2	55.2	33.0	17.7	15.2	14.6
Jamaica	31.6	22.4	26.5	23.3	32.0	17.4	20.8	20.5	18.4	27.3	24.9	16.2	24.3	22.0	21.3
Barbados	9.5	9.8	9.7	8.0	8.1	8.8	8.7	8.6	16.9	12.3	9.4	8.6	9.2	9.9	8.6
Antigua and Barbuda	9.3	9.5	14.6	32.6	7.6	2.4	9.0	7.6	3.9	1.7	3.4	4.9	7.1	6.5	7.4
Average	**21.6**	**20.9**	**23.4**	**25.2**	**21.1**	**16.0**	**17.6**	**19.0**	**19.4**	**21.4**	**23.2**	**15.7**	**14.5**	**13.4**	**12.9**
The Bahamas	3.0	7.1	1.7	1.1	1.0	1.5	1.0	2.8	4.0	1.7	2.3	2.8	2.1	2.0	2.0
Belize	44.5	32.6	37.7	38.4	16.4	82.8	14.1	11.5	8.9	10.6	8.7	7.1	7.9	7.3	7.5
Dominica	6.9	6.2	7.8	9.0	13.4	12.7	10.5	13.5	9.9	10.8	11.7	10.0	13.0	11.2	24.5
Grenada	8.6	9.7	11.0	5.2	5.6	5.3	6.2	9.4	16.8	14.2	11.7	16.3	18.3	21.1	23.4
Guyana	9.0	8.9	7.7	6.4	3.8	2.3	2.1	1.8	2.6	2.9	18.5	2.3	2.4	3.0	4.0
St. Lucia	14.6	9.8	12.6	11.8	17.9	25.2	14.2	14.7	20.5	12.0	20.4	21.7	22.8	28.2	24.6
St. Vincent and the Grenadines	6.7	7.7	11.5	11.4	13.4	12.9	13.0	15.3	17.5	17.4	17.2	16.2	15.1	14.3	13.9
Average	**13.3**	**11.7**	**12.9**	**11.9**	**10.2**	**20.4**	**8.7**	**9.9**	**11.5**	**10.0**	**12.9**	**10.9**	**11.7**	**12.4**	**14.3**
Suriname	11.0	7.8	3.9	4.1	4.1	8.8	1.0	2.4	1.0	1.1	2.0	1.5	1.8	1.8	2.1
Trinidad and Tobago	2.4	1.7	1.7	2.1	0.1	0.6	0.6	2.9	0.1	1.5	2.0	1.9	1.6	1.3	1.0
Average	**6.7**	**4.8**	**2.8**	**3.1**	**2.1**	**4.7**	**0.8**	**2.7**	**0.6**	**1.3**	**2.0**	**1.7**	**1.7**	**1.6**	**1.6**
Caribbean mean	**14.9**	**13.5**	**14.6**	**14.6**	**12.3**	**16.6**	**10.2**	**11.6**	**12.2**	**12.1**	**14.4**	**11.0**	**11.0**	**11.1**	**11.9**
Caribbean median	**9.3**	**9.5**	**11.0**	**9.0**	**8.1**	**8.8**	**9.0**	**9.4**	**9.9**	**10.8**	**11.7**	**8.6**	**9.2**	**9.9**	**8.6**

Source: Countries' debt sustainability analyses from IMF staff reports.

APPENDIX TABLE 3.7

Selected Terms of New External Commitments by Country, 2003–11

	2003	2004	2005	2006	2007	2008	2009	2010	2011
Average grant element on new external commitments *(In percent of the amount committed)*									
Antigua and Barbuda	...	...	...	...	...	...	...	...	...
The Bahamas	...	...	...	...	...	...	...	...	...
Barbados	...	...	...	...	...	...	...	...	...
Belize	4.9	21.8	27.3	17.9	44.3	36.9	54.7	55.0	46.7
Dominica	43.2	61.0	55.3	0.0	78.4	60.0	59.5	50.0	42.2
Grenada	43.1	39.2	52.0	56.0	55.2	42.7	54.7	47.8	60.2
Guyana	55.9	69.0	69.1	61.9	74.8	60.2	61.6	63.2	61.8
Jamaica	17.5	3.2	15.0	32.4	21.0	27.1	35.1	57.9	23.6
St. Kitts and Nevis	16.1	48.9	52.4	30.8	22.4	54.9	42.4	50.3	...
St. Lucia	28.2	59.7	56.8	17.6	78.6	56.1	25.5	68.4	60.0
St. Vincent and the Grenadines	18.3	25.8	23.0	0.0	78.9	4.8	49.5	49.5	58.1
Suriname	...	...	...	...	...	...	...	...	...
Trinidad and Tobago	...	...	...	...	...	...	...	...	...
Average grace period on new external commitments *(In years)*									
Antigua and Barbuda	...	...	...	...	...	...	...	...	...
The Bahamas	...	...	...	...	...	...	...	...	...
Barbados	...	...	...	...	...	...	...	...	...
Belize	6.2	7.2	1.4	2.4	12.0	4.8	4.6	5.3	5.1
Dominica	6.3	13.9	7.6	0.0	10.0	6.6	8.4	5.5	3.4
Grenada	5.8	9.6	5.3	8.3	7.5	3.3	6.8	5.9	2.1
Guyana	8.5	8.7	9.2	7.6	9.0	4.1	4.7	4.9	4.5
Jamaica	3.3	7.6	9.9	15.4	20.9	7.0	3.3	5.2	9.7
St. Kitts and Nevis	4.4	3.5	4.1	3.5	4.8	5.0	2.2	6.7	...
St. Lucia	2.1	7.3	7.8	10.3	10.1	5.9	2.2	7.8	0.3
St. Vincent and the Grenadines	1.1	3.0	2.8	0.0	10.3	0.5	5.6	4.7	1.8
Suriname	...	...	...	...	...	...	...	...	...
Trinidad and Tobago	...	...	...	...	...	...	...	...	...
Average interest rates on new external debt commitments *(In percent)*									
Antigua and Barbuda	...	...	...	...	...	...	...	...	...
The Bahamas	...	...	...	...	...	...	...	...	...
Barbados	...	...	...	...	...	...	...	...	...
Belize	6.3	3.0	0.0	2.9	5.1	3.8	1.9	2.0	3.1
Dominica	1.6	0.8	2.4	0.0	0.8	1.2	2.1	2.4	3.5
Grenada	3.5	2.4	2.8	1.8	2.6	2.6	2.6	3.1	1.5
Guyana	3.0	1.4	1.3	1.9	1.0	1.6	1.6	1.2	1.2
Jamaica	5.2	3.9	4.1	1.7	3.2	4.1	3.7	1.4	0.8
St. Kitts and Nevis	6.1	2.1	2.0	5.1	6.4	2.0	2.0	2.3	2.3
St. Lucia	1.2	1.7	2.5	0.0	0.8	2.3	3.4	1.3	1.1
St. Vincent and the Grenadines	4.5	2.2	4.7	0.0	0.8	0.0	2.8	2.5	1.0
Suriname	...	...	...	...	...	...	...	...	...
Trinidad and Tobago	...	...	...	...	...	...	...	...	...

Source: World Bank, Global Development Finance.

APPENDIX TABLE 3.8

Public External Debt Arrears by Country, 2003–11

	2003	2004	2005	2006	2007	2008	2009	2010	2011
Principal arrears on public and publicly guaranteed external debt *(In percent of total public and publicly guaranteed external debt)*									
Antigua and Barbuda	...	...	...	...	...	...	...	...	...
The Bahamas	...	...	...	...	...	...	...	...	...
Barbados	...	...	...	...	...	...	...	...	...
Belize	0.0	0.0	0.2	0.0	0.1	0.1	0.1	0.1	0.1
Dominica	1.0	0.7	1.6	1.0	1.6	1.4	1.4	1.5	1.3
Grenada	2.0	2.1	2.4	2.3	2.8	4.4	5.3	5.6	6.0
Guyana	5.2	6.1	6.3	8.2	12.9	11.1	10.0	9.3	7.8
Jamaica	2.6	2.4	2.6	3.6	2.3	2.1	2.6	2.0	2.0
St. Kitts and Nevis	...	...	...	...	...	...	...	...	...
St. Lucia	0.0	0.0	0.0	0.0	0.1	0.0	0.7	1.1	0.5
St. Vincent and the Grenadines	1.3	1.3	1.2	0.1	0.1	0.1	0.4	0.1	0.1
Suriname	...	...	...	...	...	...	...	...	...
Trinidad and Tobago	...	...	...	...	...	...	...	...	...
Interest arrears on official external debt *(In percent of GDP)*									
Antigua and Barbuda	...	...	...	...	...	...	...	...	...
The Bahamas	...	...	...	...	...	...	...	...	...
Barbados	...	...	...	...	...	...	...	...	...
Belize	0.1	0.1	0.5	0.5	0.4	0.4	0.6	0.4	0.5
Dominica	0.1	0.0	0.2	0.1	0.1	0.1	0.0	0.0	0.0
Grenada	0.6	0.7	0.2	0.4	0.5	0.7	0.9	1.0	1.0
Guyana	8.6	9.1	8.8	5.2	4.7	4.4	4.3	4.1	3.7
Jamaica	1.3	1.4	1.7	1.7	1.6	1.4	1.5	1.3	1.2
St. Kitts and Nevis	0.0	0.1	0.0	0.0	0.0	0.0	0.1	0.1	0.1
St. Lucia	0.0	0.0	0.0	0.0	0.0	0.0	0.1	0.1	0.2
St. Vincent and the Grenadines	0.1	0.1	0.1	0.1	0.2	0.0	0.0	0.0	0.0
Suriname	...	...	...	...	...	...	...	...	...
Trinidad and Tobago	...	...	...	...	...	...	...	...	...

Source: World Bank, Global Development Finance.

APPENDIX TABLE 3.9

Estimated Selected Contingent Fiscal Liabilities, 2012 *(In percent of GDP, unless otherwise stated)*

	Selected Explicit Contingent Liabilities						Selected Implicit Contingent Liabilities		
	Nationalization and contract cancellation costs awaiting court judgments	Guarantees[a]	PetroCaribe	Bank resolution	Estimated hurricane mitigation spending	Total explicit contingent liabilities	Gross exposure CLICO/BAICO	Total implicit contingent liabilities	Total contingent liabilities
Antigua and Barbuda		14.6	6.6	10	3.3	34.5	13.5	13.5	48.0
The Bahamas		14.1	. . .		3.3	17.4	0.4	0.4	17.8
Barbados		9.4			3.3	12.7	4.4	4.4	17.1
Belize	16.3	2.6	1.1		3.3	23.3	0	0.0	23.3
Dominica		11.5	7.3		3.3	22.1	11	11.0	33.1
Grenada		6.2	7.6		3.3	17.1	16.5	16.5	33.6
Guyana		na	12.8		3.3	16.1	1.3	1.3	17.4
Jamaica		6.2	13.8		3.3	23.3	0	0.0	23.3
St. Kitts and Nevis		34.5	. . .		3.3	37.8	7.0	7.0	44.8
St. Lucia		2	. . .		3.3	5.3	5.0	5.0	10.3
St. Vincent and the Grenadines		8.7	4.4		3.3	16.4	20.8	20.8	37.2
Suriname		0.5	. . .		3.3	3.8	. . .		3.8
Trinidad and Tobago		16.6			3.3	19.9	12.0	12.0	31.9
Memorandum item:									
Caribbean average	16.3	10.6	7.7	10.0	3.3	19.2	9.2	9.2	26.3

Sources: Bank of Guyana (2012); Central Bank of Belize, Information for Creditors (https://www.centralbank.org.bz/financial-system/Finformation-for-creditors); Government of Antigua and Barbuda (2014); Government of the Republic of Trinidad and Tobago (2012); Government of St. Vincent and the Grenadines (2013); IMF Country Reports (see IMF, 2011a, 2011d, 2011e, 2011f, 2011g, 2012b, 2013a, 2013b, 2013c) and IMF (2013d); Parliament of Grenada (http://www.gov.gd/egov/pdf/Grenada_2012_public_sector_debt.pdf); and IMF staff estimates.

[a]This includes letters of comfort in the case of Trinidad and Tobago.

APPENDIX TABLE 3.10

Elements of the Debt Management Framework in the Caribbean

	Legal framework	Debt Office or unit	Composition and size of the debt office	Level of training of debt officers	Objectives of debt management
Antigua and Barbuda	Finance Administration Act (2006); Treasury Bill Act (2005); the Antigua and Barbuda (General Loans) Act (2002); The ATG (development loan) Act (2002).	A debt unit within the Ministry of Finance and the Economy.	Four persons; provides analysis, recording and reporting functions. A theoretical segregation of duties (front office, middle office, and back office functions) recording, reporting, and analysis.	Originally trained in the CS-DRMS system. Technical skills of technicians are now being enhanced through the CANEC DMAS project.	Adopted in 2006, the overarching aim of the debt management strategy is to achieve a debt to GDP target in two stages: 80 percent by 2012 and 60 percent by 2020. The Government of Antigua and Barbuda also intends to target a debt service burden of no more than 20 percent of current revenue. The objectives of the Debt Strategy: establish a sustainable debt service profile consistent with the government's medium-term payment capacity outlook; resolve contractual principal and interest arrears and normalize relations with creditors; resume payment of contributions and resolve arrears owed to the statutory bodies; address the large stock of earmarked liabilities; improve the market perception of Antigua and Barbuda to rehabilitate its credit rating and regain access to international capital markets.
The Bahamas	Several pieces of legislation	Debt is managed by the central bank.	N.A.	Original training through CS-DRMS	N.A.
Barbados	Several pieces of legislation	Functions performed as part of the general functions of the ministry of finance.	N.A.	Original training through CS-DRMS	Emphasis will continue to be placed on accessing long-term funds from international financial institutions to finance public sector infrastructural projects, although there may be selective recourse to external commercial borrowing. In addtion, the debt management strategies over the medium term will include: establishment of strong debt management capacity within the ministry of finance that will ensure debt sustainability; greater use of domestic sources of financing rather than foreign resources; and

(Continued)

APPENDIX TABLE 3.10 ***(Continued)***

Elements of the Debt Management Framework in the Caribbean

	Legal framework	Debt Office or unit	Composition and size of the debt office	Level of training of debt officers	Objectives of debt management
					greater use of IFI sources of concessionary and grant funds rather than going to the market. Over the medium term it is expected that government will access approximately 40 million euros in grant funds; make greater use of amortized payment schedules rather than bullet loans; seek to refinance debt at lower interest rates where possible; make greater use of public-private sector partnership (PPP) arrangements in financing capital projects when such arrangements do not increase the debt.
Belize	Several pieces of legislation, including the Treasury Bill Act (amended in 2010) and the Finance and Audit (Reform) Act 2005.	Functions performed by the central bank and the Ministry of Finance.	No single debt unit with segregation of duties.	Original training through CS-DRMS	N.A.
Dominica	Several pieces of legislation, including the Constitution (1978); the Finance Act (1994); the Loans (Amendment) Act (1996); the Treasury Bills Act (2010); the Loans Act (1986); the International Financial Organizations Act (1978).	Debt unit.	A theoretical segregation of duties (front office, middle office, and back office functions) recording, reporting, and analysis.	Originally trained in the CS-DRMS system. Technical skills of technicians are now being enhanced through the CANEC DMAS project.	N.A.

Grenada	The requirement for Parliament to approve new debt contracted by government save and except treasury bills; the legal authority for issuance of treasury bills is the revised Treasury Bills Act, which limits new treasury bills issuance to no more than 40 percent of estimated revenues in a given fiscal year; the 2007 Public Finance Management Act gives authority to the minister of finance to contract debt on the country's behalf.	Debt unit	A theoretical segregation of duties (front office, middle office, and back office functions) recording, reporting, and analysis.	Originally trained in the CS-DRMS system. Technical skills of technicians are now being enhanced through the CANEC DMAS project.	Government's debt management strategy to reduce the cost of government borrowing by reducing reliance on the overdraft facility.
Guyana	Several pieces of legislation including the External Loans Act 1974, the Guarantee of Loans (public corporations and companies) Act 1974, the General Loans Act 1941 (amended 1965, 1975, and 1984), the Fiscal Management and Accountability Act (FMAA) 2003.	Debt unit	Three persons, who provide analysis, recording, evaluation, and reporting functions.	Originally trained in the CS-DRMS system.	To "maintain or lower its debt distress risk which is currently estimated as moderate. Although the debt relief from MDRI dropped the NPV of debt-to-revenue ratio, the longer term benefits are smaller given the decline in available resources from the World Bank and IDB. While the PetroCaribe initiative and the GRIF have filled the gap of external financing requirements, Guyana's quest to become a middle income country implies additional resources to grow the economy and improve the standards of living. This implies a number of policy options for future borrowing. Firstly, Government will continue to borrow at concessional terms and link future borrowing to development of it s most productive assets. Secondly, Government will aggressively pursue additional grant resources to finance part of its development programme; and thirdly, public-private sector partnerships (PPPs) will be aggressively pursued in the medium term. At the same time, the institutional reforms required to ensure Aid Effectiveness and international best practices of PPP

(Continued)

APPENDIX TABLE 3.10 ***(Continued)***

Elements of the Debt Management Framework in the Caribbean

	Legal framework	Debt Office or unit	Composition and size of the debt office	Level of training of debt officers	Objectives of debt management
					will be undertaken. Finally, capacity will be developed in the Ministry of Finance to conduct debt sustainability analysis on a periodic basis so as to provide the guidelines in external borrowing and management of Guyana total debt."
Jamaica	The Public Debt Law 2012 (which consolidated various debt-related acts).	Debt unit.	It provides analysis, recording, and reporting functions.	Regular training through CS-DRMS	(a) Ensuring that the financing needs and the payment obligations of the government are met at the lowest possible cost over the medium term so as to achieve the fiscal targets specified in section 48C of the Financial Administration and Audit Act, in accordance with the fiscal management principles specified in section 48D of the Financial Administration and Audit Act; (b) developing and maintaining an efficient market for government securities; (c) ensuring that the debt is managed consistent with fiscal sustainability; (d) promoting the development of the domestic debt market; and (e) ensuring that the Medium-Term Public Debt Management Strategy is compatible with the targets of the macroeconomic objectives of the government.
St. Kitts and Nevis	There is no single public debt law. Borrowing is governed by several pieces of legislation, including the Finance Administration Act 2007.	Separate debt units for St. Kitts and Nevis.	It provides analysis, recording, and reporting functions. A theoretical segregation of duties (front office, middle office, and back office functions) recording, reporting, and analysis.	Originally trained in the CS-DRMS system. Technical skills of technicians are now being enhanced through the CANEC DMAS project.	A debt management strategy is being developed, to take account of the cost-risk trade-off of alternative financing options, within the context of the overall macroeconomic environment.

St. Lucia	Several pieces of legislation: the Finance Administration Act (2001), the National Savings and Development Bonds (Amendment) Act (2005), and the Treasury Bills (Amendment) Act (2003).	Debt unit.	It provides analysis, recording, and reporting functions. A theoretical segregation of duties (front office, middle office, and back office functions) in recording, reporting, and analysis.	Originally trained in the CS-DRMS system. Technical skills of technicians are now being enhanced through the CANEC DMAS project.	To ensure that the government's financing needs and its payment obligations are met at the lowest possible cost over the medium to long run, consistent with a prudent degree of risk.
St. Vincent and the Grenadines	Several pieces of legislation, including the Finance Administration Act (2004); the Treasury Bill Act; the Caribbean Development Bank Loans Act; the International Organizations Act (1980); other acts for borrowing from other international organizations; the General Local Loans Act; the Government Guarantee of Loans Act.	Debt unit	Debt management functions have been centralized in the debt management unit of the Ministry of Finance, Planning and Development. The debt unit performs all debt management activities and provides policy advice on the overall debt management strategy of St. Vincent and the Grenadines. There is also a theoretical segregation of function in the debt unit (front office, middle office, and back office function).	Originally trained in the CS-DRMS system. Technical skills of technicians are now being enhanced through the CANEC DMAS project	To achieve a sustainable debt ratio the government is pursuing the following measures: Establishing limits on the contraction of new debts and ensuring that the projects to be financed are feasible in terms of their contributions to economic development and poverty reduction. Sound governance practices will dictate that these limits be strictly adhered to in accordance with a well documented Debt Management Strategy; increasing GDP, average annual nominal GDP growth; reducing contingent or guaranteed debt liabilities by closer monitoring and control of the borrowings by state-owned enterprises, and obtaining parliamentary approval for all borrowings in cases where an existing Act of Parliament does not authorize the loan.

(Continued)

APPENDIX TABLE 3.10 *(Continued)*

Elements of the Debt Management Framework in the Caribbean

	Legal framework	Debt Office or unit	Composition and size of the debt office	Level of training of debt officers	Objectives of debt management
Suriname	The Suriname Debt Management Office (SDMO) was established by the Public Debt Act of August 2002 (SB 2002 no. 27). It establishes a ceiling on domestic and external debt (article 3); makes the Minister of Finance solely responsible for contracting debt (Article 4); voidability of obligation (Article 9).	Debt management office.	This debt office consists of nine persons. The debt management office provides the following services: loan negotiation and borrowing, debt recording and monitoring, debt policy and strategy formulation, and debt payment.	The initial design and set-up was done with the help of Crown Agents, UK and financed through a grant from the IDB.	N.A.
Trinidad and Tobago	Debt management is enhanced by having the authority incur loans vested in a single authority: the Minister of Finance. This is governed by several pieces of legislation: the Treasury Bills Act 1960; the Treasury Notes Act 1995; the Government Savings Bonds Act 1962; the Development Loan Act 1964; the External Loans Act 1967.	Debt unit	Debt is monitored using the DMFAS system and regularly reconciled and reported on with respect to stock and debt service.	Originally training through CS-DRMS	The debt management objectives of the Government of Trinidad and Tobago are to minimize over the long term the cost of meeting its financing needs, while containing its exposure to risk; to facilitate the development of a well-functioning domestic capital market, with the creation and maintenance of a local interest rate yield curve; and to ensure that debt management policy is consistent with the objective of monetary policy, fiscal policy, and other macroeconomic policies. Debt management is based on a debt management strategy with regular, accurate, and timely reporting and monitoring of the debt stock.

Sources: Government of Antigua and Barbuda, Antigua and Barbuda Debt Profile Review 2006 to 2010, August 2011; Government of Barbados, Medium-Term Fiscal Strategy 2010–2014; Government of Belize, budget presentation for fiscal year 2013/2014, March 1, 2013; Government of Grenada, prospectus for series A EC$60 million 91-treasury bills, and series B EC$60 million 91-treasury bills, March 2011; Government of Guyana, Poverty Reduction Strategy Paper 2011–2015; Government of Jamaica, PEFA-PFM Performance Measurement Report for Jamaica, 2007 (Final Report, June 2007), and House of Parliament, The Public Debt Management Act, 2012, www.japarliament.gov.jm; Government of Trinidad and Tobago Information Memorandum, May 17, 2013; Government of St. Lucia, prospectus for EC$70 million bond, February 2012; Government of St. Vincent and the Grenadines, prospectus for treasury bill issue of EC$48 million, August 2004; IMF staff reports; Republic of Trinidad and Tobago Public Financial Management Performance Assessment Report (Final Report 2009); and Suriname Debt Office.

Note: CS-DRMS = the Commonwealth Secretariat Debt Recording and Management System; GRIF = the Guyana REDD+ Investment Fund; IDB = the Inter-American Development Bank; IFI = international financial institution; MDRI = the Multilateral Debt Relief Initiative; N.A. = not available; NPV = net present value.

REFERENCES

Bank of Guyana, 2012, *Annual Report* (Georgetown). http://www.bankofguyana.org.gy.

Eastern Caribbean Central Bank, 2013, "ECCU Countries Discuss Action Plan for Further Strengthening Institutional Structure." Press Release, April 11, 2013. http://www.eccb-centralbank.org/News/press2.asp?pressID=432.

Government of Antigua and Barbuda, 2011, "Antigua and Barbuda Debt Profile Review 2006 to 2010" (St. John's).

———, 2014, "Building a New Economy for Growth and Prosperity," Budget Speech (St. John's).

Government of Guyana, 2011, "Poverty Reduction Strategy Paper 2011–2015" (Georgetown).

Government of the Republic of Trinidad and Tobago, 2012, *Economic Review, 2012: Stimulating Growth, Generating Prosperity.* http://www.finance.gov.tt/content/Review-of-the-Economy-2012.pdf.

Government of St. Vincent and the Grenadines, 2013, "Building a Sustainable, Resilient Economy in Challenging Times," Budget Speech (Kingstown).

International Monetary Fund (IMF), 2010, "Grenada: Fifth Review Under the Extended Credit Facility, Request for Waivers of Nonobservance of Performance Criteria and Request for a Three-Year Arrangement Under the Extended Credit Facility and Financing Assurance Review, 2010," Country Report No. 10/139 (Washington).

———, 2011a, "The Bahamas: Staff Report for the 2011 Article IV Consultation," Country Report No. 11/338 (Washington).

———, 2011b, "Guyana: Staff Report for the 2011 Article IV Consultation," IMF Country Report No. 11/152 (Washington).

———, 2011c, "St. Kitts and Nevis: 2011 Article IV Consultation and Request for Stand-By Arrangement—Staff Report; Staff Supplements; Public Information Notice and Press Release on the Executive Board Discussion; and Statement by the Executive Director for St. Kitts and Nevis," Country Report No. 11/270 (Washington).

———, 2011d, "St. Lucia: Request for Disbursement Under the Rapid Credit Facility and Emergency Natural Disaster Assistance," Staff Report, Staff Supplement, Press Release and Statement by the Executive Director for St. Lucia, Country Report No. 11/278 (Washington).

———, 2011e, "St. Vincent and the Grenadines: Staff Report for the 2011 Article IV Consultation," Country Report No. 11/343 (Washington).

———, 2011f, "Belize: Staff Report for the 2011 Article IV Consultation," IMF Country Report No. 11/340 (Washington).

———, 2011g, "Jamaica: Third Review Under the Stand-By Arrangement—Staff Report, Information Annex; Staff Supplement, and Press Release on the Executive Board Discussion," IMF Country Report No. 11/49 (Washington).

———, 2012a, "Barbados: Staff Report for the 2012 Article IV Consultation," Country Report No. 12/7 (Washington).

———, 2012b, "Suriname: Staff Report for the 2012 Article IV Consultation." IMF Country Report No. 12/281 (Washington).

———, 2013a, "Antigua and Barbuda: Staff Report for the 2013 Article IV Consultation and Financing Assurances Review, Request for Waiver of Nonobservance of Performance Criterion, and Request for Waiver of Applicability," Country Report No. 13/76 (Washington).

———, 2013b, "Dominica: Staff Report for the 2013 Article IV Consultation," Country Report No. 13/31 (Washington).

———, 2013c, "St. Kitts and Nevis: Fourth Review Under the Stand-By Arrangement, Financing Assurances Review, and Request for Waivers of Applicability—Staff Report and Press Release," IMF Country Report No. 13/42 (Washington).

———, 2013d, "Caribbean Small States: Challenges of High Debt and Low Growth," IMF Policy Paper (Washington).

Prasad, A., M. Pollock, and Y. Li, 2013, "Small States Performance in Public Debt Management." Poverty Reduction and Economic Management Network. Working Paper 6356 (Washington: The World Bank).

Robinson, M., 2010, "Towards Sound Debt Management." Available at http://Michelerobinson.net/reports_and _publications.

CHAPTER 4

Global Large Debt Reduction: Lessons for the Caribbean

CHARLES AMO-YARTEY AND JOEL CHIEDU OKWUOKEI

The global financial crisis has led to renewed interest in the issue of debt reduction for many governments. Low economic growth, low budgetary revenues, and stimulus spending to prop up economic activity have resulted in a sizable accumulation of debt, especially by the developed world. For instance, the ratio of general government debt to GDP increased from 50 percent in 2007 to 90 percent during the crisis in advanced economies. In the Caribbean, the ratio of public debt to GDP increased by about 15 percentage points between 2008 and 2010.

Rising debt not only raises the risk of a fiscal crisis but also imposes costs on the economy by keeping borrowing costs high, discouraging private investment, and constraining fiscal flexibility. Empirical evidence points to a nonlinear relationship between public debt and growth, suggesting that public debt beyond certain levels can have negative effects on economic activity. Greenidge and others (2012) address the use of threshold effects between public debt and economic growth in the Caribbean. Their results show that, at debt levels lower than 30 percent of GDP, increases in the debt-to-GDP ratio are associated with faster economic growth. However, the effect on growth diminishes rapidly as debt rises beyond 30 percent of GDP, and in fact beyond 55 percent of GDP debt becomes a drag on growth.

This chapter investigates the determinants of global large debt reduction using a data set that spans more than four decades for a large sample of developed and developing economies. The analysis uses a panel data set of about 160 countries to estimate the probability that a large debt reduction will be initiated using the logit regression approach. More specifically, the chapter attempts to answer the following questions: How have large debt reductions occurred in practice? What factors determine the probability of a large debt reduction? And, what lessons can we draw for future large debt reduction in the Caribbean?

Most studies in the literature have examined debt reduction within the context of fiscal consolidation (Giavazzi and Pagano, 1990; and Alesina and Perotti, 1995). According to this approach, only public debt reductions resulting from sizeable improvements in either the primary balance or the cyclically adjusted primary balance were considered. This approach ignores other potential determinants of public debt reductions, such as business cycle developments and the magnitude of debt servicing costs. Using a sample of 15 European Union countries for the period 1985–2009, Nickel, Rother, and Zimmermann (2010) analyzed the determinants of large debt reductions. Their main findings were that major debt reductions are primarily driven by strong GDP growth and decisive and lasting fiscal consolidation efforts focused on reducing government expenditure, particularly by cuts in social benefits and public wages. This chapter extends the work of Nickel, Rother, and Zimmermann by analyzing the factors determining large debt reductions using a large data set of 160 countries for the period 1970–2009.

Our result shows that global large debt reduction is associated with robust economic growth, decisive and lasting fiscal consolidation, and a favorable external environment characterized by strong global growth. Fiscal rules are found to be positively associated with a higher probability of debt reduction because they increase fiscal discipline and the credibility of fiscal policy and help secure the gains of fiscal consolidation. The initial level of debt and debt servicing cost appears to play a disciplinary role by enhancing the incentives of governments to consolidate aggressively. The results are robust to alternative estimation methodologies and alternative thresholds for identifying large debt reduction episodes. We conclude that future large debt reduction programs in the Caribbean need to be based on credible fiscal plans to increase primary balances, fiscal rules to enhance fiscal credibility, and structural reforms to promote growth.

LITERATURE REVIEW

Theoretically, countries have a number of options to reduce their debt levels, including economic growth, fiscal consolidation, inflation, debt restructuring and defaults, and privatization. Their pluses and minuses can be summed up this way (IMF, 2003):

- Reducing debt through economic growth would generally be the preferred option of policymakers, but growth is virtually nonexistent in the Caribbean at present.
- Reducing debt through explicit defaults entails reputation costs that could influence future borrowing and constrain fiscal policy.
- High inflation has enormous growth and welfare costs, while privatization, though debt reducing, does not change the net worth of the government.
- Reducing debt through fiscal consolidation maintains the credibility of the government, but it is often politically difficult, and the gains need to be maintained over a long period of time.

The Size and Duration of Debt Reductions

What constitutes a large debt reduction episode? There is no standard definition of what constitutes a large reduction in the public-debt-to-GDP ratio. Existing literature explaining the dynamics of these reductions has analyzed episodes in terms of the magnitude of debt reduction over a specific period of time. Nickel, Rother, and Zimmermann (2010) define an episode as one in which the debt-to-GDP ratio declines by more than 10 percentage points in 5 consecutive years. In their analysis, Finger and Sadikov (2010) consider cases associated with debt-to-GDP ratio reduction of more than 20 percentage points. The IMF (2003) identifies cases in which this debt ratio was reduced by at least 18 percentage points over a three-year period. In a more recent study, the IMF (2012) analyzes cases in which the ratio exceeded the 100 percent threshold and discusses the debt dynamics 15 years following the event. Bandiera (2008) considers debt reductions on the order of 30 to 190 percentage points of GDP measured in net present value (NPV) terms. Baldacci, Gupta, and Mulas-Granados (2012) examine a debt-to-GDP ratio decline from a high level to a prudent threshold of 60 percent of GDP for advanced economies and 40 percent for emerging economies.

Examining a sample of 15 European Union countries during 1985–2009, Nickel, Rother, and Zimmermann (2010) find that the total debt reduction per country, on average, stood at about 37 percent of GDP over a relatively long period, ranging from 5 to14 years. In a large sample of countries covering 1980–2010, Baldacci, Gupta, and Mulas-Granados (2012) identify 104 episodes of public debt reduction, excluding debt relief cases lasting 2 to 13 years. Half of these episodes achieved a debt-to-GDP reduction of at least 20 percentage points, while in more than a third debt reduction was higher than 40 percentage points of GDP. The IMF (2012) identifies 26 episodes in advanced countries spanning almost 100 years; it finds that more than half of the 22 countries studied had at least one high-debt reduction episode between 1857 and 1997.

In its earlier study, the IMF (2003) identifies about 26 episodes of public debt reduction in emerging market economies during 1970–2002, of which 19 were associated with a default or restructuring. Excluding the restructuring cases, the IMF further finds that the median decline in the public debt ratio was 34 percent of GDP over three years. According to Baldacci, Gupta, and Mulas-Granados (2012), it took about 6 years, on average, during which public debt was reduced by about 29 percent of GDP. A key message that emerges from these experiences is that debt reduction takes time. It is even more difficult, and sometimes impossible, for countries emerging from a crisis. Reflecting higher uncertainty and the difficulty of fiscal adjustment in a postcrisis environment, Baldacci, Gupta, and Mulas-Granados (2010) find that lowering public debt takes about 10 years, on average, for a successful episode.

Factors that Contribute to Debt Reduction

There are diverse views in the literature about what has helped reduce debt substantially in various countries. Evidence suggests that large debt reductions are associated with a combination of factors, and the contribution of the respective factors to debt reduction differs. Findings in the literature point to the following factors: real GDP growth, fiscal adjustment, inflation or hyperinflation, interest rate, real exchange rate changes, debt restructuring or default, debt relief, and sale of government assets. On top of these, some studies have argued for an appropriate policy mix and deep-rooted structural reforms to boost competitiveness and growth.

In general, findings give prominence to robust real growth and fiscal consolidation.

The Role of Growth

Growth is mostly helpful as it allows countries to easily "grow their way" out of debt. However, the growth factor is often missing, especially in many advanced economies today, and in such cases, countries have relied on others factors to reduce public debt significantly. In emerging market economies, Baldacci, Gupta, and Mulas-Granados (2012) find that in addition to higher growth, the bulk of debt reduction in the period 1980–2010 was driven by lower interest rates. Over the period 1970–2002, strong growth performance averaging 8.5 percent of GDP and fiscal consolidation largely through expenditure restraint contributed to debt reduction in these economies (IMF, 2003).

In advanced economies, the correlation between growth and debt reduction is less clear (IMF, 2012). However, excluding hyperinflation cases, a relatively stronger growth performance is associated with debt reduction. Finger and Sadikov (2010) note that while favorable debt dynamics played a lesser role in reducing public debt in advanced economies, countries with already high debt levels tended to rely more on favorable macroeconomic conditions than on fiscal adjustment, and the episodes were less sustained.

In a study of middle-income countries, Reinhart, Rogoff, and Savastano (2003) find only one debt reduction case solely associated with real GDP growth. Badiera (2008) finds that GDP growth was the main factor in all large debt reduction episodes in seven low-income countries. Results from the World Bank (2005) indicate that primary fiscal surpluses and real GDP growth contributed to the reduction in the average public-debt-to-GDP ratio in all 15 countries covered.

The Role of Fiscal Consolidation

A number of studies have attributed large debt reductions to fiscal consolidation, implying that any serious plan for a major debt reduction must include a credible fiscal consolidation strategy. Indeed, evidence suggests that fiscal adjustments have been needed to reduce debt-to-GDP ratios to prudent levels and that these past episodes serve as a lesson for countries facing high debt levels today. Nickel, Rother, and Zimmermann (2010) and Amo-Yartey and others (2012) find that fiscal consolidation efforts must be decisive and call for reductions in government expenditure, in particular in wages and transfers. IMF (2012) lends support to this, arguing that successful debt reduction requires fiscal consolidation and a policy mix that supports growth.

Evidence from Baldacci, Gupta, and Mulas-Granados (2012) indicates that about half of the decline in public debt has emanated from stronger primary balances, especially in Africa. In oil exporting countries, the primary balance contribution to debt reduction was greater than the contribution from favorable debt dynamics, reflecting revenue booms following improvements in terms of trade

(Finger and Sadikov, 2010). Additional findings from Finger and Sadikov suggest that middle-income countries have relied more on favorable debt dynamics than on fiscal consolidation. Yet significant fiscal adjustment has been needed to set off the debt reduction episode. In their analysis of major episodes of large debt changes in a sample of 19 advanced economies over 1880–2009, Ali Abbas and others (2011) find that debt reduction was accounted for by the primary balance and the growth-interest differential components in roughly equal proportions.

While fiscal consolidation is favored in the absence of growth, Bandiera (2008) notes that it was not a key factor for the seven cases he studied. No country was able to run fiscal surpluses consistently over time. Similarly, most countries covered in Finger and Sadikov (2010) were noted to have run primary deficits of about 2 percent of GDP on average over the debt reduction episode. In these cases, the countries involved benefited from debt restructuring and relief that contributed substantially to debt reduction. For the low-income cases, the debt relief option appeared unsustainable in the absence of fiscal and structural reforms and a good debt management policy, as the countries soon found themselves back in rapidly increasing debt, which reinforces the earlier finding by the IMF (2003) that unless accompanied with sound macroeconomic policies, default is not a long-term solution for a large debt problem. Indeed, evidence suggests that debt reduction via restructuring or default is a common phenomenon even in emerging markets and several advanced economies, particularly for external debt (Reinhart and Rogoff, 2011).

Other Factors

Turning to other factors, research on the relationship between inflation and debt reduction is inconclusive. One view is that generally, inflation is not associated with debt reduction, apart from exceptional cases of hyperinflation (IMF, 2012). Citing the experience of the United States after World War II, the IMF finds that high rates of surprise inflation combined with low nominal interest rates, largely reflecting financial repression, helped the United States to reduce debt significantly. Similarly, Finger and Sadikov (2010) finds no evidence of systemically higher inflation for countries with a lower share of foreign-currency debt. However, the IMF (2003) finds that in some emerging market cases, moderate inflation and exchange rate appreciation were helpful in reducing debt levels. For the serial debt defaulters, two-thirds of the cases involved real exchange rate appreciation (Reinhart, Rogoff, and Savastano, 2003).

The literature on debt reduction has also emphasized the appropriateness of the policy mix, sound macroeconomic policies, pro-growth structural reforms, and the need to have the right environment for a sustained debt reduction, such as supportive monetary conditions and a friendly external environment. An inappropriate policy mix—severe fiscal austerity and tight monetary policy—hurts growth and raises debt, as the IMF (2012) observes in the case of the United Kingdom after World War I. The view is that debt reductions are larger when fiscal measures are permanent or structural rather than temporary and when they are anchored in fiscal frameworks, including fiscal rules. The findings of Baldacci, Gupta, and Mulas-Granados (2012) also reflect the importance of combining supply-side structural reforms with policies to ameliorate debt dynamics.

GLOBAL LARGE DEBT REDUCTIONS: STYLIZED FACTS AND ANATOMY

In our analysis for this chapter, we define a *large* debt reduction episode as occurring if the debt-to-GDP ratio declines by at least 15 percent of GDP over five consecutive years. Using this definition, we recorded about 206 episodes of large debt reductions around the world between 1970 and 2009 (Figure 4.1). These are among the key findings:

- About 100 (48 percent) of the debt reduction episodes were achieved through debt restructuring or default.
- About 106 (52 percent) of the debt reduction episodes were achieved through higher GDP growth, higher inflation, or fiscal consolidation (see Appendix 4.1).
- Of the debt reduction episodes achieved through fiscal consolidation, about 25 percent were preceded or accompanied by the existence of fiscal rules.
- Most of the large debt reduction episodes lasted over a relatively long period of time, ranging from 4 years in Panama to 18 years in Australia. The average duration of large debt reduction episodes not achieved through debt restructuring was about 7 years.
- The average decline in the debt-to-GDP ratio was 35 percent of GDP.

FACTORS BEHIND THE DECLINE IN THE PUBLIC-DEBT-TO-GDP RATIO

How have large public sector debt reductions occurred in practice? To answer this question, we used data for advanced, emerging market, and developing economies

Figure 4.1 Number of Global Debt Reduction Episodes by Year and Nature, 1970–2009

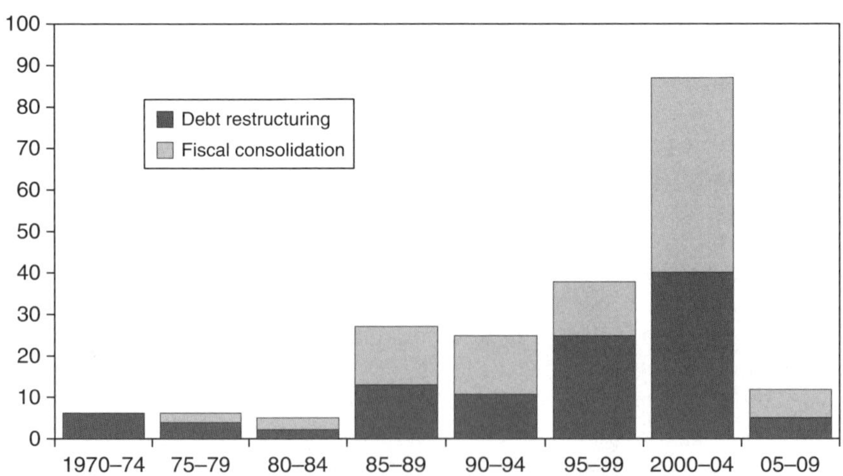

Source: Authors' calculations.

for the period 1970–2010. We identify cases where public debt was reduced over a five-year period by 15 percentage points, dropping cases in which the debt stock at the end of the period was still above the level three years prior to the event.

This section illustrates the potential drivers of large debt reduction. In particular, we examine the behavior of macroeconomic factors, as depicted in Figures 4.2 to 4.7, such as primary balance, GDP growth, government spending, government revenue, inflation, and the composition of public spending before and after the onset of a large debt reduction. Among our key findings are the following:

- In the 106 cases in which large debt reduction was not due to a restructuring, the median decline in the debt-to-GDP ratio was 26.4 percent over a five-year period (Figure 4.2).
- A strong economic performance seems to have contributed significantly to the reduction in the debt-to-GDP ratio. Real GDP growth starts to pick up one year before the event and averaged about 5 percent per year during the first five years of the debt reduction episode.
- A strong fiscal effort appears to have played an important role in the debt reduction. The primary balance starts to improve significantly at least two years before the large debt reduction episode, and the improvement continues to be sustained during the first five years of the episode (Figure 4.3).
- The fiscal improvements were due to a combination of revenue-enhancing measures and expenditure restraints. The median decline in the ratio of government spending to GDP was 3 percentage points of GDP over the five-year period (Figure 4.4).

Figure 4.2 Public Debt, 106 Global Study Cases[a] *(percent of GDP)*

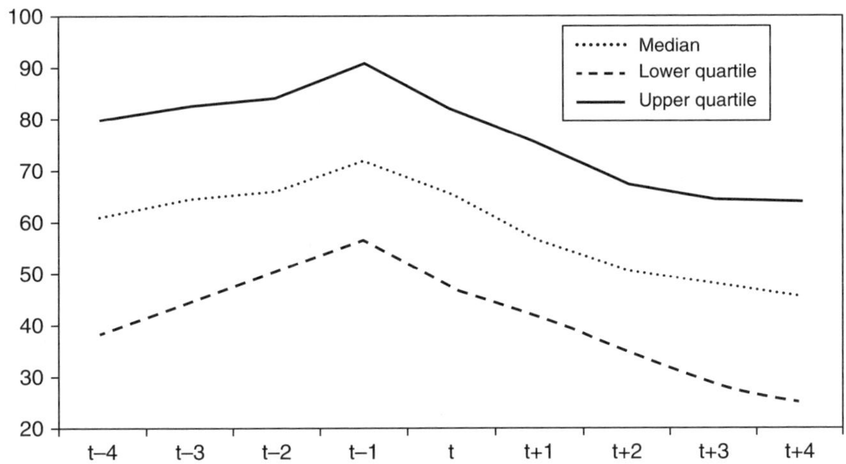

Source: Authors' calculations.
[a]Consist of cases where public debt was reduced over a five-year period by 15 percentage points or more without restructuring.

Figure 4.3 Primary Balance, 106 Global Study Cases *(percent of GDP)*

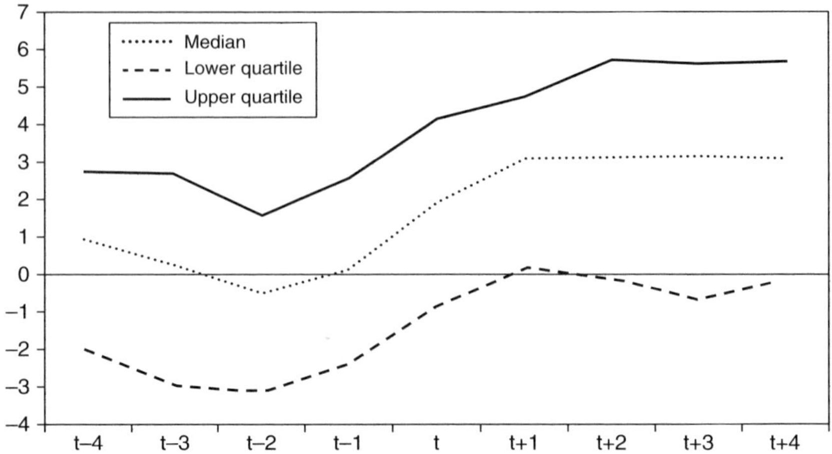

Source: Authors' calculations.

Figure 4.4 Government Spending, 106 Global Study Cases *(percent of GDP)*

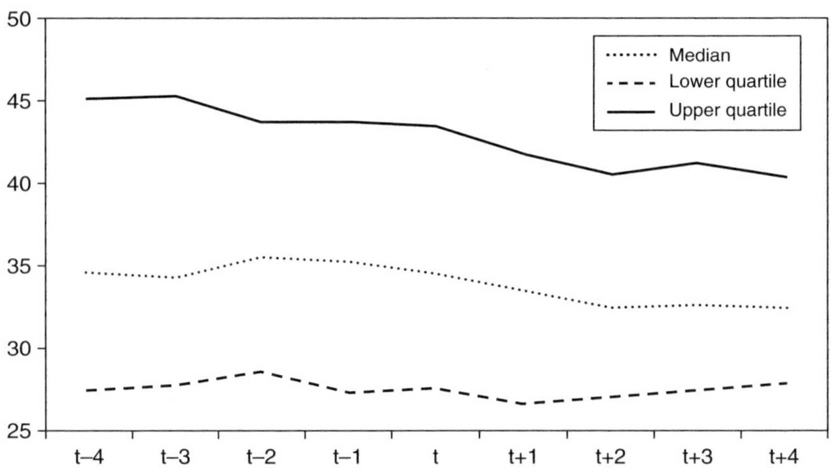

Source: Authors' calculations.

- The reduction in total spending came mainly from cuts in current spending, with capital spending remaining broadly flat over the five-year period (Figures 4.6 and 4.7).
- Moderate inflation also contributed to the decline in the debt-to-GDP ratio, with inflation averaging 5 percent over the five-year period.

Figure 4.5 Government Revenues, 106 Global Study Cases *(percent of GDP)*

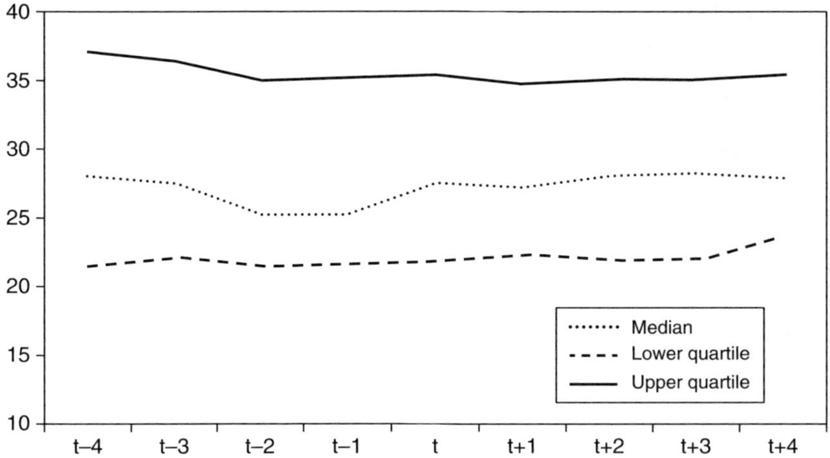

Source: Authors' calculations.

Figure 4.6 Current Spending, 106 Global Study Cases *(percent of GDP)*

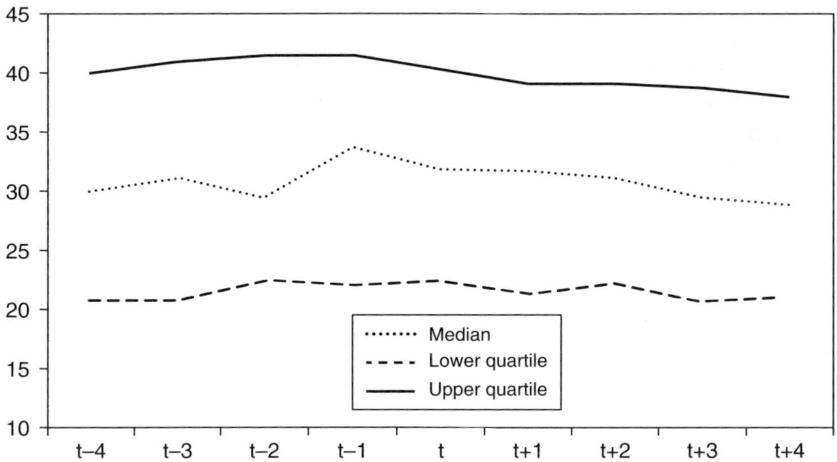

Source: Authors' calculations.

Figure 4.7 Capital Spending, 106 Global Study Cases *(percent of GDP)*

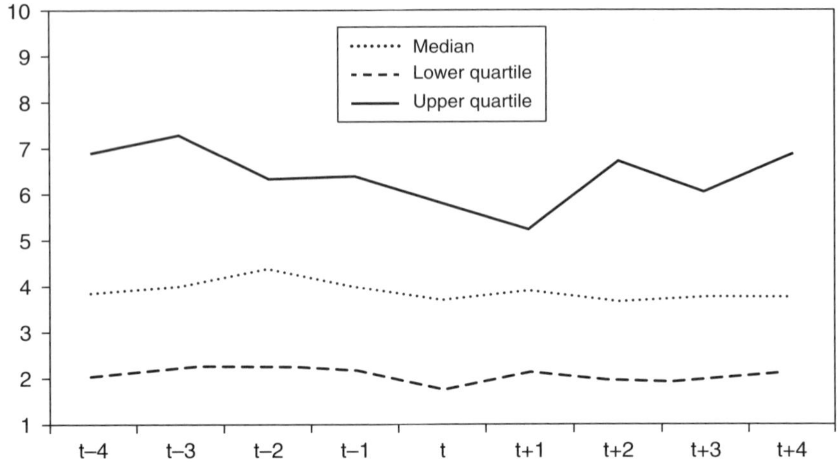

Source: Authors' calculations.

PUBLIC DEBT REDUCTION: TALES FROM SEVEN COUNTRIES[1]

This section analyzes the experience of seven countries that have succeeded in reducing their debt levels substantially during different periods of time: Brazil, Canada, Denmark, Lebanon, New Zealand, South Africa, and Vanuatu. The aim is to further examine the factors that promote debt reduction, including the specific measures implemented by these countries over the course of their debt reduction episodes. As with the analyses for the full sample, we analyze for these country cases, the behavior of public debt, growth, primary balance, government revenue, government spending and the composition of public spending before and during the debt reduction episodes.

Brazil, 2002–08

In a space of five years, covering 2002–07, the public-debt-to-GDP ratio fell by 15 percentage points from its peak of 80 percent in 2002. Over the debt reduction episode, real GDP expanded by 4 percent on average, while the primary-balance-to-GDP ratio was consistently above 3 percent of GDP (Figure 4.8). Brazil's story reflects the country's adherence to a well-established macroeconomic policy framework based on a high primary surplus objective, skillful debt management, inflation targeting, and a flexible exchange rate regime.

Debt reduction was also boosted by a favorable external environment: improved commodity prices and enhanced access to foreign financing. The country

[1]The section draws from IMF staff reports on the respective countries.

Figure 4.8 Brazil: Public Debt, Real GDP Growth, and Primary Balance, 1999–2007 *(percent of GDP)*

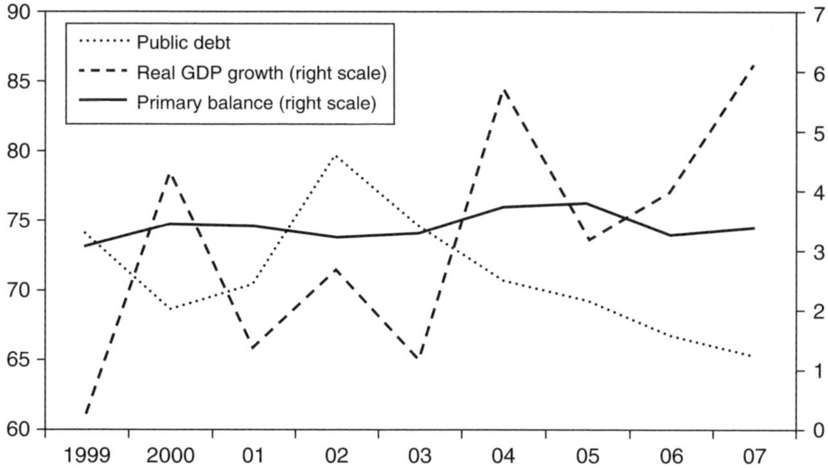

Sources: National authorities; and authors' calculations.

successfully implemented the 2002–05 IMF-supported programs that helped restore confidence and improve market conditions following its 1998–99 currency crisis.

Fiscal adjustment was essentially revenue based. The record high primary surpluses reflect strong revenue performances mainly through higher tax revenue at both the federal and subnational government levels. Expenditure measures included efforts to strengthen the social safety net and pension reform to reduce generous benefits. Current spending came down in 2002 following the start of consolidation but started rising in 2005, partly reflecting entitlement spending, while capital spending became flat. Fiscal adjustment appeared to have been achieved at the expense of a high tax burden and limited public investment.

A budget guideline law introduced in 2007 maintained the primary surplus target, eliminated ceilings on government revenues and expenditure set a year earlier, and outlined targets for reducing current expenditure. There was a debt restructuring agreement between the federal and the subnational governments and legislation limiting personnel expenditures and debt levels at all levels of government, paving the way for a comprehensive fiscal responsibility law.

Canada, 1997–2007

On the back of robust growth and fiscal consolidation, the public-debt-to-GDP ratio in Canada came down by 35 percentage points over an episode that lasted for 10 years starting from 1997 (Figure 4.9). Macroeconomic policy measures implemented since the early 1990s put the economy on a strong footing and underpinned the buoyancy of economic activities. The country has a fiscal

Figure 4.9 Canada: Public Debt, Real GDP Growth, and Primary Balance, 1993–2001
(percent of GDP)

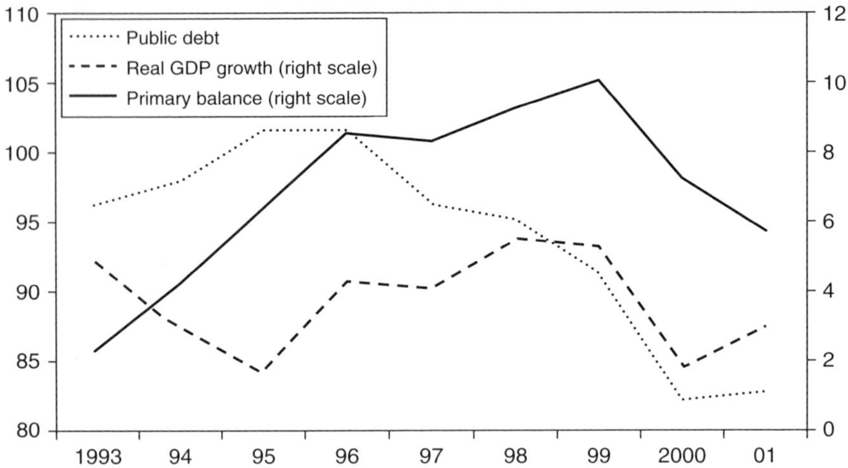

Sources: National authorities; and authors' calculations.

framework that targets a budget balance over a rolling two-year period based on conservative fiscal assumptions.

The idea is to build sufficient savings to stem future pressures on public finances associated with an aging population. This approach proved quite successful as it appeared to have provided the authorities with the flexibility to respond to changing circumstances while delivering exceptionally high fiscal surpluses and sustaining the social consensus to reduce the debt level.

Decisive fiscal consolidation, which started in the mid-1990s, was sustained. It saw government expenditure declining substantially, largely on account of lower public consumption, reduced unemployment benefits, less capital spending, and lower wage bill and transfers to provinces. Thus, with tax rates already high, fiscal adjustment had an expenditure focus, complemented by some revenue measures including higher excises and a broadening of both the personal income tax and corporate income tax bases. There were structural reforms in many key areas, including employment insurance, a public old-age pension scheme, education, and trade.

Fiscal consolidation was extended to lower-level governments. Within the period, provinces raised education and health fees and excises and broadened the corporate income tax base. With the return to fiscal surpluses, however, the government launched a five-year tax reduction plan in 2000, which significantly lowered statutory tax rates on personal income and corporate income, and it took steps to increase the contribution limits for tax-deferred retirement savings plans and cut capital gains taxes. Some provinces also lowered marginal income tax rates as well for both households and businesses.

Denmark, 1998–2007

Denmark cut the public-debt-to-GDP ratio by almost 40 percentage points over a period of nine years starting from 1998, reflecting buoyant economic activity and fiscal consolidation. Real GDP growth averaged 2 percent during 1994–2002, while primary surpluses averaged 4 percent of GDP (Figure 4.10). Prior to the debt reduction episode, the economic fundamentals seemed strong. The memory of bad times and the gains from earlier consolidation in the 1990s helped build a nationwide consensus about the importance of prudent fiscal policies. Fiscal adjustment consisted of a mix of revenue and expenditure measures, with emphasis on expenditure control, especially on transfers given the very high expenditure-to-GDP ratio. Caps on expenditure growth in real terms led to a gradual reduction in the expenditure-to-GDP ratio. To contain spending overruns, the counties were legally required to comply with budget targets beginning in 2003. At the same time, capital spending virtually disappeared.

As in the case of Canada, the government was committed to a strategy of running fiscal surpluses and lowering public debt to avert future spending pressures owing to changing demographics. To this end, fiscal policy has been explicitly guided by a medium-term fiscal framework since the early 1990s, initially motivated by the need to meet the European Union's deficit targets, debt ceilings, and convergence programs.

There were also labor market reforms, including reductions in labor taxes and flexibility of hiring and dismissal, which resulted in significant increases in employment while maintaining high standards of social security for the unemployed. In 2006, the political parties reached a welfare agreement and included various measures aimed at later retirement and increasing labor supply in the short term.

Figure 4.10 Denmark: Public Debt, Real GDP Growth, and Primary Balance, 1994–2002 *(percent of GDP)*

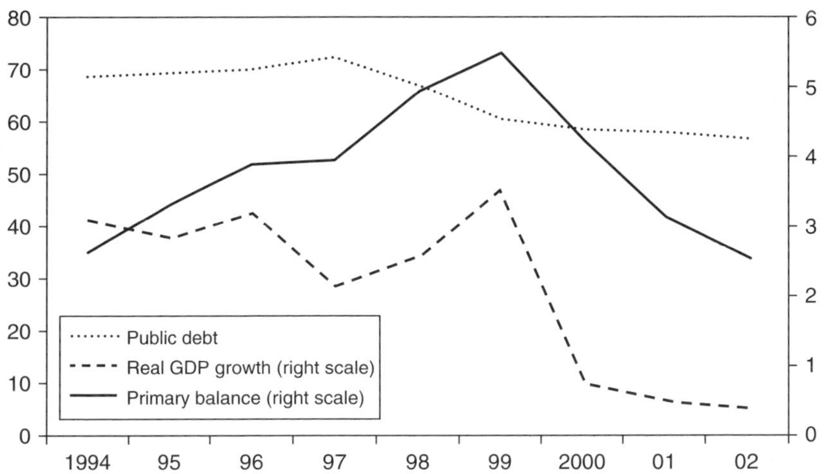

Sources: National authorities; and authors' calculations.

Lebanon, 2006–10

Economic activity has been adversely affected by civil conflicts since 1990. However, real GDP growth rebounded in 2007 and registered 8½ percent during 2006–11. This was facilitated by a new and ambitious fiscal reform and financial support from donors for reconstruction, permitting the government to raise primary surpluses in the range of 1½ to 3 percent, thereby reducing the public-debt-to-GDP ratio by 45 percentage points in four years from a very high level in 2006 (Figure 4.11). The country benefited from Emergency Post-Conflict Assistance (EPCA) from the IMF in 2007 and 2008, which helped in improving macroeconomic stability and public finances.

Under a medium-term fiscal adjustment program adopted in 2007, referred to as the Paris III Agenda, a number of measures were planned for implementation in phases. On the revenue side, the value added tax (VAT) rate increased from 10 percent to 12 percent in 2008, and then to 15 percent in 2010 bringing it in line with the regional average. A global income tax was introduced in 2008, in addition to raising gasoline excises to their pre-capping levels of 2004. Tax on interest income was also raised, from 5 percent to 7 percent, in January 2008.

Other revenue measures included improvement in revenue from government properties and reforms in property tax administration. Revenue administration reforms included the introduction of a medium-sized taxpayer office and new audit procedures, and changes to the property tax evaluation system. On the expenditure side, measures included reforms that aimed at a nominal freeze in the wage bill and structural reforms in the energy and social sectors to curb fiscal leakages. Efforts to strengthen public financial management involved introducing

Figure 4.11 Lebanon: Public Debt, Real GDP Growth, and Primary Balance, 2003–11 *(percent of GDP)*

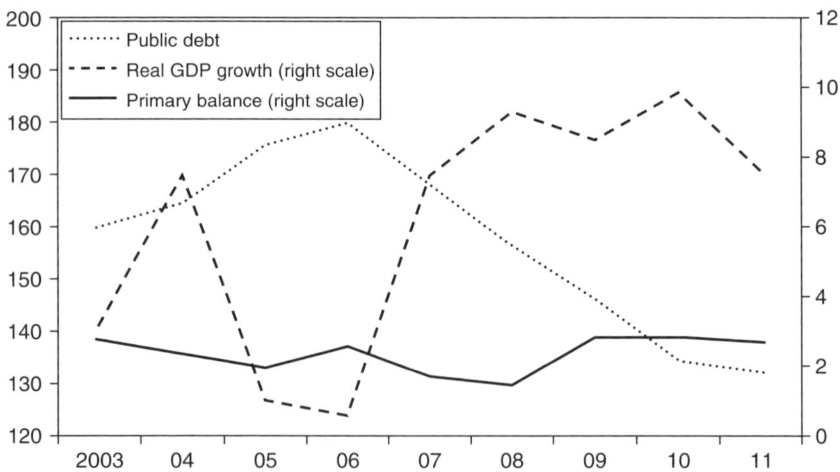

Sources: National authorities; and authors' calculations.

medium-term planning. In 2008, a public debt directorate was created and a single treasury account was proposed.

However, some of the planned fiscal consolidation and structural reforms have been delayed repeatedly due to the difficult security situation and political tensions between the government and the opposition party, especially since 2010. Progress in introducing a global income tax, increasing the VAT rate, and implementing a single treasury account has been slow. Notably, however, the cabinet has approved the reform of the energy sector. Legislation has been passed for investments in the electricity sector, and reforms in tax administration and public financing management have been making progress. Despite the challenging circumstances, the government appears committed to pursuing fiscal consolidation and reducing debt further, including by implementing the key measures of the Paris III Agenda.

New Zealand, 1992–2007

Public debt fell from about 65 percent of GDP in 1992 to 17 percent in 2007 (Figure 4.12). During 1992–97, real GDP grew by about 4 percent on average while the primary balance averaged 5 percent. The economic expansion can be traced to radical structural reforms that commenced in 1985—institutional reforms that effected a strong medium-term orientation to monetary and fiscal policies to achieve macroeconomic stability; privatization and labor market deregulation to enhance competition and efficiency; and efforts to raise the productivity of core government services.

Fiscal consolidation focused on limiting expenditures. For example, expenditure reduction accounted for approximately 40 percent of the improvement in the

Figure 4.12 New Zealand: Public Debt, Real GDP Growth, and Primary Balance, 1989–1997 *(percent of GDP)*

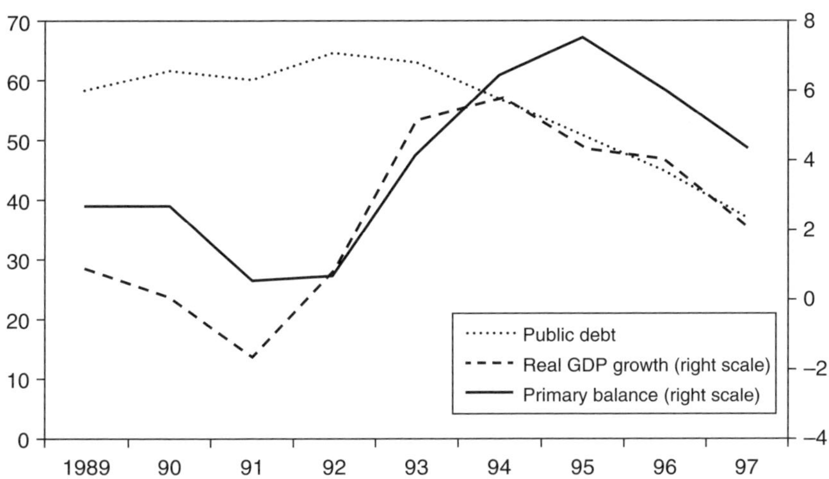

Sources: National authorities; and authors' calculations.

Figure 4.13 New Zealand: Government Revenue and Spending, 1989–1997 *(percent of GDP)*

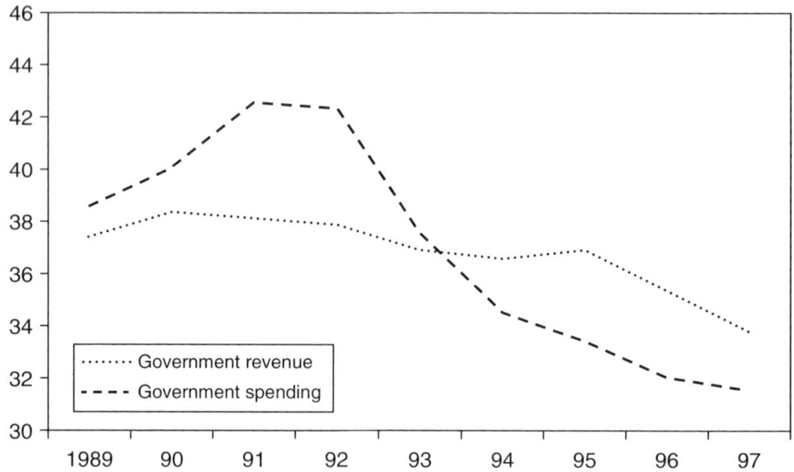

Sources: National authorities; and authors' calculations.

primary balance of about 1.4 percent of GDP in 2003. Caps on current expenditure led to a gradual reduction in the expenditure-to-GDP ratio (Figure 4.13). During the period, the government reiterated its commitment to the principles of medium-term budgeting and emphasized the need for higher savings in the light of future pension and health care obligations. Lower interest rates significantly reduced the cost of debt servicing, and a debt management office established in 1998 helped manage the public debt portfolio. As a result, the share of foreign-currency-denominated debt fell from 58 percent in 1992 to 22 percent in 2001. Moreover, a new monetary policy framework brought inflation down from an average of 8.3 percent during 1986–91 to 1.9 percent during 1992–97.

The productivity of the public sector was substantially enhanced by reforms that placed department heads on performance contracts in return for flexibility to manage financial and human resource inputs. Building on the comprehensive public sector reforms, a Fiscal Responsibility Act was introduced in 1994, emphasizing the accountability and transparency of government fiscal operations. The tax system was also overhauled to broaden the tax base, lower marginal rates, and shift tax incidence from income to consumption. Most tax exemptions were abolished. The personal income tax brackets were reduced from five to two brackets, with the top rate of 33 percent the same as the company income tax rate. A VAT of 12½ percent replaced a range of indirect taxes.

The social welfare system was streamlined, while targeting was improved; eligibility requirements were tightened and the level of benefits was lowered for a broad range of programs. The national pension scheme was made partly income dependent, and its eligibility age was set to increase gradually from age 60 to age 65 over a 10-year period. A major labor market reform introduced a legal framework for a highly decentralized wage-bargaining system, so that individual contracts became prevalent in many sectors. This enhanced labor flexibility and remuneration, and moderated the spillover of wage pressure across firms and sectors.

In 2005, the incumbent party was reelected with a mandate for continued fiscal consolidation. Continuing with the medium-term budget framework that it had introduced in 1994, for example, after the elections in 2005 the government set out explicitly its long-term fiscal objectives, including reducing net public debt on a sustained basis to remain between 20 percent and 30 percent of GDP, restoring government net worth to positive levels, and reducing expenditure to below 30 percent of GDP.

South Africa, 1999–2008

The public-debt-to-GDP ratio came down by 19 percentage points over an episode that lasted for nine years commencing in 1999 (Figure 4.14). Real GDP growth averaged 3 percent from 1996 to 2004. Over the same period, the primary balance averaged 2.6 percent of GDP. South Africa undertook a wide range of structural reforms beginning in the early 1990s, which laid the basis for improvement in macroeconomic performance and in public finances many years later, including the period of debt reduction. Key structural reforms adopted at various times included trade liberalization, tax base broadening and lower rates for income taxes, revenue administration reforms, a medium-term budget framework, and expenditure planning and financial management. Income tax rates and import duties were cut as incentives for investment and job creation.

Revenue administration reforms covered the creation of a Revenue Authority in 1997 accompanied by a reorganization of revenue administration, modernization

Figure 4.14 South Africa: Public Debt, Real GDP Growth, and Primary Balance, 1996–2004 *(percent of GDP)*

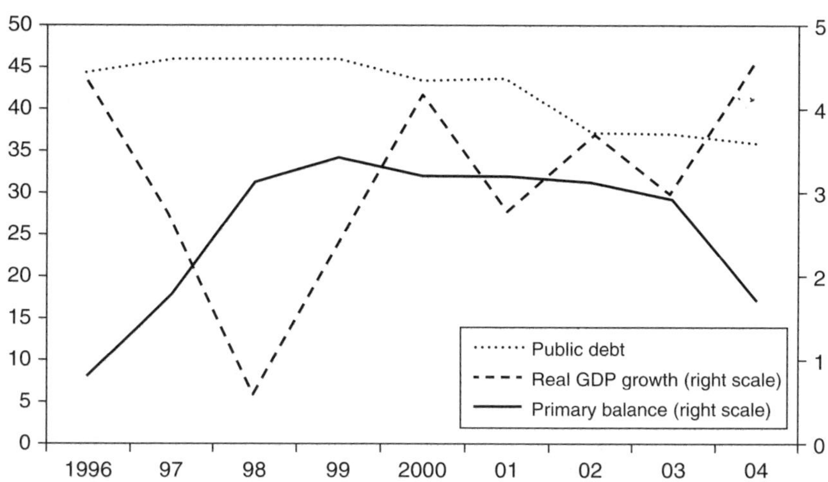

Sources: National authorities; and authors' calculations.

of the information system, and strengthening of audit and collection capacity. Public finance management legislation introduced in 2000 boosted financial accountability and improved internal controls at the national and provincial levels. On top of these reforms, there was an improvement in treasury control, and a centralization of personnel spending at the provincial level.

Fiscal consolidation focused on expenditure, with deliberate efforts to reduce the overall fiscal deficit. Expenditure measures targeted cuts in the wage bill and in subsidies and transfers and allowed a marginal increase in capital expenditures. Following fiscal adjustment, current and total expenditure were reduced while revenue improved, although the initial gains from expenditure reduction were later reversed.

The reduction of budget deficits over the years was accompanied by a reorientation of spending toward poverty reduction and social projects. The public financial management framework helped strengthened national and provincial capacity through provisions for multiyear budgeting and strategic planning. Beginning in 2000, state-owned enterprises, especially the four largest, which accounted for about 91 percent of assets of the top 30, restructured to increase their efficiency through improved governance and competition.

Vanuatu, 2002–07

After years of sub-par economic performance, Vanuatu's economy is currently one of the fastest growing among all the small islands in the Pacific. Real GDP growth averaged 6 percent over the period 2003–2007. The strong growth performance can be explained by a booming tourism sector combined with foreign direct investment in real estate. At the same time, the country lowered its public debt by 23 percentage points of GDP in the five years following 2002 (Figure 4.15). Political

Figure 4.15 Vanuatu: Public Debt, Real GDP Growth, and Primary Balance, 1999–2007
(percent of GDP)

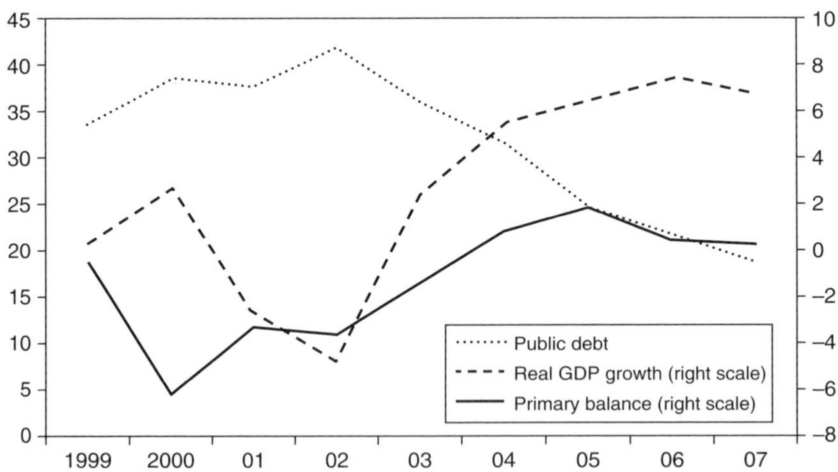

Sources: National authorities; and authors' calculations.

stability, largely absent since the early 1990s, boosted confidence and has enabled the government to undertake structural and fiscal reforms. Macroeconomic management has improved and has created the right environment for economic activity to thrive.

The strong fiscal position in recent years is credited to the buoyant economic activity and important reforms, including a widening of the tax base, improvement in tax compliance, and strengthened expenditure control. Other reforms have included the introduction of a VAT, capacity strengthening at the tax office, strengthened regulation of the state-owned utility company, and fiscal transparency through more frequent financial reporting. In addition, the government liberalized the telecommunication sector in 2006 by offering a second telecommunication license. Furthermore, technical assistance to the central bank, especially from the Pacific Financial Assistance Centre, has helped build capacity and enhanced the transparency of the country's monetary policy operations.

ESTIMATING THE PROBABILITY OF A LARGE DEBT REDUCTION

Methodology

To examine the determinants of a large debt reduction, we use a data set spanning over three decades for a large sample of developed and developing economies. The analysis uses a panel data set of about 160 countries to estimate the probability that a large debt reduction will be initiated using the logit regression approach:

$$Y_{it} = \alpha_i + \beta X_{it} + \partial G_t + \upsilon_{it}, \qquad (4.1)$$

where Y is the log of the odds ratio, or more specifically the log odds of large debt reduction. The variable i stands for the ith country and t for the tth time period, α_i is an idiosyncratic fixed effect which accounts for intercountry differences as long as these differences are constant over time. The explanatory variables X_{it} and G_t—representing macroeconomic variables and measures of fiscal rule, respectively—are measured either at the beginning of the previous five-year period or during the previous five-year period.

The analysis uses a panel data set of 160 countries for eight five-year periods (1970–74, 1975–79 . . . , 2005–09) to estimate the probability that a large debt reduction would be initiated in each five-year period using the logit regression approach. The logit is interpreted as follows: the slope coefficient measures the change in Y for a unit change in any of the explanatory variables, demonstrating how the log odds change as the explanatory variables change by a unit.[2]

[2]The odds in favor of a large debt reduction initiation are the ratio of the probability of a large debt reduction to the probability of "no debt reduction" in any given five-year period. The odds ratio is written mathematically as $\rho / (1 - \rho)$.

The predicted probability of a large debt reduction can be computed using the estimated coefficient of the above regression:

$$\hat{Y}_{it} = \alpha_i + \beta \hat{X}_{it} + \partial \hat{G}_t + \upsilon_{it}, \tag{4.2}$$

The probabilities for hypothetical observations can be calculated by first finding the average values for all explanatory variables for a subset of countries and taking this to represent a typical country within the subset and then using the following formula:

$$\rho_{it} = \frac{e^y}{(1+e^y)} = \frac{1}{(1+e^{-y})}, \tag{4.3}$$

However, when the dependent variable is observed as a qualitative variable and there are few time series observations per cross-section units and no autoregressions, fixed-effect models gives inconsistent estimates of the slope parameter. Andersen (1973) and Chamberlain (1980) argue that for large N and a small number of observations, the maximum likelihood estimation of the fixed-effects model gives inconsistent estimates of the parameters. They recommend the use of the conditional maximum likelihood (conditioning on the fixed effects). The main principle is to consider the likelihood function to be conditional on sufficient statistics for the incidental parameter α_i (Maddala, 1987). In our logit model in equation (4.1), these sufficient statistics are $\sum_t y_{it}$ for α_i. Maddala (1987) argues that for the logit model the conditional likelihood approach results in a computationally convenient estimator. The conditional maximum likelihood estimator of β is consistent, provided that the conditional likelihood function satisfies regularity conditions, which impose mild restrictions on the α_i.

Chamberlain (1980) demonstrates that the standard errors obtained by the usual conditional logit programs can be used as the asymptotic standard errors for the conditional maximum likelihood estimator of β. In the conditional fixed-effects logit approach, alternative sets for which $\sum_t y_{it} = 0$ or $\sum_t y_{it} = T$ are discarded because they do not contribute to the likelihood function. In order to test for a fixed individual effect, one can perform a Hausman-type test based on the difference between the conditional maximum likelihood estimator and the standard logit maximum likelihood, ignoring country differences:

$$H = (\beta_{CFE} - \beta_{SL})'(V_{CFE} - V_{SL})^{-1}(\beta_{CFE} - \beta_{SL}) \tag{4.4}$$

The test statistics are asymptotically χ^2 distributed with k degrees of freedom.

The Data

The dependent variable is the probability of a large debt reduction (*Debtred*). The variable takes the value of 1 if a large debt reduction occurs and a value of zero otherwise. If a large debt reduction occurs in period t and continues in t+1, the value of *Debtred* is recorded as missing.

The explanatory variables are measures of fiscal consolidation, macroeconomic variables, political and institutio]nal variables, and fiscal rules.

Fiscal consolidation: Fiscal consolidation is measured by the ratio of cyclically adjusted primary balance to potential GDP.

GDP growth: Real GDP growth is expected to be important in raising government revenues.

Inflation: Higher inflation could inflate the debt away, but it also has a significant negative effective on economic growth and welfare. Lucas (2003) estimates that the gains from completely removing the inflation rate of 200 percent are in excess of 5 percent of GDP in the long run.

Global economic conditions: We use global real GDP growth as a measure of global economic conditions. Many analysts believe that global economic conditions could influence the success of fiscal consolidation and debt reduction efforts.

Interest cost: This cost is measured as interest payments as a ratio to GDP. This measure is used to determine whether interest cost has a disciplinary effect on debt. High debt servicing cost could negatively affect growth and investment.

Fiscal rules: A dummy variable is used to capture fiscal rules. The dummy takes the value of 1 if a fiscal rule exists when the episode starts or during the episode and a value of zero otherwise. The literature suggests that fiscal rules are estimated to have affected several dimensions of fiscal consolidation and that the size of fiscal consolidation was significantly larger when fiscal rules were present. We also investigate whether the type of fiscal rules matters for a large debt reduction. To this end, we examine the impact of expenditure rules, debt rules, revenue rules, and a balanced budget rule in explaining the probability of a large debt reduction.

Estimation Results

First, it is important to examine some comparative statistics. Table 4.1 presents comparative statistics for *large debt reduction countries* and *no large debt reduction countries* during the sample period. The data shows that as compared with countries that did not experience a large debt reduction during the period, those countries that did experience a large debt reduction—

- had a much higher debt
- had much higher growth on average
- had much better fiscal performance
- had much lower inflation
- had a much higher interest cost, and, finally
- were more likely to have fiscal rules (in whichever form).

It is not surprising that the main finding from these comparative statistics is that countries that experienced a large debt reduction were on average able to achieve a higher GDP growth and larger primary surpluses and were more likely to have fiscal rules than countries that did not experience a large debt reduction.

TABLE 4.1

Comparative Statistics: Determinants of Global Large Debt Reduction

	Large Debt Reduction		No Large Debt Reduction	
	Mean	**Standard deviation**	**Mean**	**Standard deviation**
Debt reduction	1	0	0	0
Debt	68.5	34.1	60.9	60.69
GDP growth	4.9	4.11	3.72	3.6
Primary balance	1.62	5.3	−0.004	6
Interest cost	3.8	3.1	2.77	2.2
Inflation	6.9	9.4	10.94	14.69
Political risk	65	12.5	66.5	13.6
Fiscal rules	0.26	0.44	0.15	0.36
Expenditure rule	0.11	0.32	0.05	0.21
Balance budget rule	0.25	0.43	0.13	0.33
Debt rule	0.19	0.4	0.11	0.31
Revenue rule	0.04	0.2	0.016	0.13

Source: Authors' calculations.

Table 4.2 provides the logit estimates for nine different models. Model 1 is the standard logit regression for the data that are pooled over time, and model 2 is the conditional fixed-effects logit model. When looking at the regression results, it is important to note that the fixed-effect estimator does not use information provided by intercountry comparisons of debt reduction. Consequently, the probability of a large debt reduction is identified by countries that change debt reduction status during the period. In fact, in the conditional fixed-effect model, all countries with unchanged outcomes drop out of the conditional likelihood function.

In our sample, we observed 217 countries that changed their debt reduction status at least once during the period 1970–2009. It is evident therefore that the number of informative observations is substantially lower than the total sample size, since the superior properties of the fixed-effects estimators in terms of bias need to be traded for less precise estimates in terms of higher standard errors. A comparison between the standard logit model and the conditional fixed-effects logit shows that the fixed-effect model performs better. A Hausman test statistic of 23.50 with a *p* value of 0.0014 leads to a rejection of the model without fixed effects.

The main results from the conditional fixed-effects logit model are that global large debt reductions are positively associated with strong economic growth, with a favorable external environment, with lasting fiscal consolidation, and with weaker initial conditions. The probability of a large reduction tends to increase when initial debt levels are high, since high debt levels tend to make fiscal consolidation needs more pressing in our sample of countries.

Strong economic growth also increases the probability of a large debt reduction, as the implementation of sound polices helps countries grow themselves out of debt. The results also show that global large debt reductions are driven by decisive and lasting fiscal consolidation. As expected, inflation does not contribute to major debt reductions and is actually negative and significant in the

TABLE 4.2

Regression Results: Determinants of Global Large Debt Reduction *(Dependent variable: the probability of a large debt reduction)*

	(1) GLS	(2) Random Effects	(3) Fixed Effects	(4) Fixed Effects	(5) Fixed Effects	(6) Fixed Effects	(8) Fixed Effects	(9) Fixed Effects
Interest cost	0.1810	0.1672***	0.1810	0.4803**	0.2284	0.5500**	0.6233**	0.2510
	(0.1671)	(0.0561)	(0.1671)	(0.2328)	(0.1793)	(0.2546)	(0.2673)	(0.1845)
Inflation	−0.0692**	−0.0226	−0.0692**	−0.0436	−0.0659*	−0.0442	−0.0326	−0.0661*
	(0.0333)	(0.0202)	(0.0333)	(0.0361)	(0.0342)	(0.0350)	(0.0364)	(0.0338)
Global growth	0.9006*	0.6304	0.9006*	1.2181**	0.9749*	1.3896**	1.4011**	1.0819**
	(0.4996)	(0.4187)	(0.4996)	(0.6039)	(0.5149)	(0.6303)	(0.6428)	(0.5326)
Primary balance	0.1418**	0.0561**	0.1418**	0.1535**	0.1411**	0.1600**	0.1476**	0.1394**
	(0.0624)	(0.0260)	(0.0624)	(0.0623)	(0.0620)	(0.0689)	(0.0667)	(0.0626)
Debt-to-GDP ratio	0.0572***	−0.0000	0.0572***	0.0483***	0.0558***	0.0519***	0.0455***	0.0560***
	(0.0171)	(0.0029)	(0.0171)	(0.0179)	(0.0175)	(0.0178)	(0.0173)	(0.0174)
GDP growth	0.1131**	0.0477	0.1131**	0.1271**	0.1144**	0.1396***	0.1382***	0.1166**
	(0.0481)	(0.0297)	(0.0481)	(0.0494)	(0.0483)	(0.0519)	(0.0521)	(0.0483)
Fiscal rules				3.0087***				
				(1.0787)				
Expenditure rule					1.0147			
					(0.8789)			
Debt rule						5.3949**		
						(2.0981)		
Balanced budget rule							5.4797***	
							(1.9784)	
Revenue rule								1.7689
								(1.3734)
N	217	469	217	217	217	217	217	217
Log likelihood	−52.6156	−153.5913	−52.6156	−45.9339	−51.8868	−44.0946	−42.6553	−51.6386

Source: Authors' calculations.
Notes: Standard errors in parentheses. ***, **, and * denote significance at the 1, 5, and 10 percent levels, respectively.

conditional fixed-effects logit specification. Debt servicing costs also play a disciplinary role, as high debt servicing costs are positively associated with the probability of a large debt reduction.

Our results also show that fiscal rules tend to increase the probability of a large debt reduction because they help strengthen the fiscal framework and improve fiscal transparency. Which types of fiscal rules are more successful in debt reduction? We found that debt rules and balanced budget rules are important in explaining the probability of such debt reductions. Fiscal rules based on revenue and expenditure do not appear to have any significant impact on the probability of a large debt reduction.

TABLE 4.3

Robustness Tests: Determinants of Global Large Debt Reduction *(Dependent variable: the probability of a large debt reduction)*

	Alternative Definition of Debt Reduction			Excluding Oil Exporters		
	Model 1	**Model 2**	**Model 3**	**Model 4**	**Model 5**	**Model 6**
Interest cost	0.50430 (0.22121)**	0.53438 (0.0)**	0.56349 (0.23435)**	0.29272 -0.25080	0.31031 (0.25730)**	0.29679 (0.25682)
Inflation	-0.03796 (0.03483)	-0.03832 (0.03327)	-0.03991 (0.03260)	-0.08113 (0.04930)*	-0.07962 (0.04945)*	-0.08292 (0.04892)
World growth	1.58845 (0.59345)***	1.67717 (0.60020)***	1.57595 (0.62130)***	2.15448 (0.84615)***	2.18990 (0.83808)***	2.23625 (0.85083)***
Primary balance	0.14228 (0.05988)**	0.13833 (0.06170)**	0.15033 (0.06471)**	0.34035 (0.13085)***	0.34080 (0.13139)***	0.33940 (0.13295)**
Initial debt	0.04598 (0.01743)***	0.04555 (0.01746)***	0.04832 (0.01749)***	0.09870 (0.02995)***	0.09911 (0.02994)***	0.10102 (0.02986)***
GDP growth	0.12465 (0.04861)***	0.12506 (0.04870)***	0.13226 (0.04938)***	0.33741 (0.15349)**	0.33195 (0.15219)**	0.34562 (0.15358)**
Fiscal rules	2.24256 (0.78523)***			2.33547 (0.9494492)**		
Budget balance rule		2.64213 (0.97406)***			2.52412 (1.06235)**	
Debt rule			3.53640 (0.12566)***			2.48407 (1.06354)**
Log likelihood	-51.23484	-51.1829	-51.23484	-33.83596	-33.90281	-34.11112
No. of observations	231	231	231	189	189	189

Source: Authors' calculations.
Note: Standard errors in parentheses. ***, **, and * denote significance at the 1, 5, and 10 percent levels of significance, respectively.

Robustness Tests

How robust are these results? The robustness of our results is tested by the following measures. First, we use a variety of estimation techniques. Second, we restrict the sample period to the period 1990–2009. Third, we exclude oil exporters from the full sample. And fourth, we use an alternative definition of a "large debt reduction" episode. Some of the results of our robustness analysis are presented in Table 4.3.

We examine whether our benchmark regression results are robust to changes in the definition of large debt reduction. We then define a large debt reduction as occurring when the debt-to-GDP ratio declines by at least 10 percentage points over a five-year period. Using this definition, we can identify 12 more episodes of global large debt reduction. We then estimate our benchmark model using the new definition of large debt reduction as the dependent variable. The results show that the estimated coefficients are largely unchanged, even though the standard errors, as expected, are larger in the model that uses fewer observations. Higher primary surpluses, strong global growth, robust real GDP growth, and fiscal rules are all positive and significant factors explaining the probability of global large debt reduction. We also exclude oil exporters from our baseline regression, and find that the results are statistically similar to our baseline regression results.

SUMMARY AND CONCLUSION

Highly indebted Caribbean countries should generally aim to lower their debt levels in order to reduce vulnerability and to create a better platform for growth. The results of this chapter show that major debt reductions are mainly driven by decisive and lasting fiscal consolidation efforts focused on reducing government expenditure.

Our analyses also show that robust real GDP growth increases the likelihood of a major debt reduction, because it helps countries grow their way out of indebtedness. Since growth in the current environment is virtually nonexistent, significant fiscal consolidation in the Caribbean is inevitable.

Fiscal consolidation in the Caribbean needs to be credible in order to anchor market expectations about fiscal sustainability. It is essential to strengthen the fiscal framework by adopting fiscal rules and independent fiscal agencies to guide budget processes and improve fiscal transparency. The literature on fiscal rules shows that when such rules are present, the size of fiscal consolidation is significantly larger and the consolidation efforts are sustained longer. The adoption of a spending rule on top of a budget balance rule helps in the achievement and maintenance of a primary balance that is sufficient to stabilize the debt-to-GDP ratio.

Caribbean countries could create a stable general fiscal rule to strengthen the current fiscal framework by defining the rule in terms of primary deficit for general government, which could take the form of expenditure ceilings and revenue floors. It is also essential to support the fiscal rule by creating an independent fiscal council to assess macroeconomic projections underlying the budgeting process and assess the compatibility of the fiscal framework with fiscal rules and general government policies.

Fiscal consolidation needs to be completed by a comprehensive policy to reduce public debt, including reforming tax policy, improving the efficiency of government spending, containing contingent liabilities, rationalizing the public sector, actively managing debt, restructuring debt, and making growth-enhancing structural reforms. Key areas for reforms include increasing labor market flexibility, achieving greater regional cooperation, and creating an enabling environment for private sector development.

APPENDIX 4.1

APPENDIX TABLE 4.1

Episodes of Large Debt Reduction without Debt Restructuring

Country	Period	Duration (Years)	Public Debt (percent of GDP)		Change in debt ratio	Fiscal rules?
			Peak	Trough		
Angola	1999–2007	8	89.9	22.7	-67.2	Yes
Antigua	2002–2008	8	124.9	62.1	-62.8	Yes
Armenia	1999–2007	8	38.4	16.1	-22.3	No
Australia	1994–2007	18	31.5	9.6	-21.8	Yes
Bahrain	1987–1994	9	26.8	6.8	-20.1	No
Bahrain	2003–2008	5	36.9	14.6	-22.3	No
Belgium	1994–2007	13	132.1	84.2	-47.9	Yes
Belize	1985–1990	5	68.8	39.8	-29.0	No
Bhutan	2004–2008	4	81.8	63.0	-18.8	No
Botswana	1976–1980	4	45.7	13.3	-32.3	No
Botswana	1985–1990	5	39.8	17.1	-22.7	No
Brazil	2002–2008	6	79.8	65.2	-14.6	Yes
Bulgaria	2001–2008	7	68.6	15.5	-53.1	Yes
Canada	1997–2007	10	101.7	66.5	-35.2	Yes
Chile	1993–2000	7	47.4	13.7	-33.7	Yes
Colombia	2003–2008	5	45.6	30.8	-14.8	No
Comoros	1985–1993	8	115.9	69.9	-45.9	No
Croatia	2002–2008	6	48.7	28.5	-20.2	No
Cyprus	2004–2008	4	70.2	48.3	-21.9	Yes
Denmark	1998–2007	9	72.4	34.1	-38.3	Yes
Egypt	2003–2008	5	114.8	74.7	-40.1	No
Equatorial Guinea	2000–2008	8	34.4	0.7	33.7	Yes
Fiji	1997–1999	12	56.6	36.0	-20.6	No
Finland	1994–2002	8	56.6	41.5	-15.1	Yes
Gabon	1978–1984	6	80.1	23.9	-56.2	No
Ghana	1972–1978	6	28.7	9.4	-19.2	No
Grenada	1970–1979	9	136.4	26.2	-110.2	No
Hungary	1995–2001	6	82.4	52.0	-30.4	No
Iceland	1995–2000	5	58.9	41.0	-17.9	No
India	2004–2010	6	83.9	68.1	-15.8	Yes
Iran	1988–1993	5	59.7	24.1	-35.6	No
Iran	1994–1997	3	45.7	23.0	-22.7	No
Iran	2003–2010	7	26.5	11.1	-15.4	No
Ireland	1993–2006	13	94.1	24.8	-69.3	Yes
Israel	1989–1997	8	147.4	99.4	-48.0	Yes
Israel	2003–2008	5	100.2	76.8	-23.4	Yes
Jamaica	2002–2007	5	106.8	82.8	-24.0	No
Kazakhstan	1993–1996	3	38.9	12.7	-26.2	No
Kazakhstan	1999–2007	8	27.2	5.9	-21.2	No
Korea	1985–1996	11	21.5	6.8	-14.6	No
Kuwait	1994–2008	14	114.5	10.0	-104.5	No
Lao PDR	1990–1995	5	202.6	118.5	-84.2	No
Lao PDR	1998–2001	3	187.6	140.2	-47.4	No
Lao PDR	2002–2008	6	144.9	58.0	-86.9	No
Lebanon	1990–1993	3	98.5	50.8	-47.7	No

APPENDIX TABLE 4.1

Episodes of Large Debt Reduction without Debt Restructuring *(continued)*

Country	Period	Duration (Years)	Public Debt (percent of GDP) Peak	Trough	Change in debt ratio	Fiscal rules?
Lebanon	2006–2010	4	179.9	134.1	–45.8	No
Lesotho	2001–2007	6	126.1	44.9	–81.2	No
Libya	1994–2003	9	78.5	44.9	–33.7	No
Malaysia	1991–1997	6	72.2	31.8	–40.4	No
Maldives	1981–1990	9	88.1	45.5	–42.6	No
Mali	1970–1973	3	79.3	52.4	–26.9	No
Malta	1971–1978	6	38.2	18.2	–20.0	No
Mauritius	1985–1989	4	71.8	48.5	–23.3	No
Mongolia	2003–2007	4	95.8	40.7	–55.1	No
Morocco	2000–2009	9	73.7	47.7	–26.0	No
Myanmar	2000–2008	8	140.9	42.4	–98.5	No
Nepal	2002–2010	8	64.3	35.9	–28.4	No
Netherlands	1995–2002	7	76.1	50.5	–25.6	Yes
New Zealand	1992–2007	5	64.6	17.4	–47.2	Yes
Norway	1993–1999	6	61.3	31.0	–30.4	Yes
Oman	1998–2008	10	38.6	5.1	–33.5	No
Panama	2004–2008	4	62.3	39.2	–23.1	Yes
Papua New Guinea	1987–1988	11	62.1	42.1	–20.0	No
Papua New Guinea	2002–2007	5	62.6	32.9	–29.7	No
Paraguay	2002–2009	7	72.6	18.0	–54.6	No
Peru	2003–2008	5	41.3	25.0	–16.2	Yes
Phillipines	2003–2007	4	67.7	46.1	–21.6	No
Qatar	2001–2008	7	58.2	8.6	–49.6	No
Samoa	1985–1990	5	77.5	63.0	–14.5	No
Samoa	1994–1998	4	121.7	72.8	–48.9	No
Samoa	2003–2005	2	67.2	44.8	–22.4	No
Saudi Arabia	2002–2008	6	96.9	13.2	–83.7	No
Seychelles	1987–1990	3	90.6	72.9	–17.8	No
Seychelles	2003–2006	3	160.6	132.7	–27.8	No
Singapore	1979–81	2	89.0	59.7	–29.3	No
Singapore	1987–1990	3	89.0	73.1	–15.9	No
Slovak Republic	2003–2008	5	42.4	27.8	–14.6	Yes
Solomon Islands	1991–1997	6	67.4	41.2	–26.2	No
Solomon Islands	2002–2010	8	87.0	25.7	–61.3	No
South Africa	1977–1984	7	45.3	23.2	–22.1	No
South Africa	1999–2008	9	45.9	27.3	–18.7	No
Spain	1996–2007	11	67.4	36.1	–31.3	Yes
St. Kitts and Nevis	2005–2008	3	168.1	138.0	–30.1	Yes

APPENDIX TABLE 4.1

Episodes of Large Debt Reduction without Debt Restructuring *(continued)*

Country	Period	Duration (Years)	Public Debt (percent of GDP)		Change in debt ratio	Fiscal rules?
			Peak	Trough		
St. Vincent and the Grenadines	1994–1997	3	57.0	41.3	−15.7	No
Suriname	2000–2008	8	69.4	18.0	−51.4	No
Sweden	1984–1990	6	70.9	46.3	−24.6	No
Sweden	1996–2008	12	84.4	38.8	−45.6	Yes
Switzerland	1977–1989	12	46.9	31.0	−15.9	No
Switzerland	2004–2008	4	71.9	54.8	−17.1	Yes
Syria	1998–2002	4	150.4	131.2	−19.2	No
Syria	2003–2008	5	133.5	37.4	−96.1	No
Tajikistan	2002–2008	6	79.1	30.2	−48.8	No
Thailand	1986–1996	10	53.0	10.7	−42.2	No
Thailand	2001–2007	6	57.2	37.3	−19.8	No
Trinidad and Tobago	2002–2008	6	58.7	24.1	−34.6	No
Tunisia	2001–2010	9	62.5	40.4	−22.0	No
Turkey	1970–1974	4	39.8	19.0	−20.8	No
Turkey	2001–2007	6	77.6	39.4	−38.1	No
Turkmenistan	1998–2008	10	64.4	2.4	−62.0	No
United Kingdom	1970–1975	5	73.2	46.7	−26.6	No
United Kingdom	1997–2005	8	57.9	42.1	−15.8	Yes
United States	1993–2001	8	72.4	54.7	−17.7	Yes
Uzbekistan	2001–2010	9	59.4	9.8	−49.6	No
Vanuatu	2002–2007	5	41.9	18.7	−23.3	No
Vietnam	1998–2001	3	79.3	39.9	−39.4	No
Zimbabawe	1998–2002	4	88.0	20.1	−67.8	No
Average		**6.6**	**77.9**	**41.8**	**−35.5**	
Median		**6.0**	**70.9**	**38.8**	**−27.8**	

Source: Authors' calculations.

REFERENCES

Ali Abbas, S. M., Nazim Belhocine, Asmaa El Ganainy, and Mark Horton, 2011, "Historical Patterns of Public Debt—Evidence from a New Database," Presented at a Conference on Fiscal Policy, Stabilization and Sustainability, June 6–7, Florence, Italy.

Alesina Alberto, and Roberto Perotti, 1995, "Fiscal Expansions and Fiscal Adjustments in OECD Countries," NBER Working Paper No. 5214 (Cambridge, Massachusetts: National Bureau of Economic Research).

Amo-Yartey, Charles, Machiko Narita, Garth Peron Nicholls, Joel Chiedu Okwuokei, Alexandra Peter, and Therese Turner-Jones, 2012, "The Challenges of Fiscal Consolidation and Debt Reduction in the Caribbean," IMF Working Paper 12/276 (Washington: International Monetary Fund).

Andersen, Erling, 1973, *Conditional Inference and Models for Measuring* (Copenhagen: Mentalhygiejnisk Forsknings Institut).

Baldacci, Emmanuele, Sanjeev Gupta, and Carlos Mulas-Granados, 2010, "Getting Debt Under Control," *Finance and Development*, Vol. 47, No. 4, pp. 18–21 (Washington: International Monetary Fund).

———, 2012, "Reassessing the Fiscal Mix for Successful Debt Reduction," *Economic Policy*, Vol. 27, Issue 71, pp. 365–406, July.

Bandiera, Luca, 2008, "Public Debt and Its Determinants in Low-Income Countries—Results From Seven Country Case Studies," (Washington: World Bank). Available at SSRN: http://ssrn.com/abstract=1143511.

Chamberlain, Gary, 1980, "Analysis of Covariance with Qualitative Data," *Review of Economic Studies*, No. 47, pp. 225–38.

Finger, Harald, and Azim Sadikov, 2010, "Lowering Public Debt," *Finance and Development*, Vol. 47, No. 2, pp. 36–38 (Washington: International Monetary Fund).

Giavazzi, Francesco, and Marco Pagano, 1990, "Can Severe Fiscal Contractions Be Expansionary? Tales of Two Small European Countries," *NBER Macroeconomics Annual*, Vol. 5, pp. 75–111 (Cambridge, Massachusetts: National Bureau of Economic Research).

Greenidge, Kevin, Roland Craigwell, Chrystol Thomas, and Lisa Drakes, 2012, "Threshold Effects of Sovereign Debt: Evidence from the Caribbean," IMF Working Paper 12/157 (Washington: International Monetary Fund).

International Monetary Fund (IMF), 2003, "Public Debt in Emerging Markets: Is It Too High?" in *World Economic Outlook* (September) (Washington).

———, 2012, "The Good, the Bad, and the Ugly: 100 Years of Dealing With Public Debt Overhangs," in *World Economic Outlook* (October) (Washington).

Lucas, E. Robert, 2003, "Macroeconomic Priorities," *The American Economic Review*, Vol. 93, No. 1, pp. 1–14.

Maddala, G. S., 1987, "Limited Dependent Variable Models Using Panel Data," *The Journal of Human Resources*, Vol. 22, No. 3, pp. 307–38.

Nickel, Christiane, Philipp Rother, and Lilli Zimmermann, 2010, "Major Public Debt Reductions: Lesson from the Past, Lessons for the Future," Working Paper No. 1241 (Frankfurt: European Central Bank, September).

Reinhart, M. Carmen, and Kenneth S. Rogoff, 2011, "A Decade of Debt," NBER Working Paper No. 16827 (Cambridge, Massachusetts: National Bureau of Economic Research).

Reinhart, M. Carmen, Kenneth S. Rogoff, and Miguel Savastano, 2003, "Debt Intolerance," *Brookings Papers on Economic Activity*, Vol. 2003, No. 1, pp. 1–62.

World Bank, 2005, *Public Debt and its Determinants in Market Access Countries: Results from 15 Country Case Studies* (Washington).

CHAPTER 5

Fiscal Consolidation: Country Experiences and Lessons from the Empirical Literature

JOEL CHIEDU OKWUOKEI

Governments facing high debt levels and seeking to undertake fiscal consolidation are often confronted with a number of interrelated questions. What promotes a successful fiscal consolidation? How large should the adjustment be and how fast? Should one adjust now or later, and what are the consequences of postponing adjustment? Should one cut expenditures, raise revenues or do both? Which components of expenditures or revenues should one adjust, and does the composition of adjustment really matter? Would the adjustment be self-defeating? Is there a political price for fiscal adjustment?

Following two approaches, this chapter attempts to answer many of these questions that policymakers may have in their quest for fiscal consolidation. First, the chapter undertakes a comprehensive survey of a large body of mostly empirical literature on fiscal consolidation, covering industrial, emerging market, and developing economies. Second, it explores specific country experiences with fiscal consolidation dating back to the 1990s, examining 25 case studies, consisting of 14 advanced, 8 emerging market, and 3 developing economies, including Barbados and Jamaica. In doing this, it focuses on the prevailing economic and political conditions preceding fiscal consolidation, the various measures adopted, the composition of adjustments, and the achievements.[1] The ultimate goal is to draw useful lessons on the determinants of a successful fiscal consolidation.

To motivate the discussions, the chapter first lays out the theoretical background to the debate on fiscal consolidation before discussing the evidence from the empirical literature.[2] It next examines country experiences with fiscal

[1]Over the period in focus, many of the countries had fixed exchange regimes, and thus share similar features with Caribbean countries.

[2]The majority of the studies focus on advanced economies and in particular member countries of the Organisation for Economic Co-operation and Development (OECD), perhaps due to data availability.

consolidation.[3] It ends with a summary of the main lessons from the literature and country experiences and concluding remarks.

THE FISCAL CONSOLIDATION DEBATE: THEORETICAL BACKGROUND

The debate over fiscal consolidation is a long-standing one and will continue to attract attention in the future. Despite the often-cited long-term benefits of fiscal adjustment, there continues to be concern about the short-term costs. More so, fiscal consolidation appears unavoidable in the current environment of low growth, high debt, and deteriorating fiscal performance. In any case, as de Rato (2004, p. 1) points out, "the reality is that countries that decide to postpone fiscal reform and adjustment for fear of the political and economic consequences usually end up paying a much higher price when economic necessity forces them to act."

The debate stems from the standard Keynesian proposition that fiscal adjustment has a contractionary effect on economic activity in the short run. Lower government expenditures and increases in taxation both reduce aggregate demand and therefore output via the multiplier. This conventional wisdom is questioned by Giavazzi and Pagano (1990), who point to two episodes in Denmark and Ireland in the 1980s in which a sharp fiscal consolidation was associated with a surprisingly large expansion in private domestic demand. These were the so-called expansionary fiscal contractions. Following subsequent studies, there appears to be a consensus that fiscal consolidation is not always self-defeating, and several theoretical justifications of its non-Keynesian effects have been offered in the literature.

The question then is what makes fiscal contractions expansionary? A prominent view—one firmly rooted in rational expectation theory[4]—suggests that there is a strong private sector response to fiscal consolidation on the demand side, operating through wealth effects on consumption and credibility effects on interest rates. First, the wealth effect on consumption implies that fiscal restraint may give rise to expectations about future tax cuts and hence a higher permanent income for households, which in turn would stimulate private consumption and investment and therefore output.

A second channel of wealth effects identified in the literature arises from the decline in interest rates that may accompany fiscal adjustment. In the view of Alesina and Perotti (1997), fiscal consolidation, particularly a strong one in a high-debt country, may have far-reaching credibility effects on interest rates by

---

[3]This draws mainly on two studies: Kumar, Leigh, and Plekhanov (2007) and Tsibouris and others (2006). Kumar, Leigh, and Plekhanov analyzed 14 cases in the OECD, including Canada, Denmark, Finland, France, Germany, Ireland, Italy, Japan, the Netherlands, New Zealand, Spain, Sweden, the United Kingdom, and the United States. Tsibouris and others focused on large adjustments, examining a much wider sample, including Brazil, Cote d'Ivoire, Jamaica, Lebanon, Lithuania, Nigeria, Russia, South Africa, and Zambia.

[4]The key characteristics of the expectations view is that nonstandard effects of fiscal policy are explained by the role of current policy in shaping expectations about future policy (see Bertola and Drazen, 1993).

lowering risk premiums, which can be of two types: inflation risk premiums and default (or consolidation) risk premiums. To these authors, the default risk premium is non-trivial for a high-debt country. They argue that decisive steps to reduce fiscal deficits and public debt are capable of bolstering market confidence through a fall in the sovereign risk premium, thereby crowding in private investment and consumption, notably investments and consumption that are sensitive to interest rates.[5]

Further, as highlighted by Alesina, Prati, and Tabellini (1989) citing the case of Italy, countries facing high levels of debt with short term maturity may face a self-fulfilling confidence crisis. That is, if the public expects that in the future the government will be unable to roll over the maturing debt, the public may refuse to buy debt today and choose to hold foreign assets instead.

The confidence effect is visible in the favorable responses to fiscal consolidation of the stock market and real estate prices. It is especially pronounced if solvency is an issue or policy credibility is low (de Rato, 2004), in which case fiscal consolidation must be understood as part of a credible plan designed to permanently reduce the government deficit and therefore future tax liabilities (Giavazzi and Pagano, 1995; and Giavazzi, Jappelli, and Pagano, 2000). Put simply, the government must be able to signal a break from the past to attract financial markets and the public. However, according to Hjelm (2002a), a strong private sector response to fiscal consolidation may be due to country-specific factors. Thus, the expectation view may not be true in general.

While the wealth effects on private consumption emanating from permanent reductions in government expenditure are expansionary, there is a concern that the same wealth effects could affect labor supply through substitution effects.[6] As Alesina and Perotti (1997) note, if both consumption and leisure are normal goods, then a wealthier consumer would want more of both and therefore work less. Thus, an alternative view—the supply side or labor market channel—underscores the importance of adjustment composition, suggesting that income tax increases and wage and transfer cuts have opposite effects on private sector labor costs and therefore on competitiveness and growth (Ardagna, 2004; and Alesina and Perotti, 1995). Alesina and Perotti (1997) make the case that the labor cost channel may be more empirically relevant for consumption than the wealth effects and credibility channels.[7] Under different exchange rate regimes, Lane and Perotti (2003) analyze the impact of fiscal policy through the labor cost and

[5]Barro (1981) and Baxter and King (1993) distinguish the impact of temporary and permanent changes in government spending on output and real interest rates.

[6]Typically, higher labor income taxes should reduce labor supply. Thus, one expects a permanent reduction in government spending financed by a tax cut to have two opposite effects on labor supply: the wealth effect, which reduces the impact of fiscal policy, and the substitution effect, which raises the impact; the former is expected to be dominant (see Alesina and Perotti, 1997; Barro, 1981; and Baxter and King, 1993).

[7]The effects on labor supply may depend on the structure of the labor market. Alesina and Perotti (1997) notes that with unionized labor markets, a permanent increase in labor taxation shifts the union's aggregate labor supply because it reduces the after-tax at any before-tax wage.

exchange rate channels, and conclude that wages and prices need to be partially flexible for both channels to be effective. When wages and prices are fully flexible, the exchange rate channel breaks down. On the other hand, if wages and prices are fully rigid, there are no short-term adjustment costs.

Nonetheless, the short-term adjustment costs and distributional effects cannot be ignored. Indeed, Coenen, Mohr, and Straub (2008) develop a theoretical model to demonstrate that irrespective of the strategy adopted, adjustment costs are evident. The distributional effects can be pronounced, depending on the adjustment strategy and, in particular, on the extent to which households differ with regard to their ability to participate in asset markets and their dependence on fiscal transfers. Similarly, analyzing fiscal consolidation in a small open economy, Almeida and others (2011) find short-term costs, notably on output, consumption, and welfare.

Over the medium to long term, fiscal consolidation can be good for growth, and hence may not trigger an economic slowdown. Coenen, Mohr, and Straub (2008) identify positive long-term impacts on macroeconomic aggregates, such as output and consumption, when the resulting improvement in the budgetary position is used to lower distortionary taxes. Their conclusion is supported by Almeida and others (2011), who note that the consolidation gains are boosted if the strategy also involves a tax reform that shifts the tax burden away from labor income and toward final goods consumption. The creation of fiscal space after debt reduction in the long term would permit cuts in corporate income taxes (Kumar, Leigh, and Plekhanov, 2007).

FISCAL CONSOLIDATION: A SURVEY OF EMPIRICAL EVIDENCE

Turning now to the empirical literature, evidence broadly supports the view that fiscal consolidation can be expansionary under certain circumstances (Alesina and Perroti, 1995; Alesina, 2010). Alesina, Favero, and Giavazzi (2012), for example, examine whether fiscal consolidation causes large output losses. They demonstrate that adjustments based on spending cuts are much less costly in terms of output losses than tax-based adjustments. An analysis of the short- and long-term effects of fiscal adjustment in the OECD economies by Kumar, Leigh, and Plekhanov (2007) indicates that short-term negative effects are moderate and are not generally widespread. The contractionary effects, they find, are lower when consolidation involves increases in consumption taxes, and are largest when it involves cuts in productive expenditure.

Probit regression estimates by Giudice, Turrini, and in't Veld (2007) indicate that episodes in the European Union that turned out to be expansionary were more likely to start in periods with output below potential. According to Alesina and Perotti (1995) and Alesina and others (1998), fiscal adjustments crowded in business investment and improved competitiveness and therefore growth. Guajardo, Leigh, and Pescatori (2011) examine historical records to identify fiscal policy changes intended specifically to reduce budget deficits. Using a somewhat different measure than the conventional definitions of fiscal stance, they provide contrasting evidence that fiscal consolidation has short-term contractionary effects on private domestic demand and output. Estimates based on conventional measures of fiscal stance support the expansionary view, but the authors claim that the effects may be overstated in the literature.

What Really Triggers Fiscal Consolidation?

Evidence suggests that fiscal consolidation occurs when government finances are in bad enough shape to threaten fiscal sustainability (Ahrend, Catte, and Price, 2006; Price, 2010; Kumar, Leigh, and Plekhanov, 2007). In their studies of large adjustments across a wide range of countries, including developing economies, Tsibouris and others (2006) show that many large fiscal adjustments have been initiated against the backdrop of difficult macroeconomic conditions, including sluggish growth, higher debt, and high inflation. In extreme cases, fiscal consolidation is undertaken when the level of inflation, the exchange rate, and unemployment suggest a crisis situation (Ahrend, Catte, and Price, 2006).

Guichard and others (2007) analyze the OECD experience dating back to the late 1970s and provide evidence on the macroeconomic conditions and policy set-ups that have aided and sustained fiscal consolidation. Their main findings are that large initial deficits and high interest rates were important in initiating fiscal consolidation and also in boosting the size and duration of fiscal adjustments. The presence of a systemic financial crisis, which calls for banking sector repair, signals the need for consolidation (Barrios, Langedijk, and Pench, 2010). Alesina, Ardagna, and Trebbi (2006), and Drazen and Grilli (1993) argue that sometimes crisis situations are desirable because they force the government to undertake necessary reforms needed to improve economic welfare.

What Promotes a Successful Fiscal Consolidation?

Findings concerning what promotes a successful fiscal consolidation—and therefore debt reduction—point to a range of factors. In terms of positive growth effects, evidence suggests that fiscal consolidation is far more likely to succeed when countries approach a critical level of macroeconomic instability, whether arising from a chronic tendency to increase budgetary expenditures, debt problems, or balance of payment difficulties (de Rato, 2004). Ardagna (2004) suggests that while higher GDP growth matters, it does not drive the success of consolidation. Alesina (2010) argues that high inflation (or the hyper type) and sustainable growth may not occur often enough to reduce debt. In a study of 25 emerging market economies, Gupta and others (2003) find that sustained fiscal adjustments are affected by the legacy of past fiscal failures, the size of the deficit, the initial debt stock, exchange rate movement, inflation, and the unemployment rate. Perotti (1999) provides considerable support for the finding that when debts are initially at critical levels, fiscal consolidation is more likely to succeed, whereas Heylen and Everaert (2000) disagree, arguing that the success of consolidation is not clearly affected by initial debt conditions.

Do the Composition and Size of Fiscal Adjustment Matter?

Regarding the composition and size of fiscal adjustments, the general consensus is that for a fiscal adjustment to be credible it must be of considerable size. Numerous studies suggest that there are size and composition effects of successful fiscal consolidations, as they signal commitment and raise the probability of success. For example, examining a panel of OECD countries, Ardagna (2004) finds that the larger the initial adjustment, measured by the change in primary fiscal balance, the larger is the likelihood of success.

While other studies indicate that the composition is fundamental for success (Alesina and Perotti, 1995; Alesina and Ardagna, 2009; Alesina and others, 1998; Lane and Perotti, 2003), Ardagna (2004) argues that success depends more on the size and less so on the composition. Controlling for exchange rate depreciation and changes in money supply, Hjelm (2002b, 2004) concludes that the composition effect disappears. It is believed that the effects of composition on growth works mostly through the labor market channel rather than the expectations channel. Bi, Leeper, and Leith (2012) introduce uncertainty over the timing and composition of adjustment in the context of a nonlinear DSGE specification; they find that, among other things, the nature of fiscal consolidation, its duration, and the expectations of its likelihood of occurring and composition are all significant.

Which Is More Effective, Expenditure Cuts or Revenue Increases?

There is strong evidence that expenditure reductions outweigh revenue increases on successful fiscal consolidation. As pointed out by Price (2010), it is probably because expenditure measures reflect greater commitment, make substantial consolidation more feasible, and can lead to efficiency gains. Spending cuts are more important than tax increases in boosting confidence, and are more effective when they involve permanent reduction in outlays (de Rato, 2004). But it is also acknowledged that such cuts will be difficult in countries with urgent social needs and infrastructure deficiencies. In such cases, better expenditure targeting becomes crucial. Furthermore, according to Alesina (2010), lowering spending is also much more effective than increasing taxes in stabilizing the debt and avoiding economic downturns. Successful consolidations are based on expenditure reductions as opposed to major tax increases, or in conjunction with very modest increases in tax revenue (Darby, Muscatelli, and Roy, 2005; Alesina and Perotti, 1995).

Other studies confirm the conclusion that expenditure-focused adjustments are superior. Expenditure cuts constituted three-quarters of the total efforts in sustained adjustment (Tsibouris and others, 2006) and are associated with larger adjustments (Guichard and others, 2007). Alesina, Carloni, and Lecce (2012) emphasize that large, credible, and decisive expenditure-based consolidation is less likely to cause a recession. In their analyses of the fiscal expansions and consolidation experiences of industrial countries, McDermott and Wescott (1996) emphasize that focusing on the expenditure side, especially on transfers and wages, is more likely to succeed in reducing the debt ratio than tax-based consolidation. In their studies, Giavazzi and Pagano (1990, and 1995) find that spending reductions (including cuts in transfers) and tax increases were accompanied by a private consumption boom following large fiscal consolidations. A recent study by Guajardo, Leigh, and Pescatori (2011) confirms the earlier findings of Giavazzi and Pagano (1990).

The empirical literature also finds reductions in transfer programs and government wage expenditures to be more effective than capital expenditure cuts. In particular, de Rato (2004) stresses that cutting programs that have survived in the past for economic reasons can add credibility to the fiscal adjustment and increase the probability that it will have expansionary effects. In their study, Von Hagen, Hallet, and Strauch (2002) demonstrate that adjustments that lasted longer were driven by reductions in wages and transfers, with transfers and subsidies contributing about 86 percent on average to successful cases. The findings of Nickel, Rother, and Zimmermann (2010) support this conclusion, as they report that major debt reductions were influenced by durable fiscal consolidation with a focus on expenditures, especially cuts in social benefits and public wages. Two-thirds of successful adjustments have come with spending cuts, specifically in transfers and government wages (Alesina and others, 1998). In a panel study of selected OECD countries, Biggs, Hasset, and Jensen (2010) find that reductions in non-wage expenditures and government investments contribute little to success. Heylen and Everaert (2000), however, disagree that cuts in wages will bring about a successful consolidation, and argue that government should cut transfers instead.

What Role Do External and Domestic Conditions Play?

Supportive external and domestic conditions are essential. Findings by Kumar, Leigh, and Plekhanov (2007) suggest that a supportive domestic and international growth environment facilitates adjustment efforts. Heylen and Everaert (2000) also find that the chances of a consolidation's success rise with a favorable external environment, high economic growth, and low interest rates.

Evidence further suggests that in a federal setting, involving lower-level governments is helpful. Exploring the implications of fiscal decentralization for fiscal consolidation across the OECD countries, Darby, Muscatelli, and Roy (2005) find that involving subnational governments is critical in achieving expenditure cuts, especially with regard to reducing the overall size of the wage bill. Also, controlling grants to the subnational governments improves the success of fiscal consolidation. They note that, if fiscal consolidation is done in isolation, subnational governments behave differently; they focus on revenue increases and cuts in capital expenditure rather than on areas that are more durable in achieving fiscal consolidation.

How Does the Perception of Sovereign Risk Affect Fiscal Consolidation?

Agna and Igan (2013) analyze fiscal consolidation and corporate loan behavior in a sample of 16 advanced economies, and find that loan spreads increase with fiscal consolidation, especially for small firms, domestic firms, and firms with limited alternative sources of finance. However, when fiscal consolidations are large, the adverse effect of increasing loan spread can be mitigated, and it can be avoided altogether if consolidations are also accompanied with more adaptable macroeconomic policies and implemented by a stable government. In a study of the channel through which sovereign risk raises private sector funding costs, Corsetti and others (2012) find that if the monetary policy is constrained, the private sector's belief that an economy would weaken becomes self-fulfilling. Further results indicate that while sovereign risk worsens the effects of negative cyclical shocks, fiscal consolidation could help curb the risk of macroeconomic instability, and even stimulate economic activity.

It is generally understood that monetary easing could be helpful in lowering interest costs, although the likelihood of enhancing fiscal consolidation has been debated. Ardagna (2004) disagrees that successful and expansionary fiscal consolidations are the result of accompanying expansionary monetary policy. Another view is that monetary policy reaction may depend on the credibility of the consolidation plan. In their study, Guajardo, Leigh, and Pescatori (2011) find that the conduct of monetary policy may differ depending on the type of adjustment, with the central bank aggressively cutting interest rates following spending-based consolidations, in turn stimulating private demand and therefore output growth.

How Does Exchange Rate Devaluation Affect Fiscal Consolidation?

Empirical findings on the impact of exchange rate depreciation or devaluation on fiscal consolidation remain largely inconclusive. There is ample evidence that the prevailing exchange rate regime determines the impact of fiscal adjustment on the economy (Giavazzi and Pagano, 1990; Lane and Perotti, 2003; Hjelm, 2002b, 2004; Lambertini and Tavares, 2005; Mati and Thornton, 2008).

In particular, Lambertini and Tavares, 2005, controlling for other determinants of successful fiscal consolidation in a study of the OECD, find that a depreciation of the nominal effective exchange rate of one standard deviation of the sample mean in the two years before an adjustment increases the probability of success by 2 percentage points. Devaluation is found to have a positive and significant impact when the adjustment comprises reductions in transfers and taxes and increases in public investment (Heylen and Everaert, 2000). Others find that exchange rate devaluation enhances fiscal consolidation and sustains growth, especially when accompanied with moderate wage increases (Alesina, Ardagna, and Gali, 1998). The impact of devaluation may depend on adjustment composition (Heylen and Everaert, 2000; Alesina, Ardagna, and Gali, 1998).

In contrast, some studies consider exchange rate depreciation or devaluation as irrelevant (Barrios, Langedijk, and Pench, 2010; Ardagna, 2004; Alesina and others, 1998; and Gupta and others, 2003). For very small open economies, Worrell (2012) argues that the depreciation of the exchange rate would not be helpful for stabilization and growth purposes, simply because these economies are different. There is a binding foreign exchange constraint and little scope for import substitution, and thus exchange rate depreciation may not increase output, since it does not enhance price competitiveness. However, while the Worrell paper acknowledges that fiscal adjustment matters, it offers little discussion of the importance of structural reforms, including reforms in the labor market, on competiveness and growth.

Are Fiscal Adjustments a Political Liability?

Evidence also suggests that, overall, fiscal adjustment may not be a political liability. For example, Alesina (2010) finds no evidence of a systematic electoral penalty or fall in popularity for governments that adopt a restrained fiscal policy. In another study, Alesina, Carloni, and Lecce (2012) find 13 changes of government and 26 "no change of government" in the elections held during periods of fiscal adjustment, which implies relatively few changes in government associated with the adjustments.

Recent events in the euro area, however, have tested the validity of these conclusions, as voters in France and Greece vented their frustrations at the polls over difficult austerity measures. It should be further noted that a coalition government is much less likely to succeed in fiscal consolidation than a single party. In a study by Alesina and Perotti (1995), out of 23 strong adjustments initiated by coalition governments, only 3 were successful. Meanwhile, the success rate for single-party governments was 64.3 percent, and for minority party governments it was 53.3 percent. This confirms the finding of Alesina and Drazen (1991) that in more polarized political systems and societies it is difficult to reach a consensus. On the other hand, Brender and Drazen (2008), in a study of a large panel of countries consisting of different subgroups, find no evidence that an increased budget deficit during an election year helps the reelection prospects of incumbents. Indeed, they find that in developed countries and established democracies, election-year deficit spending and tax cuts are punished at the polls.

What Role Do Fiscal Rules Play in Successful Fiscal Consolidation?

In the context of successful fiscal consolidation and debt reduction, empirical evidence generally associates the presence of fiscal rules with stronger fiscal performance (Schaechter and others, 2012; FAD, 2009; Guichard and others, 2007). Fiscal rules supported several large fiscal adjustments and debt reduction episodes in a large sample of OECD, G-20 and EU countries (FAD, 2009). In particular, budget balance and debt rules have improved budgetary outcomes (Larch and Turini, 2011). Evidence also points to the increasing adoption of fiscal rules, particularly as a result of the global financial and economic crisis (Schaechter and others, 2012). Indeed, the crisis provided the platform for countries to review their existing rules, complementing them with new ones. Multiple fiscal rules are now a common practice and are mostly a combination of those rules that are closely linked to fiscal and debt sustainability.

When supported with a stronger monitoring mechanism and wider coverage, a combination of budget balance and expenditure rules appears to have been more effective (Price, 2010; FAD, 2009). It is also noted that key requirements for the effectiveness of fiscal rules include transparency, flexibility, commitment, and credible punishment for noncompliance (Guichard and others, 2007; Price, 2010). Although fiscal rules have been noted to create incentives to artificially achieve targets, other supporting features have been proposed, including independent fiscal councils and fiscal responsibility laws.

COUNTRY EXPERIENCES WITH FISCAL ADJUSTMENT

The basis of fiscal adjustment for a sample of advanced and emerging market economies is presented in Table 5.1.

Advanced Economies

Canada, 1994–97

Before its fiscal consolidation episode, the Canadian economy was characterized by slow recovery, low inflation, a high output gap, high unemployment, exchange rate deprecation, and an improving current account balance. In the fiscal sphere, the country had a sizable deficit and debt stock, a large share of short-term debt by nonresidents, a high tax-to-GDP ratio, and expanding entitlements. A majority government was elected in 1993 with a mandate to address these fiscal concerns, and this was followed by similar election outcomes in 1994–95 in the two largest provinces.

Fiscal adjustment had an expenditure focus, complemented by some revenue measures. Expenditure reduction accounted for about 85 percent of the fiscal adjustment and covered cuts in the wage bill, unemployment benefits, defense spending, agricultural and business subsidies, and transfers to provinces. There were also cuts in the provincial wage bill, capital spending, and transfers to municipalities totaling 1.7 percent of GDP in fiscal year 1993–94. Revenue measures included higher excises, a broadening of the personal and corporate income tax bases, and increases in corporate income tax rates.

In addition, provinces raised education and health fees and excises and broadened their corporate income tax base. These measures led to an improvement in the cyclically adjusted primary fiscal balance (CAPB) of 6.6 percent of GDP over 1994–97. The period saw the introduction of a medium-term budget framework, tax reforms, pension reforms, and unemployment insurances reforms.

Denmark, 2004–05

The economic slowdown in Denmark that started in 2001 continued into the period with the unemployment rate gradually rising, although the country had a moderate

TABLE 5.1

Basis of Fiscal Adjustment, Selected Countries

Revenue	Expenditure	Mixed
Brazil, Cote d'Ivoire, France, Jamaica, Nigeria, Ireland, United States, Zambia	Canada, Chile, Finland, Germany, Lebanon, Lithuania, Netherlands, South Africa, Spain, Sweden, United Kingdom	Barbados, Denmark, Japan New Zealand, Russia

Source: Author's compilation.

level of public debt (about 50 percent of GDP), and a near-balanced budget. At the same time, the ruling center-right coalition entered the second half of its term with waning public support. Fiscal adjustment consisted of a mix of revenue and expenditure measures with emphasis on expenditure restraint, which accounted for approximately half of the 2.9 percent improvement in the CAPB over the period. Tax revenues exceeded expectations, largely owing to rising oil and gas prices, in spite of a reduction in personal income tax rates in 2004 and a tax freeze in effect since 2002.

Furthermore, caps on expenditure growth in real terms led to a gradual reduction in the expenditure-to-GDP ratio. A broader reform of governance at the subnational level, involving a drastic reduction in the number of municipalities, was agreed during the period. Notwithstanding that the ruling center-right coalition entered the second half of its term with diminishing public support, the success of the fiscal consolidation in the 1990s helped build a national consensus about the importance of prudent fiscal policies. Since 2001, fiscal policy has been explicitly guided by medium-term objectives.

Finland, 1998

By 1998, the Finnish economy had recovered from a deep recession in the early 1990s and enjoyed a growth rate well above the EU average. Nevertheless, the fiscal position was characterized by high deficit and medium-level but rapidly increasing debt, a high tax-to-GDP ratio, and expanding entitlement programs. Both of the coalition governments elected respectively in 1991 and 1995 had a clear mandate to achieve European Monetary Union (EMU) membership. Following fiscal consolidation, the cyclically adjusted primary fiscal balance improved by about 1.7 percent in 1998 and by a cumulative 10 percent of GDP over the 1992–2000 period due to expenditure reductions that accounted for about 85 percent of the improvement.

There were across-the-board reductions in social benefits, transfers to municipalities, subsidies, wages, and capital spending. In addition to the reduction in transfers from the center, municipalities also reduced their wage bills and capital spending and raised property taxes, thereby improving their fiscal balances by 2.3 percent of GDP in 1994–95. Revenue measures included broadly revenue-neutral tax reforms involving raising payroll taxes and user fees. As part of structural reforms, efforts were made to broaden the tax base, raise rates, and reform the pension scheme.

France, 1996–97

The expansionary policy response to the 1993 recession left France with a large fiscal deficit and a rapidly rising public debt, falling short of the EMU criteria. Fiscal consolidation was launched on the back of a slow recovery from the recession. However, to ensure that the new government had a clear mandate for fiscal consolidation, parliamentary elections were scheduled to be held a year earlier than usual. Fiscal consolidation was rooted in revenue measures, which accounted for more than 85 percent of the 3 percent improvement in the cyclically adjusted primary fiscal balance to GDP over 1996–97.

Revenue measures covered a broadening of the tax base, temporary profit tax surcharges, an increase in the VAT rate in 1996, and one-off dividend payments.

The above measures were combined with reductions in capital spending and in health care and defense expenditures. The consolidation largely lacked support at the subnational level, although there was a public consensus that fiscal consolidation was necessary to achieve EMU membership. Proposals to reform public pensions and railways triggered protracted strikes in late 1995.

Germany, 2003–05

Germany had witnessed three years of slow growth, high unemployment, and heavy losses in the financial sector. In addition, the fiscal deficit widened to about 3.7 percent of GDP in 2002, with public debt at around 60 percent of GDP. A coalition led by the Social-Democratic Party narrowly won the elections in September 2002. In March 2003, a comprehensive, multiyear reform plan was unveiled, designed to gradually bring labor market outcomes, public finances, and the welfare system back on track by 2010. The improvement in the cyclically adjusted primary fiscal balance was in the range of 0.6–6 percent of GDP over 2003–05 mainly as a result of expenditure measures, which included reduction in health care spending, and tightened unemployment benefit entitlements. However, income tax cuts partly offset savings achieved through expenditure measures. The 2002 Internal Stability Pact failed to reach an agreement on the division of responsibilities between the central and subnational governments in compliance with the Stability and Growth Pact, and the attempts to reform intergovernmental relations ended in political gridlock. Although the proposed spending cuts were widely criticized by the opposition and by organized social groups, including the unions, voters seem to have been sharing a general sense of crisis, one requiring drastic measures.

Ireland, 2003–04

After a decade of strong growth performance, economic activity in Ireland decelerated markedly in 2002 and remained subdued in 2003. Despite the relatively low public debt, around 35 percent of GDP, and a near-balanced budget, the country undertook fiscal consolidation. Revenue measures, including increases in VAT and excises, and changes in capital gains taxation accounted for more than 90 percent of the 2.9 percent improvement of the CAPB to GDP over the period. On the expenditure side, capital expenditure was reduced, while the 2003 wage agreement moderated wages.

Structural reforms included the introduction of rolling multiyear capital expenditure budgeting and preparation of long-term fiscal projections. The central government traditionally held tight administrative control over subnational governments, although no specific adjustment measures were introduced at that level during the period. The coalition government had enjoyed a strong parliamentary majority since 2002, despite some differences of views within the coalition. Public support for fiscal consolidation was partial, with strong opposition from the trade unions. The government responded to a rapid fall in its popularity by substantially reshuffling the cabinet in September 2004, which revitalized the reform agenda.

Italy, 1997

Fiscal consolidation in Italy was preceded by electoral reforms at both the central and regional levels, which resulted in political stability. The fiscal consolidation occurred at a time when growth turned negative after a strong performance in 1995. Inflation was declining, but unemployment remained high. The debt was very high, over 115 percent of GDP in 1997, and had been rising in spite of fiscal consolidation efforts since the early 1990s. A public consensus emerged that fiscal consolidation was necessary to achieve EMU membership. Expenditure and revenue measures, approximately equally, contributed to the improvement in the CAPB by about 2 percent in 1997 (and by a cumulative 3.5 percent of GDP over 1994–97).

A number of temporary and permanent measures, including a personal income surtax, a levy on severance payment funds, and an increase in VAT rates in 1998, boosted revenues to a record high of over 47.5 percent of GDP. To lower expenditure, the government curtailed capital spending, reduced transfers to subnational governments, and halted the persistent increases in pension and health care outlays. Other reforms included tighter control over intergovernmental transfers since 1996, clearer delineation of expenditure responsibilities between the tiers of government, and electoral reform, which increased accountability.

Japan, 2004

During the fiscal consolidation episode, Japan's economy was gradually recovering, with contributions from both exports and domestic demand. However, a decade of high fiscal deficits (about 8 percent of GDP in 2003) led to a rapid accumulation of public debt, which reached 160 percent of GDP in 2003 while social security spending kept rising. The cyclically adjusted primary fiscal balance improved by about 1.3 percent of GDP in 2004, mainly as a result of higher revenues combined with expenditure restraint.

Revenue measures included a rollback of past income tax cuts, while the higher-than-expected tax revenues were saved. A gradual reduction in capital spending, containment in the growth of social security expenditures, and across-the-board cuts in discretionary spending programs were helpful. A devolution of tax and spending responsibilities to the subnational governments led to a cut in subsidies and a modest net savings. The ruling coalition had been in power since 2000, but it lost positions in both houses of parliament in 2004 as the government's approval rating plummeted, partly due to the passage of pension reform legislation.

The Netherlands, 2004–05

The Dutch economy had experienced a significant downturn in activity since 2000, accompanied by a sharp deterioration in its fiscal position as the 3 percent Maastricht deficit ceiling was breached in 2003. The general government balance worsened by almost 5½ percentage points during the first three years of the decade, as a result of the 2001 tax reform, increases in health care and education spending, and a higher deficit among local governments (reaching 0.6 percent of

GDP). Activity began to pick up in 2004; growth was projected at about 1 percent in 2004 and 1¾ percent in 2005. The challenge was to nurture the emerging recovery while ensuring fiscal sustainability.

Against this background, fiscal consolidation was initiated by a new government and consisted mainly of expenditure measures, which accounted for more than 75 percent of the improvement in the structural deficit-to-GDP ratio. As a result, the structural deficit narrowed by about 2.3 percent of GDP over 2004–05. There were modest base-broadening tax policies, while natural gas revenues increased. Expenditure measures included a significant cut in civil service employment, a general cut in subsidies, a freeze of public sector wages and social security benefits, and a reduction in the coverage of the basic public health care package. Earlier reforms in the 1990s had established a strong institutional framework for medium-term budgeting, which incorporated long-term projections of pension and social welfare spending.

At the subnational level, there were more explicit constraints on the operation of the local governments, including limitations on how much they could borrow and a strong emphasis on closer cooperation between the central and local governments. Local governments supported the consolidation effort by improving their balances in 2004–05. The government was determined to comply with the 3 percent deficit limit. To this end, debt and deficit reduction objectives were put into multiyear perspective using a medium-term fiscal framework. The role of the Bureau for Economic Policy Analysis was seen to be important in bringing consensus on the needed measures.

New Zealand, 2003

The macroeconomic environment in New Zealand was characterized by solid and accelerating economic growth, a narrowing current account deficit, unemployment at a 16-year low, a slight budget surplus, and a moderate level of public debt (about 40 percent of GDP), which nevertheless exceeded the government's long-term target of 30 percent of GDP. The political environment was competitive, with the opposition calling on the ruling Labor Party to introduce more tax cuts and improve the quality of health and education services. Nevertheless, following the September 2005 elections there was no significant relaxation of fiscal policy, and the incumbent party was re-elected with a confirmed mandate for continued fiscal consolidation.

Fiscal adjustment measures were mixed. Tax revenues and surpluses of public enterprises turned out to be higher than expected. Expenditure restraint accounted for approximately 40 percent of the improvement in the cyclically adjusted primary fiscal balance of about 1.4 percent of GDP in 2003 (and a cumulative 3.3 percent improvement since 2000). Caps on current expenditure led to a gradual reduction in the expenditure-to-GDP ratio. The government reiterated the importance of its commitment to the principles of medium-term budgeting established earlier (including the need to achieve an average surplus over the cycle) and emphasized the need for higher savings in the light of future pension and health care obligations.

Spain, 1996–97

Elected in March 1996, Spain's coalition government had a mandate for fiscal consolidation. The economy experienced a relatively rapid recovery after the recession, which had culminated in negative GDP growth in 1993. However, while economic activity was on the rise and inflation gradually subsided, high unemployment (at above 20 percent of the labor force) persisted. Public finances deteriorated gradually after 1988, with the fiscal deficit exceeding 7 percent of GDP in 1995 and public debt rising rapidly to over 70 percent of GDP.

The focus of fiscal consolidation was on expenditure reduction, complemented by some revenue measures. Expenditure cuts accounted for about 60 percent of the improvement in the cyclically adjusted primary fiscal balance of about 2.8 percent in over 1996–97 (and by a cumulative 4.1 percent of GDP since 1993). Reductions in current expenditure included cuts in social transfers, the wage bill, and health care spending. Tax reforms aimed at simplifying the tax code and reducing the burden on small businesses, coupled with strengthened tax administration, resulted in a significant improvement in tax buoyancy.

Structural reforms included gradual improvements in budgeting and monitoring, privatization, a reorganization of public enterprises, and the strengthening of tax administration. In 1992, Spain adopted a cooperative approach to regulating subnational public finances, whereby subnational fiscal targets were negotiated between the central and regional governments. The fiscal consolidation enjoyed only partial support at the regional level, although there was public consensus that it was necessary to achieve EMU membership.

Sweden, 1994–98

The Swedish economy had witnessed the deepest recession since the 1930s, accompanied with high inflation, rising unemployment, and exchange rate depreciation. The fiscal deficit exploded to over 12 percent of GDP, as a result of the cyclical downturn and the underfinanced tax reform of 1990–91, with public debt reaching 80 percent of GDP. Fiscal consolidation was largely expenditure-based, complemented with significant revenue measures. Expenditure cuts accounted for approximately 75 percent of the improvement in the cyclically adjusted primary fiscal balance of about 11 percent of GDP over 1994–98.

There were reductions in pension and welfare spending, including unemployment benefits and cuts across a broad range of spending programs. The country saw increases in social security fees, full taxation of dividends and capital gains, and increases in personal income tax rates. The unemployment benefits were reformed, with emphasis on shifting from cash payments to training. In 1993, the mechanism of distributing relief grants to municipalities was revised, which alleviated the problem of soft budget constraint. The consolidation was supported at the local level in 1995 and 1997–98. Fiscal consolidation was unpopular, as reflected in the outcome of the September 1998 elections in which the ruling party suffered major losses, despite retaining the majority in parliament.

The United Kingdom, 1995–98

After 18 years of being in opposition, the Labor Party won elections in the United Kingdom in May 1997 with an overwhelming majority in Parliament. The new government confirmed the course of fiscal consolidation and introduced a number of new policy reforms, including transferring the responsibility for setting interest rates from the Treasury to the Bank of England. The economy had experienced three successive years of solid economic growth, led by private consumption. Unemployment was falling rapidly, while inflation remained relatively low. The public sector fiscal deficit had increased to over 7 percent of GDP by 1994, the debt-to-GDP ratio was on the rise and already exceeded the target level of 40 percent by about 8 percentage points.

Adjustment efforts in the period 1995–98 were focused on expenditure restraint, which accounted for about 75 percent of the improvement in the cyclically adjusted primary fiscal balance of 6.4 percent of GDP over the period. Expenditure measures included containing increases in health care and education spending. On the other hand, revenue measures covered increases in indirect taxes and some duties, while for equity reasons the VAT on some items was lowered. Advanced corporation tax rebate was abolished, accompanied by a small reduction in the corporate tax rate. There was a one-off windfall levy on profits earned by privatized utilities.

Unemployment benefits were reformed, including the institution of a "welfare work" scheme to reduce youth unemployment. However, the central government maintained its traditional tight administrative control over subnational government spending. A new government in 1997 reiterated its preelection commitment to the golden rule and its intention to reduce the general government fiscal deficit of 4 percent of GDP in fiscal year 1996–97, while at the same time implementing tax reform to encourage investment.

The United States, 1994

Economic activity in the United States had been weak, and unemployment was rising. The federal government's fiscal situation had deteriorated rapidly with a fiscal deficit that was almost 5 percent of GDP. In nominal terms, federal debt had quadrupled over the 1980–92 period, and the debt ratio was projected to continue rising at a high rate. Consolidation focused on revenue measures and a multiyear adjustment, aimed at improving the structural deficit by 2½ percentage points of GDP over the next three years.

Measures included increases in income tax rates (on the top 1.2 percent of taxpayers) and in the corporate tax rate, and a social security tax increase for the top 15 percent of social security recipients. There were virtually no expenditure measures. In particular, there were no cuts in social and health care spending. The adjustment was carried out entirely at the federal government level. Consolidation was accompanied with intensive discussions regarding health care reform, as the costs were rising at a very fast pace and taking up sizable part of the budget. Right from the beginning, President Clinton emphasized the need to reduce the deficit, in spite of the concerns that it could further depress still weak economic activity.

However, there was a recognition that an adjustment could lead to a decline in interest rates that could outweigh the contractionary effect of the deficit reduction. The deficit reduction package was passed with an extremely narrow vote in the Congress. When the Democratic majority was lost in the 1994 mid-term elections, the President demonstrated a strong commitment to his original position of continued fiscal discipline, opposed plans by some to provide a stimulus through a large tax cut, and withstood a budget crisis in Congress in November 1995.

Emerging Market Economies

Chile, 1990–2000

Following a default on its external debt in the 1980s, Chile has since implemented strong and sustained fiscal and other economic reforms. The government reduced its debt from 54 percent of GDP in 1990 to 21 percent in 2002, owing to expenditure restraint, improvement in revenue collection, and reform of loss-making state enterprises. Privatization proceeds helped reduce debt, while real exchange rate appreciation reduced the external-debt-to-GDP ratio. Structural reform since the return of democracy in 1990 was enhanced by a high degree of political cohesiveness.

In the absence of fiscal rules, other institutional factors were useful in maintaining fiscal discipline. They included allocating more powers to the Finance Ministry than other ministries or the legislature, including over subnational finances, prohibiting the central bank from extending credit to the government, and preventing lower-level governments from borrowing. The degree of central government control over subnational finances contrasted sharply with the cases of Argentina, Brazil, and Mexico. The ban on revenue earmarking rendered fiscal policy more flexible. The country's fiscal policy strategy has permitted it to set medium-term objectives for social development and public investment.

The central government adopted a structural balance rule, targeting an annual surplus of 1 percent of GDP. These sustained fiscal policy actions improved financial market confidence, resulting in significantly lower interest rate spreads below the regional norm. Over the period, Chile enjoyed uninterrupted access to capital markets, reinforcing confidence in its economic management and avoiding forced pro-cyclical policies observed in other countries in the region.

Brazil, 1999–2003

There was broad consensus for fiscal consolidation in Brazil, bolstered by new governments elected in 1999 and 2003. The platform for fiscal consolidation was provided by external and fiscal crises stemming from contagion from Asia, a rising current account deficit, loose fiscal policy, sharp exchange rate devaluation in early 1999, and the adoption of a flexible exchange rate. The economy also experienced low growth, inflation, increasing primary fiscal deficits at all levels of government, and a rise in public debt.

Other economic weaknesses included fiscal indiscipline at the subnational level, loss-making public enterprises, labor market rigidities, a somewhat restricted trade system, a cumbersome tax system, generous pensions, and significant budget rigidities. Fiscal adjustment was essentially revenue based, targeting increases in the primary surplus of 3 percent of GDP in 1999 and gradually to 4.25 percent of GDP in 2003, which led to the nonfinancial public sector revenues increasing by 8 percent of GDP in the period 1999–2003. At the same time, total expenditure in the nonfinancial public sector increased by 7 percent of GDP, despite measures to contain entitlement spending.

The public sector primary balance improved from a 1 percent of GDP deficit in 1998 to a 4.4 percent of GDP surplus in 2003, boosted by improvement in revenue administration, privatization, and an increasingly commercial orientation of public enterprises. Expenditure measures included efforts to strengthen the social safety net and pension reform to reduce generous benefits. The primary balance targets were consistently met throughout the period. Furthermore, there was a well-established framework for developing, implementing, and monitoring the annual budget law.

The fiscal framework was anchored in the Fiscal Responsibility Law, the constitutional provisions on public financial management, and the budget guidelines, which set targets for three years ahead on a rolling basis. All levels of government contributed to the turnaround in fiscal outcomes. There was a debt restructuring agreement between the federal and the subnational governments and legislation limiting personnel expenditures and debt levels at all government levels.

Jamaica, 1998–2001

Jamaica witnessed four successive electoral victories for the People's National Party from 1989, including a strong majority victory in late 1997. The economy experienced high inflation and stagnant output in the early 1990s, a financial crisis in 1996–97, and a high current account deficit amidst exchange stability and lower inflation. Fiscal balances worsened by 8 percent in 1996–97, partly reflecting support for troubled financial institutions. Public debt rose to 155 percent of GDP in 2003. The interest bill was high, while wage bill pressures mounted.

Other issues included a large and growing informal sector, high crime rates, vulnerability to tourism receipts, and volatility in bauxite prices. The targeted improvement in the public sector primary balance was 7.8 percent of GDP over two years, with gains of 3.8 percent of GDP expected through tax administration, higher fuel taxes, and user fees. Expenditure measures targeted cuts in capital expenditure equivalent to 2.2 percent of GDP and cuts in non-wage goods and services equivalent to 1 percent of GDP, as well as a moderate wage increase equivalent to 0.2 percent of GDP.

The 2000 Staff Monitored Program targeted cost recovery in health and education and a rationalization of safety nets, while the 2002 Staff Monitored

Program focused on enterprise reforms. The fiscal impact was an overall improvement of central government and public sector primary balances by 6.0 percent of GDP, one-third of which came from revenue gains and two-thirds from cuts in non-interest expenditures. However, while public sector primary surpluses averaged 10.5 percent of GDP during the period 1999–2000 to 2001–02, there was little scope for further improvement due to the high interest burden (14 percent of GDP) and high wage bill. The adjustment effort was derailed by revenue weaknesses, wage increases, and security and tourism spending in 2001–03.

Lebanon, 1998–2002

Lebanon's public debt grew from 30 percent of GDP in 1992 to over 100 percent in 1997 in the face of moderate growth. Real exchange rate appreciation and lack of structural reforms affected competitiveness and export growth. These were compounded by a narrow tax base (15 percent of GDP), high spending on rebuilding the economy (9 percent of GDP per year during 1995–97), a high wage bill (11 percent of GDP), and debt service obligations. The overall fiscal deficit was 27 percent of GDP in 1997, with a primary deficit of 12 percent of GDP. Earlier adjustment had been undermined by weak support, high oil prices, and civil conflict in the south of the country. A new government in 1998 supported fiscal adjustment focused on expenditure, targeting an 11 percent of GDP reduction in the primary balance in 1998 and a 14 percent reduction over five years.

Revenue measures included higher customs tariffs, a new tax on hotel and restaurant services, higher receipts from cellular contracts, and increases in fees and excises. On the expenditure side, a 7 percent cut in non-interest spending was envisaged based on reducing public investment, transfers, and the number of teachers and contractual employees, as well as a wage freeze bill. Following the adjustment measures, the primary balance improved by 13.9 percent of GDP during 1998–2002. Revenue increased by 5.7 percent, boosted by VAT introduction in 2002. Non-interest expenditure fell by 8.1 percent of GDP, although the wage bill increased by 0.7 percent of GDP. Structural reforms included improved expenditure forecasting and tax and customs administration reforms.

Lithuania, 1999–2003

The Lithuanian economy experienced a deep recession following the 1998 financial crisis in Russia, with growing unemployment, a high current account deficit, and low inflation. Its currency was pegged to the U.S. dollar. Its fiscal deficit worsened in 1998–99, reflecting this recession as well as increased household transfers and lending to the state oil company. Other economic problems included poor expenditure management, a large stock of payment arrears, high debt burdens, labor market rigidities, energy tariffs below cost recovery, trade restrictions, and excessive agriculture subsidies. Fiscal adjustment was expenditure based, targeting reduction of the overall deficit by 5.7 percent of GDP in the first year and by 2.8 percent (to a balanced position) in the second year.

Revenue measures targeted 1.2 percent of GDP through increases in payroll taxes and fuel and tobacco levies. Expenditure reductions amounted to 4.5

percent of GDP through cuts in net lending and in household transfers, capital spending, and nominal wages. The deficit was reduced by 6.7 percent of GDP, even further than originally targeted, through larger expenditure cuts. Important structural reforms included strengthened treasury and commitment controls and the consolidation of extra budgetary funds, while the Fiscal Reserve Fund, an organic budget law, and a medium-term framework facilitated the adjustment. Low wage growth and labor market reforms improved competitiveness.

Russia, 1999–2002

In the years leading up to Russia's fiscal consolidation, its economy had suffered major economic problems. In 1992–94, it experienced severe contraction and hyperinflation, with the inflation rate exceeding 300 percent in 1994 and output declining by 13.5 percent. The fiscal deficit increased from 6.5 percent in 1993 to 11.5 percent in 1994 due to the growth of subsidies to industry and agriculture. Following violence in October 1993, the political landscape was characterized by a succession of prime ministers and, eventually, the resignation of President Yeltsin in 1999.

The country had a severe financial crisis in 1998, defaulting on its debt, while the domestic currency depreciated. Central government tax revenues declined through the mid-1990s, reaching 9 percent of GDP in 1998 due in part to depressed oil prices. The targeted adjustment in 1999 was 2.75 percent of GDP, half from revenues and half from expenditure cuts. Tax collection from oil companies was strengthened, boosted by the introduction of new oil taxes, a rationalization of the tax structure, and high oil prices.

Although there was no specified real cut in expenditure, expenditure control was improved by limiting some ministries' access to special funds. Transfers to subnational governments were cut by 1.5 percent of GDP and there was a further social spending reduction of 5 percent of GDP. The central government's fiscal balance improved from a deficit of 6 percent of GDP in 1998 to surpluses in 2000–02, largely on account of revenues increasing by about 7 percent of GDP, following the recovery of oil prices and currency depreciation. The interest bill declined sharply as a result of the default, while the primary balance improved by 8 percent of GDP to a surplus of over 5 percent in 2000–02.

South Africa, 1993–2001

The economy of South Africa experienced recession during 1990–92 with high inflation, capital flight, and concerns over the transition from apartheid to majority rule. The fiscal deficit had worsened during that period by 5 percentage points, due to revenue weakness and high social spending. Public debt increased, although it remained moderate at 40 percent of GDP. There were calls for structural reforms in the labor market, trade, public enterprises, and public administration. The international trade and financial sanctions of the apartheid era were lifted in October 1993.

Fiscal adjustment adopted an expenditure focus, targeting a 4 percent of GDP deficit reduction over five years—2 percent in the first year and 0.5 percent annually thereafter. Subsequent efforts announced in 1996 targeted a further deficit reduction by 2 percent of GDP from the 1995–96 out-turn.

Revenue measures were neutral from 1994–95, with the elimination of exemptions, an extension of the tax base, and lower tax rates. The VAT rate was raised from 10 to 14 percent in 1993–94, while tax policy and administration reform continued. Expenditure measures targeted cuts in the wage bill and in subsidies and transfers, as well as a 1 percent of GDP increase in capital expenditures. Following fiscal adjustment, the overall deficit was reduced by 6.5 percent of GDP in 2002–03. Revenue gains accounted for 3 percentage points, while spending reductions amounted to 3.5 percent. The primary balance was strengthened by 6.5 percent of GDP in 1999–2000. Following the decline in the interest bill, social and capital spending were increased. Key structural reforms included base broadening and lower rates for income taxes, revenue administration reforms, a medium-term budget framework, improved expenditure planning, and management accounting.

Nigeria, 1994–2000

Nigeria witnessed many years of military rule prior to its 1999 democratic transition. There were numerous allegations of corruption, fraud, and theft during the Abacha regime (1993–98). GDP growth slowed from nearly 9 percent per year in 1988–90 to 1.9 percent in 1993 and 0.3 percent in 1994. Inflation increased over the same period, exceeding 70 percent in 1994. The overall balance weakened from a surplus of 2.9 percent of GDP in 1992 to an 11.2 percent deficit in 1993. The non-oil primary deficit was in excess of 40 percent of GDP. A dual exchange rate system, a large informal sector, corruption and weak governance, oil dependency, and subsidies were all major issues of concern.

Fiscal consolidation, which began in 1994 was revenue based. The introduction of VAT in 1993 and oil price increases during the period improved government revenue, while the removal of a fertilizer subsidy and a reduction in the wage bill moderated the rising government spending. Unfortunately, higher wages in 2000 offset the earlier reduction. The primary balance improved by 9 percent of GDP during 1995–97. Similarly, the non-oil primary balance as a percentage of non-oil GDP improved by 20 percentage points.

Barbados, 1991–93

In 1990, Barbados faced severe balance of payment difficulties caused by a bunching of external debt obligations, loosened financial policies, and a steep drop in tourism receipts. During the ensuing recession, output contracted, inflation accelerated, and unemployment worsened, while foreign reserves fell to a very low level, just 1⅓ weeks of import in September 1991. High expenditure outlays in the face of weak revenue growth further widened the fiscal deficit to an unsustainable level in 1991, while public debt remained at about 31 per cent of GDP. The country undertook fiscal adjustment and economic reforms to restore financial stability and foster conditions for economic growth.

Under an IMF Stand-By Arrangement, Barbados undertook broad-ranging economic policy measures, including major increases in taxes and charges for public sector goods and services, as well as a large scale-back in expenditures. Among other revenue measures, the consumption tax was raised three times, increasing from 10 to 17 percent; a stabilization tax of 4–5 percent was imposed; and public utility tariffs and charges were raised by as much as 75 percent. The expenditure and income policies included an 8 percent wage cut for public employees, an 11 percent cut in the public workforce, cuts in transfers to public corporations, and wage freezes. Although initially the economy contracted more sharply than expected, the fiscal deficit narrowed from 7.3 to 0.7 percent of GDP, while current account deficit also improved from 4.4 to 0.3 percent of GDP, bolstering foreign reserves.

Developing Economies

Cote d'Ivoire, 1993–2000

Cote d'Ivoire experienced political instability following the death in 1993 of President Houphouët-Boigny, who had governed for 33 years. Growth had stagnated during 1987–93, partly due to strong currency and a high and increasing public debt of more than 170 percent of GDP in 1993. The fiscal deficit was equally high at 12 percent of GDP in 1992–93. Tax revenues had declined from 20–22 percent of GDP in the late 1980s to less than 15 percent, wages were 11 percent of GDP in 1992–93, and interest bills were 9.5 percent of GDP.

Within the context of an IMF program, fiscal adjustment was revenue focused, with the primary balance targeted to improve by 5 percent of GDP in 1994, by 1.2 percent in 1995, and by 0.5 percent in 1996. Another three-year IMF program (1998–2000) targeted 1.5 percent of GDP improvement in the primary surplus. There was a maximum tariff cut from 195 to 35 percent and a VAT rate cut from 25 to 20 percent, while export taxes on coffee and cocoa were reintroduced. Tax exemptions were eliminated, a minimum 5 percent import tax was introduced, and property tax was extended. Expenditure measures comprised reductions in the real wages of civil servants, a 1.5 percent reduction in personnel, and a reorientation of spending on health, education, rural development, and basic infrastructure.

The general government primary balance improved by 10 percent of GDP, 7.8 percent due to spending cuts. The public debt ratio decreased from nearly 200 percent of GDP in 1994 to just over 100 percent during 1994–2001, reflecting lower interest payments and a lower wage bill. Key structural reforms included the creation of a large taxpayer unit and improved customs administration. Economic performance improved following the CFA devaluation, with GDP growth of over 7 percent in 1995–96, 5.7 percent in 1997, and 4.8 percent in 1998.

Zambia, 1989–1994

Zambia had high inflation and external arrears, while the fiscal deficit averaged over 11 percent of GDP during 1987–89 due to poor revenues and increasing expenditures. Structural issues included price controls, agricultural subsidies, and a large informal sector. The fiscal adjustment was revenue-based, covering measures such as removal of import tax exemptions, adjustment of personal income tax brackets, reduction of the top marginal rate, extension of sales tax, introduction of a copper windfall levy, increased fees, and mandatory dividends from state-owned enterprises.

Furthermore, a sales tax on fuel was introduced, while the collection of tax arrears from parastatals improved. Expenditure measures included reducing maize and fertilizer subsidies and reorienting spending from investment to spending on operation and maintenance and on essential goods and services. The overall balance improved by 9.6 percent of GDP from 1988 to 1998 and the primary balance improved by nearly 15 percent of GDP, largely reflecting external grants. Tax revenue improved by 4.3 percent of GDP during 1989–90 before slipping. Nevertheless, little progress was made in privatization, in reducing maize subsidies, or in civil service reform, and there was overspending on the wage bill. Also, a substantial exchange rate depreciation led to a sharp increase in the public debt ratio in 1990, and the adjustment was further undermined by drought in 1992.

THE MAIN LESSONS FROM SUCCESSFUL FISCAL CONSOLIDATIONS

It is easier to build broad consensus about the need for fiscal consolidation in difficult times. Fiscal consolidations were initiated during periods of economic recession or at the early stages of a recovery—periods often characterized by macroeconomic imbalances in the form of worsening fiscal deficits, high debt levels, current account deficits, high unemployment, and high inflation. More than 75 percent of the episodes in the 14 advanced countries were initiated against the background of weak growth, except in the cases of United Kingdom and New Zealand.

Significant fiscal consolidations were initiated by new governments. In particular, about three-quarters of the episodes in advanced countries were started by new governments, many with an explicit mandate for fiscal consolidation. In emerging economies, a sizable number of the fiscal consolidation episodes were started by new governments. In Brazil, for example, consensus on the need for fiscal consolidation was bolstered by new governments elected in 1999 and 2003. In South Africa, consolidation coincided with the transition to majority rule that marked the end of the apartheid era. New governments are favored to undertake fiscal adjustment because for them it comes at a low political cost, they are expected to propose new approaches in addressing existing problems, and they have scope to develop a medium-term strategy for fiscal adjustment with maximum ownership.

Fiscal consolidation based on expenditure reductions have tended to be more effective than tax-based consolidations. A probable reason is that expenditure measures reflect greater commitment, make substantial consolidation more feasible, and can lead to efficiency gains (Price, 2010). The composition of the adjustments was generally a mixture of revenue and expenditure measures, with many countries leaning toward expenditure-based reductions. Expenditure measures accounted for an 85 percent improvement in fiscal balances in Canada and Finland and 75 percent improvements in the Netherlands, Sweden, and the United Kingdom. In New Zealand, the adjustment was a combination of revenue (60 percent) and expenditure (40 percent) measures. In the wider sample considered by Tsibouris and others (2006), findings indicate that expenditure cuts made up three-quarters of the total effort in the sustained large adjustments.

In several successful episodes, spending cuts adopted to reduce deficits were associated with economic expansions rather than recessions. The more successful expenditure-based consolidations focused on cuts in transfers and wages, the so-called politically sensitive budget items. Country experiences show that expenditure-based adjustments, especially focusing on current expenditure—such as reductions in the wage bill and social spending—were more sustainable. Expenditure cuts were spread across multiple spending categories and institutions. Sizable reductions in the wage bill and social security spending and in transfers, healthcare, and unemployment benefits made important contributions to fiscal adjustment, especially in Canada, Finland, Spain, and the Netherlands.

Frontloaded adjustments emphasized revenue measures, while gradual adjustments relied on lowering primary current spending. Gradual adjustments were more successful in advanced countries and sometimes extended up to a decade, for example in Finland, Sweden, and Spain. This approach reflects efforts to anchor policy objectives within a medium-term framework with a credible commitment to adopted strategies. However, in a wider sample, including emerging markets and developing economies, frontloaded and gradual adjustments were equally likely to succeed, with enduring frontloaded cases emphasizing revenues more than the gradual cases did, particularly trade taxes and non-tax revenues.

Successful revenue measures focused on broadening the tax base and making reforms to simplify tax administration and reduce the tax burden. Base broadening measures were common in countries with more developed revenue administrations and longer periods of implementation, including Brazil, Canada, Finland, New Zealand, and South Africa. In some cases, tax reforms resulted in tax buoyancy and higher revenues over the medium term. Revenue-based adjustment was sustained when the revenue-to-GDP ratio was low. Tax measures focused on higher fees, excise taxes, and commodity taxes—as in Barbados, Jamaica, and Russia—which appear to be relatively easy to evade. Measures that relied on a narrow tax base and weak administration were unsuccessful.

Adjustment efforts were also enhanced by broad political consensus and public support. The presence of an external political or economic anchor influenced fiscal adjustments, especially in Europe in the 1990s where the need to achieve membership in the EMU was the motivating factor. In that context, the introduction of a broad medium-term strategy was important in mobilizing public support. Strong political leadership was needed to ensure continuity to fiscal consolidation, as the experiences of the United States and Japan illustrate.

Structural reforms included the introduction of medium-term fiscal policy frameworks, organic budget laws, and tax and institutional reforms. They also included reforms of healthcare, pensions, and unemployment benefits. A medium-term expenditure framework helped countries set and meet multiyear priorities and build credibility. Such budgeting reforms were implemented in Brazil, Canada, Lithuania, New Zealand, and South Africa. Expenditure management and treasury operations were strengthened in Lebanon, Lithuania, Russia, and South Africa. Some countries incorporated long term fiscal sustainability analyses into their medium-term policy frameworks. Tax reforms were also very common: Canada, Finland, and New Zealand reduced personal and corporate tax rates, eliminated exemptions, and taxed previously non-taxed income sources. Value-added taxes were introduced as well, for example in Nigeria and Russia. Several other countries strengthened tax administration, including Cote d'Ivoire, Russia, South Africa, and Zambia.

The size of the initial adjustment may determine the success of fiscal consolidation. The empirical literature finds that there appears to be a size effect in successful fiscal consolidations. The larger the initial adjustment, measured by the change in primary fiscal balance, the larger is the likelihood of success (Ardagna, 2004). In addition, initial conditions, particularly large initial deficits and high interest rates, have boosted the size and duration of fiscal adjustments (Guichard and others, 2007). Higher GDP growth matters as well, but it does not drive the success of consolidation (Ardagna, 2004).

Supportive external and domestic conditions are essential. The findings of Kumar, Leigh, and Plekhanov (2007) suggest that a supportive domestic and international growth environment facilitates adjustment efforts. Heylen and Everaert (2000) also note that the chances of a consolidation being successful rise with a favorable external environment, high economic growth, and low interest rates.

The chance of success for consolidation also differs according to political arrangements, with a coalition government being much less likely to succeed than a single-party government. Alesina and Perotti (1995) find that out of 23 strong adjustments initiated by coalition governments, only three were successful, which translates to a success rate of just 8.7 percent, while the success rate for single-party governments was 64.3 percent.

The effects of fiscal consolidation depend on the composition of adjustment. Large, credible, and decisive expenditure-based consolidation is less likely to cause a recession (Alesina and Ardagna, 2009; Alesina, 2010; and Alesina, Carloni, and Lecce, 2012). Indeed, spending cuts led to higher GDP growth (Ardagna, 2004). In contrast, adjustments based on tax increases and cuts in public investment are not durable and are contractionary. In particular, consolidation implemented mainly through tax increases rather than cutting expenditure induces a sharper decline in private demand (Guajardo, Leigh, and Pescatori, 2011). A combination of spending cuts and tax increases was accompanied by a private consumption boom following two large fiscal consolidations (Giavazzi and Pagano, 1990).

Fiscal consolidations do come with short-term adjustment costs and have distributional effects. In contrast with previous findings, Coenen, Mohr, and Straub (2008) find that short-term costs are independent of the fiscal consolidation strategy used. However, their study further concludes that the distribution effects may be pronounced depending on the type of adjustment strategy, and in particular on the extent to which households differ with regard to their ability to participate in asset markets and their dependence on government transfers.

SUMMARY AND CONCLUSIONS

This chapter has attempted to answer many of the questions that policymakers may have in their quest to pursue a prudent fiscal consolidation strategy. It presented a comprehensive survey of a large body of mostly empirical literature on fiscal consolidation, covering industrial, emerging market, and developing economies. It also explored specific country experiences with fiscal consolidation dating back to the 1990s, examining a total of 25 case studies, consisting of 14 advanced, 8 emerging market, and 3 developing economies, including Barbados and Jamaica.

From the country experiences in regions outside the Caribbean one may surmise certain economic and political conditions and approaches that have contributed to successful fiscal consolidations. Specifically:

- Expenditure-based adjustments, especially those focused on current expenditure, were more successful.
- Both the size and the composition of the adjustment affected the probability of success.
- Adjustment efforts were enhanced by broad political consensus and public support.
- The effects of fiscal consolidation on growth depended on the composition of the adjustment.
- Expenditure-based consolidation is less likely to cause a recession.

On the empirical front, evidence suggests that large fiscal adjustments have been initiated under difficult macroeconomic conditions: sluggish growth, high budget deficits, high inflation, high unemployment, high debt, and balance of payment crises. Generally, initial conditions influence the design of the adjustment program and may determine the success of the consolidation plan as well, along with supportive external and domestic conditions. It is also generally understood that monetary easing could be helpful in lowering interest costs, although the likelihood that this will enhance a fiscal consolidation is uncertain.

Contrary to conventional wisdom, findings indicate that fiscal consolidation can be expansionary in the short term. Nevertheless, there are adjustment costs and distributional consequences. Evidence suggests that expansionary fiscal consolidation operates through wealth effects on consumption and credibility effects on interest rates. An alternative channel of expansionary adjustment emphasizes supply-side considerations through effects on labor costs and competitiveness. But, it should be noted that fiscal consolidation must be understood as part of a credible plan designed to permanently reduce a government deficit and therefore future tax liabilities.

Looking at successful fiscal consolidation and debt reduction, the empirical evidence generally associates the presence of fiscal rules with stronger fiscal performance. Key requirements for the effectiveness of fiscal rules include transparency, flexibility, commitment, and credible punishment for noncompliance. Although fiscal rules create incentives to artificially achieve targets, other supporting features, including independent fiscal councils and fiscal responsibility laws, have been adopted as well.

Finally, it is worth noting also that findings in the literature suggest that governments which undertake fiscal adjustments are not necessarily voted out of office. However, the success of fiscal consolidation differs across political arrangements—a coalition government is much less likely to succeed than a single party.

REFERENCES

Agna, Senay, and Denise Igan, 2012, "Fiscal Consolidation and the Cost of Credit: Evidence from Syndicated Loans," IMF Working Paper 13/36 (Washington: International Monetary Fund).

Ahrend, Rudiger, Pietro Catte, and Robert Price, 2006, "Interactions Between Monetary and Fiscal Policy: How Monetary Conditions Affect Fiscal Consolidation," Economics Department Working Paper No. 5 (Paris: Organization for Economic Co-operation and Development).

Alesina, Alberto, 2010, "The Political Economy of Fiscal Adjustment" (Delhi: National Council of Applied Economic Research). Available at www.ncaer.org/popuppages/.../E18.../Alberto-Alesina-presentation.pdf.

———, and Silvia Ardagna, 2009, "Large Changes in Fiscal Policy: Taxes Versus Spending," NBER Working Paper No. 15438 (Cambridge, Massachusetts: National Bureau of Economic Research).

Alesina, Alberto, Silvia Ardagna, and Jordi Gali, 1998, "Tales of Fiscal Contractions," *Economic Policy*, Vol. 13, No. 27, pp. 487–545.

Alesina, Alberto, Silvia Ardagna, and Francesco Trebbi, 2006, "Who Adjusts and When? The Political Economy of Economic Reforms," *IMF Staff Papers*, Vol. 53, Special Issue (Washington: International Monetary Fund).

Alesina, Alberto, Dorian Carloni, and Giampaolo Lecce, 2012, "The Electoral Consequences of Large Fiscal Adjustments," NBER Working Paper No. 17655 (Cambridge, Massachusetts: National Bureau of Economic Research).

Alesina, Alberto, and Allan Drazen, 1991, "Why Is Stabilization Delayed?" *American Economic Review*, Vol. 81, No. 5, pp. 1170–1188.

Alesina, Alberto, Carlo Favero, and Francesco Giavazzi, 2012, "The Output Effects of Fiscal Consolidation," NBER Working Paper No. 18336 (Cambridge, Massachusetts: National Bureau of Economic Research).

Alesina, Alberto, and Roberto Perotti, 1995, "Fiscal Expansions and Fiscal Adjustments in OECD Countries," NBER Working Paper No. 5214 (Cambridge, Massachusetts: National Bureau of Economic Research).

———, 1997, "Fiscal Adjustments in OECD: Composition and Macroeconomic Effects," *IMF Staff Papers*, Vol. 44, No. 2, pp. 210–48 (Washington: International Monetary Fund).

Alesina, Alberto, Roberto Perotti, Jose Tavares, Maurice Obstfeld, and Barry Eichengreen, 1998, "The Political Economy of Fiscal Adjustment," *Brookings Papers on Economic Activity*, Vol. 1998, No. 1, pp. 197–266.

Alesina, Alberto, Alessandro Prati, and Guido Tabellini, 1989, "Public Confidence and Debt Management: A Model and A Case Study of Italy," NBER Working Paper No. 3135 (Cambridge, Massachusetts: National Bureau of Economic Research).

Almeida, Vanda, Gabriel Castro, Ricardo Mourinho Felix, and Jose Francisco Maria, 2011, "Fiscal Consolidation in a Small Euro Area Economy," Working Paper No. 5, Economics and Research Department (Lisbon: Banco de Portugal).

Ardagna, Silvia, 2004, "Fiscal Stabilizations: When Do They Work and Why," *European Economic Review*, Vol. 48, Issue 5, pp. 1047–74.

Arrellano, Jose Pablo, 2006, "Structural Adjustment in Chile: From Fiscal Deficits to Surpluses," in *Challenges to Fiscal Adjustment in Latin America: The Cases of Argentina, Brazil, Chile and Mexico*, ed. by Luiz de Mello (Paris: Organization for Economic Co-operation and Development), pp. 113–33.

Barrios, Salvador, Sven Langedijk, and Lucio Pench, 2010, "EU Fiscal Consolidation after the Financial Crisis: Lessons from Past Experiences," Economic Paper No. 418 (Brussels: European Commission).

Barro, Robert, 1981, "Output Effects of Government Purchases," *Journal of Political Economy*, Vol. 89, No. 6, pp. 1086–1121.

Baxter, Marianne, and Robert G. King, 1993, "Fiscal Policy in General Equilibrium," *American Economic Review*, Vol. 83, No. 3, pp. 315–34.

Bertola, Guiseppe, and Allan Drazen, 1993, "Trigger Points and Budget Cuts: Explaining the Effects of Fiscal Austerity," *American Economic Review*, Vol. 83, No. 1, pp. 11–26.

Bi, Huixin, Eric M. Leeper, and Campbell B. Leith, 2012, "Uncertain Fiscal Consolidation," NBER Working Paper No. 17844 (Cambridge, Massachusetts: National Bureau of Economic Research).

Biggs, Andrew G., Kelvin A. Hasset, and Matthew Jensen, 2010, "A Guide for Deficit Reduction in the United States Based on Historical Consolidations that Worked," AEI Economic Policy Working Paper No. 2010–04 (Washington: American Enterprise Institute for Public Policy Research).

Brender, Adi, and Allan Drazen, 2008, "How Do Budget Deficits and Economic Growth Affect Reelection Prospects? Evidence from a Large Panel of Countries," *American Economic Review*, Vol. 98, No. 5, pp. 2203–20.

Coenen, Gunter, Matthias Mohr, and Roland Straub, 2008, "Fiscal Consolidation in the Euro Area: Long-Run Benefits and Short-Run Costs," ECB Working Paper No. 902 (Frankfurt: European Central Bank).

Corsetti, Giancarlo, Keith Kuester, Andre Meier, and Gernot J. Mueller, 2012, "Sovereign Risk, Fiscal Policy, and Macroeconomic Stability," IMF Working Paper 12/33 (Washington: International Monetary Fund).

Darby, Julia, V. Anton Muscatelli, and Graeme Roy, 2005, "Fiscal Consolidation and Decentralization: A Tale of Two Tiers," *Fiscal Studies*, Vol. 26, No. 2, pp. 169–95.

de Rato, Rodrigo, 2004, "Benefits of Fiscal Consolidation," Remarks to the Real Academia de Doctores, Barcelona, Spain, November 25.

Drazen, Allan, and Vittorio Grilli, 1993, "The Benefits of Crises for Economic Reforms," *American Economic Review*, Vol. 83, No. 3, pp. 598–607.

Giavazzi, Francesco, Tullio Jappelli, and Marco Pagano, 2000, "Searching for Non-Linear Effects of Fiscal Policy: Evidence from Industrial and Developing Countries," *European Economic Review*, Vol. 44, pp. 1259–89.

Giavazzi, Francesco, and Marco Pagano, 1990, "Can Severe Fiscal Contractions Be Expansionary? Tales of Two Small European Countries," *NBER Macroeconomics Annual*, Vol. 5, pp. 75–111 (Cambridge, Massachusetts: National Bureau of Economic Research).

———, 1995, "Non-Keynesian Effects of Fiscal Policy Changes: International Evidence and the Swedish Experience," NBER Working Paper No. 5332 (Cambridge, Massachusetts: National Bureau of Economic Research).

Giudice, Gabriele, Alessandro Turrini, and Jan in't Veld, 2007, "Non-Keynesian Fiscal Adjustments? A Close Look at Expansionary Fiscal Consolidations in the EU," *Open Economies Review*, Vol. 18, No. 5, pp. 613–30.

Guajardo, Jaime, Daniel Leigh, and Andrea Pescatori, 2011, "Expansionary Austerity: New International Evidence," IMF Working Paper 11/158 (Washington: International Monetary Fund).

Guichard, Stephanie, Mike Kennedy, Eckhard Wurzel, and Christopher Andre, 2007, "What Promotes Fiscal Consolidation: OECD Country Experiences," OECD Economics Department Working Paper No. 553 (Paris: Organization for Economic Co-operation and Development).

Gupta, Sanjeev, Emmanuele Baldacci, Benedict Clements, and Erwin R. Tiongson, 2003, "What Sustains Fiscal Consolidation in Emerging Markets?" IMF Working Paper 03/224 (Washington: International Monetary Fund).

Heylen, Freddy, and Gerdie Everaert, 2000, "Success and Failure of Fiscal Consolidation in the OECD: A Multivariate Analysis," *Public Choice,* Vol. 105, pp. 103–24.

Hjelm, Goran, 2002a, "Is Private Consumption Growth Higher (Lower) During Periods of Fiscal Contractions (Expansions)?" *Journal of Macroeconomics,* Vol. 24, pp. 17–39.

———, 2002b, "Effects of Fiscal Contractions: The Importance of Preceding Exchange Rate Movements," *Scandinavian Journal of Economics*, Vol. 104, No. 3, pp. 423–41.

———, 2004, "When Are Fiscal Contractions Successful? Lessons for Countries Within and Outside the EMU," Working Paper No. 92 (Stockholm: The National Institute of Economic Research).

Kumar, Manmohan, S., Daniel Leigh, and Alexander Plekhanov, 2007, "Fiscal Adjustments: Determinants and Macroeconomic Consequences," IMF Working Paper 07/178 (Washington: International Monetary Fund).

Lambertini, Luisa, and Jose Tavares, 2005, "Exchange Rates and Fiscal Adjustments: Evidence from the OECD and Implications for the EMU," *Contributions to Macroeconomics*, Vol. 5, No. 1.

Lane, Phillip, and Roberto Perroti, 2003, "The Importance of Composition of Fiscal Policy: Evidence from Different Exchange Rate Regimes," *Journal of Public Economics*, Vol. 87, pp. 2253–79.

Larch, Martin, and Alessandro Turrini, 2011, "Received Wisdom and Beyond: Lessons from Fiscal Consolidation in the EU," *National Institute Economic Review,* Vol. 217, R1.

McDermott, C. John, and Robert F. Wescott, 1996, "An Empirical Analysis of Fiscal Adjustments," *IMF Staff Papers*, Vol. 43, No. 4, pp. 725–53 (Washington: International Monetary Fund).

Mati, Amine, and John Thornton, 2008, "The Exchange Rate and Fiscal Consolidation Episodes in Emerging Market Economies," *Economic Letters*, Vol. 100, pp. 115–18 (Washington: International Monetary Fund).

Nickel, Christiane, Philipp Rother, and Lilli Zimmermann, 2010, "Major Debt Reductions: Lessons from the Past, Lessons for the Future," Working Paper No. 1241/September (Frankfurt: European Central Bank).

Perotti, Roberto, 1999, "Fiscal Policy in Bad Times," *Quarterly Journal of Economics*, Vol. 114, No. 4, pp. 1399–1436.

Price, Robert, 2010, "The Political Economy of Fiscal Consolidation," OECD Economics Department Working Paper No. 776 (Paris: Organization for Economic Co-operation and Development).

Schaechter, Andrea, Tidiane Kinda, Nina Budina, and Anke Weber, 2012, "Fiscal Rules in Response to the Crisis—Toward the 'Next-Generation' Rules. A New Dataset," IMF Working Paper 12/187 (Washington: International Monetary Fund).

Tsibouris, George C., Mark A. Horton, Mark J. Flanagan, and Wojciech S. Maliszewski, 2006, *Experience with Large Fiscal Adjustments*, IMF Occasional Paper No. 246 (Washington: International Monetary Fund).

Von Hagen, Jurgen, Andre Hughes Hallet, and Rolf Strauch, 2002, "Budgetary Consolidation in Europe: Quality, Economic Conditions, and Persistence," *Journal of the Japanese and International Economies,* Vol. 16, pp. 512–35.

Worrell, Delisle, 2012, "Policies for Stabilization and Growth in Small Very Open Economies," Occasional Paper No. 85 (Washington: Group of Thirty).

CHAPTER 6

Fiscal Sustainability and Public Debt Limits in the Caribbean: An Illustrative Analysis

GARTH PERON NICHOLLS AND ALEXANDRA PETER

This chapter reviews different concepts of debt sustainability and gives illustrative results on debt limits for economies based on macroeconomic characteristics prevailing in the Caribbean region. In particular, we deal with three important policy-related issues: First, we delineate key aspects of the different approaches to measure fiscal sustainability and public debt limits; second, we measure the sustainability of fiscal policy and the extent of over- or under-borrowing by the public sector over the last two decades; and third, we derive debt benchmarks through illustrative scenarios, using reasonable assumptions about growth and interest rate shocks from the region's economies.

After 50 years of leading Caribbean economic transformation, the public sector is overburdened with debt and is restraining economic recovery. This has instigated a policy debate on the sustainability of fiscal policy and public debt amid new strains created by the global financial and economic crisis, which exposed longstanding structural weaknesses in the region. In particular, in 2011 the median public debt ratio was about 71 percent of GDP, having risen from about 65 percent before the global crisis in 2008.[1] Importantly, many in the Caribbean now recognize that their fiscal policy is headed down an unsustainable path, their public debt is too high, and fiscal adjustment strategies are required to lower public debt ratios to a level that would restore sustainability and promote growth. Without adjustment, the region would remain highly indebted for a long time owing partly to the slow recovery of key trading partners and continuing fiscal deficits. Yet some important questions need to be answered, including questions about the pace of fiscal consolidation, the short-term costs of consolidation, and the levels to which the region's economies should reduce their debt ratios over the medium term.

The literature on fiscal and debt sustainability is vast and expanding, but it yields no single agreed-upon definition. Fiscal sustainability concepts range from simple to complex approaches. Simple approaches include, as an example, the debt stabilizing primary balance, whereas complex approaches aim to measure

[1]It must be emphasized that individual country circumstances vary greatly using this measure.

optimal debt levels within welfare-maximizing frameworks. In addition to the lack of a single definition of fiscal sustainability, a number of other gaps remain in the existing literature as well. These include the general absence or inadequacy of the treatment of economic uncertainty in existing debt sustainability models and the over-concentration of empirical work on developed and large emerging market economies.

Overall, the results suggest that the region is pursuing policies that are not in accord with a sustainable path for fiscal policy and that it has over-borrowed relative to the calibrated debt limits for the region.[2] Owing to this, Caribbean governments will need to adopt ambitious fiscal adjustment or other debt reduction strategies over the medium term to reduce the drag of high public debt on economic activity.

This chapter begins by describing the Caribbean context that motivates the analysis of fiscal sustainability. It then sketches definitions of fiscal sustainability and debt limits, with a discussion of their operational measures and implications for public debt ratios. After that, it discusses some illustrative results based on macroeconomic characteristics of the countries analyzed. It ends with concluding comments.

CONTEXT AND MOTIVATION

The public sector in Caribbean economies has been a key driver of growth and transformation for a long time. For historical reasons, the original leading role of this sector was focused on two goals: the creation of public goods and the transformation of the economy and society from a colonial orientation to a modern one. In this context several indicators of human well-being have indeed improved, revealing strong social, economic, and political progress, including high per capita incomes and health standards, a high ranking on the United Nations' human development index, and thriving and competitive parliamentary democracies.

However, in the last 20 years the public sector has also been used to somewhat compensate for the collapse of traditional export sectors, including sugar and banana exports, as competitive pressures have intensified. This enhanced role for the public sector, facilitated by deficit financing, caused a rapid growth in public debt, sometimes financing projects without a direct cash return (including poorly managed public enterprises). Added to this has been the very high cost of coping and rebuilding after destructive natural events, such as annual hurricanes. These factors have contributed to high public debt levels, which have increased further

---

[2]We should stress that while we take every effort to calibrate the necessary parameters carefully, the results should be taken as illustrative scenarios subject to the caveats related to the different methods. In particular, the fiscal sustainability measures are highly dependent on the underlying assumptions about growth and interest rates. Therefore, these calculations should not be seen as the ultimate debt target, but should be seen as a way to think about the high debt levels and fiscal sustainability and how it is affected by prevailing and prospective macroeconomic conditions.

as a consequence of the global crisis and brought the sustainability of fiscal policy and public debt to the forefront of the policy debate.

Today, large public debt imposes a high cost on the region's economies and puts at risk the social and developmental gains made over the last 50 years. There are several channels through which these costs and risks are transmitted to the economy, described next.

Higher Debt May Lower Growth

There is some empirical evidence that high public debt reduces long-run economic growth (see, e.g., Kumar and Woo, 2010; and Greenidge and others, 2012). For the region's countries, Greenidge and others (2012) show that gross debt beyond a threshold of 55–56 percent of GDP is associated with lower economic growth. Indeed, there is a nonlinear relationship between debt and growth. Excessive public debt crowds out private sector investment and lowers economic growth; higher debt requires higher taxes to service the debt, which reduces investment and growth. Further increases in government expenditure financed by higher debt from already elevated levels are likely to be self-defeating, leading to lower long-term growth, as public sector debt crowds out private investment.

Higher Debt Heightens Roll-Over Risks

Higher public debt is likely to increase the public sector borrowing requirement for two reasons. First, a higher debt ratio requires a larger share of GDP to service this debt. Second, as the debt ratio becomes larger, investors are likely to demand higher interest rates and shorter maturities, as has happened for some of the region's countries (see Chapter 3). As the size and frequency with which the government needs to tap the debt market increases, this directly increases the roll-over risk.

Higher Debt Increases Vulnerability Through Sovereign–Bank Interlinkages

High public debt held largely by the domestic banking system increases a country's vulnerability to shocks. For example, a shock that negatively affected the sovereign's ability to repay its debt would impact the domestic banking system, which could lead to a negative feedback loop. Further, where the debt is largely held by domestic banks, in the event of a debt restructuring the scope for debt relief is reduced considerably (see Chapter 3).

Higher Debt Reduces Policy Flexibility and Increases Vulnerability

A high debt ratio reduces the space for policy flexibility and the ability to respond to shocks. Countries that had a high debt ratio at the time of the global crisis were unable to respond with countercyclical fiscal policies due to the lack of fiscal space. Instead, many countries had to tighten their fiscal stance to stave off a financing crisis, thus pursuing procyclical policies. Furthermore, increases in interest rates raise the debt service burden and may hasten debt distress.

Two policy questions are worth answering: Taking into account their stage of development and vulnerability to shocks, what public-debt-to-GDP ratio should the region's economies adjust to? And what should be the speed of adjustment to that ratio? While theory offers little or no guidance on these matters, some Caribbean countries adopted a 60 percent debt ratio before the global crisis, and most considered a 60 percent debt ratio as a safe medium-term public debt target. Yet many countries have encountered fiscal and debt distress and are unlikely to meet these medium-term targets without ambitious adjustments. Against this background, it would appear that a total rethinking of fiscal sustainability and safe debt limits for all of the region's economies is required.

DEBT SUSTAINABILITY AND DEBT LIMITS: THEORY

Definitions

Debt sustainability is an elusive concept. Determining whether a government's debt is sustainable is not a straightforward matter (Chalk and Hemming, 2000). In the context of IMF programs, a government's fiscal policy is regarded as sustainable if its path does not imply an abrupt change in primary balances, and the government has sufficient financial resources to meet all of its maturing obligations. In addition, the fiscal adjustment path pursued by the government must be economically and politically feasible.

The concept of a *debt limit* is closely associated with fiscal sustainability. It represents the explicit stock implications to the flow variables that are used to calibrate fiscal sustainability. There are at least three ways debt limits can be defined: First, a debt limit can be the debt ratio to which the economy converges in the steady state (see, e.g., Blanchard, 1990; and Blanchard and others, 1990). Second, it could be the level of debt that the economy can service or carry without generating debt distress and requiring debt restructuring. Third, a debt limit could be the optimal level of debt given an economy's policy objectives, stage of development, and policy environment.

A number of countries have adopted debt limits to anchor fiscal policy. They have done so in the context of fiscal responsibility legislation, which provides the legal basis for a medium-term macroeconomic framework. Some of these debt limits or targets have been adopted after a major crisis, others to protect prudent countries from the spillover effects of other countries' fiscal distress, typically in a monetary and financial integration arrangement. Examples of the latter include the limits adopted by the euro area and the Eastern Caribbean Currency Union (ECCU). Both have a 60 percent debt-to-GDP-ratio limit on public debt. This limit is included in the accession principles for the euro area, whereas for the ECCU countries the limit is a target to which they are aiming to reduce their debt by 2020.[3] However, there is no theory underpinning their adoption of such limits. Instead, their adoption largely rests on the degree of comfort policymakers feel with particular targets relative to where their own country's debt ratios currently stand.

Measures of Fiscal Sustainability

Several indicators have been proposed in the literature to measure fiscal sustainability. These include, among others, the debt stabilizing primary balance, the reaction of fiscal policy to higher public debt, and debt benchmarks. The first two are discussed here, whereas debt benchmarks and debt limits are presented in the next section.

Debt Stabilizing Balances and Fiscal Efforts

This approach involves calculating the primary budget balance that would stabilize public debt at its current level, thus "debt stabilizing primary balance" (see Box 6.1).[4] Fiscal sustainability is then determined by comparing the actual primary balance with the debt stabilizing primary balance. If the actual balance is less than the debt stabilizing one, this implies that public debt is rising and unsustainable. This approach is consistent with the IMF framework for assessing sustainability.

Although this measure of fiscal sustainability has many advantages, it also has some important drawbacks. One advantage is its simplicity: it is simple and easy to apply and the results are easy to interpret. This model, however, does not incorporate uncertainty and its key parameters—growth, interest rate, and the primary balance—are assumed to follow deterministic paths. As a result, there is no presumed feedback from the debt stock to fiscal policy or the environment within which policy is made. Finally, the model presumes that the authorities would be able, somehow, to achieve the required primary surplus and therefore avoid defaulting on the country's public debt obligations.

Fiscal Policy Reaction to Debt Levels

Another way of assessing debt sustainability is to look at the reaction of fiscal policy to rising debt levels. Under this approach, the primary balance adjusted for the effects of temporary factors is presumed to respond to public debt, where a positive response to debt implies a policy with long-term solvency (Bohn, 1998). By taking account of the constraints and objectives of policy, this framework is more flexible than the simple debt stabilizing primary balance approach.

A number of studies on fiscal sustainability apply this approach. These include Melitz (1997), Égert (2010), and Ghosh and others (2013) for OECD countries; Debrun and Wyplosz (1999) and Gali and Perotti (2003) for the euro area; and

[3]Actually, the euro convergence criteria include a "debt criterion" that provides for a limit on gross government debt of 60 percent of GDP or, if the debt ratio is higher, it shall at least be found to have "sufficiently diminished and must be approaching the reference value at a satisfactory pace" (see European Monetary Institute, 1995).

[4]See, for example, IMF (2003) for an application to emerging market and industrial economies.

BOX 6.1

The Long-Run Fiscal Sustainability Condition

This approach uses the government's flow budget constraint

$$b_t = (1+r)b_{t-1} - x_t - \sigma_t, \tag{B1}$$

where b_t is real government debt, r_t the real interest rate, x_t the real primary balance, and s_t real seigniorage.

Forward iteration on (B1) combined with the condition

$$\lim(1+r)^{-(j+1)}b_{t+j} = 0 \tag{B2}$$

implies

$$b_{t-1} = \sum_{i=0}^{\infty}(1+r)^{-(j+1)}(x_{t+1} + \sigma_{t+1}). \tag{B3}$$

This equation is the government's lifetime budget constraint, thus the government finances its debt at the end of the period $t-1$ by raising seigniorage revenue and running primary surpluses with an equal present value.

The most basic tool for fiscal sustainability analysis uses a steady-state version of the lifetime budget constraint. Equation (B3) can be rewritten in terms of stocks and flows expressed as fractions of GDP. Letting y_t represent real GDP and defining $\bar{b}_t = \frac{b_t}{y_t}$, $\bar{x}_t = \frac{x_t}{y_t}$, $\bar{\sigma}_t = \frac{\sigma_t}{y_t}$ equation (B3) can be rewritten as follows:

$$\bar{b}_{t-1} = \sum_{i=0}^{\infty}(1+r)^{-(i+1)}(\bar{x}_{t+i} + \bar{\sigma}_{t+i})\frac{y_{t+i}}{y_{t-1}}. \tag{B4}$$

In steady state, real GDP grows at a constant rate g, and the primary surplus ($\bar{x}$) as a fraction of GDP and seigniorage ($\bar{\sigma}$) as a fraction of GDP are constant. As a result, (B4) reduces to

$$\bar{b}_{t-1} = \sum_{i=0}^{\infty}\left(\frac{1+g}{1+r}\right)^{i+1}(\bar{x} + \bar{\sigma}). \tag{B5}$$

Assuming that r > g, equation (B5) becomes

$$\bar{b}_{t-1} = \bar{b} = (\bar{x} + \bar{\sigma})/\bar{r}, \tag{B6}$$

where $\bar{r} = (r - g)/(1 + g)$.

Two measures of fiscal sustainability can be derived from this equation. First, using medium-term values of $\bar{x}, \bar{\sigma}, r,$ and g we can derive an estimate of $\bar{b}$. If the government's actual stock of debt exceeds this estimate, then a government's finances are unsustainable. Second, by rearranging equation (B6) to

$$\bar{x} = \bar{r}\bar{b} - \bar{\sigma}, \tag{B7}$$

we can use equation (B7) to determine the necessary size of the primary balance to ensure fiscal sustainability given estimates of $\bar{\sigma}$, $\bar{r}, g,$ and $\bar{b}$.

This box is adapted from Burnside (2004).

Burger and others (2011) for South Africa. A key drawback, however, is that this approach is silent on when and how fiscal policy should adjust to rising debt. It only requires the policymaker to commit to adjust at some time in the future. Therefore, the reliance on the credibility of the policy framework and the policymaker has to be considered. As a result, it may take a very long time to achieve fiscal sustainability, in particular if the market does not believe the policymaker's commitment.

Debt Limit Measures

Debt limits are meant to reflect the maximum level of debt that can be contracted without imposing undue welfare costs or instigating debt distress and default. The literature distinguishes between the optimal debt level, a normative concept, and the crisis-free debt level—the so-called "safe debt" level.[5] We follow this distinction and discuss these two broad concepts separately. First, we discuss the safe debt concept, starting with debt benchmarks, before turning to debt thresholds based on uncertainty and probabilistic methods (natural debt limits, value-at-risk and fair spread approaches). Second, we briefly touch on the literature about optimal debt. The concepts under the first category are used in the illustrative scenarios later in this chapter, and the comparison with actual debt ratios will give a sense of over- and under-borrowing.

Debt Benchmarks

Debt benchmarks can be used to judge whether a country has over-borrowed and may face debt distress at some time in the future. A country's debt benchmark is derived using historical values for its ratio of revenues to GDP (T/GDP) and its ratio of primary spending to GDP (G/GDP), both of which are discounted by the differential between its real interest (r) and GDP growth (g) rate. Thus, each country's debt benchmark has the following form:

$$b_{bm} = \frac{T/GDP - G/GDP}{r-g} = \frac{PB/GDP}{r-g}. \tag{6.1}$$

Of the different approaches to calculate debt benchmarks, we will discuss four methods. The first approach is the long-term debt benchmark, also referred to as the Blanchard ratio (see, e.g., Blanchard, 1990; and Blanchard and others, 1990). This standard approach is based on steady-state or long-term values for the fiscal indicators. Basically, a country's historical track record forms the basis for the interest rate, growth rate, and primary balance paths.

Second, there is an approach based on the exceptional fiscal performance of a country. This approach uses the maximum primary surplus during a predefined period and discounts it with the average interest and growth performance.

A third approach is the signal approach. It relies on the signaling effect of debt distress and uses the debt ratio at which a country experiences debt distress as the debt benchmark. Thus, this ratio is based on a country's history with debt

---

[5]See the discussion on debt limits in IMF (2013b).

distress. For example, if a country experienced debt distress above a debt ratio of 50 percent of GDP, then a debt ratio of 50 percent or higher is considered unsafe. In such a scenario, there is a signal that a crisis is likely. If the country's debt level does not exceed this threshold then there is no signal of debt distress.

The fourth approach unifies the fiscal reaction function methodology and the long-term approach to measuring fiscal sustainability. Based on the parameters of the fiscal reaction function and estimates of the interest rate-growth differential, a country's debt limit and its associated fiscal space is calibrated (see Ghosh and others, 2011). This approach makes a distinction between the long-term public debt to which an economy converges in the steady state, on the one hand, and the maximum sustainable public debt, the level of debt immediately before a country loses market access, on the other.

Later in this chapter we will provide illustrative scenarios based on the long-term and exceptional fiscal performance debt benchmarks.

Debt Thresholds Based on Uncertainty and Probabilistic Methods

Debt limits based on probabilistic methods explicitly take into account that governments face high amounts of uncertainty regarding their revenues and expenditures and how these affect sustainable debt ratios. Since fiscal revenues and expenditures are subject to shocks, a steady-state level of public debt that ignores downside risks might not give a full picture of sustainable debt. Instead, the methods discussed here ask whether a current debt ratio is sustainable given the current macroeconomic environment and future prospects. In addition, interest and exchange rate movements add to the uncertainties. However, one caveat should be kept in mind: While these methods relax some of the problematic assumptions used in the steady-state methods, new assumptions have to be added, making them susceptible to criticism as well (see Burnside, 2004).

Strategies for Including Macroeconomic Uncertainty

There are different strategies for including macroeconomic uncertainty in the assessment of fiscal sustainability. Each of the approaches is specialized and looks at a particular aspect of fiscal sustainability. We will consider three approaches: the natural debt limit based on Mendoza and Oviedo (2009), the value-at-risk (VaR) approach, and the fair spreads approach.[6]

Natural Debt Limit Approach

The natural debt limit, based on Mendoza and Oviedo (2009), takes into account the uncertainty and risks faced by policymakers. In particular, it considers that volatile revenues and expenditures can have a devastating effect on debt sustainability

---

[6]For a detailed overview of these approaches, see Burnside (2004) and Tanner (2013). Additional probabilistic methods include approaches that formally model stochastic processes for the macro determinants of debt ratios. These estimates are then used to simulate corresponding debt ratios and to derive their probability distributions. For applications to selected emerging market economies see, for example, Celasun, Debrun, and Ostry (2006), Tanner and Samake (2006), and di Giovanni and Gardner (2008).

if negative shocks are realized. A government that wants to credibly commit to service its debts in the future under all circumstances has to bear in mind that it could be faced, for example, with a prolonged period of below-average revenues. To account for this uncertainty, the natural debt limit is calculated by adjusting average revenues and expenditures downward by two standard deviations:

$$b_{nl} = \frac{T^{Min} / GDP - G^{Min} / GDP}{r - g}. \tag{6.2}$$

To further take into account growth and interest rate shocks, we propose an additional measure for the natural debt limit. This measure—our preferred one—adjusts real interest rates upward and growth rates downward by one standard deviation:

$$b_{nl} = \frac{T^{Min} / GDP - G^{Min} / GDP}{r^{Max} - g^{Min}}. \tag{6.3}$$

The key idea is that the minimum primary balance generated indicates the fiscal stance that the authorities can credibly commit to in the presence of economic shocks going forward. The advantage of the debt limit approach is that it explicitly incorporates uncertainty in the assessment of fiscal/debt sustainability. Therefore, it takes into account the possibility of default when the primary balance cannot be increased beyond a certain level.

Value-at-Risk Approach

The approach used by Barnhill and Kopits (2004) adapts the value-at-risk (VaR) methodology, which is commonly used to assess the risk of financial assets, to the government's net worth. In particular, this measure of the government's net worth compares the value of outstanding debt to the present value of net flows used to service the debt. However, it excludes measures that are only used to close the budget constraint, as this concept is an ex-ante assessment of a government's finances (Burnside, 2004). By modeling the government's net worth as a stochastic process, the probability of the net worth becoming negative can be assessed, and that can be interpreted as the probability of a government default. Thus, in this approach fiscal risks and their impacts on the government's net worth position are modeled and estimated explicitly, showing the vulnerability of the net worth. While in theory this approach can factor in contingent liabilities, it requires a vast amount of information from public sector balance sheets, thus precluding its application to a large set of countries.[7]

Fair Spreads Approach

The method by Xu and Ghezzi (2003) proposes to compute "fair spreads" on public debt to assess default probabilities. The flows of the government budget are modeled as stochastic processes, which are used to estimate default

---

[7]Barnhill and Kopits (2004) apply their model to Ecuador. For an application to Brazil see da Costa, Silva, and Baghdassarian (2004), and da Costa (2010).

probabilities. These probabilities are then mapped into term structure models to compute fair spreads. However, in contrast to the other approaches discussed, this measure is more closely linked to liquidity than to pure solvency (Burnside, 2004).

The Optimal Debt Level

The literature on optimal debt levels contains two strands (IMF, 2013b). The first strand focuses on calibrating an absolute level of the debt-to-GDP ratio. Most of the models attempting this have faced difficulties modeling the complex interplay of objectives, costs, and distributive effects in a tractable way and have instead opted for a simple approach, modeling just one aspect of the issue from which welfare costs and gains are then derived. An important work belonging to this strand is that of Aiyagari and McGrattan (1998), who calibrate the optimal debt level for the U.S. economy. Their results are based on certain special assumptions about the behavior of the government, households, and borrowing constraints. At the time of their work (1998), their result suggested that the debt level of the United States then was optimal and that further increases over a wide policy space did not seem to yield measurable welfare costs.

Another recent strand of the literature on optimal debt ratios looks into the optimal debt profile. These models essentially focus on the tax smoothing properties of rolling over debt, in the spirit of Barro (1979).

ILLUSTRATIVE RESULTS OF FISCAL SUSTAINABILITY AND DEBT LIMITS FOR CARIBBEAN ECONOMIES

In this section, we apply some of the fiscal sustainability and debt limit concepts discussed above to illustrate scenarios based on the 13 Caribbean countries. This will give us illustrative results about how high the debt limits are and how they depend on underlying macroeconomic characteristics. First, we discuss debt stabilizing primary balances, before turning to debt limits.

Debt Stabilizing Balances and Fiscal Efforts

An analysis of debt stabilizing primary balances for the region shows that policies in many countries are not in line with a sustainable fiscal policy. The stabilization of public-debt-to-GDP ratios at 2011 levels would require adjustment in seven countries (Table 6.1). The fiscal adjustment efforts required range from 1.3 percent of GDP for Barbados to 5.6 percent in St. Lucia. Since the 2011 debt ratios are high, stabilizing at this level would not help to lower the vulnerability to shocks, particularly in the highly indebted countries. In this context, it would be important for most countries to reduce their debt ratios to levels that make them less vulnerable to shocks and bring fiscal policy onto a sustainable path. We choose 60 percent of GDP by the end of the decade as the debt ratio limit, since the ECCU countries have committed themselves to reduce their debt ratios to this level by 2020.

Reducing public debt ratios to 60 percent of GDP by 2020 would require large fiscal adjustments (above 2 percent of GDP) in eight countries. Of these, five countries—Antigua and Barbuda, Barbados, Grenada, Jamaica, and St.

TABLE 6.1

Debt Stabilizing Balances: Illustrative Fiscal Adjustments *(In percent of GDP)*

		Stabilizing Debt in 2011		Reducing Debt to 60% by 2020	
Countries	Primary balance in 2011	Primary balance needed	Fiscal effort needed	Primary balance needed	Fiscal effort needed
Antigua and Barbuda	−1.0	0.7	1.7	4.3	5.3
The Bahamas	−2.3	0.1	2.4	...	...
Barbados	1.1	2.5	1.3	7.2	6.1
Belize	2.3	0.3	...	2.9	0.6
Dominica	−2.9	0.0	2.9	1.3	4.2
Grenada	−2.3	2.2	4.6	6.7	9.0
Guyana	−1.5	−2.3	...	...	...
Jamaica	3.2	2.1	...	10.8	7.6
St. Kitts and Nevis	8.3	0.6	...	10.9	2.6
St. Lucia	−3.7	1.9	5.6	2.9	6.6
St. Vincent and the Grenadines	−1.4	0.1	1.6	1.0	2.5
Suriname	1.8	−0.9	...	...	...
Trinidad and Tobago	2.2	−0.5	...	...	...
Caribbean Average	**0.3**	**0.5**	**2.9**	**5.3**	**4.9**

Source: Authors' calculations.

Lucia—would require a fiscal adjustment above 5 percent of GDP relative to their primary balances in 2011. In particular, Barbados would require an adjustment of 6.1 percent of GDP. The fiscal adjustment would be somewhat smaller in the other three countries (Dominica, St. Kitts and Nevis, and St. Vincent and the Grenadines), ranging between 2 and 4 percent of GDP. One country would need an adjustment below 2 percent (Belize).

Debt Limits

In this section, we show illustrative results based on the region focusing on two debt limit concepts: long-term debt benchmarks and natural debt limits. In addition to deriving results under various specifications, we compare the calculated debt ratios with the actual ones as of end-2011 to convey a sense of whether countries have over- or under-borrowed. Finally, we also show debt benchmarks for exceptional fiscal performance.

For the calculation of these concepts, we construct three groups based on the macroeconomic characteristics of the region:

- Group 1: countries with debt ratios above 90 percent of GDP
- Group 2: countries with debt ratios between 60 and 90 percent of GDP, and
- Group 3: countries with debt ratios below 60 percent of GDP.

In addition, we calculate the average for the Caribbean. We use data on revenues, primary expenditures, and real growth rates from the October 2012 World Economic Outlook database. Ideally, we would like to use averages over the last 20 years to derive steady-state values for the key parameters. However, since in some cases the available data is limited to a shorter horizon, we use the longest available data for each country case (Table 6.2, column 2). Table 6.2 gives an overview of the averages for revenues, primary expenditures, and real GDP growth rates.

TABLE 6.2

Measures of Debt Sustainability: Illustrative Underlying Variables *(In percent of GDP)*

									Lowest Primary Surplus		Highest Primary Surplus	
Countries	Years	Average Revenues	Coefficient of Variation of Revenues	Average Primary Expenditures	Coefficient of Variation of Primary Expenditures	Average Primary Balance	Average Real Growth Rate	Real Interest Rate	Primary Balance	Year	Primary Balance	Year
Group 1: Debt ratio above 90 percent		**25.5**	**9.4**	**25.5**	**16.3**	**0.1**	**2.1**	**5.4**			**6.3**	
Country A	1997–2011	19.8	8.0	25.9	20.3	−6.0	2.0	5.2	1.9	2010	1.9	2010
Country B	1991–2011	23.3	7.1	24.9	11.5	−1.6	3.1	4.0	0.3	2003	5.2	2004
Country C	1994–2011	33.7	6.6	33.5	12.6	0.2	1.6	5.2			5.5	1999
Country D	1990–2011	24.8	7.7	17.4	17.5	7.4	1.0	7.3			10.5	2003
Country E	1990–2011	26.0	17.8	25.7	19.5	0.3	3.0	5.2			8.3	2011
Group 2: Debt ratio between 60 and 90 percent		**26.4**	**8.9**	**26.7**	**12.2**	**−0.4**	**3.0**	**4.2**			**4.0**	
Country A	1997–2011	27.0	7.8	27.6	16.8	−0.6	2.4	4.0	0.6	2001	4.2	1999
Country B	1990–2011	25.3	7.1	25.7	9.0	−0.4	2.9	4.0	0.03	2003	2.4	1996
Country C	1995–2011	30.4	13.5	30.3	13.9	0.1	2.4	4.0			5.2	2005
Country D	1996–2011	24.9	8.4	25.5	10.5	−0.6	4.5	5.2	0.1	1996	4.2	2008
Country E	1990–2011	24.4	7.7	24.6	11.0	−0.3	2.7	4.0	0.1	1996	3.8	1998
Group 3: Debt ratio below 60 percent		**23.1**	**13.0**	**22.4**	**16.0**	**0.7**	**3.2**	**5.7**			**5.0**	
Country A	1990–2011	22.2	12.9	23.2	17.1	−1.0	2.7	5.2	0.2	2004	3.7	1994
Country B	1999–2011	31.7	15.8	28.2	18.7	3.5	5.1	6.8			9.8	2008
Country C	1991–2011	15.4	10.3	15.8	12.1	−0.4	1.8	5.2	0.1	2006	1.5	1995
Caribbean average		**25.3**	**10.1**	**25.3**	**14.7**	**0.1**	**2.7**	**5.0**			**5.1**	

Source: Authors' calculations.

Another important parameter for the calculation is the real interest rate. However, these rates are hard to measure, as debt instruments differ in their characteristics.[8] Another complication for measuring real interest rates in the region's countries arises from the lack of fully developed debt management practices and underdeveloped capital markets, in particular for domestic debt. This might lead to a downward bias in the interest rates paid on domestic debt instruments, as risk factors are not properly taken into account. Using average interest rates on public debt, calculated as expenditure on interest divided by the previous period's debt stock—as is done in debt sustainability analyses—might not give an adequate picture of the risks associated with government debt. To estimate real interest rates, we use the average of JPMorgan's Central American and Caribbean Index for the period 2002–11, discounted by the U.S. GDP deflator and, where available, we use yields to maturities on a country's bonds (see Table 6.2). We also explore the effects of increasing or decreasing the interest rate in a sensitivity analysis.

However, a number of countries in the Caribbean can borrow on concessional terms, which might render a real interest rate oriented at the market rate too high. Therefore, we consider that countries that are eligible for concessional assistance from the IMF's Poverty Reduction and Growth Trust might be subject to lower real interest rates.

Long-Term Debt Benchmarks

First, we focus on the long-term debt benchmark (compare equation 6.1). The derivation of the long-term debt benchmark raises two issues: The average primary balance needs to be in surplus and the real interest rate needs to be higher than the real GDP growth rate in order to get meaningful debt benchmarks. If the average primary balance is negative, the growth rate would need to exceed the real interest rate in order to get a positive debt benchmark. The case of growth rates exceeding real interest rates, also known as "dynamic inefficiency," implies that there would not be a need to generate primary surpluses in order to achieve fiscal sustainability (see Blanchard and others, 1990). However, in the long run it is expected that real interest rates would be higher than real growth rates.

Thus, the primary balance needs to be, on average, in surplus. However, for quite a few Caribbean countries, average primary balances were negative over the observation period. Nevertheless, to calculate the debt benchmark we use the smallest positive primary balance over the observation period (see Table 6.2). This means the calculated long-term debt benchmark should be interpreted as an upper limit, since on average the primary balance is actually lower.[9]

In the baseline case, long-term debt benchmarks are on average 40.3 percent of GDP (Table 6.3, column 4). However, there are big differences across countries

---

[8]See Mendoza and Oviedo (2009) for a discussion.

[9]An alternative way to derive the primary balance would be to adjust tax revenue and government spending as was done for the natural debt limit by Mendoza and Oviedo (2009). The results for the natural debt limit in the Mendoza and Oviedo formulation can be found in Appendix Table 6.1.

TABLE 6.3

Measures of Debt Sustainability: Illustrative Long-Term Debt Benchmarks *(In percent of GDP)*

			Baseline		Sensitivity		
					Interest rate	Growth rate	Combined shock
Countries	Years	Debt ratio in 2011	Long-term debt benchmark	Over-/under-borrowing	Long-term debt benchmark		
Group 1: Debt ratio above 90 percent		**120.2**	**46.6**	**2.6**	**35.6**	**62.0**	**19.9**
Country A	1997–2011	93.4	58.6	1.6	44.5	69.5	15.9
Country B	1991–2011	103.7	35.6	2.9	16.4	85.6	4.0
Country C	1994–2011	106.9	6.6	16.2	5.2	7.7	2.9
Country D	1990–2011	142.9	117.4	1.2	101.3	127.4	72.5
Country E	1990–2011	154.3	15.1	10.2	10.4	19.6	4.2
Group 2: Debt ratio between 60 and 90 percent		**71.7**	**13.7**	**5.2**	**7.8**	**25.8**	**2.9**
Country A	1997–2011	65.2	36.1	1.8	22.3	52.2	8.9
Country B	1990–2011	68.1	3.3	20.8	1.7	6.2	0.5
Country C	1995–2011	71.2	7.3	9.8	4.5	10.6	1.8
Country D	1996–2011	83.6	13.1	6.4	5.4	45.8	1.5
Country E	1990–2011	70.1	8.7	8.1	4.9	14.3	1.6
Group 3: Debt ratio below 60 percent		**33.2**	**74.2**	**0.4**	**42.1**	**93.0**	**14.7**
Country A	1990–2011	19.1	8.8	2.2	6.3	11.1	2.8
Country B	1999–2011	31.1	209.6	0.1	131.3	298.4	42.1
Country C	1991–2011	49.5	4.1	12.1	3.2	4.8	1.5
Caribbean average		**81.5**	**40.3**	**2.0**	**27.5**	**57.9**	**12.3**

Source: Authors' calculations.

with different characteristics. For example, a country with exhaustible natural resources would be able to generate high primary surpluses more easily than other countries. However, such a country would also need to run primary surpluses, since the revenue stream would be based on a finite and possibly price-sensitive resource and it would be necessary to build buffers for the future. In addition, the natural resource boom in the years leading up to a financial crisis also would have helped in generating strong GDP growth.

This combination of factors leads to a high long-term debt benchmark as exemplified by country B in group 3. However, we need to keep in mind that the long-term debt benchmark might not capture all aspects in a country with exhaustible natural resources. Similarly, country D in group 1 shows that high primary surpluses would lead to a long-term debt benchmark above the Caribbean average. Now, we can compare the derived long-term debt benchmark with actual debt-to-GDP ratios at the end of 2011. This gives a sense of whether countries are over- or under-borrowing. A ratio higher than 1 shows that a country has over-borrowed compared to its debt benchmark, while a ratio lower than 1 shows that a country has under-borrowed.[10] On average, Caribbean countries have borrowed twice as much as the long-term debt benchmark would suggest. However, the over-borrowing ratios vary considerably by country characteristics and depend on the specific combination of fiscal performance and growth and interest rates. The illustrative results also show that, on average, over-borrowing ratios are not necessarily higher in countries with high debt ratios (group 1) than they are in countries with somewhat smaller debt ratios (group 2).

Next, we explore the effects of the discount factor, that is, the effect of real interest and growth rates on the debt benchmarks. From a simple, comparative static point of view, a higher interest rate would lead to a lower debt benchmark, all else being equal, while a higher growth rate would lead to a higher debt benchmark.[11] Of course, by taking this perspective, we ignore the effects that the interest rate or GDP growth might have on the primary balance. For example, one would expect higher GDP growth to have a positive effect on tax revenue, while certain expenditure categories might be lower, thus increasing the primary balance. Because these effects depend on each country's economic structure, taking them into account would be beyond the scope of this chapter. Instead, we will keep the primary balance constant and just vary interest and growth rates.

In a first step, we analyze by how much the debt benchmark in each country changes if in turn the interest rate is raised by 1 percentage point or the average real GDP growth rate increases by half a percentage point. Secondly, we explore how a negative shock would affect the debt benchmark, by shocking both the real interest rate and the real GDP growth rate. To take into account the volatility of

---

[10] See IMF (2003) for an overview of over-borrowing ratios in emerging market and industrial countries.

[11] This can be seen by computing the marginal derivatives of equation (6.1) with respect to the interest and growth rates, respectively.

each country, the interest rate is increased by one standard deviation, while the GDP growth rate is decreased by one standard deviation.

The sensitivity analysis of the long-term debt benchmarks is displayed in Table 6.3, columns 6–8. On average, debt benchmarks decrease by 13 percentage points of GDP for a 1 percentage point increase in real interest rates, while a higher average GDP growth of half a percentage point increases the debt benchmark by 18 percentage points of GDP. For the interest rate increase, the average debt benchmark falls to 27.5 percent of GDP, down from 40.3 percent of GDP, which shows the high sensitivity of the debt benchmark to interest rate changes. This also drives up over-borrowing ratios. On the other hand, higher growth has a beneficial impact on debt benchmarks, bringing the average up to about 57.9 percent of GDP.

A negative shock, raising interest rates and lowering average growth rates at the same time, leads to considerable lower debt benchmarks compared to the baseline case (see last column in Table 6.3). This negative shock paints a particularly dire picture as the Caribbean average drops to 12.3 percent of GDP; depending on country characteristics the debt benchmark may even fall below 10 percent of GDP. This shows that an increase in interest rates coupled with subdued GDP growth would pose a high risk for sustainability in Caribbean countries.

Natural Debt Limits

The second debt limit we focus on is the concept of a *natural* debt limit as described earlier (see equation 6.3).[12] This takes into account the volatility of revenues and expenditures, as well as the volatility of growth and interest rates. The average natural debt limit for the Caribbean is 30 percent of GDP (Table 6.4). Thus, taking into account the volatility of fiscal and macroeconomic variables reduces the debt levels that could be sustained. Natural debt limits vary across different country characteristics, but overall they are below 100 percent of GDP. On average, higher revenue variability leads to a lower natural debt limit. For example, country E in group 1 has a very high coefficient of variation of revenues (see Table 6.2), while its natural debt limit is only about 14.3 percent of GDP.

As for long-term debt benchmarks, we can calculate over- and under-borrowing ratios. For the Caribbean average, the over-borrowing ratio increases to almost 3, that is, the average actual debt ratio is three times higher than the suggested natural debt limit. There is a high variability of these ratios across countries. Again, some country characteristics suggest an under-borrowing (country B of group 3 and country A of group 2). There are also examples of countries with relatively low over-borrowing ratios of less than 2 (countries C and D of group 1 and country A of group 3). The highest ratio is found for country C in group 3, which has a relatively high revenue and relatively low expenditure variability.

---

[12]For completeness, we also report the country group medians for the natural debt limit in the Mendoza-Oviedo formulation in Appendix Table 6.1. However, as it does not take into account growth and interest rate volatility, we focus our discussion on the adjusted natural debt limit.

TABLE 6.4

Measures of Debt Sustainability: Illustrative Natural Debt Limits *(In percent of GDP)*

			Baseline		Sensitivity			
					Low interest rate		High interest rate	
Countries	Years	Debt ratio in 2011	Natural debt limit	Over-/under-borrowing ratio	Natural debt limit	Over-borrowing ratio	Natural debt limit	Over-borrowing ratio
Group 1: Debt ratio above 90 percent		**120.2**	**36.8**	**3.3**	**47.4**	**2.5**	**30.1**	**4.0**
Country A	1997–2011	93.4	11.7	8.0	14.3	6.5	10.0	9.4
Country B	1991–2011	103.7	10.8	9.6	14.9	6.9	8.5	12.2
Country C	1994–2011	106.9	55.2	1.9	75.0	1.4	43.7	2.4
Country D	1990–2011	142.9	91.7	1.6	113.1	1.3	77.1	1.9
Country E	1990–2011	154.3	14.3	10.8	19.5	7.9	11.3	13.7
Group 2: Debt ratio between 60 and 90 percent		**71.7**	**24.1**	**3.0**	**35.8**	**2.0**	**18.2**	**3.9**
Country A	1997–2011	65.2	73.1	0.9	108.7	0.6	55.1	1.2
Country B	1990–2011	68.1	11.3	6.0	17.2	4.0	8.5	8.0
Country C	1995–2011	71.2	5.6	12.8	8.3	8.6	4.2	17.1
Country D	1996–2011	83.6	9.3	9.0	14.3	5.8	6.8	12.2
Country E	1990–2011	70.1	21.3	3.3	30.5	2.3	16.4	4.3
Group 3: Debt ratio below 60 percent		**33.2**	**27.5**	**1.2**	**39.5**	**0.8**	**21.1**	**1.6**
Country A	1990–2011	19.1	16.1	1.2	22.2	0.9	12.7	1.5
Country B	1999–2011	31.1	63.6	0.5	92.9	0.3	48.4	0.6
Country C	1991–2011	49.5	2.7	18.5	3.4	14.4	2.2	22.7
Caribbean average		**81.5**	**29.8**	**2.7**	**41.1**	**2.0**	**23.4**	**3.5**

Source: Authors' calculations.

Figure 6.1 Over- and Under-Borrowing, Natural Debt Limit—Interest Rate Scenarios[a]

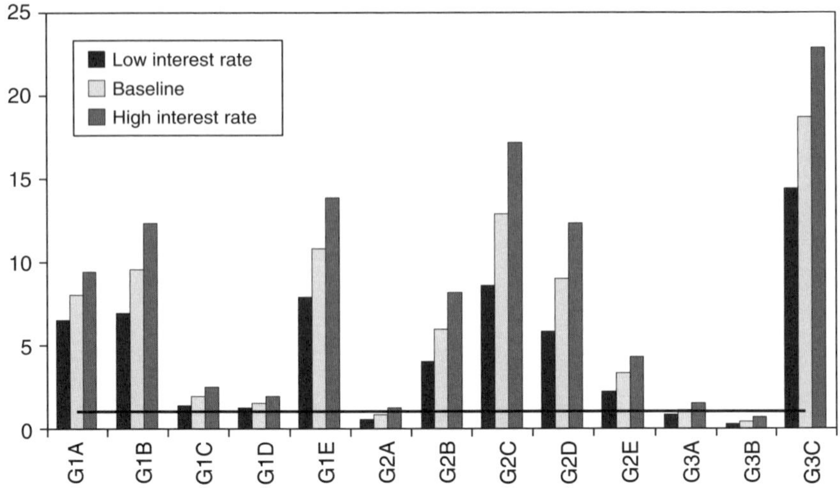

Source: Authors' calculations.

[a]The abbreviations correspond to the grouping from Table 6.2, which means G1A corresponds to Group 1, Country A, and so on.

The Caribbean average of natural debt limits is higher compared to the one for long-term debt benchmarks (by 10 percentage points of GDP), while correspondingly the over-/under-borrowing ratios are higher as well (see Table 6.5). Turning to individual countries, a comparison shows that for the majority of cases the natural debt limit is smaller than the long-term debt benchmark. This would be expected if a high volatility of revenues would restrain governments in their repayment capacity. However, there are also some cases for which the natural debt limit is higher than the long-term debt benchmark. These include countries with relatively low revenue volatility, for example country C of group 1 and country B of group 2. Some country characteristics can also lead to the case where the two debt ratios are quite close, with a difference of less than one percentage point (country E in group 1).

In a next step, we conduct a sensitivity analysis by varying the real interest rate. In particular, we show how the natural debt limits change for a low interest rate scenario (2 percentage points lower than the baseline) and a high interest rate scenario (2 percentage points higher than the baseline). On average, natural debt limits are 5 percentage points of GDP higher for the low interest rate case, while they are 3 percentage points of GDP lower for the high interest rate case. Figure 6.1 depicts the corresponding over- and under-borrowing ratios for the different interest rate scenarios. Only one case, country B in group 3, shows under-borrowing even for the high interest rate case. All other countries are more or less very susceptible to interest rate increases.

An important question surfaces. The analysis of long-term debt benchmarks and natural debt limits for the Caribbean average and different country cases raises one important issue: *Why is the actual average debt ratio in the Caribbean two or three times as high as the respective debt benchmark?* These discrepancies might be due to factors that the debt sustainability measures are unable to capture but that are specific characteristics of the Caribbean region.

One of these factors might be related to the interest rates on government debt. We have mentioned that it is complicated to measure real interest rates in the Caribbean due to the lack of fully developed debt management and underdeveloped capital markets. This, coupled with further distortions in domestic financial markets, might shelter these governments from real capital costs and allow them to borrow more than the debt benchmarks would suggest. Indeed, the sensitivity analysis hints at the possibility that this issue exists by showing that reducing the real interest rate by 200 basis points would increase the average natural debt limit by 10 percent of GDP.

Underdeveloped capital markets also imply that domestic investors (like banks, nonbank financial institutions, and national insurance schemes) lack viable and profitable investment alternatives and therefore invest heavily in government debt instruments. In addition, foreign investment options are often limited due to capital controls or foreign investment caps. All of this would limit the power of interest rates to work as true indicators for market rates.

While the high domestic investor base might, on the one hand, lead to adverse sovereign–bank interlinkages in cases where the sovereign faces debt distress, on the other hand it might also help to sustain a higher debt ratio. Arslanalp and Tsuda (2012) show that for a set of advanced economies, countries with a high share of domestic investors (domestic banks or central banks) have a low risk of pressures from financial markets. In several Caribbean countries, domestic investors hold a large share of government debt (see Chapter 3).

The issue of low real interest rates also touches upon the previously mentioned "dynamic inefficiency" issue. If a government were sheltered from facing the true interest rate costs, it might not have needed to run fiscal surpluses. But instead, the combination of real interest rates lower than the (albeit low) average growth rates might have lead to a negative discount factor combined with a primary deficit. Normally, market mechanisms would have led over time to rising interest rates; however, distortions might have suspended this mechanism from working correctly. Thus, governments may have been able to borrow above the debt benchmarks based on the measures for real interest rates that we have used in this analysis. Indeed, Escolano, Shabunina, and Woo (2011) find that persistently negative interest rate-growth differentials in non-advanced economies are related to captive financial markets, financial repression, and lack of financial development.

However, even though a negative interest rate-growth differential should play a debt-stabilizing role, keeping debt stable even in the presence of persistent primary deficits, debt has increased strongly over the last years in the Caribbean region (see Chapter 2). This casts doubt on whether this mechanism was at play.

Exceptional Fiscal Performance

As a third measure, we look at a debt benchmark based on exceptional fiscal performance and compare it to the long-term debt benchmark as well as the natural debt limit. This measure uses the highest attained primary surplus of each country together with the baseline interest and growth rate differential. The exceptional fiscal performance debt ratio shows the highest possible debt limit a country could commit to if fiscal outcomes were particularly favorable. However, we have to stress that this is based on the fiscal outcome of one particular year, and maintaining such primary surpluses over a longer period of time or raising average primary balances to such dimensions would be a different story. In particular, Chapter 7 of this book shows that maintaining fiscal consolidation efforts in the Caribbean is not an easy endeavor.

In this case, the average debt ratio for the Caribbean is almost 300 percent. However, the adjustments from the average to the highest attained primary balance are substantial for some cases. A comparison between the Caribbean average of average primary surpluses and the highest attained primary surpluses shows a difference of 5 percentage points of GDP (see Table 6.2). For individual countries, the differences vary between 1.9 percentage points (country C of group 3) and 8 percentage points (countries A and E of group 1). Therefore, the results on exceptional fiscal performance should be seen as illustrative, showing that debt problems could be mitigated by embarking on strong fiscal consolidation.

Most Caribbean countries would not run into debt problems if they would maintain their highest ever attained fiscal surplus (see Table 6.5).[13] However, in some cases, even using the exceptional fiscal performance measures indicates overborrowing compared to actual debt ratios. Examples include country A in group 1 and country C in group 3.

Fiscal Contingent Liabilities

The analysis of over- and under-borrowing ratios so far has only taken into account actual debt ratios as of end-2011 but has not included contingent fiscal liabilities. However, these liabilities can be high and can add a substantial amount of debt to already high debt ratios, jeopardizing fiscal sustainability. Recent examples include Antigua and Barbuda and Belize. For the latter, IMF staff estimate that gross contingent liabilities are about 17 percent of GDP (see IMF, 2011). However, since a big part of these contingent liabilities stems from nationalized companies and their valuation is surrounded by a great deal of uncertainty, the value of Belize's contingent fiscal liabilities is also uncertain. Similarly, in Antigua and Barbuda contingent liabilities from state-owned enterprises pose fiscal risks, with the government-guaranteed debt of these enterprises amounting to 14.6 percent of GDP (see IMF, 2013a).

We check how our illustrative results would change if contingent liabilities were included. Results so far have already shown substantial amounts of overborrowing for the Caribbean average. Including contingent liabilities would only exacerbate this situation. Table 6.6 shows an illustrative scenario for the way

[13]In addition, we need to stress that this measure does not take into account possible positive or negative effects such as those that strong fiscal consolidation would have on growth in the short and medium term.

TABLE 6.5

Measures of Debt Sustainability: Illustrative Results—Comparison of Different Measures *(In percent of GDP)*

			Long-Term Debt Benchmark		Natural Debt Limit		Exceptional Fiscal Performance	
Countries	Years	Debt ratio in 2011	Debt ratio	Over-borrowing ratio	Debt ratio	Over-borrowing ratio	Debt ratio	Over-borrowing ratio
Group 1: Debt ratio above 90 percent		**120.2**	**46.6**	**2.6**	**36.8**	**3.3**	**273.5**	**0.4**
Country A	1997–2011	93.4	58.6	1.6	11.7	8.0	58.6	1.6
Country B	1991–2011	103.7	35.6	2.9	10.8	9.6	608.0	0.2
Country C	1994–2011	106.9	6.6	16.2	55.2	1.9	154.2	0.7
Country D	1990–2011	142.9	117.4	1.2	91.7	1.6	166.2	0.9
Country E	1990–2011	154.3	15.1	10.2	14.3	10.8	380.7	0.4
Group 2: Debt ratio between 60 and 90 percent		**71.7**	**13.7**	**5.2**	**24.1**	**3.0**	**341.3**	**0.2**
Country A	1997–2011	65.2	36.1	1.8	73.1	0.9	258.5	0.3
Country B	1990–2011	68.1	3.3	20.8	11.3	6.0	226.2	0.3
Country C	1995–2011	71.2	7.3	9.8	5.6	12.8	321.4	0.2
Country D	1996–2011	83.6	13.1	6.4	9.3	9.0	600.2	0.1
Country E	1990–2011	70.1	8.7	8.1	21.3	3.3	300.2	0.2
Group 3: Debt ratio below 60 percent		**33.2**	**74.2**	**0.4**	**27.5**	**1.2**	**258.7**	**0.1**
Country A	1990–2011	19.1	8.8	2.2	16.1	1.2	146.8	0.1
Country B	1999–2011	31.1	209.6	0.1	63.6	0.5	584.9	0.1
Country C	1991–2011	49.5	4.1	12.1	2.7	18.5	44.4	1.1
Caribbean average		**81.5**	**40.3**	**2.0**	**29.8**	**2.7**	**296.2**	**0.3**

Source: Authors' calculations.

TABLE 6.6

Measures of Debt Sustainability: Illustrative Results—Over-/Under-Borrowing and Contingent Liabilities

	Baseline			Including Contingent Fiscal Liabilities		
Countries	Debt ratio in 2011	LTDB O. B. ratio	NDL O. B. ratio	Debt ratio including contingent liabilities	LTDB O.B. ratio	NDL O.B. ratio
Group 1: Debt ratio above 90 percent	**120.2**	**2.6**	**3.3**	**135.2**	**2.9**	**3.7**
Country A	93.4	1.6	8.0	108.4	1.9	9.2
Country B	103.7	2.9	9.6	118.7	3.3	11.0
Country C	106.9	16.2	1.9	121.9	18.5	2.2
Country D	142.9	1.2	1.6	157.9	1.3	1.7
Country E	154.3	10.2	10.8	169.3	11.2	11.9
Group 2: Debt ratio between 60 and 90 percent	**71.7**	**5.2**	**3.0**	**86.7**	**6.3**	**3.6**
Country A	65.2	1.8	0.9	80.2	2.2	1.1
Country B	68.1	20.8	6.0	83.1	25.4	7.3
Country C	71.2	9.8	12.8	86.2	11.8	15.5
Country D	83.6	6.4	9.0	98.6	7.5	10.6
Country E	70.1	8.1	3.3	85.1	9.8	4.0
Group 3: Debt ratio below 60 percent	**33.2**	**0.4**	**1.2**	**48.2**	**0.7**	**1.8**
Country A	19.1	2.2	1.2	34.1	3.9	2.1
Country B	31.1	0.1	0.5	46.1	0.2	0.7
Country C	49.5	12.1	18.5	64.5	15.8	24.2
Caribbean average	**81.5**	**2.0**	**2.7**	**96.5**	**2.4**	**3.2**

Source: Authors' calculations.

Note: LTDB = long-term debt benchmark; NDL = natural debt limit; O.B. ratio = over-/under-borrowing ratio.

over- and under-borrowing ratios would increase for the hypothetical case of adding contingent liabilities of 15 percent of GDP to each country's debt ratio. In this case, the average of the over-borrowing ratio would be about 2.4 in the case of the long-term debt benchmark (up from 2) and about 3.2 in the case of natural debt limits (up from 2.7). Once more, this scenario illustrates the high vulnerability of many Caribbean economies to any type of debt shock.

POLICY IMPLICATIONS AND CONCLUSIONS

In this chapter, we have discussed measures of fiscal sustainability and related the concepts to fiscal performance and debt ratios in the Caribbean. The illustrative results have revealed an over-borrowing ratio for the Caribbean average of 2, casting doubt on the sustainability of public debt in the Caribbean region. Several sensitivity analyses have shown the high vulnerability to negative shocks from interest rates and contingent liabilities, but they have also shown that higher growth and fiscal consolidation could lead the way back to sustainable paths.

There are several important implications for policy that follow from these insights. In particular, policy needs to refocus on reducing public debt to sustainable levels. Moreover, these sustainable levels are likely to be different for each country, given their varying growth prospects and the volatility of revenues and spending. Further, public debt policy needs to target a debt ratio in normal times that would not create financing difficulties in the presence of negative economic shocks. Finally, the authorities need to develop a comprehensive framework to fully account for all public debt obligations, including contingent fiscal liabilities. This is important to fully determine debt sustainability.

APPENDIX 6.1

APPENDIX TABLE 6.1

Measures of Debt Sustainability: Illustrative Natural Debt Limits *(In percent of GDP)*

		Mendoza-Oviedo Formulation	
Countries	**Debt ratio in 2011**	**Natural debt limit**	**Over-/under-borrowing ratio**
Group 1: Debt ratio above 90 percent	106.9	92.1	1.2
Group 2: Debt ratio between 60 and 90 percent	70.1	74.6	0.9
Group 3: Debt ratio below 60 percent	31.1	47.6	0.7
Caribbean median	71.2	74.6	1.0

Source: Authors' calculations, based on the Mendoza-Oviedo (2009) formulation.

REFERENCES

Aiyagari, S. Rao, and Ellen McGrattan, 1998, "The Optimum Quantity of Debt," *Journal of Monetary Economics*, Vol. 42, pp. 447–69.

Arslanalp, Serkan, and Takahiro Tsuda, 2012, "Tracking Global Demand for Advanced Economy Sovereign Debt," IMF Working Paper 12/284 (Washington: International Monetary Fund).

Barnhill Jr., Theodore M., and George Kopits, 2004, "Assessing Fiscal Sustainability Under Uncertainty," *The Journal of Risk,* Vol. 6, No. 4, pp. 31–53.

Barro, Robert, 1979, "Optimal Debt Management," NBER Working Paper No. 5327 (Cambridge, Massachusetts: National Bureau of Economic Research).

Blanchard, Olivier J., 1990, "Suggestions for a New Set of Fiscal Indicators," OECD Working Paper No. 79 (Paris: Organization for Economic Co-operation and Development).

Blanchard, Olivier J., Jean-Claude Chouraqui, Robert P. Hagemann, and Nicola Sartor, 1990, "The Sustainability of Fiscal Policy: New Answers to Old Questions," *OECD Economic Studies*, No. 15 (Autumn), pp. 7–36.

Bohn, Henning, 1998, "The Behavior of U.S. Public Debt and Deficits," *Quarterly Journal of Economics*, Vol. 113, pp. 949–63.

Burger, Philippe, Alfredo Cuevas, Ian Stuart, and Charl Jooste, 2011, "Fiscal Sustainability and the Fiscal Reaction Function for South Africa," IMF Working Paper 11/69 (Washington: International Monetary Fund).

Burnside, Craig, 2004, "Assessing New Approaches to Fiscal Sustainability Analysis," unpublished, Duke University, September 2004.

Celasun, Oya, Xavier Debrun, and Jonathan D. Ostry, 2006, "Primary Surplus Behavior and Risks to Fiscal Sustainability in Emerging Market Countries: A 'Fan-Chart' Approach," IMF Working Paper 06/67 (Washington: International Monetary Fund).

Chalk, Nigel, and Richard Hemming, 2000, "Assessing Fiscal Sustainability in Theory and Practice," IMF Working Paper 00/81 (Washington: International Monetary Fund).

da Costa, Carlos Eugenio, 2010, "Public Debt Sustainability," in *Public Debt: the Brazilian Experience*, ed. by Anderson Caputo Silva, Lena Oliveira de Carvalho, and Otavio Ladeira de Medeiros (Brasília: National Treasury Secretariat and World Bank).

da Costa, Carlos Eugênio, Anderson Caputo Silva, and William Baghdassarian, 2004, "Assessing Three Models for the Analysis of Debt Sustainability," unpublished, Getúli Vargas Foundation, April 2004.

Debrun, Xavier, and Charles Wyplosz, 1999, "Onze Gouvernements et une Banque Centrale," *Revue d'Economie Politique*, Vol. 109 (May–June), pp. 387–424.

di Giovanni, Julian, and Edward Gardner, 2008, "A Simple Stochastic Approach to Debt Sustainability Applied to Lebanon," IMF Working Paper 08/97 (Washington: International Monetary Fund).

Égert, Balázs, 2010, "Fiscal Policy Reaction to the Cycle in the OECD: Pro- or Countercyclical?" OECD Economics Department Working Paper No. 763 (Paris: Organization for Economic Co-operation and Development).

Escolano, Julio, Anna Shabunina, and Jaejoon Woo, 2011, "The Puzzle of Persistently Negative Interest Rate-Growth Differentials: Financial Repression or Income Catch-Up?" IMF Working Paper 11/260 (Washington: International Monetary Fund).

European Monetary Institute, 1995, "Progress Towards Convergence" (November 1995). www.ecb.int/pub/pdf/othemi/emiprogresstowardsconvergence199511en.pdf.

Gali, Jordi, and Roberto Perotti, 2003, "Fiscal Policy and Monetary Integration in Europe," *Economic Policy*, Vol. 18, No. 37, pp. 533–72.

Ghosh, Atish R., Jun I. Kim, Enrique G. Mendoza, Jonathan D. Ostry, and Mahvash S. Qureshi, 2013, "Fiscal Fatigue, Fiscal Space and Debt Sustainability in Advanced Economies," *Economic Journal*, Vol. 123, No. 566, pp. F4–F30.

Greenidge, Kevin, Roland Craigwell, Chrystol Thomas, and Lisa Drakes, 2012, "Threshold Effects of Sovereign Debt: Evidence from the Caribbean," IMF Working Paper 12/157 (Washington: International Monetary Fund).

International Monetary Fund (IMF), 2003, "Public Debt in Emerging Markets: Is It Too High?" Chapter 3 in *World Economic Outlook,* September (Washington).

———, 2011, "Belize 2011, Article IV Consultation," IMF Country Report No. 11/340 (Washington).

———, 2013a, "Antigua and Barbuda, Staff Report for the 2012 Article IV Consultation, Seventh Review under the Stand-By Arrangement and Financing Assurance Review, Request for Waiver of Nonobservance of Performance Criterion and Request for Waiver of Applicability," IMF Country Report No. 13/76 (Washington).

———, 2013b, *Fiscal Monitor,* April (Washington).

Kumar, Manmohan, and Jaejoon Woo, 2010, "Public Debt and Growth," IMF Working Paper 10/174 (Washington: International Monetary Fund).

Melitz, Jacques, 1997, "Some Cross-Country Evidence about Debt, Deficits and the Behaviour of Monetary and Fiscal Authorities," CEPR Discussion Paper No. 1653 (Washington: Center for Economic Policy Research).

Mendoza, Enrique, and Marcelo Oviedo, 2009, "Public Debt, Fiscal Solvency and Macroeconomic Uncertainty in Latin America," *Economia Mexicana*, Vol. 18, No. 2, pp. 133–73.

Tanner, Evan, 2013, "Fiscal Sustainability: A 21st Century Guide for the Perplexed," IMF Working Paper 13/89 (Washington: International Monetary Fund).

Tanner, Evan, and Issouf Samake, 2006, "Probabilistic Sustainability of Public Debt: A Vector Autoregression Approach for Brazil, Mexico, and Turkey," IMF Working Paper 06/295 (Washington: International Monetary Fund).

Xu, David, and Piero Ghezzi, 2003, "From Fundamentals to Spreads: A Fair Model for High Yield Emerging Markets Sovereigns," Deutsche Bank, July.

CHAPTER 7

Fiscal Consolidation in the Caribbean: Past and Current Experiences

JOEL CHIEDU OKWUOKEI, CHARLES AMO-YARTEY, AND MACHIKO NARITA

Countries in the Caribbean have undertaken fiscal consolidation at various times with the primary objective of putting the debt-to-GDP ratio on a sustainable downward trajectory. Yet public debt levels in most of these countries remain high today, suggesting that past and ongoing fiscal consolidation efforts have not yielded durable benefits. Some questions immediately come to mind. Why are public debts levels not falling as one would expect? Would it be connected with the Caribbean approach to fiscal consolidation, country-specific circumstances, or some challenges unique to the region? What are the characteristics of fiscal consolidation in the region, and how different are they from the experiences around the world?

This chapter takes a broad look at the Caribbean experience with fiscal consolidation, covering a sample of 14 countries, including six in a currency union, over three decades, 1980–2011.[1] The aim is to provide useful insights into the nature of fiscal consolidation across the region and their possible implications for policy. In addition, the chapter assesses current fiscal consolidation efforts in the region with case studies of Barbados, Jamaica, and St. Kitts and Nevis. Further, it identifies a number of challenges to successful consolidation.

The analysis provides ample evidence of fiscal consolidation in the region, although the durations have generally been short, about a year on average, perhaps reflecting the difficulty in sustaining fiscal efforts. Concerning debt reduction, the success rate has been substantially higher, on average, than the consolidation rate, suggesting that it would be desirable for the authorities to engage in more fiscal consolidation as they tend to be successful nearly half the time. The findings also show that consolidation has been more successful in commodity-exporting

[1]The sample includes Antigua and Barbuda, The Bahamas, Barbados, Belize, Dominica, the Dominican Republic, Grenada, Guyana, Jamaica, St. Kitts and Nevis, St. Lucia, St. Vincent and the Grenadines, Suriname, and Trinidad and Tobago.

countries than in tourism-intensive economies.[2] The common challenges to fiscal consolidation include the already high debt, fiscal rigidity, high exposure to global economic conditions, and natural disasters.

The chapter begins by defining fiscal consolidation to identify consolidation episodes in the region. It then analyzes the features of those episodes and examines current consolidation efforts as well. Following that analysis, it extends the discussion to selected countries—Barbados, Jamaica, and St. Kitts and Nevis. Lastly, the chapter lays out the challenges to fiscal consolidation and offers a summary with some concluding observations.

DEFINING AND IDENTIFYING FISCAL CONSOLIDATION[3]

The standard approach is to relate fiscal consolidation to a specific improvement in the cyclically adjusted primary balance (CAPB) as a percentage of potential GDP over a specific period. Nevertheless, the definitions of fiscal consolidation in the literature vary, partly reflecting different study objectives (Box 7.1). We adopt the following definition:

- Fiscal consolidation is said to occur when the ratio of CAPB to potential GDP improves by at least one percentage point in one year, or over two consecutive years.
- A consolidation episode continues as long as the CAPB improves, and it terminates if the change in the CAPB becomes zero or negative.
- Fiscal consolidation is successful if after four years, the debt-to-GDP ratio drops 5 percentage points below its level prior to the start of consolidation.[4]
- The size of a fiscal consolidation refers to the improvement in the CAPB in a year or over the course of an episode.

FEATURES OF FISCAL CONSOLIDATION IN THE CARIBBEAN

On average, the likelihood of fiscal consolidation occurring appears moderate, and consolidation tends to succeed nearly half of the time. In 352 observations, the study identified 107 cases of fiscal consolidation, which represents 30.4 percent of the sample (Table 7.1). Of these 107 cases, 51 of them, about 47 percent, were

---

[2]Tourism-intensive economies include Antigua and Barbuda, The Bahamas, Barbados, Belize, Dominica, the Dominican Republic, Grenada, Jamaica, St. Kitts and Nevis, St. Lucia, and St. Vincent and the Grenadines. Commodity-exporting countries include Guyana, Suriname, and Trinidad and Tobago.

[3]For the purpose of duration analysis, multiyear fiscal adjustment will constitute a single episode.

[4]The sample includes cases in which the reduction in the debt-to-GDP ratio was reversed.

BOX 7.1

Defining a Fiscal Consolidation Episode: Alternative Views from the Literature

There is no standard definition of fiscal consolidation. Reflecting a change in the underlying fiscal stance, fiscal consolidation is commonly defined as a specific improvement in the ratio of the cyclically adjusted primary balance (CAPB) to potential GDP (Alesina, Ardagna, and Gali, 1998; Larch and Turrini, 2011; and Alesina, Carloni, and Lecce, 2012). An alternative measure relates to changes in the ratio of the primary balance to GDP (Lambertini and Tavares, 2005; and Tsibouris and others, 2006). In addition to that last measure, Tsibouris and others (2006) consider changes in the ratio of the primary balance to government expenditure. Giavazzi, Jappelli, and Pagano (2000), defined consolidation as a persistent improvement in the fiscal impulse.

An episode is deemed to occur when the improvement in the CAPB or a related measure falls within a specified threshold. Studies of large fiscal adjustments impose tighter conditions and require an improvement of the CAPB or other measures by at least 1.5 percentage points in a year or in two consecutive years (Barrios, Langedijk, and Pench, 2010; Biggs, Hasset, and Jensen, 2010; Alesina, Carloni, and Lecce, 2012; and Larch and Turrini, 2011). Alternatively, the more gradual approaches consider an improvement of at least 1 percentage point (Ahrend, Catte, and Price, 2006; Kumar, Leigh, and Plekhanov, 2007) or by at least 1.25 percentage points (Von Hagen, Hallett, and Strauch, 2002). Generally, the episode continues as long as the measure of fiscal consolidation improves.

To assess the success of fiscal consolidation, alternative approaches have been adopted, including using the primary balance, debt, and growth as criteria. The *primary balance approach* aims to safeguard fiscal consolidation by requiring that the improvement in the CAPB, or in the primary balance a few years after the event, remains within a given threshold (Larch and Turrini, 2011; Lambertini and Tavares, 2005). This criterion excludes as successful a consolidation not arising from fiscal efforts. The *debt approach*, which is commonly applied, considers fiscal consolidation as a necessary condition for debt reduction and therefore ties success to the reduction in the debt-to-GDP ratio of some 5 percentage points over a three- to five-year period. In this context, a very successful fiscal consolidation is one that reduces debt over a three-year period. A third approach, also referred to as the expansionary criterion, proposes that GDP growth should improve after a consolidation (Hernandez de Cos and Moral-Benito, 2012; and Giudice, Turrini, and in't Veld, 2007).

successful. This suggests that, on average, the likelihood of fiscal consolidation occurring in the Caribbean would appear moderate, but the chance of success is much higher.[5]

Although the frequency of fiscal consolidation in the region has consistently declined over time, the experience has been broadly comparable to what findings

[5]The primary source of data is the World Economic Outlook database. This was supplemented with data compiled by IMF desk economists. The sample size differs across countries, reflecting data availability. The data that are available are primarily from the 1990s. The debt data, most of which cover general government debt, were obtained from the IMF Historical Public Debt Database compiled by the Fiscal Affairs Department.

TABLE 7.1

Fiscal Consolidation in the Caribbean, 1980–2011

Country	Sample Period	No. of Cases	Years	No. of Successes	Years
Antigua and Barbuda	1992–2011	8	1995, 1996, 1998, 2000, 2003–04, 2007, 2010	4	1998, 2003–04, 2007
The Bahamas	1988–2011	5	1992, 1994, 1996, 1998, 2003–04	1	1996
Barbados	1985–2011	8	1988, 1991–92, 1994, 1997–98, 2003, 2011	2	1994, 1997
Belize	1980–2011	11	1983, 1986–88, 1990, 1995–96, 2002, 2004–06	6	1986–88, 2004–06
Dominica	1986–2011	10	1991–93, 1995–96, 2001–03, 2005, 2010	4	1995–96, 2002, 2005
Dominican Republic	1980–2011	7	1984–85, 1989, 1991, 1995, 2004–05	6	1984, 1989, 1991, 1995,
Grenada	1990–2011	8	1991–93, 1995, 2003–04, 2008, 2010	3	2004–05 1991–92, 1995
Guyana	1991–2011	6	1999, 2002, 2004, 2007–08, 2010–11	4	1999, 2002, 2004, 2007
Jamaica	1983–2011	9	1984–86, 1988–89, 1998–2000, 2003	5	1985–86, 1988–89, 2003
St. Kitts and Nevis	1990–2011	6	1992–93, 2001, 2003, 2005, 2009, 2011	3	1992–93, 2005, 2011
St. Lucia	1983–2011	8	1984–85, 1987, 1997–98, 2003, 2007, 2009	0	
St. Vincent and the Grenadines	1990–2011	7	1993, 1994, 1995–96, 1998–99, 2000, 2008, 2011	3	1993, 1994, 1995–96
Suriname	1990–2011	7	1992–94, 2001, 2003, 2005, 2007	6	1992–94, 2001, 2003, 2005
Trinidad and Tobago	1988–2011	7	1989–90, 1993, 1999, 2000–01, 2005, 2010	4	1990, 1993, 2001, 2005
Total		**107**		**51**	

Source: Authors' calculations.

show for consolidations in advanced countries.[6] The consolidation rate in the region declined from 38 percent in 1980–89 to 28 percent in 2000–11 (Figure 7.1). Similarly, the success rate declined from 50 percent to 45 percent in 2000–11.

Focusing on large adjustments (1.5 percent improvement in the CAPB) outside the Caribbean region, findings by Larch and Turrini (2011) indicate a consolidation rate of about 25 percent and a success rate of 33 percent in 27 EU member countries. In a sample of 19 Organization for Economic Co-operation and Development (OECD) member countries, Alesina, Carloni, and Lecce (2012) find a 45.5 percent consolidation rate for any improvement in the fiscal position, and a 9 percent rate for large adjustments.[7]

[6]The findings in the literature are not easily comparable because of varying definitions of fiscal consolidation and their successes.

[7]In a study by Barrios, Langedijk, and Pench (2010), fiscal consolidation succeeded in only one-third of cases, about 34.5 percent, in 15 EU countries. In another study covering advanced countries, Alesina and Ardagna (2009) identified 107 fiscal consolidation episodes, representing a 15.1 percent consolidation rate, and 17 successful episodes implying a success rate of 15.8 percent.

Figure 7.1 Episodes of Fiscal Consolidation: Success Rates and Distribution by Decade, Caribbean Region, 1980–2011 *(Percent)*

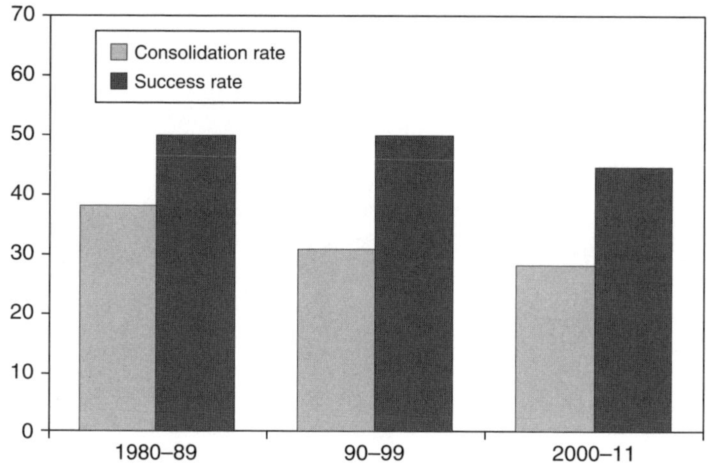

Source: Authors' calculations.

Figure 7.2 Consolidation Success Rates and Distribution by Decade, Caribbean Tourism-Intensive Economies, 1980–2011 *(Percent)*

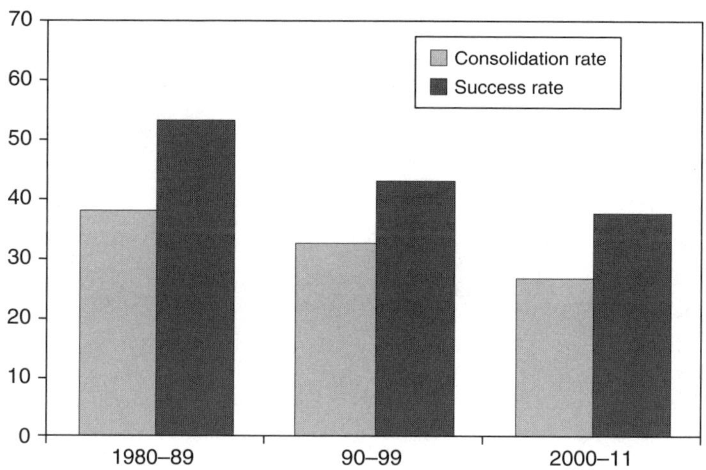

Source: Authors' calculations.

The rate of consolidation differs significantly across countries. Notably, the pattern of consolidation in tourism-intensive economies is similar to the pattern of the overall sample, declining consistently over time (Figure 7.2). The commodity-exporting economies exhibited a somewhat different pattern, with fiscal consolidation picking up in 2000–2011 (Figure 7.3). In particular, The Bahamas and the Dominican Republic have the lowest rates of consolidation, 20.9 percent and 21.8 percent, respectively (Figure 7.4). The rate is high for Antigua and Barbuda

Figure 7.3 Consolidation Success Rates and Distribution by Decade, Caribbean Commodity-Exporting Economies, 1980–2011 *(Percent)*

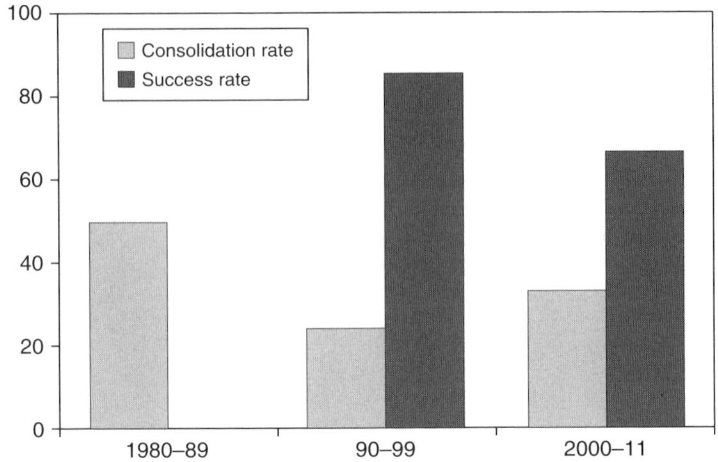

Source: Authors' calculations.

Figure 7.4 Rates of Consolidation and Success by Country, 1980–2011

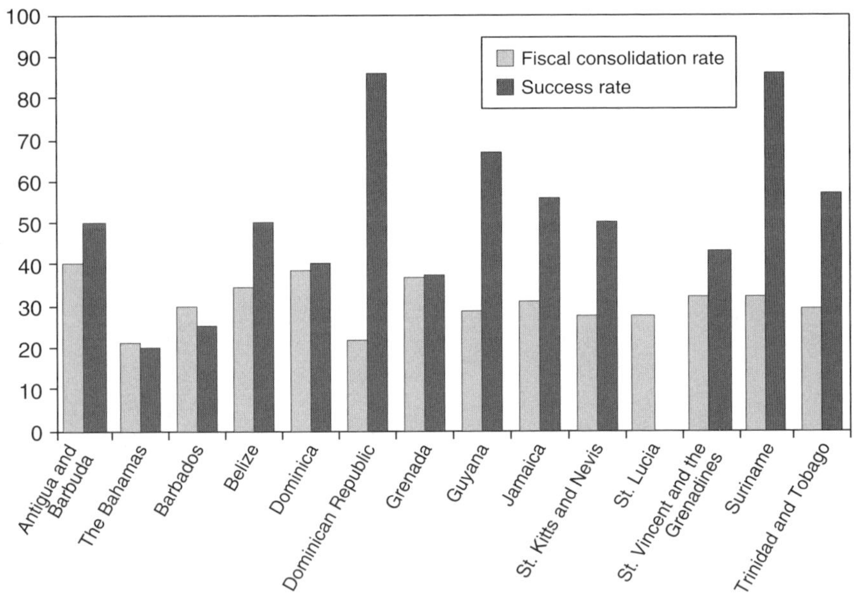

Source: Authors' calculations.

at 40 percent; Dominica, 38.5 percent; Grenada, 36.4 percent; and Belize, 34.3 percent. The prevailing economic conditions in each country, which indicate the need for fiscal adjustment, would account for the differences in the rates.

The success rates indicate mixed performances. The success rate of fiscal consolidation in the tourism-intensive economies has declined consistently over time. On average, the rate is about 5 percentage points below the average of the overall sample over the period. In contrast, the commodity-exporting economies have substantially higher success rates, exceeding the overall sample average by about 22 percentage points.

Available data further suggest that consolidation efforts have not been successful in St. Lucia, while four other countries also recorded low success rates, including The Bahamas at 20 percent, Barbados at 25 percent, Dominica at 40 percent, and Grenada at 37.5 percent. The historically low public-debt-to-GDP ratios of The Bahamas and St. Lucia could explain why fiscal consolidation as defined in the study failed to achieve significant debt reductions in those countries.

The size of fiscal consolidations is substantial but it is falling over time. Slightly more than half of the fiscal consolidation episodes recorded improvement in the CAPB in excess of 2 percent of GDP in a year during the full sample period. However, perhaps reflecting a waning appetite for consolidation, a similar sized adjustment occurred in about half of the episodes in 2000–11, as compared with 55 percent and 68 percent in 1990–99 and 1980–89, respectively (Figure 7.5). Notably, large adjustments occurred regularly in Jamaica, St. Lucia, and Suriname, and occasionally in other countries. Relative to previous findings, Tsibouris and others (2006) identified 300 episodes of fiscal adjustment exceeding 5 percent of GDP. In two-thirds of the consolidation cases identified by Larch and Turrini (2011), the CAPB improved by 1.5 percentage points.

Figure 7.5 Distribution of Consolidation Episodes by Size and Decade, Caribbean Region, 1980–2011 *(Percent)*

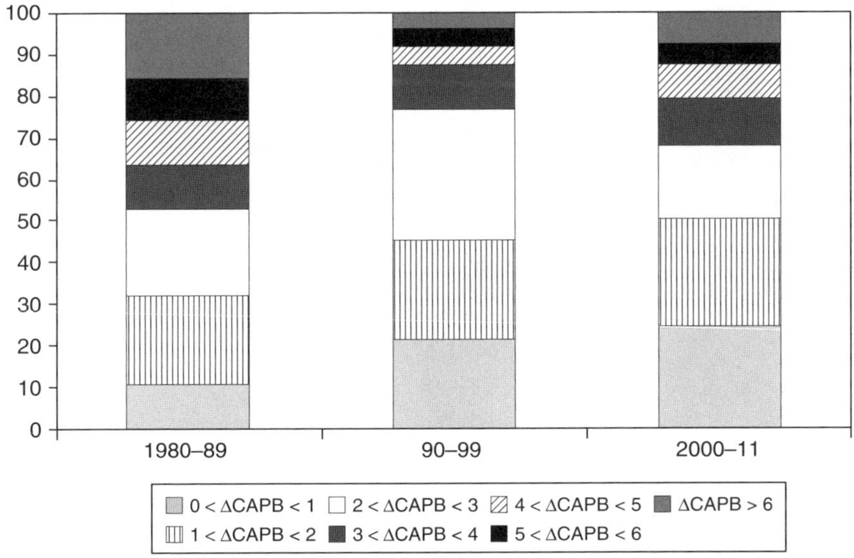

Source: Authors' calculations.

Note: ΔCAPB = change in the cyclically adjusted primary balance.

Successful fiscal consolidations are not necessarily associated with large adjustments in the year in which they occured. In some cases, the improvement in the CAPB was relatively moderate, while in others they were quite substantial. However, in many of the successful cases, the CAPB improved significantly preceding the year of success. For example, Barbados achieved a 5 percentage point debt reduction in 1994 by improving the CAPB by 1.1 percentage points that year. However, before this episode, in 1991–92, the country had recorded a higher improvement in the CAPB without significantly reducing the debt.

The adjustment duration is short, perhaps reflecting the difficulty in sustaining fiscal efforts (Figure 7.6). Half of the episodes lasted for a year, while about two-fifths lasted for two to three years. In particular, fiscal consolidation was predominantly of one to two years' duration in Antigua and Barbuda, Dominica, Guyana, and St. Lucia. It was between one and three years' duration in Barbados, Belize, the Dominican Republic, and Grenada. The episodes were of two to three years' duration in Jamaica, while in The Bahamas and Suriname they lasted one year and three years, respectively. Three countries had consolidation spells that lasted for four years: St. Kitts and Nevis (2003–2006), St. Vincent and the Grenadines (1993–1996 and 1998–2011), and Trinidad and Tobago (1999–2002). Over the longer episodes, the improvement in the fiscal position was much larger, reflecting the persistence of fiscal efforts. Figure 7.7 illustrates these varying durations alongside the frequency of episodes of each country.

The adjustment duration in the Caribbean region has been consistent with the experience in advanced countries. Tsibouris and others (2006), in a global sample of over 165 countries, find diversity in both the length and the pace of fiscal adjustments, noting that two-thirds of the adjustments were concentrated in the first year. Findings by Alesina and Ardagna (2009) from a panel of OECD countries

Figure 7.6 Distribution of Episodes by Duration, Caribbean Region, 1980–2011

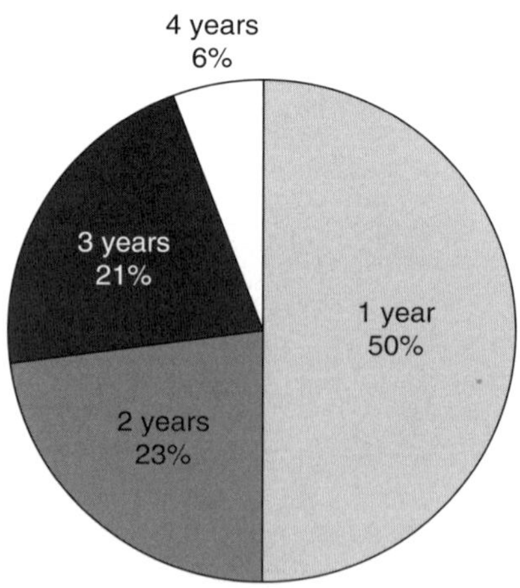

Source: Authors' calculations.

Figure 7.7 Duration and Frequency of Episodes by Country, 1980–2011

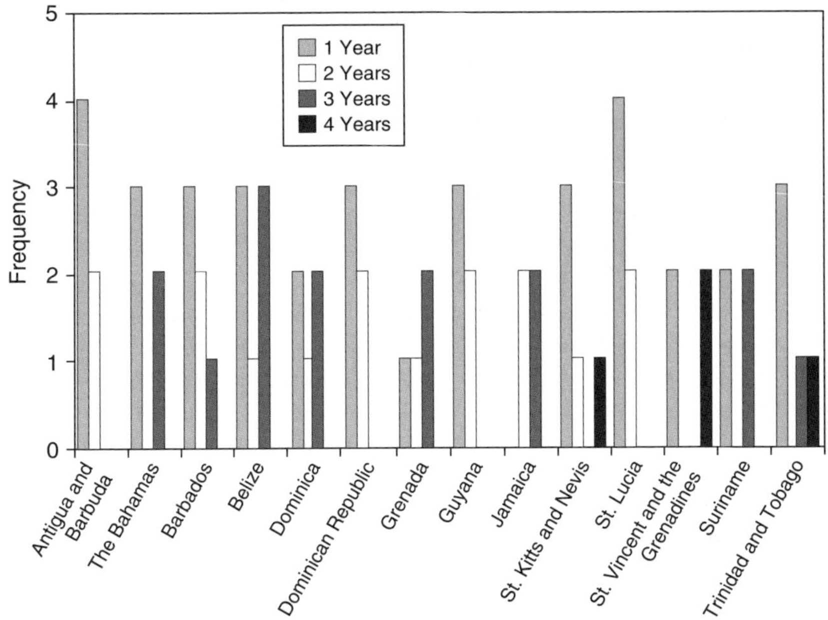

Source: Authors' calculations.

show that 65 of 107 episodes (about 60 percent) lasted for one year, 13 lasted for two years, 4 lasted for three years, and only one lasted for four years.

CURRENT EFFORTS IN THE REGION

Fiscal consolidation efforts in the Caribbean have been slow and steady. A number of countries have embarked on consolidation with the objectives of putting the debt-to-GDP ratio on a sustainable downward path and improving external stability. Recently, the emphasis has been on maintaining social stability and mitigating the impact of the global financial crisis.

These countries have adopted various tax and expenditure measures to reduce their fiscal deficits. While there is little ambiguity about the fact that they need to move swiftly to lower debt, answers to questions about how much of the adjustment should come from spending cuts or tax increases and which areas of government activity they should tackle will depend on country-specific circumstances.

In most of the region, the emphasis has been on raising revenues as opposed to making spending cuts. However, in countries with IMF-supported programs, expenditure controls have been an important aspect of the strategy, as well as reducing losses in public enterprises. In a small number of countries where spending has been restrained, countries have preferred to reduce capital spending rather than current spending.

Even though these consolidation efforts are ongoing, countries are generating much lower primary fiscal surpluses than they need to reduce their debt-to-GDP ratios. Examining the current high debt levels and fiscal prospects, we identified the fiscal adjustment needed (defined as debt stabilizing primary balance minus actual primary balance) to stabilize and reduce debt in the medium term. We found that when debt levels are high, large primary surpluses must be run to reduce the debt stock. The magnitude of the primary surpluses needed increases with interest rates and the initial debt stock, but it varies inversely with real GDP growth.

Our debt sustainability analysis suggests that stabilizing public-debt-to-GDP ratios at 2011 levels would require fiscal adjustment efforts ranging from 1.6 percent of GDP (for Barbados) to 6.0 percent (for St. Lucia) (see Chapter 6). For the average Caribbean country, the adjustment would be around 1 percent of GDP. If the adjustments were to come mainly from spending cuts, this would translate into large real spending cuts for a number of countries. Reducing public debt ratios to 60 percent of GDP by 2020 would require even stronger fiscal adjustments.

Fiscal consolidation in the Caribbean has been accompanied by debt restructuring in some countries, including Antigua and Barbuda, Belize, Jamaica, and St. Kitts and Nevis. These countries recognized that fiscal adjustment alone could not ensure debt sustainability unless accompanied by a meaningful reduction in the public debt service burden, requiring burden sharing by all stakeholders. Antigua and Barbuda reached an agreement with the Paris Club in September 2010 on the rescheduling of the country's public external debt. The goal of its debt restructuring was to reduce the government's interest bill to 4½ percent of GDP in 2010, from 9 percent of GDP. St. Kitts and Nevis undertook a comprehensive and substantive public debt restructuring. Overall, its debt restructuring was expected to yield substantial interest savings to help put public debt on a firm downward trajectory over the medium term. Similarly, early in 2013, Belize and Jamaica had debt restructurings. Of note, Belize's exchange of its "super-bond" for new U.S. dollar-denominated bonds is also expected to bring in substantial cash-flow relief.

EFFORTS IN SELECT CARIBBEAN COUNTRIES

This section reviews recent fiscal consolidation efforts in Barbados, Jamaica, and St. Kitts and Nevis and draws common lessons from their experiences. Following the global financial crisis and the resulting huge increase in the debt-to-GDP ratio, these three countries started consolidating government finances in order to reduce public debt and enhance external sustainability.

A look at their fiscal consolidation experiences reveals three commonalities: (1) a holistic approach, (2) quick implementation of short-term measures, and (3) steady progress on structural reforms. Fiscal consolidation efforts in these countries involved a holistic approach that considered all possible improvements in revenue and expenditure reduction that could help deliver the expected results.

Since multipronged consolidation efforts often take some time to materialize, quick implementation of short-term measures, such as a temporary freeze of public wages and a temporary increase of a tax rate, have been helpful in showing governments' commitments and in creating some instant fiscal space. These countries have also made steady progress on structural reforms, which is important to successful fiscal consolidation. However, weak tax administration and debt management capacities, vulnerability to spillovers from the global economy and to natural disasters, and optimistic assumptions in fiscal consolidation plans have all continued to slow the pace of fiscal reforms in these countries.

Barbados

Barbados was severely affected by the global economic crisis, the impact of which continues to be felt throughout its economy. Economic activity contracted by a cumulative 5 percent between 2008 and 2010 with adverse impacts on the labor market. The unemployment rate almost doubled from 6.7 percent to 12.1 percent in June 2011. The government responded to the economic slump by increasing current spending to limit employment losses and shield vulnerable groups. These efforts widened the fiscal deficit and have increased public debt by more than 20 percentage points of GDP since 2008, exacerbating an already high debt level (Figure 7.8). In light of the deteriorating public finances, the government developed a Medium-Term Fiscal Strategy (MTFS) in early 2010 to reduce the fiscal deficit, balance the budget and reduce the debt-to-GDP ratio. However, the MTFS went off track in the first year of implementation due to weak global conditions and low revenues.

Figure 7.8 Barbados: Fiscal Deficit and General Government Debt, 2003–12 *(Percent of GDP)*

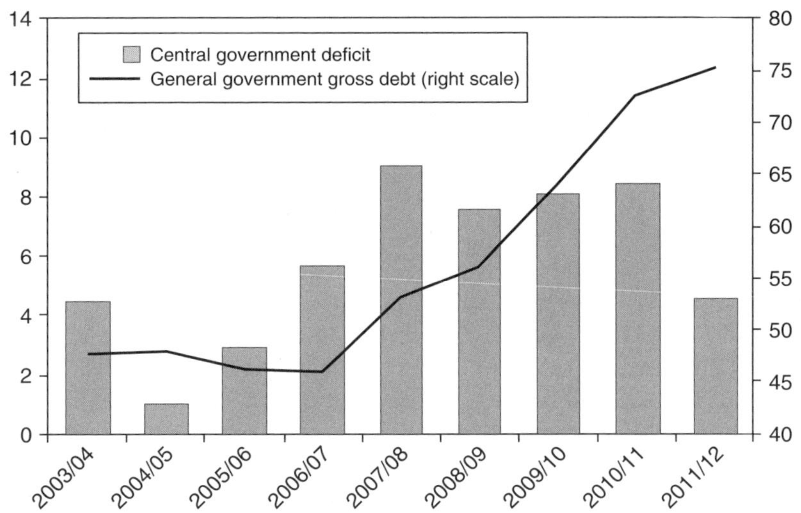

Source: Authors' calculations.

Fiscal consolidation in Barbados began with a front-loaded adjustment based on revenue enhancing measures. The government increased the value added tax (VAT) rate from 15 percent to 17.5 percent for a period of 18 months and increased excise taxes on gasoline by 50 percent. Tax-free allowances for travel and entertainment were eliminated, bus fares were raised, and some fees and charges for dispensary services were adjusted.

The government also enumerated a number of expenditure reduction measures, but political economy considerations have made their implementation very difficult. The expenditure measures outlined in the MTFS include these:

- Containing public sector wages by restricting wage growth to be equivalent to the amount normally paid as increments,
- Reducing the level of spending on goods and services by increasing the efficiency of public procurement through better sourcing, and
- Capping transfers to statutory boards, statutory corporations and state-owned enterprises and allowing some state-owned enterprises to borrow directly from the National Insurance Scheme.

Progress on lowering expenditures has been slow, and the 2012–13 budget contained no expenditure-cutting measures since expenditures were projected to broadly remain unchanged as a percent of GDP. The IMF has advised the authorities to discourage direct lending by the National Insurance Scheme to public enterprises.

Fiscal consolidation has helped improve Barbados' fiscal performance. The central government deficit in fiscal year 2011–12 narrowed to 4.5 percent of GDP from 8.3 percent of GDP in 2010–11. This outturn reflected the cuts in capital spending and lower transfers to state-owned enterprises, as a large sum (1½ percent of GDP) was taken off-budget and replaced by loans from the National Insurance Scheme directly to those enterprises. The 2012–13 budget targeted a central government deficit of 4.3 percent of GDP, but high expenditure during the 2012–13 election cycle meant that the target was missed by a wide margin.

With the country's public debt on an unsustainable path, the IMF has advised the authorities to make MTFS more ambitious and, at a minimum, to aim at reducing the public debt by about 15 percentage points of GDP over 5 years. Debt sustainability analysis suggests that the envisaged fiscal target under the MTFS would not be enough to reduce the vulnerability of public debt. Public debt would not follow a sustained downward path under most standardized shocks unless a more ambitious fiscal consolidation plan is implemented to reduce debt further in the medium-to-long term. The IMF has also stressed the need for MTFS to cover state enterprises and to be based on realistic macroeconomic assumptions. In particular, the current assumption of average GDP growth of around 2.5 percent in the medium term seems on the optimistic side.

The IMF has also recommended focusing fiscal consolidation on expenditure reduction, with revenue measures focusing on improving tax administration and reducing exemptions. Since room for further tax increases is limited, measures to contain wage spending and reduce transfers to public enterprises need to remain key elements of the MTFS. The IMF has also recommended extending the temporary increase in the VAT rate, which the authorities have implemented, and developing a plan to reduce tax exemptions estimated at 5.6 percent of GDP in 2011–12.

Jamaica

Jamaica has a history of low growth and high debt. Real GDP growth over the past three decades has been relatively low, perhaps reflecting deep-rooted competitiveness problems, exposure to natural disasters, and macroeconomic risks arising from fiscal and external imbalances. At the same time, public debt, which is very sensitive to exchange rate and interest rate shocks, remains among the highest in the world, at about 138 percent of GDP in 2011–12 (Figure 7.9).

The combination of a high interest burden, heavy wage bill, and losses from public enterprises poses further challenges. The country has maintained large primary surpluses, on average, of some 8 percent of GDP to finance the interest bill, which during 2009–10 rose to 17.1 percent of GDP (Figure 7.10). Since the mid-1990s, public sector wages in percent of GDP have fluctuated between 10 and 12.5 percent, as the government is the largest employer of labor.

In the context of the 2010 Stand-By Arrangement, the government had a domestic debt restructuring in January 2010. The Jamaican Debt Exchange, which covered domestic debt, secured close to 100 percent participation and achieved a net present value (NPV) reduction of 15–20 percent through lower coupon rates. As a result, the public sector interest bill fell to 10 percent in 2011–12 from 17 percent in 2009–10. At the same time, the maturity profile of domestic debt increased from 4.5 to 9.8 years. Positive market reception of the

Figure 7.9 Jamaica: Real GDP Growth and Public Debt, 2000–11

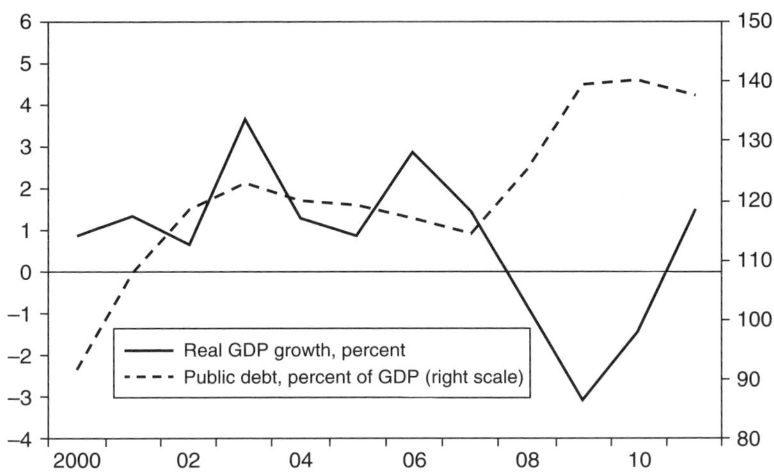

Source: Authors' calculations.

Figure 7.10 Jamaica: Interest Payments, Wage Bill, and Primary Balance, 2000–11
(Fiscal year, percent of GDP)

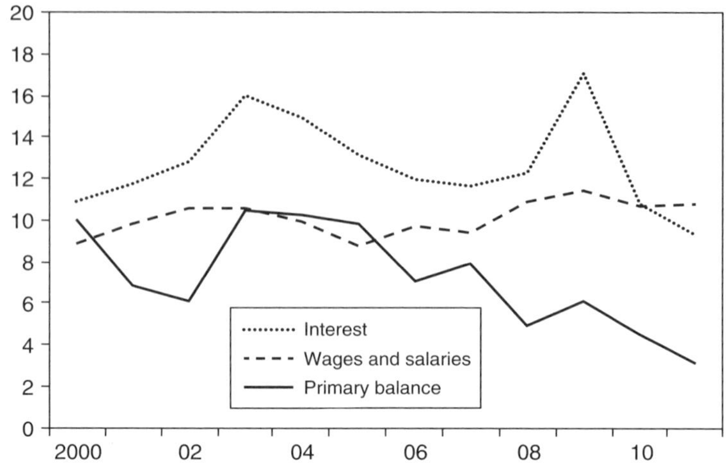

Source: Authors' calculations.

fiscal consolidation embedded in the Jamaican Debt Exchange lowered interest rates. Overall, the exchange could be considered as a temporary alleviation of the debt problem.

However, the planned fiscal consolidation failed to materialize. The 2010 Stand-By Arrangement was broadly on track, initially. However, policy slippages in 2011, especially on the fiscal front, led to program targets being missed by wide margins. The failure of fiscal consolidation reflects higher-than-anticipated public sector wages following a decision to clear the full amount of wage back-payments, lower tax revenues (associated with widespread use of tax incentives and waivers, and weak administration), and delays in the privatization of the loss-making Clarendon Alumina Plant.

Despite progress with structural reforms, more is needed to improve competitiveness and growth. The government has successfully divested from loss-making public enterprises, such as Air Jamaica and the sugar estates; a new fiscal responsibility law was passed in 2010; and a new Tax Administration Jamaica was created, which is functional. Nonetheless, key fiscal reforms have been delayed, including public sector rationalization, tax and pension reforms, a reform of the Central Treasury Management System, and divestment from the Clarendon Alumina Plant, while the new tax administration has yet to address the erosion of the tax base. Furthermore, while interim measures to cap discretionary waivers were introduced in November 2010, a more comprehensive reform to scale back incentives is lacking. The authorities have developed an economic program to address the challenges of low growth, fiscal sustainability, and high debt.

The IMF recommended a prompt and strong up-front fiscal adjustment to put public debt on a clear downward path. The strategy is based on a significantly higher and sustained primary surplus of the central government over the medium-term—7.5 percent of GDP commencing from 2012–13 and rising to 7.9 percent of GDP in 2015–16. The approach should center on high-quality measures supported by domestic ownership and broad national consensus. While the IMF emphasized the importance of early action, it noted that public debt would still remain high, with continued adverse effects on growth even after a sustained fiscal adjustment. The authorities favored a gradual approach, which aims to balance the central government budget and reduce the debt-to-GDP ratio to 100 percent by March 2016. The authorities' plan proposed a primary surplus of 5.2 percent of GDP in 2012–13, gradually rising to 6.0 percent by 2015–16.

A new government, which came into office in January 2012 following a decisive election victory in December 2011, started tightening fiscal policy in 2012–13. The government introduced a budget for the fiscal year that aimed at raising the central government primary surplus to 6 percent of GDP from 3.2 percent the previous year. A tax package, with full-year effect estimated at 1.6 percent of GDP, was passed during the year. Further, the government strengthened its Fiscal Responsibility Framework, including a sanctions regime for unbudgeted spending. Although fiscal outcomes improved during the year, preliminary IMF staff estimates indicate that the primary surplus (5¼ percent of GDP) fell short of the target due to weaker than anticipated revenues, despite recent improvement in tax collection efforts.

The authorities have developed a comprehensive economic program to address the challenges of low growth, fiscal sustainability, and high debt. The four-year program seeks to avert the immediate crisis risks and create conditions for sustained growth through significant improvement in the fiscal and debt positions. The main pillars of the program are as follows: (1) structural reforms to boost growth and employment; (2) actions to improve price and non-price competitiveness; (3) up-front fiscal adjustment, supported by extensive fiscal reforms; (4) debt reduction, including a debt exchange, to place debt on a sustainable path, while protecting financial stability; and (5) improved social protection programs, with a floor to safeguard social spending. The new reform program focuses on actions to strengthen public financial management, introduce a fiscal rule, reform the tax system, improve the business climate, move toward inflation targeting, and reform the securities dealers sector.

St. Kitts and Nevis

A series of shocks have led to a sizable accumulation of debt in St. Kitts and Nevis over the last decade. Following a succession of hurricanes in the late 1990s, the sharp drop in tourism after the September 11 attacks, and the closure of the loss-making sugar industry, the central government debt quickly increased in the early 2000s from 62 percent of GDP in 2000 to 109 percent of GDP in 2006. Although the outstanding debt in percent of GDP declined in 2007 and 2008, due to a buoyant economy and strengthened tax administration, it strongly increased again in the wake of the global economic crisis in 2008. This led to a fall in tourism and construction resulting from foreign direct investment, which had been driving growth in recent years.

Rising debt service costs have been a challenge for the government. In addition to a high debt level, the increased use of the expensive overdraft facility since 2005, which reflects the government's limited access to other forms of financing, has exacerbated the heavy debt service burden (Figure 7.11). Interest payments reached their peak at 7.6 percent of GDP in 2006 (Figure 7.12). Although the government successfully reduced the overdraft in 2008, it returned to tapping the overdraft in 2009, responding to the economic slump. High debt service costs, which have taken over 20 percent of total government revenue in recent years, leave little room for maneuver to respond to adverse shocks.

Faced with increasing fiscal imbalances, the government started to implement a strong fiscal adjustment program in 2010. On the revenue side, it introduced a VAT and implemented a number of tax reforms. Other measures implemented include streamlining import duty exemptions, strengthening the auditing and monitoring of duty-free shops, introducing an environmental levy on new vehicles, restructuring the Housing and Social Development Levy, and increasing electricity tariffs. On the expenditure side, the government froze public wages. The expected benefits from these revenue reforms and expenditure cuts started to materialize in 2011.

In order to achieve fiscal and debt sustainability, the government set up a multipronged reform agenda and requested support under a 36-month IMF program in 2011. The strategy was focused on: (1) achieving ambitious primary fiscal surpluses; (2) lowering the debt service burden; and (3) further strengthening the financial sector. Notwithstanding the fiscal adjustment, it was also agreed that a comprehensive and timely public debt restructuring was crucial for the program to be fully financed and to achieve debt sustainability. Debt

Figure 7.11 St. Kitts and Nevis: Fiscal Balance and Outstanding Debt, 2000–11
(Central government, percent of GDP)

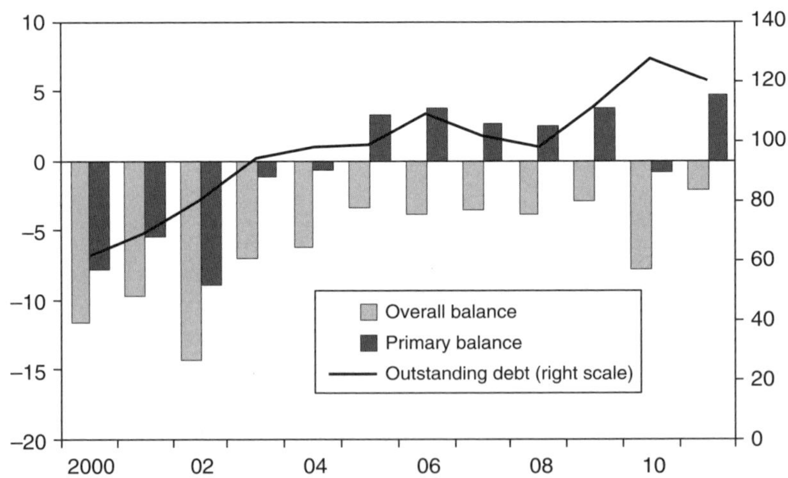

Source: Authors' calculations.

Figure 7.12 St. Kitts and Nevis: Outstanding Debt and Interest Payment, 2000–11
(Central government, percent of GDP)

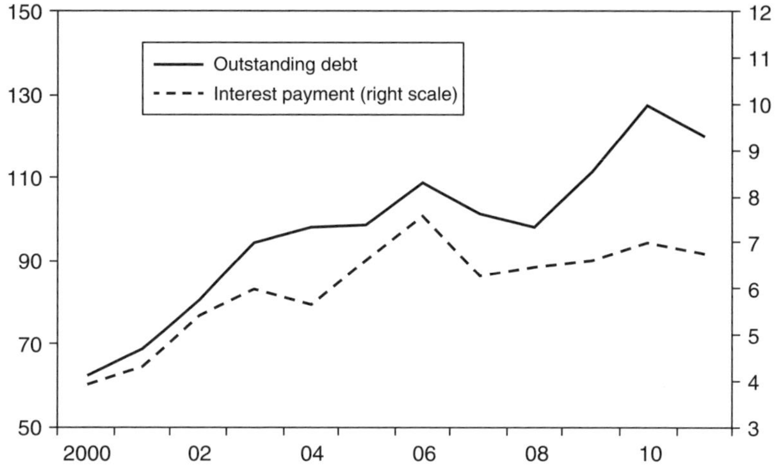

Source: Authors' calculations.

restructuring, it was argued, would complement the ongoing fiscal effort, ensuring burden sharing by all stakeholders.

Since the inception of the IMF program in July 2011, the authorities have steadfastly implemented their economic program and begun to achieve positive results. Although the economic outturn has been weaker than projected, the authorities have met all quantitative performance criteria and completed the structural benchmarks of the IMF program. They have also made progress in a comprehensive debt restructuring, including successfully completing the restructuring of bonds and external commercial debt and reaching an agreement on the debt-land swap with domestic creditors and an agreement with their Paris Club creditors. Discussions with other bilateral official creditors are aimed at obtaining comparable terms as those in the Paris Club agreement. Negotiations on debt not covered by the debt-land swap and those held by the Social Security Board are still ongoing.

Although the restructuring of the public debt is expected to place it on a declining trajectory, the debt sustainability analysis indicates that the debt trajectory could be flattened by an adverse growth shock. This highlights the importance of safeguarding the implementation of the program and planning for contingencies on an ongoing basis.

Overall, the whole debt restructuring is anticipated to lead to a sizable reduction in total public debt and to set debt on a sustainable medium-term trajectory, together with the continued strong fiscal consolidation efforts. Going forward, it will be essential to sustain the pace of both fiscal and structural reforms in order to achieve the medium-term fiscal goals, including a debt-to-GDP ratio of 112 percent in 2017, even if the sluggish global environment continues. Ongoing efforts in broadening the tax base are also encouraged to secure additional tax revenue. In addition, it is important to ensure that the debt-for-land swap does not impair the resilience of the domestic financial sector by proceeding with resulting land sales at a swift pace.

CHALLENGES IN THE REGION

Common challenges to fiscal consolidation in the region include high levels of public debt, fiscal rigidity, high exposures to global economic conditions, and natural disasters. Many countries in the Caribbean have high levels of public debt, which put pressure on expenditure by increasing the interest payment burden and could limit their capability of accessing additional financing. Limited flexibility in fiscal adjustment, which is also common, typically stems from a large share of non-discretionary spending (such as wages and interest payments). The region is highly exposed to global economic conditions through tourism and commodity prices and to natural disasters, which pose risks to continuous implementation. Fiscal consolidation is also hindered by the limited scope for significant revenue increases in some countries.

High Debt Levels

The high debt levels of the region make fiscal consolidation very difficult. Interest payments of the central government co-moved with the debt level in the Caribbean, except for the period of debt restructuring in Antigua and Barbuda and Jamaica (see Figure 7.13). For many Caribbean countries, interest payments comprise a significant proportion of total expenditure (Figure 7.14). The high debt level also implies that a substantial fiscal adjustment is needed to consolidate government finances.

Figure 7.13 Outstanding Debt and Interest Payments, Caribbean Region, 2000–11
(Central government, percent of GDP)

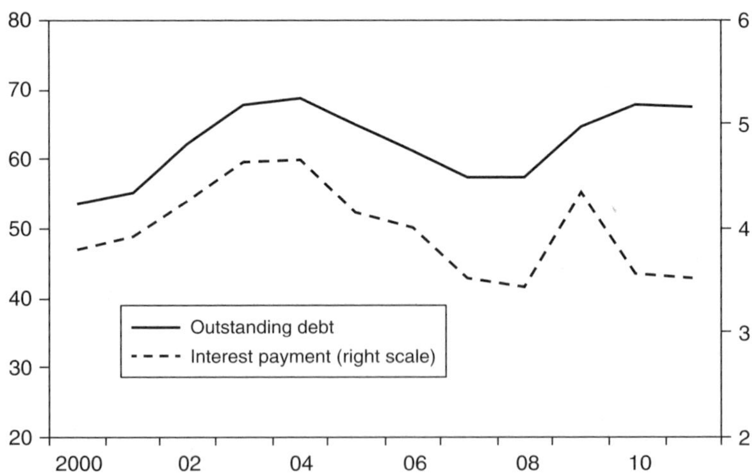

Source: Authors' calculations.

Figure 7.14 Share of Interest Payments in Total Expenditures, 2011 *(Central government, percent)*

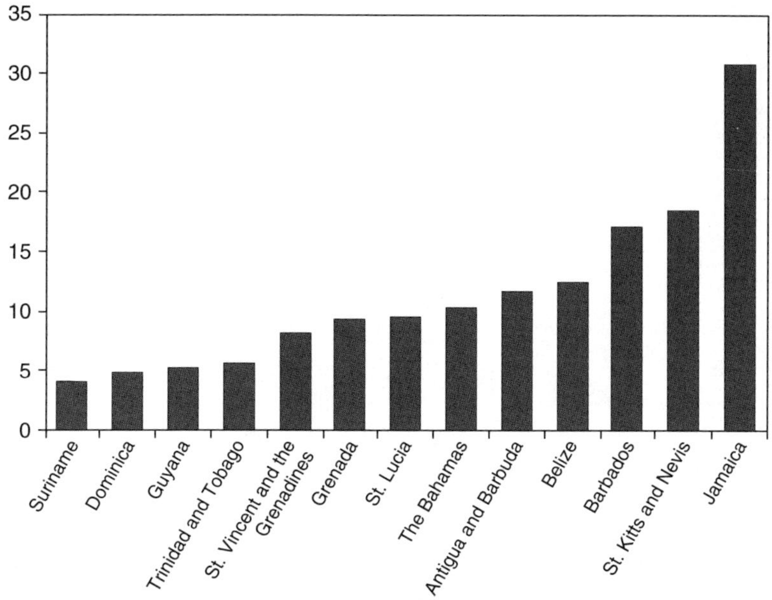

Source: Authors' calculations.

Fiscal Rigidities

In many countries in the Caribbean, fiscal expenditures are mostly committed to wages, interest payments, and social security, limiting the flexibility of fiscal adjustment. In order to quantify and compare the degrees of fiscal flexibility across countries and regions, we consider a simple index of fiscal flexibility, defined as the size of government spending that can be characterized as discretionary. We define fiscal flexibility index as:

$$\mathrm{FFI} = \left(1 - \frac{\mathrm{NDS}}{\mathrm{TGS}}\right) * 100,$$

where *TGS* is total government spending and *NDS* is nondiscretionary spending, defined as expenditure on wages and salaries, transfers, and interest payments. The maximum value of this index without any correction factor is 100, indicating total fiscal flexibility. We also consider another fiscal flexibility index, controlling for the size of government spending in the country's economy:

$$\mathrm{FFI}^* = \mathrm{FFI} * \left(1 + \frac{\mathrm{TGS}}{\mathrm{GDP}}\right).$$

This adjusted index evaluates fiscal flexibility according to the size of the government; the larger the government's size, the more the adjusted index evaluates the country's fiscal flexibility.

Figure 7.15 Simple Fiscal Flexibility Indices by Country

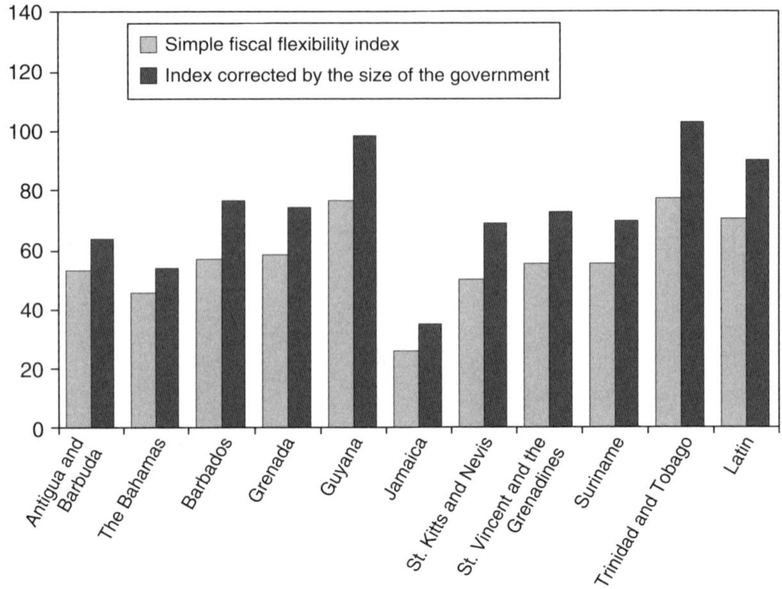

Source: Authors' calculations.
Note: "Latin" is the simple average of Brazil, Chile, Colombia, Peru, and Uruguay.

The analysis, illustrated in Figure 7.15, shows that fiscal rigidities are smaller in Latin American countries than in the Caribbean countries, making fiscal adjustment much more difficult in the region. The two flexibility indices just defined consistently show a higher flexibility for Latin American countries. Lower fiscal flexibility in the Caribbean indicates that there is less room available for relatively easy spending reductions.

The degree of actual rigidity differs across components of the government expenditures, based on historical data. Current expenditure tends to be more rigid than capital expenditure, when revenue growth slows down (see Figure 7.16). Current expenditure as a percentage of total revenues rose in a period of slow revenue growth, meaning that current expenditures were not adjusted along with revenue growth. The rise in current expenditure as a percentage of total revenue was larger during 2009–2011, when the slowdown of revenue growth was more pronounced.

Rigidity in current expenditure is accounted for by nondiscretionary expenditures, including transfers, wages and salaries, and interest payments (Figure 7.17). In 2009, all of these expenditures in percent of revenue increased by over 3 percentage points. Transfers and wages and salaries have not returned to their pre-crisis levels. The decline in interest payments in 2010 was due to the large debt restructurings in Antigua and Barbuda and Jamaica. A higher rigidity in current expenditure than in capital expenditure was observed in many countries during the crisis period from 2009 to 2011. Measured as a percent of revenue,

Figure 7.16 Caribbean Region: Current and Capital Expenditures, 2000–11 *(Percent of revenue)*

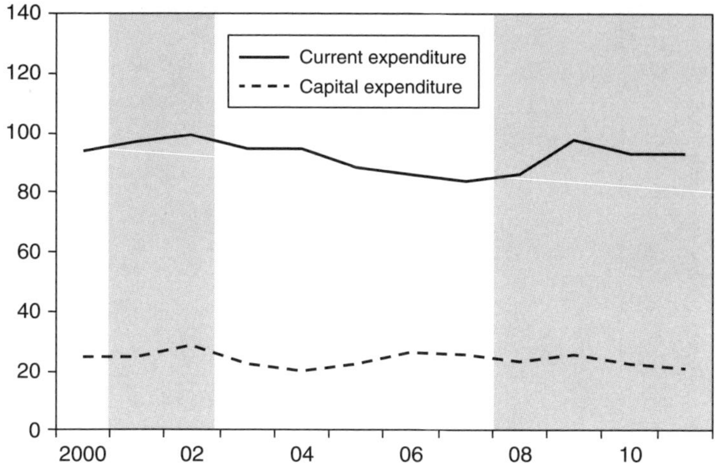

Source: Authors' calculations.
Note: Years of slow revenue growth are shaded.

Figure 7.17 Caribbean Region: Detailed Items of Current Expenditure, 2000–11 *(Percent of revenue)*

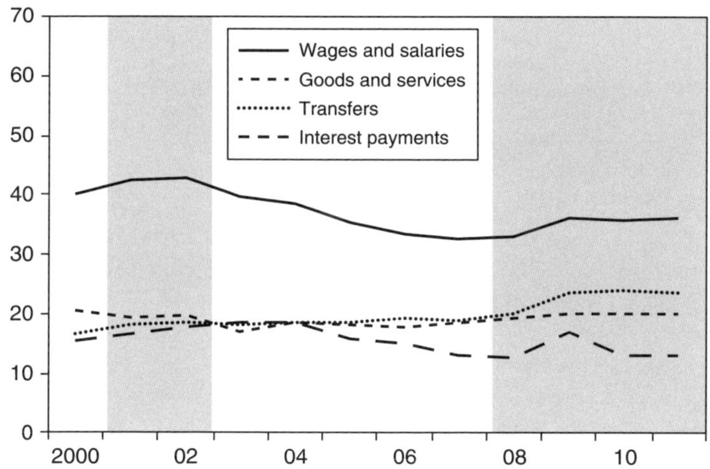

Source: Authors' calculations.
Note: Years of slow revenue growth are shaded.

current expenditure increased after the crisis in most countries, while capital expenditure in percent of revenue did not follow a similar pattern (see Figures 7.18 and 7.19).

Transfers were responsible for a greater part of the rigidity in current expenditure during the crisis. Transfers in percent of revenue sizably increased after the crisis in some countries, ranging from about 7 percent in Barbados to 15 percent

Figure 7.18 Current Expenditure to Revenue Ratio, 2006–11 *(Percent)*

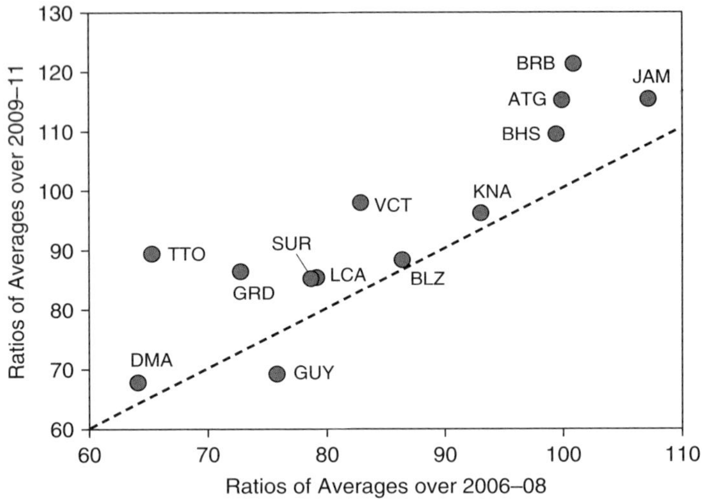

Source: Authors' calculations.

Note: ATG = Antigua and Barbuda, BHS = The Bahamas, BRB = Barbados, BLZ = Belize, DMA = Dominica, GRD = Grenada, GUY = Guyana, JAM = Jamaica, KNA = St. Kitts and Nevis, LCA = St. Lucia, VCT = St. Vincent and the Grenadines, SUR = Suriname, and TTO = Trinidad and Tobago.

Figure 7.19 Capital Expenditure to Revenue Ratio, 2006–11 *(Percent)*

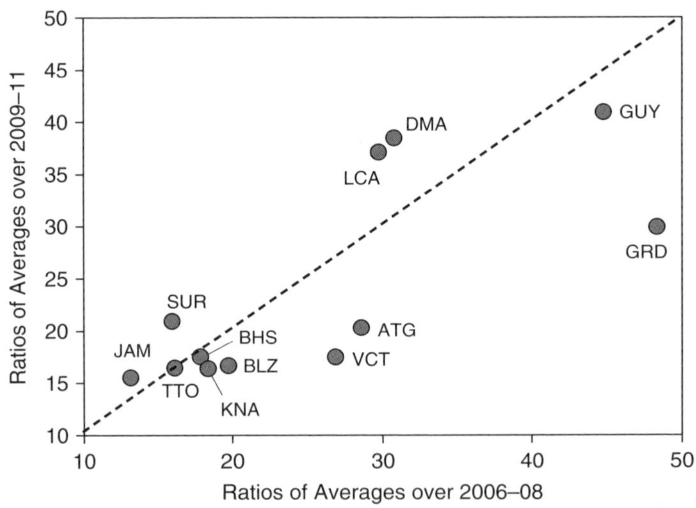

Source: Authors' calculations.

Note: ATG = Antigua and Barbuda, BHS = The Bahamas, BRB = Barbados, BLZ = Belize, DMA = Dominica, GRD = Grenada, GUY = Guyana, JAM = Jamaica, KNA = St. Kitts and Nevis, LCA = St. Lucia, VCT = St. Vincent and the Grenadines, SUR = Suriname, and TTO = Trinidad and Tobago.

in Trinidad and Tobago (see Figure 7.20). The rise in transfers in percent of revenue partly reflects countercyclical components, such as unemployment benefits. Wages and salaries in percent of revenue also increased in most countries and accounted for some of the rigidities in current expenditure (see Figure 7.21).

Figure 7.20 Transfers to Revenue Ratio, 2006–11 *(Percent)*

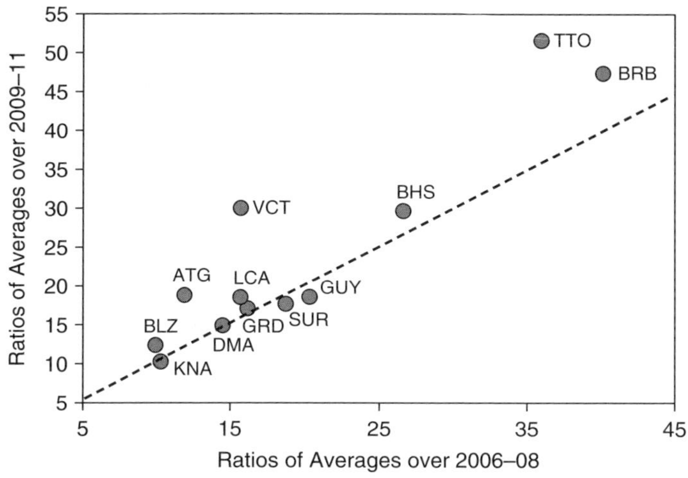

Source: Authors' calculations.
Note: ATG = Antigua and Barbuda, BHS = The Bahamas, BRB = Barbados, BLZ = Belize, DMA = Dominica, GRD = Grenada, GUY = Guyana, JAM = Jamaica, KNA = St. Kitts and Nevis, LCA = St. Lucia, VCT = St. Vincent and the Grenadines, SUR = Suriname, and TTO = Trinidad and Tobago.

Figure 7.21 Wages and Salaries to Revenue Ratio, 2006–11 *(Percent)*

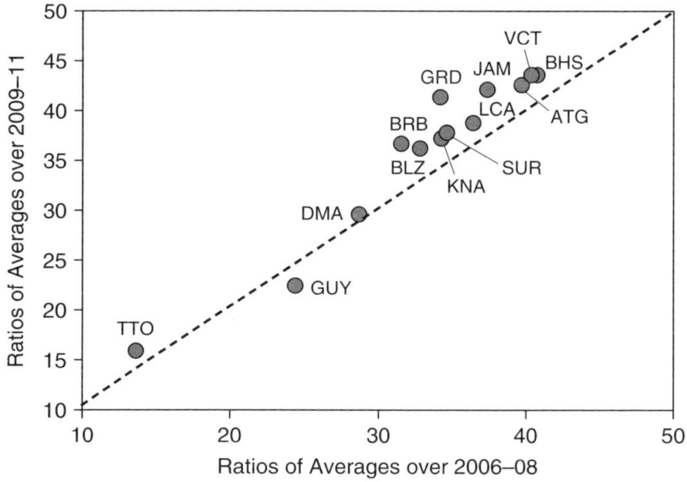

Source: Authors' calculations.
Note: ATG = Antigua and Barbuda, BHS = The Bahamas, BRB = Barbados, BLZ = Belize, DMA = Dominica, GRD = Grenada, GUY = Guyana, JAM = Jamaica, KNA = St. Kitts and Nevis, LCA = St. Lucia, VCT = St. Vincent and the Grenadines, SUR = Suriname, and TTO = Trinidad and Tobago.

Global Economic Conditions

The current weak global growth and high commodity prices raise serious concerns about how Caribbean countries can revamp growth (see Figures 7.22 and 7.23). High commodity prices continue to exert pressure on the fiscal stance and the current account for commodity-importing countries.

Figure 7.22 Commodity Prices, 2000–13 *(Index: 2005=100)*

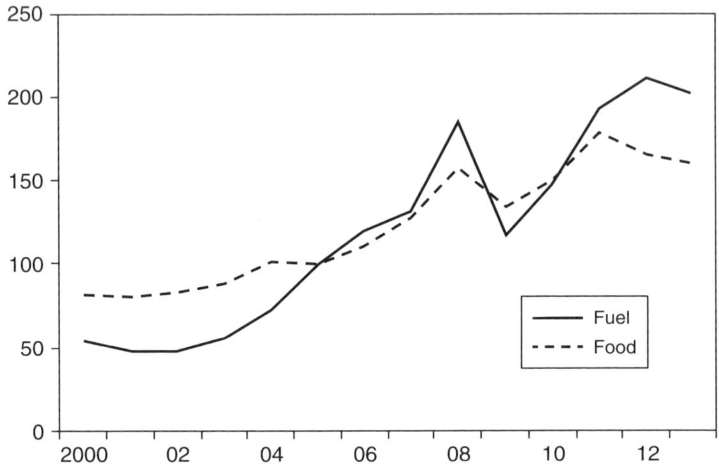

Source: World Economic Outlook database.

Figure 7.23 Economic Growth, 2000–13 *(Percent)*

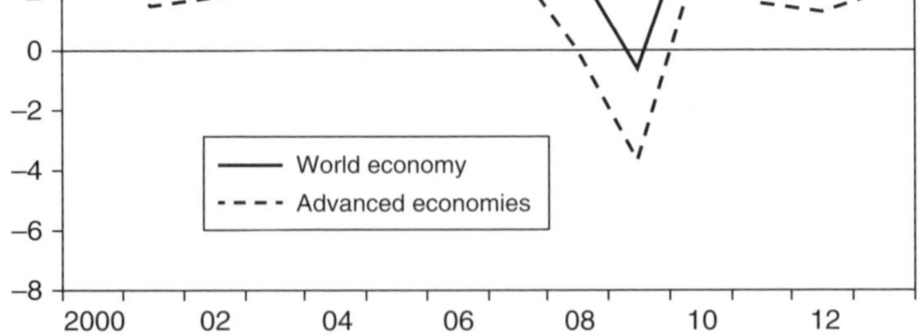

Source: World Economic Outlook database.

Figure 7.24 Tax Revenue by Country, 2011 *(Percent of GDP)*

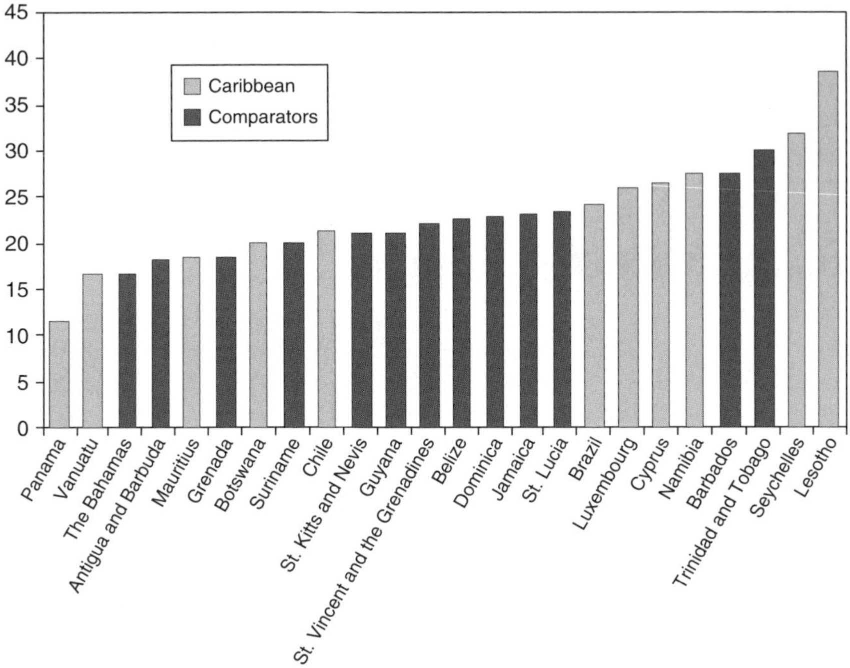

Source: World Economic Outlook database.

Limited Scope for Tax Increases

Some countries have very little room for strong fiscal efforts on the revenue side given that tax collections are already very high. Tax collection in Barbados, for instance, amounted to around 26 percent of GDP in 2011 (Figure 7.24).

Natural Disasters

The Caribbean region is prone to frequent natural disasters, such as hurricanes, tropical storms, and floods, whose social and economic impacts can be catastrophic. Hurricane Omar, which passed St. Kitts and Nevis in 2008, caused flooding in its major tourism resort and destroyed roads and coastal infrastructure. The impact on the tourism receipts in 2009 was estimated at more than 3 percent of GDP. The passage of Hurricane Sandy in 2012 also badly impacted broad economic activities in Jamaica; the hurricane's total cost there was estimated at more than US$55 million. Natural disasters pose challenges to fiscal consolidation by putting extra pressures on both the revenue side and the expenditure side. Severe disasters are followed by economic slowdowns and necessary reliefs, which reduce tax revenues, and by the rebuilding of damaged infrastructure, which increases expenditures.

Despite these challenges to fiscal consolidation, there is a need to reorient fiscal policy in the region given that debt levels are so high. Unlike in the past, there is currently no fiscal space that can be used to boost economic growth. Rather, countries need to adjust to lower their debt ratios. Fiscal multipliers in the Caribbean are quite low (see Chapter 8), suggesting that any negative impact of fiscal consolidation on growth would be smaller than in other countries. Caribbean countries can learn from successful fiscal consolidations in other regions to guide their current efforts (see Chapter 5).

SUMMARY AND CONCLUSIONS

This chapter analyzed the fiscal consolidation experiences of 14 countries in the Caribbean region, covering a sample period from 1980 to 2011, with differences in size across countries, due to data availability. It found that relative to the overall sample, the rate of fiscal consolidation in the region is 30 percent, on average, which seems moderate and broadly consistent with findings in advanced countries. The consolidation efforts, as reflected in the consolidation rate and the size of adjustment, appear to have waned over time. However, in terms of achieving a debt-to-GDP reduction of at least 5 percentage points, the success rate is 47 percent, on average. This would suggest that it would be desirable for the authorities to engage in more fiscal consolidation, since they tended to be successful nearly half the time. The analysis also reveals that fiscal consolidations have been more successful in commodity-exporting economies than in tourism-dependent economies.

Although fiscal consolidation in the region has consistently declined over time, the experience is broadly comparable with the findings for advanced countries. Likewise, as in other countries, the duration of fiscal adjustments in the Caribbean is generally short, possibly reflecting the difficulty of sustaining consolidation efforts. Meanwhile, the historically low public-debt-to-GDP ratios in some countries, such as The Bahamas and St. Lucia, could explain why fiscal consolidation, as defined in this chapter failed to achieve significant debt reductions in these countries over the period.

Even though fiscal consolidation efforts are ongoing in the region, these countries are generating much lower primary fiscal surpluses than is needed to reduce the public-debt-to-GDP ratio. Debt sustainability analysis suggests that stabilizing those ratios at 2011 levels would require a fiscal adjustment of around 1 percent of GDP. If the adjustments were to come mainly from spending cuts, this would translate into large real spending cuts for a number of countries. Reducing public debt ratios to 60 percent of GDP by 2020 would require even stronger fiscal adjustments.

Fiscal consolidation in the Caribbean therefore faces a number of challenges: high debt levels, fiscal rigidity, natural disasters, a weak global environment, and the limited scope for high revenue increases in some countries. Despite these challenges, there is a need to reorient fiscal policy in the region given that the debt levels are so high. There is currently no fiscal space that can be used to boost economic growth, however. Rather, the countries will need to adjust to lower their debt ratios. Fiscal multipliers in the Caribbean are quite low, suggesting that any negative impact of fiscal consolidation on growth would be smaller than it would be elsewhere. Caribbean countries can learn from successful fiscal consolidation in other regions to guide their current efforts.

REFERENCES

Ahrend, Rudiger, Pietro Catte, and Roberto Price, 2006, "Interactions Between Monetary and Fiscal Policy: How Monetary Conditions Affect Fiscal Consolidation," Economics Department Working Paper No. 5 (Paris: Organization for Economic Co-operation and Development).

Alesina, Alberto, and Silvia Ardagna, 2009, "Large Changes in Fiscal Policy: Taxes versus Spending," NBER Working Paper No. 15438 (Cambridge, Massachusetts: National Bureau of Economic Research).

Alesina, Alberto, Silvia Ardagna, and Jordi Gali, 1998, "Tales of Fiscal Adjustments," *Economic Policy*, Vol. 13, No. 27, pp. 487–545.

Alesina, Alberto, Dorian Carloni, and Giampaolo Lecce, 2012, "The Electoral Consequences of Large Fiscal Adjustments," NBER Working Paper No. 17655 (Cambridge, Massachusetts: National Bureau of Economic Research).

Ardagna, Silvia, 2004, "Fiscal Stabilizations: When Do They Work and Why," *European Economic Review*, Vol. 48, No. 5, pp. 1047–74.

Barrios, Salvador, Sven Langedijk, and Lucio Pench, 2010, "EU Fiscal Consolidation after the Financial Crisis: Lessons from Past Experiences," Economic Paper No. 418 (Brussels: European Commission).

Biggs, Andrew G., Kelvin A. Hasset, and Matthew Jensen, 2010, "A Guide for Deficit Reduction in the United States based on Historical Consolidations that Worked," AEI Economic Policy Working Paper No. 2010–04 (Washington: American Enterprise Institute for Public Policy Research).

Giavazzi, Francesco, Tullio Jappelli, and Marco Pagano, 2000, "Searching for Non-Linear Effects of Fiscal Policy: Evidence from Industrial and Developing Countries," *European Economic Review*, Vol. 44, pp. 1259–89.

Giudice, Gabriele, Alessandro Turrini, and Jan in't Veld, 2007, "Non-Keynesian Fiscal Adjustments? A Close Look at Expansionary Fiscal Consolidations in the EU," *Open Economies Review*, Vol. 18, No. 5, pp. 613–30.

Hernandez de Cos, Pablo, and Enrique Moral-Benito, 2012, "Fiscal Consolidations: Impact on Growth and Determinants of Success." Paper presented at the eleventh Journées Louis-André Gérard-Varet, Institute of Public Economics, Marseille (France), June 18–20.

Kumar, S. Manmohan, Daniel Leigh, and Alexander Plekhanov, 2007, "Fiscal Adjustments: Determinants and Macroeconomic Consequences," IMF Working Paper 07/178 (Washington: International Monetary Fund).

Lambertini, Luisa, and Jose Tavares, 2005, "Exchange Rates and Fiscal Adjustments: Evidence from the OECD and Implications for the EMU," *Contributions to Macroeconomics*, Vol. 5, No. 1, Article 11.

Larch, Martin, and Alessandro Turrini, 2011, "Received Wisdom and Beyond: Lessons from Fiscal Consolidation in the EU," *National Institute Economic Review*, Vol. 217, R1.

Tsibouris, George C., Mark A. Horton, Mark J. Flanagan, and Wojciech S. Maliszewski, 2006, "Experience with Large Fiscal Adjustments," IMF Occasional Paper No. 246 (Washington: International Monetary Fund).

Von Hagen, Jurgen, Andre Hughes Hallet, and Rolf Strauch, 2002, "Budgetary Consolidation in Europe: Quality, Economic Conditions, and Persistence," *Journal of the Japanese and International Economies*, Vol. 16, pp. 512–35.

CHAPTER 8

Fiscal Multipliers in the Caribbean

MACHIKO NARITA

The recent global financial crisis has drawn renewed attention to the effectiveness of fiscal policy, as many countries implemented fiscal stimulus measures to boost economic activity. The effectiveness of fiscal policy is often assessed by the size of fiscal multipliers, which measure a change in output caused by an exogenous change in government spending or tax revenue. This chapter estimates fiscal multipliers for the Caribbean using quarterly data for 14 Caribbean countries,[1] and investigates key determinants of the size of the multipliers. The results show that fiscal multipliers in the sample countries are modest, and that the high levels of trade openness and public debt account for their modest size.

FISCAL MULTIPLIERS

Different multipliers are used in the literature, depending on the time frame considered. The most frequently used measure is the impact multiplier, which is defined as $\Delta Y_t / \Delta G_t$, where ΔY_t is a change in output and ΔG_t is a change in government expenditure in period t. The impact multiplier measures the increase in output generated by an additional dollar in government spending in period t. Another frequently used notion is the cumulative multiplier, which is defined as

$$\sum_{j=0}^{N} \Delta Y_{t+j} \,/\, \sum_{j=0}^{N} \Delta G_{t+j}.$$

Since fiscal stimulus packages can only be implemented over time and there may be lags in the economy's response, the cumulative multiplier may be more accurate in capturing the impact of fiscal policy. We can define tax-revenue multipliers in the same way.

Interpreting fiscal multipliers requires caution, because they are not deep structural parameters. Instead, they consist of policy reactions and structural parameters. That is, fiscal multipliers depend on various factors that can differ from case to case, such as the fiscal policy instrument, its duration, its associated fiscal adjustments, the stance of monetary policy, and country-specific circumstances. Multipliers are therefore best interpreted as empirical summaries of average output reactions following exogenous changes in government spending or tax revenue.

[1]Appendix 8.1 shows the sample countries and periods included in the analysis.

Theories of Fiscal Multipliers

Different theories provide different mechanisms for fiscal multipliers, but they all highlight the importance of hours worked in explaining the short-run multipliers.[2] Since the capital stock cannot be adjusted instantaneously, only hours worked can increase total output in the short term. Therefore, the short-run multipliers are essentially accounted for by the response of equilibrium hours worked to a fiscal policy and the extent to which those hours translate to output.

The Keynesian tradition explains fiscal multipliers through demand-side effects. Assuming that an economy is constrained by demand, not by supply, Keynesian theory says that government spending increases demand, which raises incomes, which in turn leads to private sector spending. In the extreme case where wages and prices do not respond, the multiplier is given by $1/(1 - mpc)$ for spending and $-mpc/(1 - mpc)$ for taxes, where mpc is the marginal propensity to consume. The multipliers become smaller according to the extent of price adjustment, and zero in another extreme case where wages and prices are infinitely responsive. The multipliers also depend on the monetary policy; they become larger when the central bank keeps the nominal interest rate constant. In a new Keynesian model calibrated to the U.S. economy, Christiano, Eichenbaum, and Rebelo (2011) show that when government spending rises for 12 quarters while the nominal interest rate is kept constant, the multiplier is about 1.6 on impact and attains a peak at around 2.3.

The neoclassical tradition provides a mechanism for fiscal multipliers through supply-side effects. In neoclassical models, economic agents react to a fiscal policy if it changes the present value of income or intertemporal trade-offs. For example, a tax cut with a future tax increase in a nondistortionary way does not affect the present value of income, so its multiplier is zero (Ricardian Equivalence). On the other hand, a fiscal policy that involves distortionary adjustments can generate either positive or negative effects on output. For example, when government spending temporarily rises but a current distortionary labor tax also increases to keep the budget balanced, the impact multiplier can be negative (Baxter and King, 1993). If an increase in government spending is financed with a deficit, the impact multiplier is larger because of intertemporal substitution effects: economic agents work more today because they expect a higher tax in the future.

Empirical Studies on Fiscal Multipliers

The size of the fiscal multiplier varies with countries, time periods, and circumstances. Previous studies have suggested a number of factors that influence the size, including trade openness, public debt level, exchange rate regime, and state of the economy.[3]

---

[2]Ramey (2011) and Chinn (2013) provide comprehensive surveys of theoretical work.

[3]Baunsgaard and others (forthcoming) provides a comprehensive literature review on key determinants of the size of the fiscal multipliers.

- *Trade openness:* Fiscal multipliers are smaller for countries with a larger propensity to import (IMF, 2008; Ilzetzki, Mendoza, and Végh, 2009; Barrel, Holland, and Hurst, 2012), because additional demand created by the fiscal policy will "leak" through imports.
- *Public debt level:* Fiscal multipliers are smaller for countries with higher levels of public debt (Ilzetzki, Mendoza, and Végh, 2009; and Kirchner, Cimadomo, and Hauptmeier, 2010), because expansionary fiscal policies in countries with large public debt imply a risk to fiscal sustainability and the need for fiscal tightening in the near future.
- *Exchange rate regime:* Fiscal multipliers are larger for countries with a fixed exchange rate regime (Ilzetzki, Mendoza, and Végh, 2009). This is because the "leakage" through the currency appreciation caused by a fiscal expansion would be minimal in a country with a fixed exchange rate regime.
- *State of the economy:* Fiscal multipliers are larger during economic recessions, when there is substantial slack in the economy (Auerbach and Gorodnichenko, 2012a, 2012b; Baum, Poplawski-Ribeiro, and Weber, 2012; Blanchard and Leigh, 2013; IMF, 2012). Larger multipliers reflect larger shares of liquidity-constrained (hand-to-mouth) households and firms (Gali, López-Salido, and Vallés, 2007; Parker, 2011).

The range of estimated fiscal multipliers varies considerably. Baunsgaard and others (forthcoming) review a large number of empirical studies and report that the spending multipliers in the first year range between 0.3 and 2.1 for the United States and between 0.3 and 1.8 for the European countries. They also report a range for the tax multiplier, which is –0.7 to –1.4 for the United States and –0.5 to 0.7 for Europe. Kraay (2012) finds that the first-year spending multiplier for developing countries is around 0.4. Ilzetzki, Mendoza, and Végh (2009) find that economies with relatively low degrees of openness to trade (measured as exports plus imports as a proportion of GDP) have a cumulative multiplier of around 1.6 after 24 quarters, but relatively open economies have an almost zero multiplier. They further find that the cumulative multiplier is about 1.5 after 24 quarters for economies under fixed exchange-rate regimes, but it is essentially zero in economies under flexible exchange regimes.

Fiscal multipliers in the Caribbean are low, according to the existing empirical studies. Guy and Belgrave (2012) find that the cumulative multipliers are less than 0.3 after 24 quarters in their sample countries over the period 1980–2008. They find that the first-year spending multiplier is 0.14 for Barbados, 0.11 for Jamaica, 0.18 for Trinidad and Tobago, and negative for Guyana. The cumulative spending multiplier after 24 quarters is at 0.2 for Barbados, 0.3 for Jamaica, and negative for Guyana and Trinidad and Tobago. Guy and Belgrave (2012) argue that although public expenditures are initially increased in a downturn to stimulate productive sectors, they are typically not sustained due to the constraints of declining revenues and high debt ratios.

Gonzalez-Garcia, Lemus, and Mrkaic (2013) estimate fiscal multipliers in the Eastern Caribbean Currency Union (ECCU) and find that the multipliers of consumption and investment spending range from 0.1 to 0.3 on impact and from 0.2 to 0.62 after 24 quarters; and that only the long-run investment multiplier is statistically significantly different from zero. These modest Keynesian effects in the Caribbean countries could be due to a combination of factors discussed in the literature, such as the degree of openness[4] and high debt levels.

METHODOLOGY AND DATA

We estimate fiscal multipliers using structural vector autoregression (SVAR) models and quarterly data for Caribbean countries.[5] Specifically, we consider multipliers of spending and tax revenue of central governments, as well as those of spending components: consumption spending and capital spending. The impact and cumulative multipliers are constructed using the dynamic response of GDP to shocks in fiscal variables, which are the estimated SVAR impulse response functions. Appendix 8.1 provides data sources and definitions of variables, such as "government spending," and Appendix 8.2 describes our empirical model.

Our analysis focuses on fiscal multipliers for a group of countries instead of those for individual countries. Although fiscal multipliers in individual countries could be heterogeneous and informative, obtaining reliable estimates for them is difficult for many Caribbean countries given the limited number of observations available. In addition, Ilzetzki, Mendoza, and Végh (2009) and Gonzalez-Garcia, Lemus, and Mrkaic (2013) illustrate that panel VAR techniques are useful in providing characteristics of "average" multipliers for a group of economies and for analyzing the determinants of the size of fiscal multipliers by comparing those in different groups.

ESTIMATED FISCAL MULTIPLIERS

Effects of an Expenditure Shock

Fiscal stimulus policies boost real GDP, but their effects tend to be short-lived in the Caribbean. Figures 8.1 and 8.2 show the estimated impulse response function (solid line) and its 95 percent confidence interval (dotted lines). The results, based on the 14 Caribbean countries studied, indicate that real GDP increases for about a year after a positive shock in government spending. Specifically, a one-standard-deviation shock in government spending increases real GDP by 20 basis points per quarter for about a year, but the effect tapers off afterwards.

The spending multiplier in the Caribbean is small on impact and modest in the long run.[6] The impact multiplier of government spending is 0.13, which

---

[4]Endegnanew, Amo-Yartey, and Turner-Jones (2012) show that fiscal policies affect the current account in microstates; a strengthening of the fiscal balance improves the current account.

[5]The effects of fiscal policies are identified in a SVAR model by assuming that fiscal authorities require at least one quarter to respond to output shocks (Blanchard and Perotti, 2002).

[6]The 95 confidence intervals of the cumulative multipliers are computed by Monte Carlo simulations based on 500 replications.

means an additional dollar of government consumption generates only 13 cents of additional output in the quarter when it is implemented. The cumulative multiplier grows modestly to its peak at 0.6 in the seventh quarter and then converges to its long-run value of 0.53, which can be considered a moderate size[7] (see Figure 8.3). The cumulative multiplier converges to the long-run value in two years because the output response to a spending shock becomes almost zero after two years, as we can see in the "response" charts (Figures 8.1 and 8.2).

"Leakages" through imports are important for understanding the modest level of the spending multiplier in the region. The trade openness there, defined as exports and imports in percent of GDP, exceeds 100 percent on average during 1990–2012. In fact, the Caribbean average of trade openness is the second highest among all regions during this period (Figure 8.4). As discussed in Endegnanew, Amo-Yartey, and Turner-Jones (2012), the proportion of imports in domestic consumption is high in small states, including most Caribbean and Pacific island countries, due to their small domestic market and the tendency toward a high degree of specialization in production. The effects of a fiscal policy would be limited if the policy led to importing additional goods and services from abroad instead of stimulating domestic consumption and investment. Ilzetzki, Mendoza, and Végh (2009) empirically show that trade openness is one of the critical determinants of the size of fiscal multipliers.

Figure 8.1 Response of GDP to a Spending Shock, Caribbean Region Average

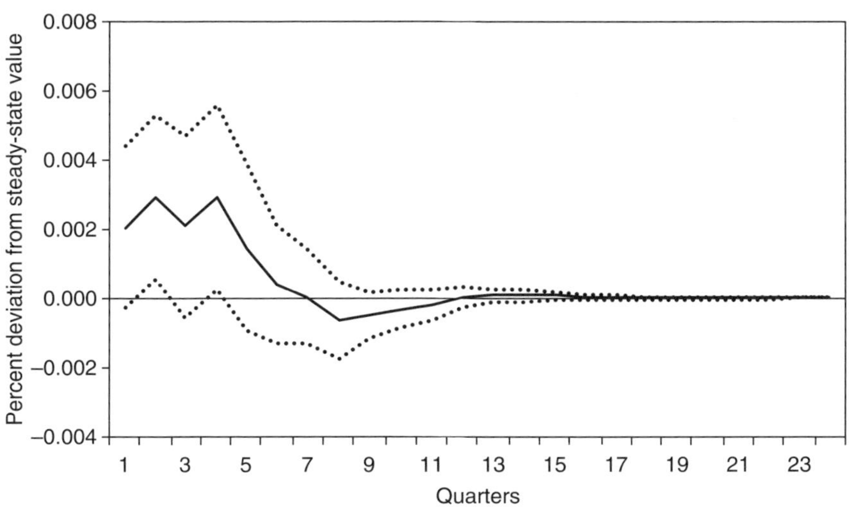

Source: Author's calculations.
Note: Dotted lines indicate the 95 percent confidence interval of the impulse response functions (solid line).

[7]The cumulative multiplier of 0.53 after 24 quarters can be considered as moderate. For example, Perotti (2005) finds that the cumulative spending multiplier ranges from 0.3 to 1.4 after 20 quarters for five Organization for Economic Co-operation and Development member countries.

Figure 8.2 Response of Spending to a Spending Shock, Caribbean Region Average

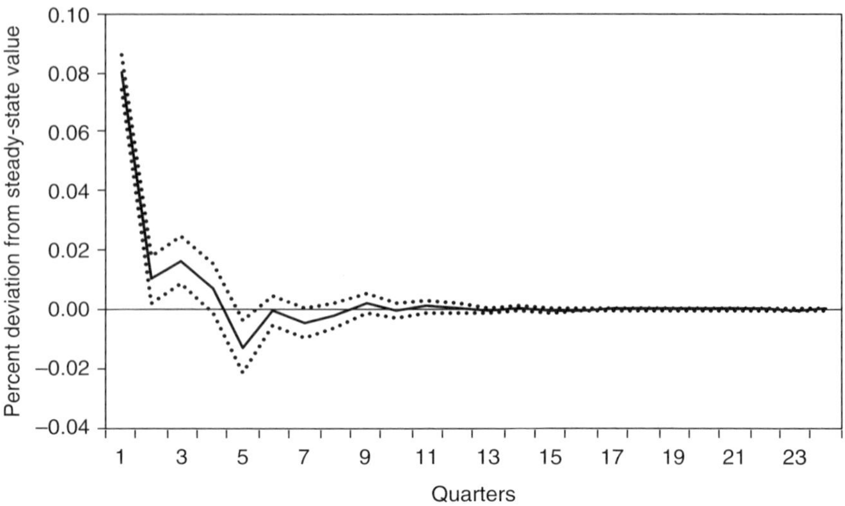

Source: Author's calculations.
Note: Dotted lines indicate the 95 percent confidence interval of the impulse response functions (solid line).

Figure 8.3 Cumulative Spending Multiplier on GDP, Caribbean Region Average

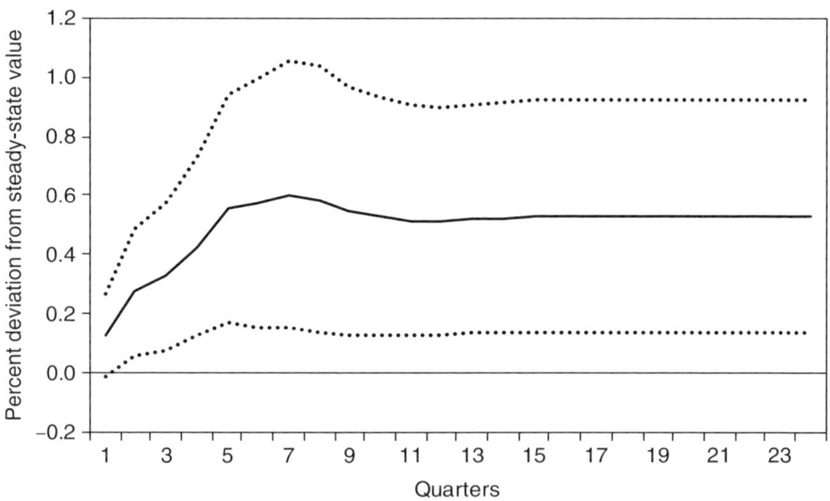

Source: Author's calculations.
Note: Dotted lines indicate the 95 percent confidence interval of the cumulative multiplier (solid line).

By contrast, the spending multiplier on imports in the Caribbean is actually sizable and significant. It is defined as the cumulative change in imports over the cumulative change in government spending at some horizon, and in our sample it is estimated for countries where quarterly import data are also

Figure 8.4 Openness to Trade by Global Region, 1990–2012 *(Average, percent of GDP)*

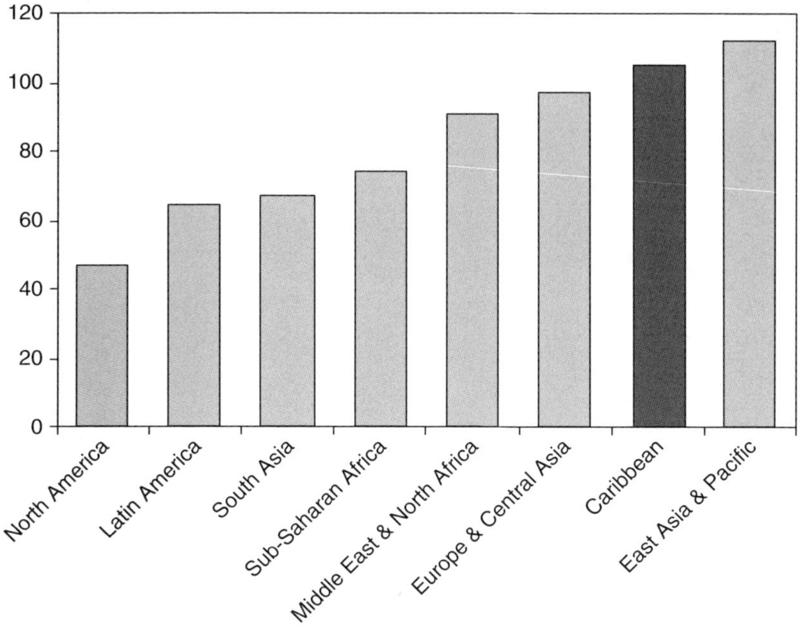

Sources: World Economic Outlook database; and author's calculations.
Note: Openness to trade is defined as exports plus imports in percent of GDP. Each bar indicates the average in each region during 1990–2012.

available.[8] The spending multiplier on imports is 0.4 on impact, increases at its peak to 0.97 in the seventh quarter, and converges to its long-run value of 0.83 (Figure 8.5). That is, the "leakage" of an additional one dollar in fiscal spending is 4 cents in the first quarter and 83 cents in the long run. This result supports the previous studies that show lower multipliers in economies that are open to trade.

The public debt level is another critical factor affecting the size of multipliers suggested in the literature and relevant for the Caribbean region. We divide the sample countries into two groups—a high-debt group and a low-debt group—and estimate and compare the multipliers across groups. The high (low) debt group includes countries whose average central government debt-to-GDP ratio during the sample period is above (below) 65 percent. Figure 8.6 identifies these two groups.

We also confirm that the level of public debt is another critical factor explaining the relatively small spending multiplier in the region.[9] Results show that the cumulative multipliers of government spending are lower for high-debt countries, which is consistent with the evidence in the literature (Figures 8.7 and 8.8). The cumulative multiplier for high-debt countries becomes essentially zero after two

[8]These countries are Antigua and Barbuda, The Bahamas, Dominica, Grenada, St. Kitts and Nevis, St. Lucia, and St. Vincent and the Grenadines.

[9]Using different thresholds, such as 50 or 60 percent of debt to GDP ratio, does not change our results.

Figure 8.5 Cumulative Spending Multiplier on Imports, Caribbean Region Average

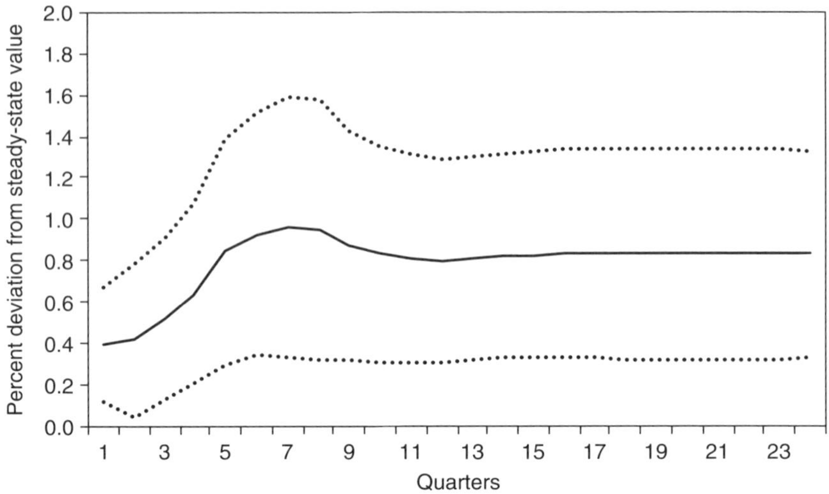

Source: Author's calculations.
Note: Dotted lines indicate the 95 percent confidence interval of the cumulative multiplier (solid line).

Figure 8.6 Central Government Debt-to-GDP Ratio by Country *(Percent)*

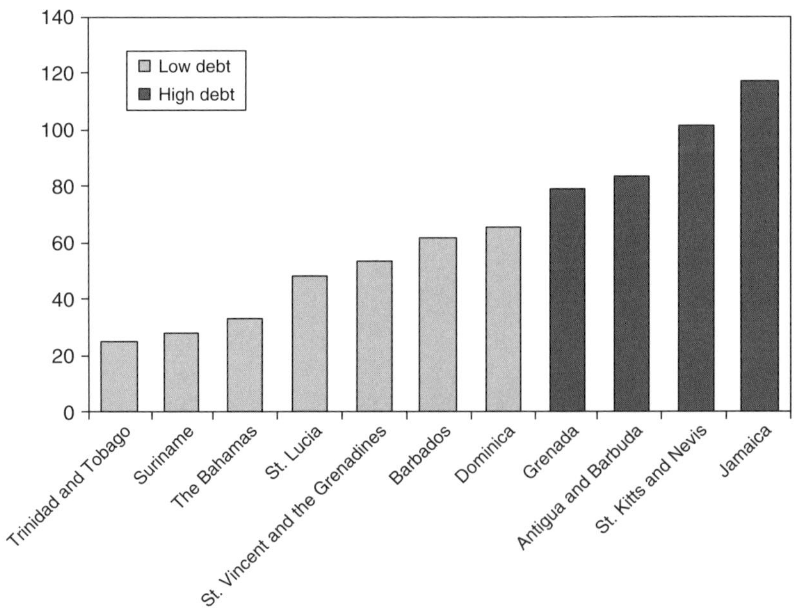

Sources: National authorities; and author's calculations.
Note: Figure shows the average of the debt-to-GDP ratio during the sample period used for the estimation: Antigua and Barbuda, 2003–11; The Bahamas, 1997–2011; Barbados, 2003–06; Dominica, 2000–11; Grenada, 2003–11; St. Lucia, 2000–11; St. Vincent and the Grenadines, 2000–11; Suriname, 2002–08; Trinidad and Tobago, 2000–11. See also Appendix Table 8.1.

Figure 8.7 Cumulative Spending Multiplier (High Debt), Caribbean Region Average

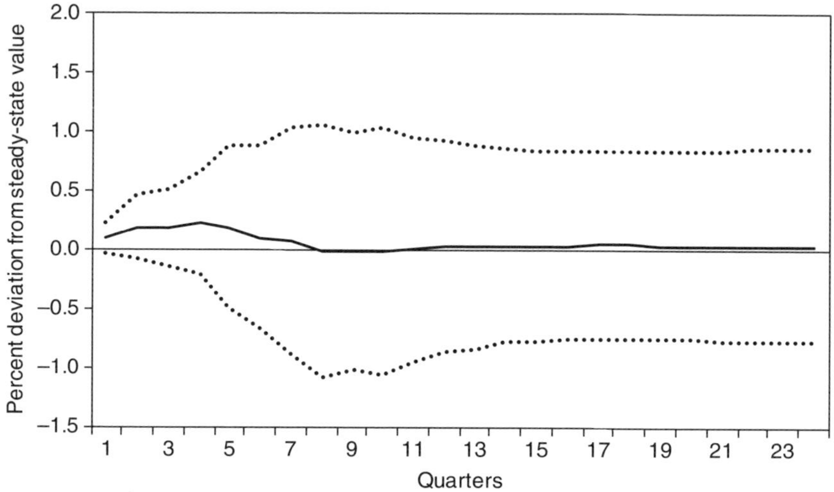

Source: Author's calculations.
Note: Dotted lines indicate the 95 percent confidence interval of the cumulative multiplier (solid line).

Figure 8.8 Cumulative Spending Multiplier (Low Debt), Caribbean Region Average

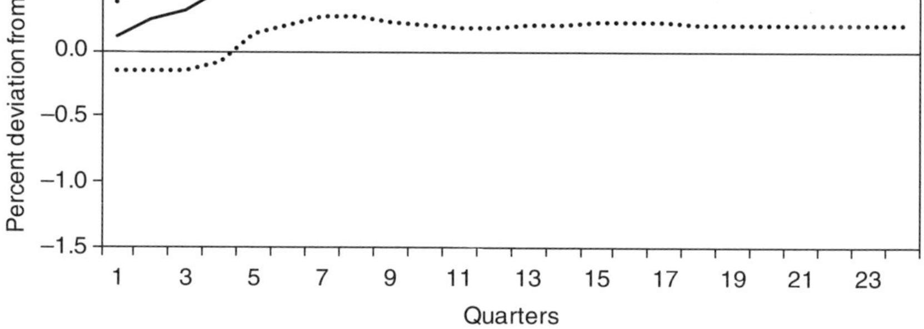

Source: Author's calculations.
Note: Dotted lines indicate the 95 percent confidence interval of the cumulative multiplier (solid line).

years, while the one for low-debt countries converges to 0.77 and is statistically significant. This result suggests that fiscal expansions may have weakened fiscal sustainability and decreased the confidence of economic agents when the public debt level is high. Consumers and investors might act in a precautionary fashion against a fiscal stimulus policy if they are concerned about debt sustainability.

Effects of a Tax Cut

In estimating the tax multiplier, we need the estimates of the within-quarter elasticity of taxes with respect to output for all countries[10] (see Appendix 8.2 for the technical explanation). In this analysis, as a bold reference, we take the tax elasticity estimate of 2.08 for the U.S. economy from Blanchard and Perotti (2002). That is, in our analysis here, we assume that tax revenue responds to unexpected output movements within the quarter at an elasticity of 2.08 (Figure 8.9). Considering that several countries in the Caribbean do not have broad-based consumption taxes and/or income taxes (dos Santos and Bain, 2004), one can argue that the within-quarter tax elasticity in the Caribbean could be much lower than that in the United States. Therefore, one can interpret our estimate of the tax multiplier as an upper bound for the actual tax multiplier in the Caribbean.

A tax cut boosts real GDP immediately, but its effect is not persistent. Figure 8.10 shows the estimated impulse response functions to a negative shock in tax revenue (solid line) along with 95 percent confidence intervals (dotted lines). Real GDP rises by 80 basis points after a one-standard-deviation negative shock in tax revenue, but the effect dies out after two years.

The estimated tax multiplier is also modest in the region (Figure 8.11). The impact tax multiplier of –0.51 indicates that a tax reduction of one dollar would

Figure 8.9 Response of GDP to a Negative Tax Shock, Caribbean Region Average

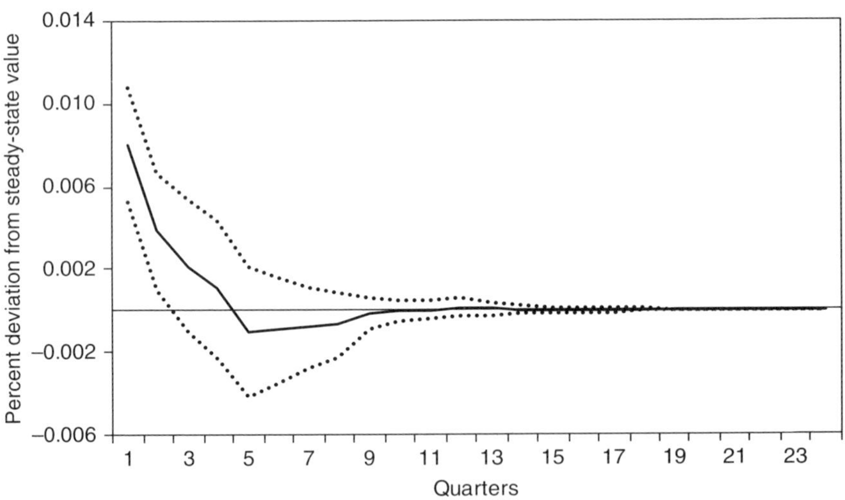

Source: Author's calculations.
Note: Dotted lines indicate the 95 percent confidence interval of the impulse response functions (solid line). The underlying elasticity of tax with respect to output is set at 2.08.

[10]The tax elasticity changes the magnitude of the initial responses.

Figure 8.10 Response of Tax Revenue to a Negative Tax Shock, Caribbean Region Average

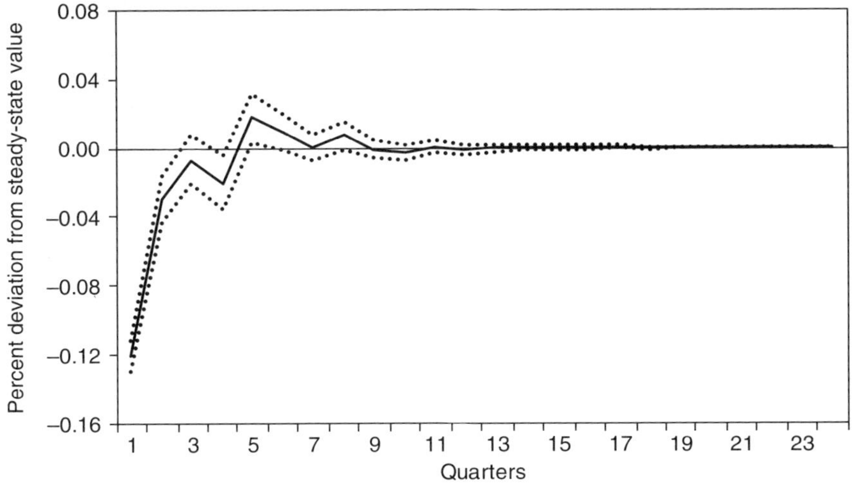

Source: Author's calculations.

Note: Dotted lines indicate the 95 percent confidence interval of the impulse response functions (solid line). The underlying elasticity of tax with respect to output is set at 2.08.

Figure 8.11 Cumulative Tax Multiplier on GDP, Caribbean Region Average

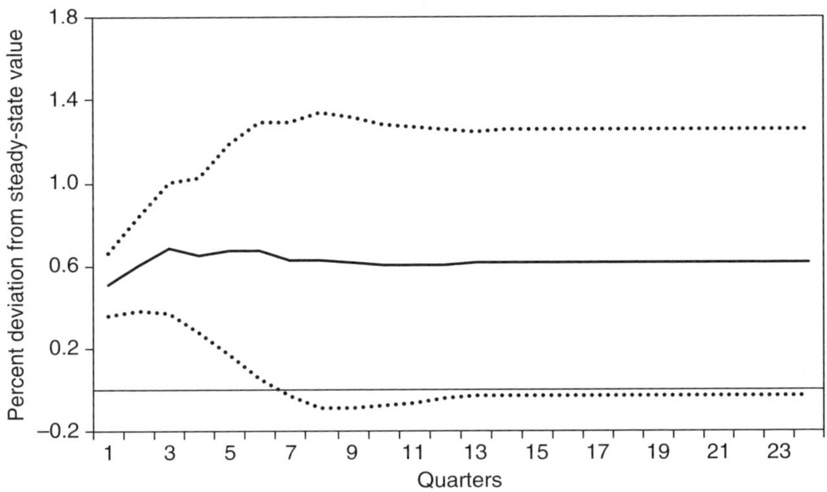

Source: Author's calculations.

Note: Dotted lines indicate the 95 percent confidence interval of the cumulative multiplier (solid line). The underlying elasticity of tax with respect to output is set at 2.08.

deliver an additional output of 51 cents. This is slightly larger than the impact multiplier of government spending and statistically significant, but it is still less than one. In addition, as discussed above, if the *true* elasticity of taxes with respect to output in the Caribbean is smaller than the U.S. elasticity of 2.08, the implied impact multiplier of tax revenue is less than 0.51. The cumulative tax multiplier quickly converges to its long-run value at 0.62 as the output response to a tax reduction tapers off after the first quarter. The point estimate of the long-run tax multiplier is larger than the long-run spending multiplier of 0.53, but it is not significantly different from zero.

SUMMARY AND CONCLUSION

This chapter addressed one of the important macroeconomic policy questions: To what extent do governments' spending expansions or tax cuts stimulate economic activities in the Caribbean? We examined this question using panel structural vector autoregression (SVAR) methods and quarterly data on 14 Caribbean countries.

The estimated fiscal multipliers in the Caribbean are modest, consistent with evidence from existing empirical studies (Guy and Belgrave, 2012; and Gonzalez-Garcia, Lemus, and Mrkaic, 2013). The impact multiplier of government spending is 0.13 and the cumulative multiplier is 0.53 after 24 quarters. The tax multiplier is 0.51 on impact and 0.62 after 24 quarters.

The modest size of fiscal multipliers can be accounted for by the region's high levels of trade openness and public debt. We find that the "leakages" through imports are actually positive and statistically significant. In addition, we find that the cumulative spending multiplier is essentially zero in the subgroup of high-public-debt countries, while it is 0.77 and statistically significant in the subgroup of low-public-debt countries.

One important caveat is that the estimated multipliers are not deep structural parameters, so their interpretation needs caution. As discussed in the opening section of this chapter, the empirical literature emphasizes that fiscal multipliers can differ with countries, time periods, and circumstances because they are made of response functions as well as deep parameters. The estimated multiplier is the average output response to an exogenous change in a fiscal policy during the sample period, and it is not necessarily the predicted effectiveness of a fiscal policy under consideration.

APPENDIX 8.1. DATA SOURCES AND PROCESSING

Data are sourced from various publications from central banks, their web sites, and the IMF's International Financial Statistics database. We construct a panel data set, which includes quarterly data of fiscal variables and GDP for 14 Caribbean countries. Appendix Table 8.1 reports the countries included in our analysis and the sample periods of main variables.

Fiscal variables used in the analysis are defined as follows. Tax revenue (*Tax*) is defined as the central government's tax revenue net of taxes on international trade. We exclude taxes on international trade because our focus is on the effects of tax cuts on domestic activities. Government spending (*Spen*) is defined as the sum of consumption spending (*Cons*) and capital spending (*Capx*) by the central government. *Cons* is defined as current expenditure net of interest payments and transfers.

For countries without quarterly GDP data, it is imputed using the interpolation method of Chow and Lin (1971). The interpolation method uses variation of quarterly series, which are relevant to the economy, in imputing the quarterly variation of real GDP. Among available quarterly series, we select a set of variables used for the imputation for each country, considering its main economic activities and the performance of the regression model. The selected variables, which are reported in Appendix Table 8.2, typically include bank credit to the private sector, the number of stay-over tourists (for tourism countries), oil prices, and some indicators of U.S. economic activities. Nominal data, such as private credit and compensation to employees, are deflated by the consumer price index (CPI) of each economy.

Series used for the SVAR estimation are deflated, seasonally adjusted, and detrended. Nominal data are deflated using the CPI index. We take the natural logarithm of all variables, use the SEATS algorithm for seasonal adjustment, and detrend the series using the Hodrick-Prescott filter.

APPENDIX TABLE 8.1

Summary of Quarterly Data Series Used for Analysis

	The Bahamas	Barbados	Belize	Jamaica	Trinidad and Tobogo
Real GDP	...	1990:Q1–2011:Q4	1994:Q1–2011:Q4	1996:Q1–2011:Q4	2000:Q3–2011:Q3
Tax revenue	1998:Q1–2011:Q4	2003:Q2–2007:Q1	2005:Q2–2011:Q4	2003:Q2–2011:Q4	1991:Q1–2011:Q4
Spending	1999:Q1–2011:Q4	2003:Q2–2007:Q1	2005:Q2–2011:Q4	2003:Q2–2011:Q4	1991:Q1–2011:Q4
Imports of goods and services	2007:Q1–2011:Q4	...	...	...	...
Policy interest rate	1990:Q1–2011:Q4	1990:Q1–2011:Q4	1990:Q1–2011:Q4	1990:Q1–2011:Q4	1990:Q1–2011:Q4
REER	1990:Q1–2011:Q4	1990:Q1–2011:Q4	1990:Q1–2011:Q4	1990:Q1–2011:Q4	1990:Q1–2011:Q4
CPI	1990:Q1–2011:Q4	1990:Q1–2011:Q4	1990:Q1–2011:Q4	1990:Q1–2011:Q4	1990:Q1–2011:Q4
	Suriname	**Anguilla**	**Antigua and Barbuda**	**Dominica**	**Grenada**
Real GDP	...	...	...	...	...
Tax revenue	2002:Q1–2008:Q4	2000:Q1–2011:Q4	2003:Q1–2011:Q4	2000:Q1–2011:Q4	2003:Q1–2011:Q4
Spending	...	2008:Q1–2011:Q4	2004:Q1–2011:Q4	2000:Q1–2011:Q4	2003:Q1–2011:Q4
Imports of goods and services	...	...	2005:Q1–2011:Q4	2000:Q1–2011:Q4	2006:Q1–2011:Q4
Policy interest rate	1990:Q4–2011:Q4	1990:Q1–2011:Q4	1990:Q1–2011:Q4	1990:Q1–2011:Q4	1990:Q1–2011:Q4
REER	1990:Q1–2011:Q4	1990:Q1–2011:Q4	1990:Q1–2011:Q4	1990:Q1–2011:Q4	1990:Q1–2011:Q4
CPI	1990:Q1–2011:Q4	1998:Q1–2011:Q4	1998:Q1–2011:Q4	1990:Q1–2011:Q4	1990:Q1–2011:Q4
	Montserrat	**St. Kitts and Nevis**	**St. Lucia**	**St. Vincent and the Grenadines**	
Real GDP	...	...	...	...	
Tax revenue	2000:Q1–2011:Q4	2000:Q1–2011:Q4	2000:Q1–2011:Q4	2003:Q1–2011:Q4	
Spending	2010:Q1–2011:Q4	2000:Q1–2011:Q4	2000:Q1–2011:Q4	2000:Q1–2011:Q4	
Imports of goods and services	...	2000:Q1–2011:Q4	2000:Q1–2011:Q4	2001:Q1–2011:Q4	
Policy interest rate	1990:Q1–2011:Q4	1990:Q1–2011:Q4	1990:Q1–2011:Q4	1990:Q1–2011:Q4	
REER	1990:Q1–2011:Q4	1990:Q1–2011:Q4	1990:Q1–2011:Q4	1990:Q1–2011:Q4	
CPI	1990:Q1–2011:Q4	1990:Q1–2011:Q4	1990:Q1–2011:Q4	1990:Q1–2011:Q4	

Sources: Real GDP, fiscal data, and imports of goods and services are sourced from various publications from central banks and their websites. Policy interest rate, real effective exchange rate (REER), and consumer price index (CPI) are sourced from the IMF, International Financial Statistics database.

APPENDIX TABLE 8.2

Variables Used in the Interpolation of Quarterly Real GDP

	Variables
The Bahamas	Private credit; stay-over tourists; oil price; U.S. real GDP.
Anguilla	Private credit; stay-over tourists; oil price; U.S. index of industrial production.
Antigua and Barbuda	Private credit; stay-over tourists; oil price; U.S. index of industrial production (–1).
Dominica	Private credit; stay-over tourists; U.S. real compensation to employees (–1); U.S. real GDP (–1).
Grenada	Private credit; stay-over tourists; oil price; U.S. index of industrial production.
Montserrat	Private credit; stay-over tourists; U.S. real compensation to employees (–1); U.S. real GDP (–1).
St. Kitts and Nevis	Private credit; stay-over tourists; U.S. real compensation to employees (–1); U.S. real GDP (–1).
St. Lucia	Private credit; stay-over tourists; Domestic exports; U.S. real compensation to employees (–1).
Suriname	Private credit; oil price; gold price; U.S. real GDP.
St. Vincent and the Grenadines	Private credit; stay-over tourists; U.S. real compensation to employees (–1); U.S. real GDP (–1).

Sources: Central banks; the U.S. Federal Reserve Economic Data; and IMF, World Economic Outlook database.
Note: (–1) refers to the variable one year earlier.

APPENDIX 8.2. STRUCTURAL VECTOR AUTOREGRESSION MODELS AND ESTIMATION METHODS

Our baseline SVAR model is the following system of equations, which is similar to the specification in Gonzalez-Garcia, Lemus, and Mrkaic (2013):

$$AY_{i,t} = \sum_{p=1}^{P} C_{t-p} Y_{i,t-p} + \sum_{p=0}^{P} D_{t-p} Z_{i,t-p} + B\varepsilon_{i,t}, \tag{A1}$$

where $Y_{i,t}$ is a two-variable vector including a fiscal variable of interest (spending, tax revenue, consumption spending, or capital spending) and GDP of country i in quarter t; $Z_{i,t}$ is an N-dimensional vector of control variables, which are exogenous to the system; and $\varepsilon_{i,t}$ is a vector of two exogenous shocks.[11] In order to control for the effects from external shocks and monetary policies, $Z_{i,t}$ includes the real effective exchange rate, the U.S. GDP, and the interest rate of monetary policy. The matrix A allows for the possible simultaneous effects across the endogenous variables $Y_{i,t}$. The matrices C_{t-p} and D_{t-p} capture the effects from the pth lag of the endogenous variables Y_{t-p} and the exogenous variables Z_{t-p} on the current endogenous variables Y_t. The matrix B is diagonal, which contains standard deviations of exogenous shocks. We estimate the system (A1) by panel OLS regression with fixed effects.

The number of lags is set at four for both endogenous and exogenous variables in all estimations. We computed five criteria in determining how many lags to include in the equation: Akaike information criterion, Schwarz information criterion, modified sequential likelihood ratio criterion, final prediction error criterion, and Hannan-Quinn criterion. However, they were not very useful because the suggested number of lags differs across methods and often takes a maximum number of lags considered. Therefore, we use four lags in all analyses because the results do not differ substantially from those using other suggested numbers of lags[12] and because it is often the choice of other related studies, including Ilzetzki, Mendoza, and Végh (2011) and Gonzalez-Garcia, Lemus, and Mrkaic (2013).

The SVAR model (1) needs additional assumptions in order to identify the effect of fiscal policies. The identification issue exists because fiscal policies and output could affect each other. We use the short-term restriction proposed by Blanchard and Perotti (2002): it takes more than one quarter for policymakers and the legislatures to learn about and to respond to a GDP shock. This implies that the contemporaneous effect of a GDP shock on government spending and tax revenue is only through automatic feedback, which is zero for government spending. For tax revenue, Blanchard and Perotti (2002) estimate within-quarter elasticity of taxes with respect to output using detailed data on taxes and tax bases from 1947:Q1 to 1997:Q4 in the United States. For the analysis in this chapter, we use their estimated elasticity in generating the baseline tax results. Therefore, the estimated tax multiplier can be overestimated because the *true* tax elasticity in the Caribbean may be smaller due to narrower tax bases, as is discussed in this chapter.

---

[11] We use imports instead of GDP when we estimate the multipliers on imports.

[12] Although the suggested number of lags varies, four lags are sometimes actually suggested.

REFERENCES

Auerbach, Alan J., and Yuriy Gorodnichenko, 2012a, "Fiscal Multipliers in Recession and Expansion," Paper prepared for the NBER conference, "Fiscal Policy after the Financial Crisis," Milan, December 2011.

———, 2012b, "Measuring the Output Responses to Fiscal Policy," *American Economic Journal*, Vol. 4, No. 2, May.

Barrel, Ray, Dawn Holland, and Ian Hurst, 2012, "Fiscal Consolidation: Part 2. Fiscal Multipliers and Fiscal Consolidations," OECD Economics Department Working Paper No. 933 (Paris: Organization for Economic Co-operation and Development, February).

Baum, Anja, Marcos Poplawski-Ribeiro, and Anke Weber, 2012, "Fiscal Multipliers and the State of the Economy," IMF Working Paper 12/286 (Washington: International Monetary Fund).

Baunsgaard, T., A. Mineshima, M. Poplawski-Ribeiro, and A. Weber, forthcoming, "Fiscal Multipliers," in *Post-Crisis Fiscal Policy*, ed. by C. Cottarelli, P. Gerson, and A. Senhadji (Boston: MIT Press).

Baxter, Marianne, and Robert G. King, 1993, "Fiscal Policy in General Equilibrium," *American Economic Review*, Vol. 83, pp. 315–34.

Blanchard, Olivier, and Daniel Leigh, 2013, "Growth Forecast Errors and Fiscal Multipliers," IMF Working Paper 13/1 (Washington: International Monetary Fund).

———, and Roberto Perotti, 2002, "An Empirical Characterization of the Dynamic Effects of Changes in Government Spending and Taxes on Output," *Quarterly Journal of Economics*, Vol. 117, pp. 1329–68.

Chinn, Menzie David, 2013, "Fiscal Multipliers," Working Paper No. 2015–02, La Follette School of Public Affairs.

Chow, Gregory, and An-Loh Lin, 1971, "Best Linear Unbiased Interpolation, Distribution, and Extrapolation of Time Series by Related Series," *Review of Economics and Statistics*, Vol. 53, pp. 372–75.

Christiano, Lawrence J., Martin Eichenbaum, and Sergio Rebelo, 2011, "When Is the Government Spending Multiplier Large?" *Journal of Political Economy*, Vol. 119, pp. 78–121.

dos Santos, Paulo, and Laurel Bain, 2004, "Survey on the Caribbean Tax Systems," Paper prepared for the 18th General Assembly and Technical Conference of the Caribbean Organization of Tax Administrators (COTA), Nassau, The Bahamas, July 2004.

Endegnanew, Yehenew, Charles Amo-Yartey, and Therese Turner-Jones, 2012, "Fiscal Policy and the Current Account: Are Microstates Different?" IMF Working Paper 12/51 (Washington: International Monetary Fund).

Galí, Jordi, J. David López-Salido, and Javier Vallés, 2007, "Understanding the Effects of Government Spending on Consumption," *Journal of the European Economic Association*, Vol. 5, No. 1, pp. 227–70.

Gonzalez-Garcia, Jesus, Antonio Lemus, and Mico Mrkaic, 2013, "Fiscal Multipliers," Chapter 8 in *The Eastern Caribbean Economic and Currency Union: Macroeconomics and Financial Systems*, ed. by A. Schipke, A. Cebotari, and N. Thacker (Washington: International Monetary Fund).

Guy, Kester, and Anton Belgrave, 2012, "Fiscal Multipliers in Microstates: Evidence from the Caribbean," *International Advances in Economic Research*, Vol. 18, No. 1, pp. 74–86.

Ilzetzki, Ethan, Enrique G. Mendoza, and Carlos A. Végh, 2009, "How Big Are Fiscal Multipliers?" *CEPR Policy Insight*, No. 39.

———, 2011, "How Big (Small?) Are Fiscal Multipliers?" IMF Working Paper 11/52 (Washington: International Monetary Fund).

International Monetary Fund, 2008, "Fiscal Policy as a Countercyclical Tool," Chapter 5 in *World Economic Outlook*, October (Washington: International Monetary Fund).

———, 2012, "Are We Understanding Short-Term Fiscal Multipliers?," Box 1.1., Chapter 1 in *World Economic Outlook*, October (Washington: International Monetary Fund).

Kirchner, Markus, Jacopo Cimadomo, and Sebastian Hauptmeier, 2010, "Transmission of Government Spending Shocks in the Euro Area: Time Variation and Driving Forces," ECB Working Paper No. 1219 (Frankfurt am Main: European Central Bank).

Kraay, Aart, 2012 "Government Spending Multipliers in Developing Countries: Evidence from Lending by Official Creditors," World Bank Policy Research Working Paper No. 6099 (Washington: World Bank).

Parker, Jonathan A., 2011, "On Measuring the Effects of Fiscal Policy in Recessions," NBER Working Paper 17240 (Cambridge, Massachusetts: National Bureau of Economic Research).

Perotti, Roberto, 2005, "Estimating the Effects of Fiscal Policy in OECD Countries," CEPR Discussion Paper No. 4842, January (London: Centre for Economic Policy Research).

Ramey, Valerie A., 2011, "Can Government Purchases Stimulate the Economy?" *Journal of Economic Literature,* Vol. 49, No. 3, pp. 673–85.

Spilimbergo, Antonio, Steve Symansky, and Martin Schindler, 2009, "Fiscal Multipliers," IMF Staff Position Note No. 09/11 (Washington: International Monetary Fund).

CHAPTER 9

Selected Debt Restructuring Experiences in the Caribbean

GARTH PERON NICHOLLS

This chapter reviews selected Caribbean debt restructuring cases. In particular, it deals with three interrelated policy questions. First, it delineates the history of resolving debt overhangs in emerging market and low-income economies generally. Second, it reviews selected Caribbean experiences with debt restructuring and associated challenges in the region. And third, it examines the needs for additional traditional debt restructuring in Caribbean economies, along with some alternative options and the role that the IMF can play in helping to restore the region's fiscal and debt sustainability.

Past attempts at tackling high debt in Caribbean economies through debt restructuring have not yielded lasting gains for all countries. Among the cases where restructuring succeeded in helping to lower public debt were the efforts in Guyana, Suriname, and Trinidad and Tobago. Certain factors contributed to their success, including favorable commodity prices in the years following the restructuring. These countries also adopted, to some extent, broader macroeconomic policy reforms that changed the way things were done.

In a number of other cases, particularly in the tourism-dependent countries, debt restructurings were not sufficient to yield sustainable debt reduction. At the same time, their small size and geographic location make them highly vulnerable to a host of frequent shocks, against which it is costly to insure. These shocks have contributed to the pile-up of their debt. As a result, these economies have had a silent debt crisis for the past two decades, contributing to a high-debt–low-growth trap. More particularly, the high public debt has constrained fiscal policy flexibility, which in an environment of growing debt intolerance can easily trigger a fiscal crisis.

Financial innovation and international cooperation have been key factors in resolving past international debt overhang cases. An important example of this was the use of Brady bonds, which reduced the debt overhang of some emerging market countries in the late 1980s while facilitating renewed international capital

---

For the purposes of this discussion, the Dominican Republic and Haiti have not been included. Some parts of this chapter draw on Gold and others (2012). The chapter has benefited from some very useful suggestions and comments from Takahiro Tsuka and Charles Kramer.

market access. Over time, this solution popularized the use of public bond markets among emerging market economies, particularly in Latin America, as a mechanism for raising money. For low income developing economies, the Heavily Indebted Poor Countries (HIPC) Initiative helped reduce their debt overhang and poverty.

However, some have argued that the public debt overhang for middle-income small island developing states represents a new challenge for the existing debt resolution mechanisms, one that has not been sufficiently studied. Notwithstanding the fact that these economies are highly indebted, most of them—many of which are small island nations in the Caribbean—have not benefited from past international programs for comprehensive debt relief. Also, many have been graduated from concessional borrowing at the World Bank given their relatively high per capita income.

That said, a number of Caribbean countries have pursued debt restructuring over the past 25 years, although the relief secured has not been sufficient by itself to restore long-term fiscal and debt sustainability. Looking ahead, the changing structure of Caribbean public debt (high levels of domestic debt held by domestic banks) necessitates more innovative debt restructuring strategies to secure sufficient debt relief without instigating a financial crisis. In addition, a credible macroeconomic framework is required to lock in the fiscal space achieved through debt restructuring.

The remainder of this chapter is organized as follows. First the international experience with debt restructuring is reviewed. Then the chapter reviews recent selected Caribbean debt restructuring cases, followed by a discussion of the challenges of debt restructuring in the region. Lastly, it discusses the case for additional traditional debt restructuring in the region along with alternative options for debt reduction and the role that the IMF can play both in debt reduction and more broadly in helping restore sustainable public finances.

INTERNATIONAL DEBT RESTRUCTURING AND DEBT RELIEF MECHANISMS[1]

The international framework for addressing debt restructuring is a collection of mechanisms—both market-based and official—that continue to evolve over time in response to different debt crises. Indeed, since the 1950s there have been more than 600 sovereign debt restructurings in 95 countries. About two-thirds of these have been Paris Club agreements for official bilateral debt. These include debt restructuring operations under the HIPC and Multilateral Debt Relief Initiative (MDRI) initiatives, which have provided extensive debt relief for highly indebted low-income countries. The remaining third have been debt exchanges with private creditors.

[1]This section is based on Das, Papaioannou, and Trebesch (2012), who examined cases that occurred between 1950 and 2010.

Commercial Bank Debt

Commercial bank debt has been restructured through a Bank Advisory Committee—better known as the London Club. These restructurings were particularly prevalent during the late 1970s and early 1980s. Notwithstanding legal, coordination, and logistical issues as well as holdouts and intercreditor disputes, there were more than 100 restructurings between 1980 and 1990. The majority of them required the recipient country to have an IMF program in place. This was done to assure creditors that the adjustment effort, together with the debt restructuring and new funding, would be adequate to close any residual financing needs and achieve debt sustainability. In this context, it is important to note that the IMF introduced some innovations as the debt crisis unfolded. In particular, "it assumed a much more active role than heretofore in arranging the total financing packages for adjustment programs. . . the standard practice for the staff before the crisis was to estimate the financing that would be provided by other private and official creditors under normal conditions and with good policies in place. The Fund would then negotiate a program that would make such financing possible, and it would provide financing (within the established access limits) to close any remaining gap" (Boughton, 2001, p. 545). However, as the debt crisis evolved in the early 1980s it became clear that in some cases private creditors wanted to reduce their exposure and in such cases IMF funding would be insufficient to close the financing gap. According to Boughton, "The solution was to require concerted lending by the banks so as to stabilize their aggregate financing" (p.545). In this regard, the IMF programs played a critical role in mobilizing resources from foreign and multilateral creditors and donors and in ensuring a viable medium-term macroeconomic strategy.

The IMF also developed procedures for monitoring adjustment programs that were not supported by IMF financing—such as enhanced surveillance. Under these procedures the IMF provided information and analysis (staff reports that evaluated non-IMF-financed programs) to private creditors.[2] Nevertheless, despite a chain of rescheduling agreements, countries generally only received short-term liquidity relief and their debt paths remained unsustainable.

The Brady Plan was launched in 1989 to address debtor insolvency and commercial bank exposure. The plan signaled a shift in the official policy stance on debt restructurings from short-term relief to face-value reductions in debt to restore debtor solvency. It had three key elements. First, banks exchanged their loans for sovereign bonds. Second, creditors were offered a menu of options with respect to instruments with different terms and implications for NPV and face-value reductions. And third, the plan provided for the capitalization of the interest arrears that were not written off by commercial banks. There were 17 deals between 1989 and 1997 under this plan, which is widely regarded as a success since it lowered the debt levels of emerging-market countries (particularly in Latin America), normalized their relations with creditors, and allowed them to regain access to capital markets. According to Boughton (2001), under the Brady

[2]See Boughton (2001, p.547).

Plan, the IMF provided the resources used for repurchasing bank loans at secondary market prices.

Sovereign Bond Debt

Sovereign bonds are typically restructured through an exchange offer. This involves identifying bond holders, verifying their claims, preparing an exchange offer (most likely after consultation with the bondholders), launching the exchange offer that sets conditions and deadlines for bondholder participation, and exchanging the debt. Sovereign bond restructurings have not always been smooth, and in some cases negotiations have been protracted. The IMF's role in these restructurings has been to provide information and assess the debt sustainability of the proposed offer.

Since 1998, there have been more than 18 bond exchanges with foreign bondholders, involving bonds with a cumulative value of about US$81.1 billion. Some countries have pursued domestic and external debt exchanges at the same time, while in other cases, such as in Jamaica (in 2010 and 2013) the focus has been only on domestic creditors. Although delays due to holdouts and litigation are possible, these have been rare in recent times (IMF, 2012b). Indeed, only Dominica (2004) and Argentina (2005) have had difficulties with creditor holdouts and with regaining access to international capital markets after the bond exchange.

Official Bilateral Debt

Official bilateral debt has generally been restructured under the auspices of the Paris Club. A country must demonstrate payment difficulties and reach an understanding with the IMF on an adjustment program in order to be considered for a Paris Club restructuring. The level of debt relief granted by the Paris Club has been aligned with the debtor financing gap identified in the IMF program, and has been related to a country's income level. Before the 1990s, most Paris Club restructurings delivered only short-term refinancing and maturity lengthening, but they did not address underlying fiscal solvency issues.[3] Overall, between 1950 and 2010, a total of 447 Paris Club agreements in 88 countries were implemented for official debt amounting to US$545 billion.

Debt Relief for Highly Indebted Poor Countries

Highly indebted poor countries have been eligible for the joint IMF- and World Bank-sponsored HIPC and MDRI initiatives. Under the HIPC initiative, launched in 1996, highly indebted poor countries could obtain relief in the context of an IMF and Bank program by following a two-step process. First, countries had to meet a set of conditions, including having a poverty reduction strategy, a track record of reform and sound policies, and a debt burden that could not be addressed through traditional mechanisms. Meeting these conditions qualified a

[3]Over time the level of debt relief granted by the Paris Club has increased somewhat. Starting in 1988, the Toronto terms provided relief of 33 percent, which increased to 67 percent under the Naples terms in 1994 and further expanded with the HIPC initiative to 80 percent under the Lyons terms and then to 90 percent under the Cologne terms by the end of the 1990s. In 2003, the focus shifted to include debt sustainability with the launch of the Evian terms, which offered debt relief to non-HIPC countries.

country to reach the HIPC decision point, where preliminary commitments for debt reduction were made. Second, the country had to meet additional conditions, including establishing a further track record of good performance under an IMF-supported program; satisfactory implementation of key reforms agreed upon at the decision point; and satisfactory implementation of its poverty reduction strategy, to reach the "completion point," when the debt relief committed at the decision point was delivered.

In 2005, as a contribution toward achieving the Millennium Development Goals (MDGs), the Group of Eight agreed that the IMF, World Bank, and African Development Bank would provide relief under the MDRI for 100 percent of their debt claims on countries that reached the completion point under the HIPC initiative.[4] Thus far, 33 countries have reached the completion point and have received or are receiving full debt relief under the HIPC and MDRI initiatives. Participation in both these initiatives was closed in 2006, with a further ring-fencing in 2011. Of the countries that reached the HIPC completion point, two are in the Caribbean: Guyana and Haiti, which also benefited from the MDRI as noted above.

The majority of Caribbean economies have relied increasingly on the evolving market-based arrangements for countries in debt distress to help reduce their debt levels and restore debt sustainability. These efforts have not been successful in all cases.

FEATURES OF SELECTED RECENT PUBLIC DEBT RESTRUCTURINGS IN THE CARIBBEAN

Caribbean economies have received many rounds of debt relief since the 1970s (see Table 9.1). Some countries, such as Jamaica, have had repeated restructurings and are still very highly indebted. Other countries, such as Suriname and Trinidad and Tobago, have been able to lock in the gains of debt relief; supported by high commodity prices, they have reduced their public debt ratios over time. Although most countries pursued debt restructurings in the context of IMF programs, in some cases, such as Belize in 2007 and 2013, debt relief operations occurred despite the absence of an IMF-supported program.

Since 2004 there have been eight episodes of sovereign debt restructuring in six Caribbean countries—Antigua and Barbuda, Belize, Dominica, Grenada, Jamaica, and St. Kitts and Nevis. Table 9.2 provides an overview of the eight debt restructurings for these six countries. There are both similarities and differences in the characteristics of these recent episodes. Six episodes were supported by IMF programs, in some cases with financing of over 300 percent of quota. These restructurings were completed within a relatively short period: less than a year and a half. In the case of Jamaica (2010), the domestic debt exchange took about two months, and in the cases of Dominica, Grenada, and St. Kitts and Nevis, it took 10 to 15 months to complete. The restructurings in Belize (2007 and 2013) and another in Jamaica (2013) did not involve an IMF program[5] (Table 9.2).

---

[4]The Inter-American Development Bank also delivered MDRI relief to some countries, including Guyana.

[5]In the case of Jamaica, however, the 2013 debt exchange operation was a prior action for an IMF program.

TABLE 9.1

Debt Restructuring in the Caribbean,1978–2013

Country	Year	Type
Antigua and Barbuda	2005	Debt relief
	2010	Commercial
	2010	Paris Club
Belize	2007	Commercial (bond exchange)
	2013	Commercial (bond exchange)
Dominica	2004	Commercial, official
Grenada	2005	Commercial (bond restructuring)
	2006	Paris Club
	2013	Commercial (bond restructuring)[a]
Guyana	1989	Paris Club
	1990	Paris Club
	1992	Commercial (buyback, donor funded)
	1993	Paris Club
	1996	Paris Club
	1999	Commercial, Paris Club
	2004	Paris Club (HIPC debt relief)
Jamaica	1978	Commercial
	1979	Commercial
	1981	Commercial
	1984	Commercial, Paris Club
	1985	Commercial, Paris Club
	1987	Commercial, Paris Club
	1988	Paris Club
	1990	Commercial, Paris Club
	1991	Paris Club
	1993	Paris Club
	2010	Commercial (debt exchange)
	2013	Commercial (debt exchange)
St. Kitts and Nevis	2012	Commercial (debt exchange)
	2012	Paris Club
St. Vincent and the Grenadines	2007	Debt relief
Suriname	2001/2002	Rescheduling of government debt
	2006	Debt relief (repayment with partial debt cancelation)
	2009	Debt relief (repayment with partial debt cancelation)
Trinidad and Tobago	1989	Commercial, Paris Club
	1990	Paris Club

Sources: Das and others (2012); and IMF staff reports.
Note: HIPC = Heavily Indebted Poor Countries.
[a]The Government of Grenada announced its intention to restructure in March 2013.

Most Caribbean debt restructuring operations are delayed until the countries face the possibility of economic collapse. In particular, the median delay in debt restructuring events from the time of establishing that their debt is unsustainable is about three years (Table 9.2). However, there are important differences among Caribbean countries. For example, while Jamaica (2010) conducted its debt exchange about two years after losing market access, it took Antigua and Barbuda

TABLE 9.2

Characteristics of Recent Sovereign Debt Restructuring in the Caribbean, Selected Countries, 2005–12

Case	Date Debt Declared Unsustainable[a]	Preemptive or Post-Default	Date of Default	Restructuring Type	Final Exchange Offer	Duration (months)	IMF Program	Total Debt Exchanged (US$ millions)	Outstanding Instruments Exchanged	Cut in Face Value (percent)	Net Present Value Haircut Estimate (percent)	Instruments Exchanged
Dominica (bonds/loans)	2001	Post-default	Jul-03	Commercial	Apr-04	15	Yes	144	External	15	54	Two bonds, short- and medium-term loans
Grenada (bonds/loans)	2001	Preemptive		Commercial	Sep-05	13	No	210	External and domestic	0.0	33.9	Five external bonds, eight domestic bonds, two external loans
				Paris Club	May-06		Yes	16	External loans	0.0	. . .[b]	
Belize (bonds)	2005	Preemptive		Commercial	Dec-06	6	No	516	External	0.0	23.7	Seven bonds, eight loans
Antigua and Barbuda (bonds/loans)	1990s	Post-default	Since the 1990s	Commercial	2010		No	989	External and domestic	15[c]	. . .[d]	
				Paris Club	Sep-10		Yes	117	External	0.0	25–30[e]	
Jamaica (bonds)	2008	Preemptive		Commercial	Jan-10	1	Yes	7,855	Domestic	0.0	20	350 instruments (U.S.-dollar- and Jamaican-dollar-denominated bonds)
St. Kitts and Nevis (bonds/loans)	2006	Preemptive		Commercial	Feb-12	10	Yes	138	External and Domestic	31.8	61–73	13 bonds (11 external and 2 domestic)
				Paris Club	May-12		Yes	5.7	External	0.0	. . .[f]	

TABLE 9.2 (Continued)

Characteristics of Recent Sovereign Debt Restructuring in the Caribbean, Selected Countries, 2005–12

Case	Date Debt Declared Unsustainable[a]	Preemptive or Post-Default	Date of Default	Restructuring Type	Final Exchange Offer	Duration (months)	IMF Program	Total Debt Exchanged (US$ millions)	Outstanding Instruments Exchanged	Cut in Face Value (percent)	Net Present Value Haircut Estimate (percent)	Instruments Exchanged
Jamaica (bonds)		Preemptive		Commercial	Feb-13	1	No[6]	9,100	Domestic	0[c]	more than 10[d]	26 U.S.-dollar- and Jamaican-dollar-denominated domestic bonds
Belize (bonds)	2010	Preemptive		Commercial	Feb-13	7	No	529.9	External	10[e]	29–31[f]	One external bond

Sources: Alleyne (2011); Government of Antigua and Barbuda, Review of Antigua and Barbuda Debt Portfolio from 2006 to 2010 (http://www.ab.gov.ag/article_details.Php?id=2729&category=114); Antigua and Barbuda Letter of Intent, Memorandum of Economic and Financial Policies, and Technical Memorandum of Understanding, May 21, 2010; Jahan (2012); IMF (2006, 2012a, and 2012b); and www.clubdeparis.org/en.

[a]Based on IMF staff reports and staff estimates.

[b]The Paris Club agreement reduced by over 90 percent the debt service due to Paris Club creditors during the IMF-supported program under the Poverty Reduction and Growth Facility. The debt was rescheduled under classic terms. Repayment of non-Official Development Assistance (ODA) credits over 12 years, with 5 years of grace. Repayment of the ODA credits over 12 years, with 5 years of grace. The agreement also deferred a large part of moratorium in interest due under the rescheduling and then deferred until 2009 through 2013 the repayment of arrears accumulated on short-term debt. In May 2009, Grenada obtained an extension of the Paris Club agreement through end-2009. (http://www.clubdeparis.org/sections/communica. . .rchives-2006/grenade/switchLanguage/en).

[c]On debt to two large statutory bodies, the Medical Benefits Scheme and the Social Security Scheme. See Review of Antigua and Barbuda Debt Portfolio from 2006 to 2010 (http://www.ab.gov.ag/article_details.Php?id=2729&category=114).

[d]The Paris Club Agreement reduced by over 86 percent the debt service due to the Paris Club creditors during the IMF-supported program under the Stand By Agreement. It rescheduled US$117 million consisting of arrears due as of August 31, 2010, as well as maturities falling due from September 1, 2010 up to April 30, 2013 to be repaid over 12 years, including 5 years of grace. The ODA loans were rescheduled at a commercial rate (http://www.clubdeparis.org/sections/communica. . .2010/Antigua-barbuda/switchLanguage/en).

[e]Review of Antigua and Barbuda Debt Portfolio from 2006 to 2010 (http://www.ab.gov.ag/article_details.Php?id=2729&category=114).

[f]The Paris Club agreement reduced by over 90 percent the debt service due to the Paris Club creditors during the IMF-supported program under the Stand By Arrangement. This included rescheduling the stock of debt over 20 years, including a 7-year grace period (http://www.clubdeparis.org/sections/communica. . .nt-christophe-nieves/switchLanguage/en).

about 20 years to deal with a clearly unsustainable public debt path. The other cases fall within these extremes. It is likely that the delays in effectively dealing with their public debt overhang have aggravated it, causing much uncertainty in the macroeconomic environment.

The range of debt relief varied widely, ranging from about a 10 percent reduction in NPV terms in the case of Jamaica (2013) to about 73 percent for St. Kitts and Nevis. Also, the cut in face value varied across countries, ranging from zero in the case of Jamaica to about 32 percent of the eligible debt for St. Kitts and Nevis. In addition, with the exception of Antigua and Barbuda and Dominica, all recent Caribbean debt restructurings were pre-emptive. Finally, Jamaica restructured only domestic debt (in both 2010 and 2013), while Belize (in 2013 and 2007) and Dominica (in 2004) restructured only foreign instruments. The remaining countries—Antigua and Barbuda, Grenada, and St. Kitts and Nevis—restructured both their domestic and external debt portfolios (see Table 9.2).

Except in the case of St. Kitts and Nevis, the recent debt restructuring operations for most countries appear to have provided mainly cash flow relief, and debt sustainability remains at risk. While gross financing needs and debt service ratios declined after the debt restructuring operations, all these countries remained highly vulnerable to debt distress, given their still high debt ratios (see Figures 9.1 and 9.2

Figure 9.1 Total Public Sector Debt, Selected Caribbean Countries, 2004–13
(Percent of GDP)

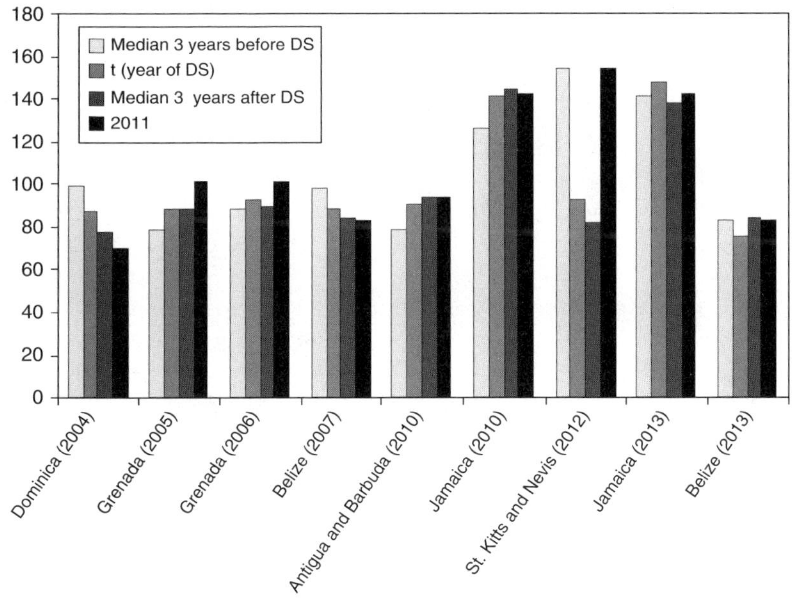

Source: Author's calculations using data from the IMF, World Economic Outlook database and individual country Debt Sustainability tables.

Note: DS = debt restructuring. Debt ratios for Antigua, Jamaica (2013), Belize (2013) and St. Kitts and Nevis include projections. These projections are based on debt restructuring agreements that have already been completed or are already in progress. For Dominica and Grenada, since the debt restructuring exercises their GDP has been rebased resulting in a higher GDP level and lower debt ratios, including before and after debt restructuring.

Figure 9.2 Debt Service, Selected Caribbean Countries, 2004–13 *(Percent of GDP)*

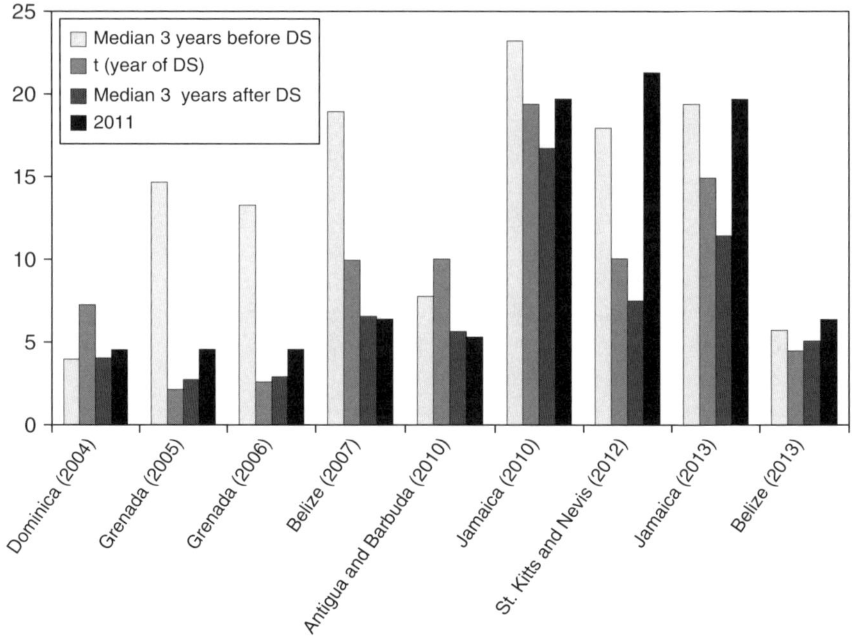

Source: Author's calculations using data from the IMF, World Economic Outlook database and individual country Debt Sustainability tables.

Note: DS = debt restructuring. For Antigua and Barbuda, Jamaica (2010), St. Kitts and Nevis, Jamaica (2013), and Belize (2013) debt service includes projections. These projections are based on debt restructuring agreements that have already been completed or are already in progress.

and Table 9.3). For St. Kitts and Nevis, however, the debt stock declined to about 87 percent of GDP the year after debt restructuring from 154 percent of GDP the year before debt restructuring. Clear evidence of debt restructuring operations that have provided insufficient debt relief includes the cases of Jamaica (2010) and Belize (2007), both of which recently repeated their debt restructuring exercises within five years. Another example is Grenada, which restructured its debts in 2005 but announced in March 2013 its intention to once again restructure its external debts. It remains to be seen whether the recent debt restructuring cases in Jamaica (2013), Belize (2013), and St. Kitts and Nevis (2012) have provided sufficient debt relief to ensure medium- to long-run public debt sustainability.

Key features of some of these debt exchanges contained elements that threatened medium-term sustainability and contributed to renewed restructuring. Of particular note is the interest rate step-up feature that characterized Belize's and Grenada's debt exchanges. These interest rate step-ups assumed improved medium-term prospects relative to the time of the debt restructuring. However, in both cases, the interest rate step-up occurred in the middle of the global financial crisis and when growth was sub-par for both countries. This timing, combined with a deterioration in the fiscal balances, caused serious financing difficulties, forcing both governments to seek additional relief from creditors.

TABLE 9.3

Outcomes Before and After Debt Restructuring (DS), Selected Caribbean Countries, 2004–13 *(In percent of GDP)*

	Total Debt				Gross Financing Needs			GDP Growth			Inflation		
	Median 3 (years before DS)	t (year of DS)	Median 3 years after	2011	Median 3 (years before S)	t (year of DS)	Median 3 years after	Median 3 years before	t year of DS	Median 3 years after	Median 3 years before	t year of DS	Median 3 years after
Restructuring of commerical debt (debt exchange)													
Median	**98.7**	**89.3**	**86.0**	**97.3**	**14.8**	**5.9**	**5.5**	**1.0**	**0.3**	**2.1**	**2.6**	**2.6**	**3.3**
Dominica (2004)[a]	99.2	86.5	77.5	70.2	5.7	5.2	0.4	0.5	0.8	3.6	1.6	2.4	2.6
Grenada (2005)[a]	78.8	88.0	88.4	101.2	13.1	4.6	6.2	3.3	12.5	1.7	2.2	3.5	4.3
Belize (2007)	98.1	87.9	83.3	83.0	18.2	5.7	3.9	4.6	1.3	2.7	3.7	2.3	2.0
Antigua and Barbuda (2010)[a,b,c]	78.8	90.6	93.3	93.3	7.9	6.1	4.8	1.5	–8.5	1.0	3.0	2.7	3.9
Jamaica (2010)[b]	125.6	140.8	143.7	141.5	17.6	14.8	11.5	–1.7	–0.6	1.1	12.4	7.8	6.8
St. Kitts and Nevis (2012)[b,c]	153.6	92.3	81.9	153.6	51.1	40.9	22.7	–1.9	–0.7	3.2	2.1	2.5	2.5
Jamaica (2013)[d]	140.8	147.0	136.7	141.6	16.6	11.5	7.5	–0.6	–0.2	1.4	8.5	7.2	9.8
Belize (2013)[e]	83.0	75.1	83.6	83.0	4.1	3.4	4.1	3.5	2.5	2.5	1.7	2.5	2.5
Restructuring of official debt (Paris Club)													
Grenada (2006)	88.0	92.6	88.9	101.2	6.1	6.2	7.0	8.6	–4.4	1.7	0.9	5.2	2.0

Sources: IMF staff reports; and author's calculations.

Note: Debt ratios for Antigua and Barbuda, Jamaica (2013), Belize (2013), and St. Kitts and Nevis include projections. These projections are based on debt restructuring agreements that have already been completed or are already in progress. For Dominica and Grenada, since the debt restructuring exercise GDP has been rebased, resulting in a higher GDP level and lower debt ratios, including before and after debt restructuring.

[a]Debt ratios have been lowered since the rebasing of the GDP (which made the level of GDP higher for countries in the Eastern Caribbean Currency Union).

[b]The averages for three years after DS for these countries include projections.

[c]The commercial and Paris Club debt restructuring occurred during the same year.

[d]The averages for three years after DS for Jamaica include projections.

[e]The averages for three years after DS for Belize include projections. It also includes additional liabilities from 2015.

On the question of market access, the story is mixed. On the domestic front, all countries were able to maintain private market access.[6] In some countries, this was secured by explicit protection of certain maturities from eligibility for restructuring, such as in St. Kitts and Nevis and Grenada, where treasury bills were declared ineligible. Even in the case of Antigua and Barbuda, which had a prolonged period of debt distress before the explicit announcement of restructuring, regional debt market access was gained and maintained within the context of the regional government securities market. On the external front, while Antigua and Barbuda, Belize, Grenada, and St. Kitts and Nevis lost market access, Jamaica maintained external credit market access after the domestic debt restructuring.

Looking at broader macroeconomic outcomes, median growth rate and inflation were higher for the region as a whole three years after debt restructuring than they had been three years before (Table 9.3).[7] Two groups of countries can be identified. The first group (Dominica, Jamaica, and St. Kitts and Nevis) are countries where growth and inflation (only for Jamaica) appear to have been better three years after the debt restructuring than three years before.[8] The second group (Antigua and Barbuda, Belize, and Grenada) are countries where GDP growth was lower and inflation higher (except for Belize) three years after the debt restructuring than three years before.[9]

On financial sector outcomes, available indicators appear to suggest that the effects of debt restructuring operations overall has been manageable. In the cases examined, capital ratios were most affected, followed by profitability. In particular, capital ratios declined in Dominica and Antigua and Barbuda after the debt restructuring operations compared with the median ratios three years before the event (see Table 9.4).[10] Although for Jamaica and St. Kitts and Nevis it may be too early to assess the impact of the recent debt restructuring on the financial sector, analysis done by IMF staff suggests that in the case of Jamaica most institutions were able to remain above the 10 percent minimum capital adequacy ratio (CAR) as excess capital helped financial institutions to absorb the initial reduction in capital (IMF, 2013c). In the case of St. Kitts and Nevis, IMF staff did a

---

[6]In the countries, that make up the Eastern Caribbean Currency Union (ECCU), three markets can be identified, the narrow domestic market (the market within the country borders); the regional government securities market (the market for the currency union); and the external or extraregional market.

[7]Two caveats need to be noted. First, in the assessment of macroeconomic outcomes, the impact of debt restructuring on expectations is not assessed. Expectations of agents can of course be an important factor in economic outcomes before and after debt restructuring. Second, care must be taken in the interpretation of these results as restructuring in some countries occurred during the 2008–09 global financial crisis, which severely affected tourist arrivals to many of these countries, causing GDP growth to contract sharply.

[8]Inflation was slightly higher in Dominica and St. Kitts and Nevis three years after the debt restructuring than three years before.

[9]Inflation was slightly lower in Belize three years after debt restructuring than three years before.

[10] It must be noted that in Antigua and Barbuda, arising out of the effects of the global economic and financial crisis, two banks had to be rescued and these may affect the observed ratios.

TABLE 9.4

Financial Sector Outcomes Before and After Debt Restructuring (DS), Selected Caribbean Countries, 2004–13 *(In percent)*

	Banking Sector Liquidity: Total Loans to Total Deposits			Banking Sector Profitability: Net Profit before Taxes to Average Assets			Banking Sector Capital Ratios: Total Capital to Risk-Weighted Assets		
	Median 3 (before DS)	t (year of DS)	Median 3 years after	Median 3 (before DS)	t (year of DS)	Median 3 years after	Median 3 years before	t year of DS	Median 3 years after
Restructuring of commercial debt (debt exchange)									
Median	**71.8**	**66.3**	**75.9**	**2.4**	**1.7**	**2.1**	**16.5**	**18.2**	**15.6**
Dominica (2004)	63.4	57.5	57.5	1.4	0.5	2.1	34.1	23.5	20.8
Grenada (2005)	68.1	66.0	75.9	2.3	1.7	2.0	16.3	15.3	15.6
Belize (2007)	97.5	99.9	92.3	3.8	3.5	2.6	18.9	23.1	20.7
Antigua and Barbuda (2010)[a]	87.7	88.5	82.7	2.4	0.1	0.5	16.5	16.1	4.0
Jamaica (2010)	71.8	66.3	67.8	3.5	2.5	3.2	16.0	18.2	15.1
Restructuring of official debt (Paris Club)									
Grenada (2006)	66.0	73.2	80.0	2.3	2.4	1.3	15.3	17.5	15.6

Sources: IMF staff reports; and author's calculations.
Note: Recent data are not available to measure the impact, if any, on the financial system of the recent debt restructuring operations in Belize (2013), Jamaica (2013), and St. Kitts and Nevis (2012).
[a]The commercial and Paris Club debt restructuring occurred during the same year.

post–debt restructuring stress test of the indigenous banking sector to illustrate the impact of the debt restructuring (including the debt/land swap). They noted that the CAR following the debt/land swap would decline from 45 percent to 20.7 percent, but still remain above the regional benchmark. They also noted that interest income would decline, but the nonperforming loans-to-total loans ratio would increase (from 6.1 percent to 15.4 percent) given the high weight of government loans with indigenous banks (IMF, 2013d).

The macroeconomic vulnerabilities associated with public debt over the medium term after debt restructuring, gauged by a debt sustainability analysis, have been somewhat mixed (Table 9.5). In particular, using the central debt projection and the results of stress tests in IMF staff reports, we find that except for Belize (2013) and Jamaica (2013), in all cases the medium-term baseline projections were below the pre–debt-restructuring debt levels. Also, except for Belize (2013) and Dominica (2004), the means of the projected debt levels of both the historical and no-policy-change scenarios for most countries at the end of the projection horizon were lower than before debt restructuring. Nevertheless, for most countries both baseline and mean debt level after debt restructuring remained high—in most cases over 100 percent of GDP. At the same time, the dispersion of the projected debt levels was higher than the pre–debt-restructuring levels for some countries, including Antigua and Barbuda, but broadly the same for Dominica (2004) and St. Kitts and Nevis (2013).

TABLE 9.5

Caribbean Economies: Medium-Term Vulnerabilities *(In percent of GDP)*

	Before Debt Restructuring			After Debt Restructuring		
	Baseline	Mean[a]	STD[a]	Baseline	Mean[a]	STD[a]
Restructuring of commercial debt (debt exchange)[b]						
Dominica (2004)	120.4	140.9	18.8	111.4	156.0	18.8
Belize (2007)	84.8	91.7	9.2	84.6	89.6	7.0
Antigua and Barbuda (2010)	93.0	116.5	28.2	71.6	106.2	36.9
Jamaica (2010)	114.9	119.8	16.5	105.3	109.7	8.0
St. Kitts and Nevis (2012)	161.5	186.8	38.1	68.1	68.7	37.2
Jamaica (2013)	152.7	...	...	126.5	143.9	6.9
Belize (2013)	72.1	74.5	5.1	86.3	85.6	0.6
Median	**106.3**	**119.8**	**16.5**	**85.5**	**106.2**	**8.0**

Sources: IMF staff reports; and author's calculations.

Note: This analysis is based on debt sustainability projections in IMF staff reports both at the time of the debt restructuring, and post-debt restructuring. The medium-term years before debt restructuring were as follows: Dominica end-2007; Belize (2007), end-2011; Belize (2013), end-2016; Antigua and Barbuda, end-2015; St. Kitts and Nevis, end-2016; Jamaica (2010), end-2013/14; Jamaica (2013), end-2016/17. The medium-term years after debt restructuring were as follows: Dominica end-2007; Belize (2007), end-2011; Belize (2013), end-2018; Antigua and Barbuda, end-2017; St. Kitts and Nevis, end-2017; Jamaica (2010), end-2014/15; Jamaica (2013), end-2016/17.

[a]Mean and standard deviation (STD) of scenarios and bound tests.

[b]Grenada is excluded as the debt sustainability analysis framework used before (market access) and after debt restructuring (low income) are not comparable.

CHALLENGES WITH DEBT RESTRUCTURING IN THE REGION

Challenges to debt restructuring in the Caribbean include the required size of debt reduction, high levels of domestically held public debt, lack of fiscal discipline, potential for spillovers and contagion, implausible optimistic growth forecasts, slow resumption of market access, and the political economy of debt restructuring.

The Required Size of the Debt Reduction

The required debt reduction to achieve lasting debt sustainability can be large in some countries (see Table 9.6). This can be shown using assumed debt sustainability target levels. For example, if Caribbean countries aspire to achieve a 60 percent debt-to-GDP ratio, the median haircut, without fiscal adjustment, amounts to about 25 percent of GDP. With this debt target, Jamaica and St. Kitts and Nevis (using their pre–debt-restructuring debt ratios) would require the largest haircuts—of 58 percent and 61 percent, respectively. On the other hand, using the natural debt limit concept of debt sustainability (see Chapter 6), and using the Caribbean average natural debt limit of about 30 percent of GDP, the median haircut, without fiscal adjustment, for public debt to achieve sustainability would be about 88 percent of GDP. With this debt target, six countries would require a haircut of over 60 percent of GDP on their public debt ratios.[11]

[11]It is important to note that this calculation is done for illustrative purposes only. It does not imply, for example, that a country must restructure once the debt level exceeds a certain level. Debt sustainability is a mix of judgmental exercises and is determined by a number of different factors, including, but not limited to, debt level, speed of debt reduction, creditor base, currency structures, interest rate structures, and liquidity conditions. Finally, it needs to be determined on a country-by-country basis.

TABLE 9.6

Illustrative Required Haircuts to Achieve Debt Sustainability by Country *(In percent of GDP)*

	Natural Debt Limit	60% Debt Ratio
Antigua and Barbuda	67.8	35.7
Bahamas	52.4	4.8
Barbados	76.1	52.2
Belize	63.9	27.7
Dominica	57.3	14.5
Grenada	70.4	40.7
Guyana	54.0	8.0
Jamaica	78.8	57.6
St. Kitts and Nevis	80.5	60.9
St. Lucia	57.8	15.6
St. Vincent and the Grenadines	55.8	11.5
Suriname	...	...
Trinidad and Tobago	3.5	...
Memorandum items:		
Mean haircut	65.0	29.9
Median haircut	60.8	27.7

Source: Author's calculations.

The Share of Public Sector Debt Held Domestically and By Multilateral Agencies

At the same time, eligible debt is largely held by domestic agents or multilateral financial institutions. As noted in Chapter 3, the structure of the public debt for the highly indebted countries in the Caribbean is skewed toward domestic debt, with the domestic financial sector being the key holder of domestic debt. Therefore, the scope for traditional approaches is limited as large debt write-offs raise the risks to financial stability. Further, in some countries a large proportion of foreign debt is held by multilateral institutions, which have only provided debt relief to the very poorest countries. Even so, except for Guyana and St. Vincent and the Grenadines, where multilateral debt represents about one-third of total public debt, the relief from reducing multilateral debt may be limited.

Access to External Private International Debt Market

Even after undergoing debt restructuring operations, a number of countries have failed to regain market access. Does this reflect the private sector's perception that the public debt remains high and the economy highly vulnerable?

The Tendency for Short-Lived Fiscal Consolidation Efforts and Weak Macroeconomic Policy Frameworks

Debt restructuring is often necessary, but it is rarely sufficient to deliver sustained debt reduction. To be successful, debt restructuring operations must be supported by credible policy reform programs to restore fiscal sustainability, maintain creditor confidence, and lock in the gains of any debt relief. The general observation in the Caribbean has been that fiscal consolidation efforts are short lived and mostly insufficient to deliver sustained reductions in the public debt ratio. In addition, macroeconomic policy has not always responded appropriately to exogenous shocks, leading to a continuous buildup of public debt.

The Potential for Spillovers and Contagion Effects

The Caribbean has a relatively high level of financial integration. As a result, a cluster of debt restructurings in one Caribbean country can impact other countries through the financial sector, including banks, social security schemes, and some insurance companies, which hold a portfolio of regional government securities. In addition, for the countries of the ECCU which have a closely connected banking system, spillovers from a debt restructuring in one country (potentially) can create a systemic banking crisis for the entire currency union if mitigation measures are not adopted.

Optimistic Projections

Debt restructuring scenarios and instrument design have not sufficiently taken into consideration the reduced long-term growth prospects and macroeconomic vulnerability of Caribbean economies. As a result, some of the new offers, post-restructuring, have been based on overly optimistic assumptions about future growth. A good example of this is the use of step-up interest rate instruments that have not worked well where they have been tried in the Caribbean. These instruments appear to have sown the seeds of additional debt restructurings/defaults in the countries where they have been used.

The Political Economy of Domestic Debt Restructuring

Domestic debt restructuring can result in income and wealth redistribution among constituents. The government can determine the distribution of these losses based on income or the capacity of the economic agents to absorb the losses on their balance sheets. Domestic debt restructuring can therefore have a high 'political cost' if not managed effectively. This can be especially so if financial stability is threatened in the restructuring process or if an important domestic constituency is adversely impacted.

IS THERE A CASE FOR FURTHER PUBLIC DEBT RESTRUCTURINGS?

High debt levels represent a significant burden on many economies in the region, and strong policy frameworks are necessary to put debt on a steady downward trend.[12] Notwithstanding debt relief and rapid growth in some Caribbean

[12] See Appendix 9.1 for some lessons from recent debt restructurings in the Caribbean.

countries in the years preceding the global economic crisis, by 2011 the average debt-to-GDP ratio had risen above its 2001 level to about 82 percent of GDP, with significant differences across countries.

As discussed in Chapter 6, Caribbean countries can be classified into three groups with respect to their public debt situation (see Figures 9.3, 9.4, and 9.5):

- *Countries that have stabilized their public debt ratios at below 60 percent of GDP* (including Suriname and Trinidad and Tobago). They have low debt-service payments of about 12 percent of total revenues, including interest payments of 8 percent of revenues. These countries are at low risk of debt distress.
- *Countries whose debt-to-GDP ratios range from 60 to 90 percent of GDP* (including Belize and St. Vincent and the Grenadines). Some of these countries have debt ratios that are stabilizing, but others, in the absence of further adjustment or debt relief, face rising debt ratios and are at risk of debt distress. A further factor that would affect the risk of debt distress is the debt structure and the amortization profile (see Chapter 3). On average, these countries have debt service payments of about 22 percent of total revenues (with interest payments of 9 percent of revenues).
- *Countries that have debt-to-GDP ratios above 90 percent of GDP* (including Barbados, Grenada, and Jamaica). Their total debt service averages about 34 percent of total revenues (with interest payments of 19 percent of revenues), and their primary balances are insufficient to reduce or stabilize their debt ratios. These countries are generally at a high risk of debt distress.

Sustained large fiscal adjustments may not be sufficient in a number of countries. While there is no consensus on a specific debt-to-GDP ratio that could serve

Figure 9.3 Changing Size of Public Debt, Caribbean Region, 2001–11 *(Unweighted average; percent of GDP)*

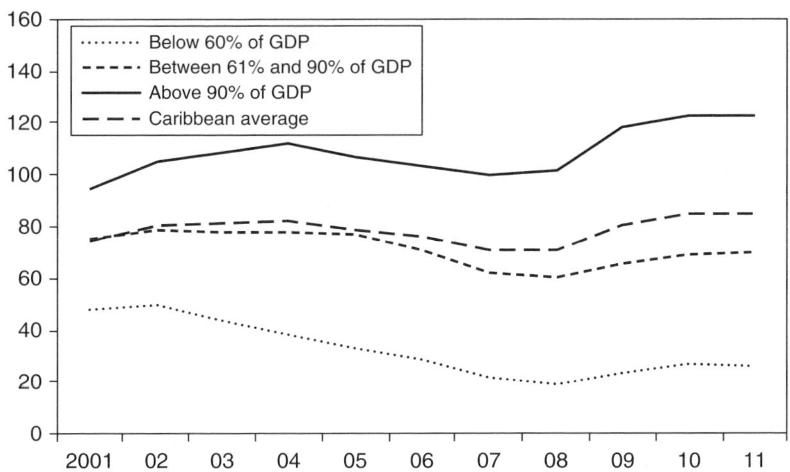

Source: Author's calculations.

Figure 9.4 Public Debt by Country, 2011 *(Percent of GDP)*

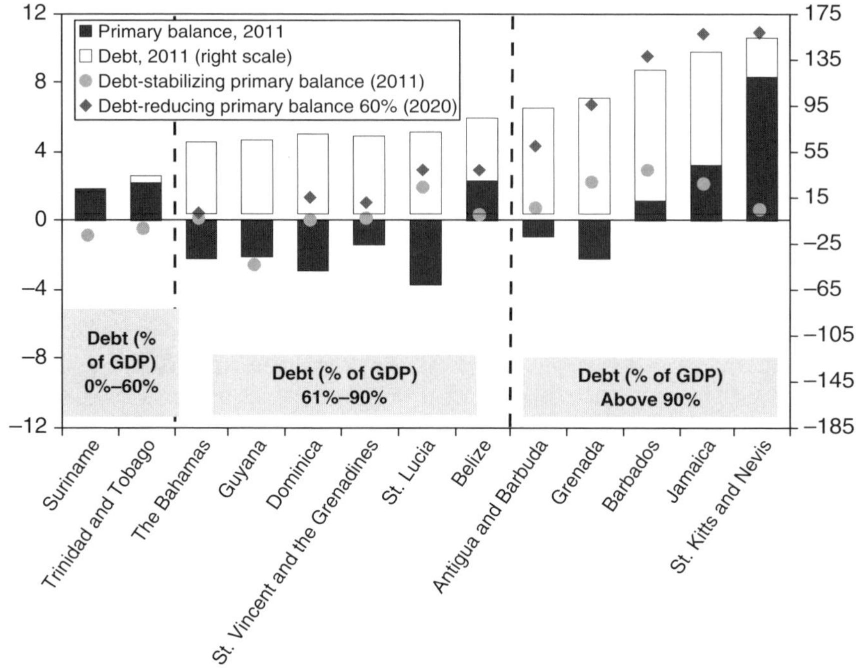

Sources: IMF staff reports; and author's calculations.

as a reference point for concern about debt sustainability, recent IMF staff studies suggest that a threshold of 60 percent should trigger a careful assessment of a country's debt sustainability to determine the risk of debt distress.[13,14] Indeed, a debt-to-GDP ratio of 60 percent has been commonly used as a ceiling in fiscal responsibility laws and in the context of regional integration agreements, including the ECCU, as discussed in Chapter 6. In a number of countries, reducing the debt ratios to 60 percent of GDP would require maintaining sizeable primary surpluses over a sustained period (averaging 7 percent of GDP over a 10-year period). Some of the required adjustments are so large over a sustained period that they may not be economically, socially, or politically feasible (see Figures 9.4 and 9.5 and Appendix Table 9.1). In addition, most countries have large negative international investment position, low average growth rates, and high debt and debt-service-to-revenue ratios (see Appendix Table 9.1).

[13]IMF (2011) indicates that based on recent empirical evidence, the reference point for public debt of 60 percent of GDP is to be used flexibly to trigger deeper analysis for market-access countries. The presence of other vulnerabilities would call for in-depth analysis even for countries where debt is below the reference point.

[14]The debt target of 60 percent of GDP has been embedded in the IMF Stand-By Arrangements for Antigua and Barbuda and for St. Kitts and Nevis.

Figure 9.5 Debt Service by Country, 2011 *(Percent of revenues)*

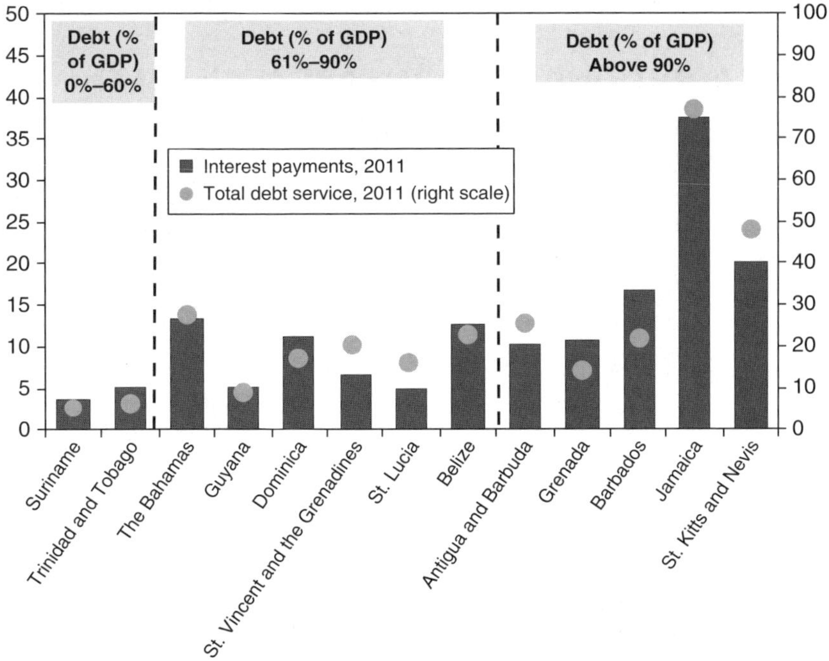

Sources: IMF staff reports; and author's calculations.

At the same time, since the onset of the global financial and economic crisis, GDP growth has decelerated sharply and the recovery is now being held back by high debt and a weak external environment. The median medium-term growth projection (for tourism-dependent economies[15]) has fallen since the global crisis from about 3.6 percent before the crisis to about 1.7 percent. In light of this, some of the assumptions upon which debt was contracted have substantially changed, and it may not be feasible to adjust the fiscal policy to correct for growth short falls.

Without reforms to boost competitiveness, sustained fiscal retrenchment will further depress economic activity. While fiscal consolidation is generally believed to lead to a real depreciation of the exchange rate, this adjustment usually takes an extended period of contraction/depression, which may not be feasible in an already depressed economy. Long-lasting improvements in competitiveness would require a number of structural reforms to improve the non-price competitiveness and business environment of the region. In this context, easing the debt

[15]Antigua and Barbuda, The Bahamas, Barbados, Belize, Dominica, Grenada, Jamaica, St. Kitts and Nevis, St. Lucia, and St. Vincent and the Grenadines.

overhang could both provide fiscal space and permit a lowering of distortionary taxes so that private enterprise could once more thrive.

WHAT ADDITIONAL OPTIONS ARE AVAILABLE?

Caribbean economies will need to develop new and innovative approaches to reduce their debt burdens and also seek to address their fiscal difficulties much sooner than they have done in the past. In particular, the countries should seek the assistance of the IMF much earlier than they have done in the past, especially when their challenge involves fiscal reform and adjustment.

Innovative Solutions to Debt Restructuring

Among the possible options are debt or equity swaps, such as those that are being pursued in St. Kitts and Nevis, and domestic debt exchange operations, such as was undertaken by Jamaica.[16] Debt conversions offer opportunities for both domestic and external debt reduction. On the domestic front, a number of public enterprises can be privatized through this mechanism. This will facilitate a reduction in public debt, an increase in private sector activity, and improved productive efficiency. On the external front, the PetroCaribe arrangement[17] already provides an option for debt repayment using goods and services; it can be used by Caribbean countries that are in a position to do so (an example is Guyana, which exports rice in exchange for a reduction of its PetroCaribe debt). It is important to emphasize that each country would have to examine its circumstances to determine a debt reduction strategy that best meets its needs given the constraints it faces.

More generally, Caribbean governments may want to consider issuing debt that is linked to GDP growth performance as a way of easing the pressure on public finances during recessions. In this way, a fall in GDP growth would mean lower debt payments and less strain on the public finances.

Leveraging the Catalytic Role of the IMF

Both in the context of IMF-supported programs and also more broadly, the IMF is playing a critical role to help mobilize the resources that countries need. This is particularly the case in two areas:

- *Resources from donors and multilateral institutions:* IMF-supported programs are designed to ensure that the adjustment efforts undertaken by the coun-

[16]In these efforts, special attention has to be given to the political economy implications of these strategies, as they may involve the shifting of the adjustment burden from one group of domestic agents to another.

[17]The PetroCaribe Arrangement is an oil purchase agreement between the government of the Republic of Venezuela and many governments in the Caribbean. Under this arrangement member countries are permitted to defer payment for up to 90 percent of the oil shipments for up to 25 years. The repayment terms include a two-year grace period, and interest rates are concessional. More broadly the arrangement provides for the repayment of oil debt through goods and services by borrowing countries.

try, together with the financing available, will be adequate to close any residual financing needs and achieve debt sustainability. In that respect, IMF programs play a critical role in mobilizing resources from foreign donors and multilateral creditors and ensuring a viable medium-term macroeconomic strategy.

- *Framework for debt restructuring:* While strong policy frameworks are necessary to put debt on a steady downward trend, in some cases they need to be supplemented with market-friendly debt restructuring. The IMF has played a role by identifying the envelope of resources available for debt service payments. Other multilaterals have also made important contributions, such as providing guarantees and financing contingency funds.

The recent experience with debt restructurings in the Caribbean provides helpful guidance as to what can be done. It also confirms the importance of close coordination with creditors to design a menu of options carefully calibrated to deliver optimal results given policy constraints in each country. Finally, it underscores the importance of effective communication of the government's economic policy and strategy. However, the structure of the Caribbean debt, in which a large share is held by the domestic financial system, imposes limitations to the scope of traditional debt restructuring.

Looking ahead, the IMF can help catalyze additional external resources to assist the region in its adjustment efforts. Greater reliance on external multilateral rather than domestic financing would reduce borrowing costs and free up resources from the domestic banking system that it can lend to the private sector, which would help finance growth.[18] These strategies would have to be buttressed with carefully calibrated policies to raise production and productivity in key export sectors.

CONCLUSION

In this chapter we discussed some key issues related to public debt restructuring in the Caribbean. Given some of these countries' high debt burdens and diminished growth prospects, a strong case may be made for debt restructuring to reduce debt and restore fiscal sustainability. This chapter has also shown that much of the past major international debt relief (such as the Brady Plan and HIPC) has not been available to the majority of the Caribbean nations, most of which are middle income. At the same time, many of these nations have had several rounds of debt restructuring, yet most are still highly indebted, and accordingly remain highly vulnerable to macroeconomic shocks. That said, there are several lessons to be learned from the successful debt restructuring cases in the Caribbean, including the need for a credible macroeconomic framework to lock in the gains of debt

---

[18]This, of course, would also need to be managed within a fully articulated debt management strategy that takes into account the cost-risk trade-off. An important risk from foreign borrowing that must be managed is the foreign exchange risk.

relief. Finally, the Caribbean should leverage the IMF's catalytic role in its adjustment efforts while adopting broad base reforms to reduce macroeconomic vulnerabilities and boost export competitiveness.

Several policy implications can be drawn from these insights. First, there is a need for a holistic economic strategy over the medium term, anchored in debt sustainability. Second, nontraditional debt reduction and restructuring strategies are likely to have a key role in restoring fiscal sustainability given the structure of the region's debt. Third, policy reforms that lock in the gains of debt relief for future generations would be essential to avoid a repeat of unsustainable fiscal outcomes.

APPENDIX 9.1. KEY ELEMENTS OF SUCCESSFUL DEBT RESTRUCTURING: LESSONS FROM RECENT EPISODES IN THE CARIBBEAN

Credible economic program: A credible policy reform program is required to restore fiscal sustainability, maintain creditor confidence, and lock in the gains of any debt relief.

Effective communication: A credible and transparent communication strategy on the government's economic policy and strategy targeted at creditors and other stakeholders is key to a successful debt restructuring. This was particularly critical in Dominica and in Jamaica, where the authorities explained to the bondholders the economic situation facing the government and the options available, along with the cost of each.

Ownership of economic policies: Country ownership of the broader economic reform strategy by the authorities is critical for successful outcomes. Antigua and Barbuda, Dominica, and St. Kitts and Nevis remained committed to fiscal adjustment, even in the face of severe contraction in GDP.

Contingency planning: A contingency fund to safeguard financial sector stability during debt restructuring operations is critical for domestic debt restructuring. These funds have been important in maintaining public confidence in the financial system and in providing liquidity in both Jamaica's and St. Kitts and Nevis' debt restructuring cases.

Case-by-case analysis: One size does not fit all countries. A menu of options, carefully calibrated to deliver optimal results given policy constraints, is required for successful debt restructuring. No single option will work for all countries; each restructuring has to be designed, case by case, based on an analysis of the objective conditions.

Multilateral support: The support of the multilateral organizations was key to the success of the recent successful debt restructurings. Of particular note is the recent innovation of providing a guarantee on restructured instruments, in the case of St.

Kitts and Nevis, and more broadly the provision of funding, as in the case of Jamaica.[1]

IMF involvement: An IMF fiscal adjustment program has been a key component in the recent debt restructuring cases of Antigua and Barbuda, Dominica, Grenada, Jamaica (2010), and St. Kitts and Nevis. This has enhanced the IMF's engagement with the countries and its role as a policy advisor with respect to assessing the sustainability of different policy options and in clarifying the financing gaps along with providing financing for three cases. The IMF also has an important review and monitoring role in the implementation of the agreed adjustment programs.

Even in cases where no formal IMF adjustment program has been agreed, the bond/loan holders look at the IMF's assessment. The private sector relies on IMF assessments to clarify the consistency and credibility of a country's economic program in restoring growth and promoting debt sustainability.

Technical team: Governments that are contemplating debt restructuring operations need to establish a strong technical team, including professionals with legal, economic, financial, negotiating, and public relations skills. Further, this technical team must have strong political support and be empowered to take decisions.

[1]In 2008 the African Development Bank provided a guarantee of restructured debt instruments for Seychelles. This model was adopted by St. Kitts and Nevis in its 2012 debt restructuring operation.

APPENDIX 9.2 SELECTED INDICATORS

APPENDIX TABLE 9.1

Caribbean Region: Selected Indicators, 2011

	Poverty (percent of population)	Gross Public Debt (% of GDP)	Debt/Fiscal Revenues	Required Primary Balance for 60% Debt Ratio	Total Debt Service/Fiscal Revenues	Total Debt Service to GDP	Last Sovereign Credit Rating[a]	Net Foreign Assets/GDP	Real GDP Growth (percent) (2007–11)
The Caribbean	**. . .**	**83.5**	**286.8**	**4.4**	**27.5**	**7.5**	**. . .**	**–128.5**	**0.9**
The Bahamas	9.3 (2004)[b]	63.0	274.0	. . .	22.0	4.0	BBB+	. . .	–0.5
Barbados	15[c]	125.5	330.0	8	23.0	8.0	BBB–	. . .	0.1
Belize	41.3 (2009)[c]	83.0	282.0	3	18.0	5.0	C	–133.5	2.0
Guyana	35 (2000-06)[d]	65.2	193.0	. . .	8.0	3.0	. . .	–83.0	4.2
Jamaica	16.5[e]	141.5	565.0	9	78.0	20.0	B–	–134.2	–0.5
Suriname	. . .	19.1	74.0	. . .	6.0	2.0	BB–	–0.9	4.2
Trinidad and Tobago	. . .	31.4	88.0	. . .	7.0	2.0	A–	–22.5	0.6
Antigua and Barbuda	18.3 (2005/06)[c]	93.3	336.0	2	41.0	8.0	. . .	–144.4	–2.2
Dominica	29 (2008/09)[c]	70.2	228.0	0	30.0	9.0	. . .	–61.7	2.4
Grenada	38 (2007/08)[c]	101.2	384.0	2	18.0	4.0	B–	–202.0	0.1
St. Kitts and Nevis	23.7 (2007/08)[c]	153.6	439.0	12	52.0	18.0	. . .	–228.7	0.2
St. Lucia	28.8 (2005)[c]	71.1	261.0	3	30.0	8.0	. . .	–186.5	1.9
St. Vincent and the Grenadines	30.2 (2007/08)[f]	67.8	275.0	1	24.0	6.0	B+	–216.0	–0.4

Sources: IMF, *World Economic Outlook* (October 2012), and International Financial Statistics database; and author's calculations.
[a]Median ratings published by Moody's, Standard and Poor's, and Fitch.
[b]The Bahamas: Staff Report for the 2012 Article IV Consultation (IMF, 2013e).
[c]Caribbean Development Bank Country Poverty Assessments, accessed at http://www.Caribank.Org/publications-and-resources/poverty-assessment-reports-2.
[d]Guyana: Staff Report for the 2010 Article IV Consultation (IMF 2010).
[e]Jamaica: First Review Under the Extended Arrangement Under the Extended Fund Facility and Request for Modification of Performance Criteria (IMF, 2013c).
[f]United Nations Development Program (2010).

REFERENCES

Alleyne, T., 2011, "The Challenges of High Debt, Addressing the Debt Overhang: The Cases of Jamaica and Antigua," unpublished (Washington: International Monetary Fund).

Boughton, J., 2001, *Silent Revolution: The International Monetary Fund 1979–1989* (Washington: International Monetary Fund).

Das, U., M. Papaioannou, and C. Trebesch, 2012, "Sovereign Debt Restructurings 1950–2010: Literature Survey, Data, and Stylized Facts," IMF Working Paper 12/203 (Washington: International Monetary Fund).

Gold, J., H. Monroe, G. P. Nicholls, and J. Park, 2012, "The Role of the International Community and the IMF," paper presented at the IMF's 2012 High-Level Caribbean Forum, Sept. 4–5, Port of Spain, Trinidad and Tobago.

Government of Antigua and Barbuda, 2011, "Antigua and Barbuda Debt Profile Review 2006 to 2010" (St. John's, Antigua).

International Monetary Fund, 2006, "Grenada: Request for a Three-Year Arrangement Under the Poverty Reduction and Growth Facility—Staff Report; and Press Release on the Executive Board Discussion," IMF Country Report No. 06/277 (Washington).

———, 2010, "Guyana: Staff Report for the 2010 Article IV Consultation," IMF Country Report No. 11/152 (Washington).

———, 2011, "Modernizing the Framework for Fiscal Policy and Public Debt Sustainability Analysis," August 8 (Washington).

———, 2012a, "St. Kitts and Nevis: Second Review Under the Stand-by Arrangement and Financing Assurances Review, and Request for Waivers of Applicability—Staff Report and Press Release," IMF Country Report No. 12/196 (Washington).

———, 2012b, "A Survey of Experiences with Emerging Market Sovereign Debt Restructurings," June 5 (Washington).

———, 2013a, "Belize—Staff Report and Press Release," IMF Country Report No. 13/227 (Washington).

———, 2013b, "Sovereign Debt Restructuring—Recent Developments and Implications for the Fund's Legal and Policy Framework" (Washington).

———, 2013c, "Jamaica: First Review Under the Extended Arrangement Under the Extended Fund Facility and Request for Modification of Performance Criteria," IMF Country Report No. 13/304 (Washington).

———, 2013d, "St. Kitts and Nevis: Fourth Review Under the Stand-By Arrangement, Financing Assurances Review and Request for Waivers of Applicability—Staff Report and Press Release," IMF Country Report No. 13/42 (Washington).

———, 2013e, "The Bahamas: Staff Report for the 2012 Article IV Consultation," IMF Country Report No. 13/100 (Washington).

———, 2013f, "Antigua and Barbuda: Staff Report for the 2012 Article IV Consultation, Seventh Review Under the Stand-By Arrangement and Financing Assurances Review, Request for Waiver of Nonobservance of Performance Criteria and Request for Waiver of Applicability," IMF Country Report No. 13/76 (Washington).

Jahan, S., 2012, "Experiences with Sovereign Debt Restructuring: Case Studies from the OECS/ECCU and Beyond," in *The Eastern Caribbean Economic and Currency Union: Macroeconomics and Financial Systems,* ed. by Alfred Schipke, Aliona Cebotari, and Nita Thacker (Washington: International Monetary Fund).

United Nations Development Program, 2010, "Social Implications of the Global Economic Crisis in Caribbean Small Island Developing States: 2008–2009 St. Vincent and the Grenadines," Country Report (New York).

CHAPTER 10

Fiscal Policy and the Current Account in Microstates

YEHENEW ENDEGNANEW, CHARLES AMO-YARTEY, AND THERESE TURNER-JONES

This chapter examines the empirical link between fiscal policy and the current account focusing on microstates, defined as countries with a population of less than 2 million between 1970 and 2009. The extent to which fiscal adjustment can lead to predictable development in the current account remains controversial, with two competing views. The traditional view argues that changes in fiscal policy are associated with changes in the current account through a number of channels that are discussed in the literature review. The traditional view is challenged by the Ricardian equivalence principle, which states that an increase in budget deficit (through reduced taxes) will be offset by increases in private saving, insofar as the private sector fully discounts the future tax liabilities associated with financing the fiscal deficit, hence not affecting the current balance.

This chapter employs panel regression and panel vector autoregression (VAR) to estimate the impact of fiscal policy on the current account. The main challenge in the empirical literature is how to measure fiscal policy that reflects deliberate policy decisions and not simply the impact of business cycle fluctuation. The conventional approach to addressing this problem is to use the cyclically adjusted fiscal data to identify deliberate changes in fiscal policy. The presumption is that cyclically adjusted changes in the fiscal balance reflect decision by policymakers to adjust tax rates and expenditure levels.[1] IMF (2010) uses an alternative approach based on identifying changes in fiscal policy directly from historical records. While this approach could be superior to the conventional approach, this chapter follows the conventional approach because of the difficulties in constructing exogenous fiscal policy measures from historical records in microstates.

Panel regression results show that a percentage point improvement in the fiscal balance improves the current account balance by 0.4 percentage points of GDP

This chapter first appeared as IMF Working Paper 12/51 and was later published in the journal *Applied Economics*, Vol. 45, No. 29, pp. 4137–51. It is reproduced here with minor editorial changes.

[1]IMF (2011) outlines a number of shortcomings of using the cyclically adjusted fiscal balance as a measure of deliberate fiscal policy changes.

(similar to the coefficient of 0.34 found for the global sample). The real effective exchange rate has no significant impact on the current account in microstates but the coefficient is significant in the global sample. Panel VAR results show that an increase in government consumption results in real exchange appreciation but the effect on the current account after an initial deterioration dies out quicker in microstates, in contrast to the global sample, where the deterioration remains for extended periods. The results imply that fiscal policy has little effect on the current account in microstates beyond its direct impact on imports. Overall, the results suggest that the weak relative price effect makes fiscal adjustment much more difficult in microstates.

The remainder of the chapter is organized as follows. The next section reviews the theoretical and empirical literature on fiscal policy and the current account. Following that the chapter reviews the literature on microstates with a focus on their characteristics that have implications for the current account. It then evaluates econometrically the relationship between fiscal policy and the current account using both panel regression and panel VAR.

LITERATURE REVIEW

This paper builds on the literature on fiscal policy and the current account and the literature on microstates. The theoretical and empirical relationship between fiscal policy and the current account is studied extensively. Theoretically, there are competing views that give different results depending on the kind of transmission mechanisms considered in the model to explain the link between fiscal policy and the current account.

Theoretical studies differentiate between intratemporal and intertemporal transmission mechanisms (Mundell, 1960; Fleming, 1962; Salter, 1959). The Mundell-Fleming model and the Swan-Salter model focus on an intratemporal (the relative price effect) mechanism. In the Mundell-Fleming model, an expansionary fiscal policy, by raising domestic demand and increasing the interest rate, leads to a real exchange appreciation through higher capital inflows to the domestic economy. In this model, financial openness and exchange rate regime can affect the effectiveness of the transmission mechanism. In the Swan-Salter model, exchange rate is defined as the relative price of tradables to nontradables. If the government spending is skewed to nontradables, the induced real exchange appreciation might worsen the trade balance by driving production away from tradables and switching consumption towards tradables.

The intertemporal approach (Frenkel and Razin, 1996; Baxter, 1995), on the other hand, suggests that declines in public saving resulting from a fiscal expansion would be offset by an equal increase in private saving, leaving the national saving unaffected. In models of the intertemporal mechanism, an increase in debt-financed government spending lead forward-looking private agents to consume less and increase labor supply to offset the future tax increases, resulting in improvements in the current account that counteract the negative effect of government spending on the current account.

New open economy models that incorporate both the intertemporal and intratemporal mechanisms have been developed recently to address empirical findings on developed countries that show positive government spending shocks resulting in an increase in private consumption and real exchange depreciation in spite of the worsening of the trade balance. Monacelli and Perotti (2006) developed an open economy model with non-separable preferences mitigating the negative wealth effect of an increase in government spending and giving rise to a positive consumption response. Furthermore, when the elasticity of substitution between domestic and imported goods is sufficiently small, the model is also successful in delivering real exchange depreciation and trade balance deterioration after government spending shocks. Ravn, Schmitt-Grohe, and Uribe (2007) offer an alternative explanation using a two-country model that incorporates a deep habit mechanism. Under deep habits, an increase in government spending in the domestic economy leads to a decline in domestic markups relative to foreign markups, which induces the real exchange rate to depreciate. At the same time, a decline in domestic markups raises labor demand, giving rise to an increase in domestic real wages. In turn, the rise in wages leads households to increase their leisure consumption strongly enough to offset the negative wealth effect stemming from the increase in government spending, resulting in an equilibrium increase in private consumption.

Empirically, the evidence is less debatable and the balance of evidence seems to support the intratemporal mechanism of a strong relationship between fiscal policy and the current account. Empirical research on the relationship between fiscal policy and the current account can be grouped into two types, according to the fiscal variable of interest and the methodology used. Studies based on the panel regression approach (for example, Chinn and Prasad, 2003) examine the effect of changes in the fiscal balance on the current account. Generally, they find evidence suggesting that fiscal expansion worsens the current account. Estimates of the impact of 1 percentage point of GDP increase in the government deficit on the current account range between 0.2 and 0.7 percentage points of GDP, depending on the sample and techniques used. Studies based on VAR (Ravn, Schmitt-Grohe, and Uribe, 2007; Beetsma, Giuliodori, and Klaassen, 2008) analyze the effect of government spending on the current account. These studies find evidence to show that an increase in government spending has a deteriorating effect on the current account, except for countries like United States, where the results are mixed (Kim and Roubini, 2008).

An important issue in the VAR literature is the identification of the government spending shocks. There are two main approaches to identify government spending shocks, namely, recursive and narrative approaches. The recursive approach assumes that government consumption does not to react to changes in other variables within a given period (Blanchard and Perotti, 2002). The narrative approach examines official documents to capture specific episodes of large exogenous changes in government spending (Ramey and Shapiro 1998; IMF, 2010, 2011). This paper uses the recursive approach, taking into account the difficulty involved in trying to apply the narrative approach in the large sample of countries considered.

Ali Abbas and others (2011) apply both the panel regression and panel VAR approaches to study the effect of fiscal policy on the current account using a large sample of advanced, emerging market, and low-income economies. They find that a strengthening in the fiscal balance by 1 percentage point of GDP is associated with a current account improvement of 0.3 percentage points of GDP. This relationship appears to be stronger in emerging market and low-income economies, when the exchange rate is flexible, in economies that are more open, when output is above potential, and when initial debt levels are above 90 percent of GDP.

Studies on the impact of the relationship between fiscal policy and the current account in microstates are sparse. Imam (2008) attempts to identify policies that help reduce the current account in microstates. The results suggest that microstates are more likely to have large current account adjustments if they are already running large current account deficits; run budget surpluses; and are less open. Interestingly, Imam (2008) finds that changes in the real effective exchange rate do not help drive reductions in the current account deficit in microstates.

CHARACTERISTICS OF MICROSTATES

This chapter defines microstates as countries with an average population of less than 2 million between 1970 and 2009 (see Table 10.1). Using this definition, about 42 microstates were identified, of which about 70 percent are islands and usually located in the Caribbean, the African region, or the Pacific. Microstates possess a wide range of characteristics such as location, climate, and size, which create a variety of comparative advantages as well as disadvantages. This section highlights some of the unique characteristics of microstates with a focus on those characteristics that have implications for the current account.

Small Size of Domestic Market

Microstates are characterized by the small size of their domestic market, making the level of domestic demand lie below the minimum efficient scale of output (Armstrong and others, 1993). Due to the small size, microstates are usually disadvantageous as a location for extensive industrial activities, especially those that could substantially raise growth. The small domestic market is less conducive for the development of indigenous technologies, limiting the growth of research and development, technical progress and technology acquisition. In addition, a small domestic market does not allow competitive firms to emerge within microstates because of the limited number of participants involved in any economic activity. As a result, prices of goods are generally higher in microstates than larger economies (Armstrong and others, 1993).

Small Domestic Resource Base

Microstates have a small and/or poor domestic resource base due to their small size. In countries where agriculture dominates economic activity, the sector tends to absorb a significant share of land endowment, thereby depriving other alternative production activities from this resource (Commonwealth Consultative Group, 1997). The relatively small population tends to make labor very scarce in microstates, and as a result output in microstates is usually enhanced through the accumulation of human or physical capital rather than through employment (Bhaduri, Mukherji, and Sengupta, 1982). The small size of the domestic market and scarce labor tend to narrow the structure of domestic output in microstates, making them dependent on a small number of activities and hampering the potential to implement import substitution industrialization strategies, thereby exposing them to exogenous shocks.

Narrow Range of Exports and Export Markets

Microstates have a narrow range of exports and export markets, due in part to the narrowness of their domestic production structures. The need for specialization tends to limit export-oriented domestic output to just a few products. Tourism and financial services are usually the main service sectors in microstates, normally complemented by an uncompetitive agricultural sector. Offshore financial services have become an important sector in microstates due to their strategic location and enabling local laws. Highly liberalized financial systems based on lax regulatory standards or strong supervisory frameworks have been a major attraction in the emergence of microstates as offshore financial centers. The export specialization of microstates renders them vulnerable to external shocks, and the vulnerability is exacerbated by reliance on export markets in just a few countries (Armstrong and others, 1998).

High Degree of Openness

Microstates are usually characterized by a high level of openness to trade. The small domestic markets and the tendency towards a high degree of specialization in output and export limit the potential for import substitution because of the adverse impacts on the price level and competitiveness. The importance of tradable goods to these economies necessitates the pursuit of a highly open trading regime. Consequently, import barriers are less important than for larger states (Selwyn, 1975). There is a substantial asymmetry between the domestic production patterns and consumption of microstates. Therefore, the proportion of imports in domestic consumption is high.

High Transport Cost and Lumpiness of Investment

Armstrong and others (1993) discussed extensively the specific problems of landlocked and island microstates, including high transport cost and a high degree of dependence of adjacent states for surface communications and port facilities and,

TABLE 10.1

Real GDP Per Capita and Population of Selected Microstates, 2009

Country	Real GDP per Capita in US$	Real GDP per Capita in Purchasing Power Parity	Population
Antigua and Barbuda	12,920	18,778	87,600
The Bahamas	16,300	22,868	341,713
Bahrain, Kingdom of	26,021	39,200	791,473
Barbados	9,244	17,504	255,872
Belize	4,062	6,628	333,200
Bhutan	1,831	5,113	697,335
Botswana	6,064	13,384	1,949,780
Cabo Verde	3,064	3,644	505,606
Comoros	812	1,183	659,098
Cyprus	31,280	30,848	871,036
Djibouti	1,214	2,319	864,202
Dominica	5,132	8,883	73,596
Equatorial Guinea	15,397	31,779	676,273
Fiji	3,326	4,526	849,218
Gabon	7,502	14,419	1,474,586
The Gambia	430	1,415	1,705,212
Grenada	6,029	8,362	103,930
Guinea-Bissau	519	1,071	1,610,746
Guyana	2,656	3,240	762,498
Iceland	38,029	36,795	319,062
Kiribati	1,306	2,432	98,045
Lesotho	764	1,468	2,066,919
Luxembourg	105,044	83,820	497,854
Maldives	4,760	5,476	309,430
Malta	19,248	24,814	414,971
Mauritius	6,735	12,838	1,275,323
Namibia	4,267	6,410	2,171,137
Oman	11,192	24,226	2,845,415
Qatar	69,754	91,379	1,409,423
Samoa	2,776	4,405	178,846
São Tomé and Príncipe	1,171	1,820	162,755
Seychelles	8,688	19,587	87,972
Solomon Islands	1,256	2,547	523,170
St. Kitts and Nevis	10,988	14,527	49,593
St. Lucia	5,496	9,605	172,092
St. Vincent and the Grenadines	5,335	9,154	109,209
Suriname	2,668	6,930	519,740
Swaziland	2,533	4,998	1,184,936
Trinidad and Tobago	15,841	25,572	1,338,585
Vanuatu	2,702	4,438	239,788

Source: World Bank, World Development Indicators.

therefore, access to export markets and import sourcing. High transport cost has the effect of reducing prices received for exports and raising prices of imports, leading the current account to deteriorate. Djankov, Freund, and Pham (2006) estimate that microstates were on the average 50 percent more distant from trading partners than larger countries. Microstates can suffer from lumpiness of investment due to small size. A single large investment project has an immediate effect on the current account, making it more volatile than it would be in larger economies.

Figure 10.1 Government Consumption in Selected Microstates and Large Emerging Market Economies, 2010 *(Percent of GDP)*

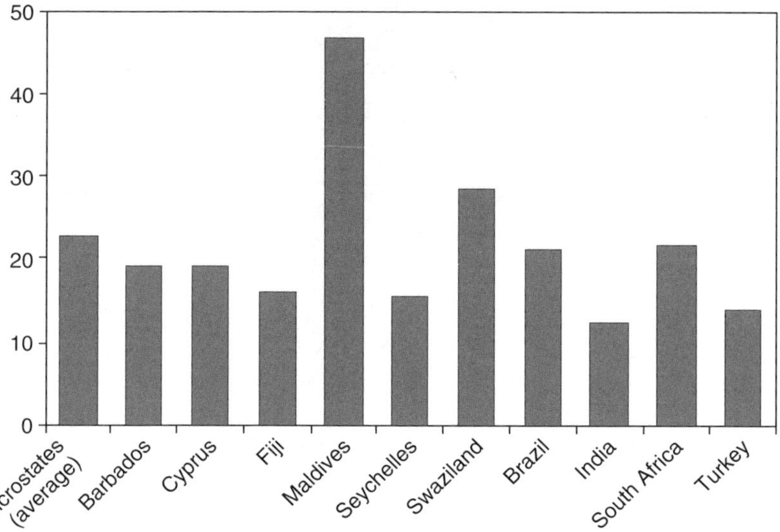

Source: Authors' calculations.

Large Size of the Public Sector

The per capita cost of supplying public goods may be higher in microstates than in larger states due to the lack of economies of scale in supplying public goods (Figure 10.1). The public sector as a share of GDP tends to be bigger. Since government spending is biased toward nontradables, and since historically microstates have had large current account deficits, the current account tends to be structurally more vulnerable in these countries (Imam, 2008).

While there is near consensus that the salient features of microstates make them disadvantageous, microstates also possess some advantages that could help external stability: greater social homogeneity and cohesion, a consequent greater flexibility and decision making efficiency, greater openness to change and the gains from greater openness (Streeten 1993). For instance, greater social homogeneity should enable adjustment to shocks to be more promptly handled because the shifting of adjustment onto other social groups is not possible (Alesina and Drazen, 1991).

PANEL REGRESSION

Data

This chapter uses data from 155 countries, of which 42 are microstates. The main data source is the IMF's *World Economic Outlook* (WEO), where we obtained most of the fiscal variables. The real GDP per capita in purchasing power parity is taken from the World Bank's World Development Indicators (WDI). We used the updated and extended version of the Lane and Milesi-Ferretti (2007) database to get data on net foreign assets. The real effective exchange rate is obtained from the IMF's Information Notice System database. The data range from 1970–2009 whenever they are available. All details can be found in Appendices 10.1 and 10.2.

The Model

The benchmark specification assumes a fixed-effects model of the form:

$$Y_{it} = (\alpha + f_i) + \beta X_{it} + \varepsilon_{it} \tag{10.1}$$

where f_i is the country fixed effects, Y is the current-account-to-GDP ratio, and X is a vector of explanatory variables including the ratio of the cyclically adjusted primary balance to potential GDP, the lagged log real GDP per capita, trade openness (ratio of imports plus exports to GDP), the ratio of lagged net foreign assets to GDP, the volatility of terms of trade, and the lagged log of real effective exchange rate.

The explanatory variables might influence the current account in the following ways.

Cyclically Adjusted Fiscal Balance

An increase in government balance could improve the current account through an increase in national saving in the absence of Ricardian equivalence. Reduction in government spending or a tax increase would lead to an increase in public saving. Unless the private sector is fully Ricardian, the total national saving would increase, thereby improving the current account. This chapter uses the cyclically adjusted primary balance (CAPB) to potential GDP ratio to capture fiscal balance. This choice is motivated by the fact that there could be some endogeneity problems between fiscal balance and the current account balance because of common reaction to the business cycle. IMF (2011) criticized what they call the conventional approach of using cyclically adjusted fiscal data on the grounds that CAPB may still include non-policy factors, or it may reflect deliberate policy responses to other developments affecting economic activity or to the current account itself. This chapter attempts to address these problems by applying a panel VAR methodology using another fiscal variable less vulnerable to the criticisms, namely government consumption, in the next section.

The CAPB is calculated by applying Hodrick-Prescott (HP) filtering to the real GDP to obtain the output gap measure and then using 1 and 0 as the elasticity of revenue and expenditure, respectively, with respect to the output gap. In this way, the CAPB becomes:

$$CAPB = R\left(\frac{Y^P}{Y}\right) - G \tag{10.2}$$

where R is revenue and grants, G is government spending less interest payment, Yp is the potential output, and Y is the actual output.

Trade Openness

Due to the high increase in international trade in the past decades, it would be interesting to study the relationship between trade openness and the current account balance. Microstates are characterized by their narrow range of exports, large proportion of imports, and high degree of openness. We would expect more trade openness in microstates to lead to more imports, implying a negative relationship between trade openness and the current account balance.

Net Foreign Assets

The relationship between net foreign assets (NFA) and the current account is ambiguous, as NFA may have two different effects. On the one hand, a negative relationship can exist between NFA and the current account, because high NFA might lead people to think that economies can afford to prolong trade deficits. On the other hand, high NFA could bring higher net income flows, resulting in a positive relationship with the current account balance.

Terms of Trade Volatility

Increased uncertainty associated with high volatility in terms of trade might lead agents in the economy to save more for precautionary reasons. Moreover, for the same reason, economies may also experience low investment. Therefore, we expect a positive relationship between high terms of trade volatility and the current account balance. The volatility of the terms of trade is constructed by taking the three-year moving standard deviation of the terms of trade of goods and services index.

Real Effective Exchange Rate

Depreciation of the real effective exchange rate makes imports more expensive and exports cheaper. As a result, the real effective exchange rate is expected to be negatively related with the current account balance.

Panel Regression Results

This section presents the panel regression results for the global sample and microstates. Tables 10.2 and 10.3 give the results obtained for the benchmark model and its variations under different specifications. To take into account cross-country differences in time-invariant characteristics of our microstates, we use a panel fixed-effects estimation as our baseline model. We also control for income levels in all specifications of our model.

The results show that in both the global sample and microstates, the fiscal balance appears to be positively associated with the current account. The size of the CAPB coefficients is 0.34 and 0.39 for the global sample and the microstates, respectively. The coefficient for microstates reflects their openness to trade and the likely impact of fiscal expansion on imports. Our results compare well with the CAPB coefficient obtained by Ali Abbas and others (2011) for a large sample of countries; they find a coefficient of 0.35 and also show that the coefficient is larger for countries with a high degree of trade openness.

TABLE 10.2

Panel Regressions: Global Sample *(Dependent variable: Current-account-to-GDP ratio)*

	Fixed Effects	Fixed Time Effects	Pooled OLS	Excluding Oil-Exporting Countries	Dynamic Panel GMM
Cyclically adjusted primary balance	0.346***	0.322***	0.367***	0.289***	0.297***
	10.61	9.76	11.41	8.63	8.57
Lagged log per capita income	−0.481	0.836	0.628***	−0.666	−1.713*
	(−1.00)	1.37	2.72	(−1.35)	(−1.93)
Trade openness	−0.0128*	−0.00328	−0.0154***	−0.00684	−0.0488***
	(−1.87)	(−0.46)	(−3.13)	(−0.98)	(−4.92)
Lagged net foreign-assets-to-GDP ratio	0.0221***	0.0263***	0.0256***	0.0203***	−0.0120***
	7.81	9.32	10.87	7.07	(−2.59)
Volatility of terms of trade	0.00152	0.00207	0.00116	0.00108	−0.00123
	0.65	0.89	0.5	0.47	(−0.13)
Lagged log of real effective exchange rate	−1.237***	−1.279***	−1.032**	−0.968**	−1.569**
	(−2.79)	(−2.71)	(−2.41)	(−2.00)	(−2.23)
Lagged current-account-to-GDP ratio					0.324***
					14.21
Constant	8.599*	−4.562	−1.586	8.219*	22.85***
	1.87	(−0.87)	(−0.53)	1.75	2.7
N	2,370	2,370	2,370	2,211	2,131

Source: Authors' calculations.
Note: GMM = generalized method of moments; OLS = ordinary least squares. t-statistics in parentheses. * $p < 0.1$, ** $p < 0.05$, *** $p < 0.01$.

TABLE 10.3

Panel Regressions: Microstates *(Dependent variable: Current-account-to-GDP ratio)*

	Fixed Effects	Fixed Time Effects	Pooled OLS	Excluding Oil-Exporting Countries	Dynamic Panel GMM
Cyclically adjusted primary balance	0.394***	0.443***	0.416***	0.313***	0.361***
	5.25	5.71	5.63	4.02	5.49
Lagged log per capita income	−1.043	2.305	1.398*	−1.607	−4.807***
	(−0.76)	1.2	1.73	(−0.92)	(−3.17)
Trade openness	−0.0537***	−0.0519***	−0.0599***	−0.0394**	−0.0335*
	(−2.84)	(−2.74)	(−3.70)	(−1.97)	(−1.88)
Lagged net foreign-assets-to-GDP ratio	0.0363***	0.0381***	0.0421***	0.0322***	0.00589
	4.57	4.53	7.59	3.87	0.78
Volatility of terms of trade	−0.000823	−0.0014	−0.000528	−0.00081	−0.00163
	(−0.27)	(−0.46)	(−0.18)	(−0.27)	(−0.72)
Lagged log of real effective exchange rate	1.599	−1.896	1.733	1.828	3.105
	−0.58	(−0.63)	0.7	0.64	1.38
Lagged current-account-to-GDP ratio					0.428***
					10.59
Constant	2.84	−7.807	−17.52	4.434	26.75
	0.14	(−0.37)	(−1.17)	0.19	1.43
N	510	510	510	472	444

Source: Authors' calculations.
Note: GMM = generalized method of moments; OLS = ordinary least squares. t-statistics in parentheses. * $p < 0.1$, ** $p < 0.05$, *** $p < 0.01$.

In line with a priori expectations, the degree of openness appears to be negatively related to the current account balance. The coefficient is statistically significant at 1 percent in microstates, while it is only significant at the 10 percent level in the global sample. One possible interpretation of this is that with the limited exports and already high trade openness in microstates, an increase in the degree of openness is likely to imply more imports. Chinn and Prasad (2003) find a similar negative relationship in the medium term between openness and the current account balance.

The coefficient of the NFA is positive and statistically significant both for the global sample and for microstates, implying that high NFA helps countries to obtain higher net income flow and that negative NFA is associated with a low current account balance due to outward interest payment. Imam (2008), however, finds a negative relationship between NFA and the current account and suggests that high NFA helps to finance and sustain a current account deficit.

The coefficient of terms of trade volatility appears to have an insignificant relationship with the current account in both the global sample and microstates. One plausible explanation is that changes in saving and investment decisions taken by agents—the main channel through which volatility affects the current account balance—could be more of a medium-term behavior that is difficult to capture in our annual data framework. Chinn and Prasad (2003) support this hypothesis by finding a strong positive relationship between terms of trade volatility and the current account in the medium term (using five-year averages) but a negligible relationship in the short term.[2]

In the global sample, the coefficient of the real effective exchange rate implies that appreciation appears to be associated with deterioration of current account balance. However, in microstates the impact is not statistically significant. As counter-intuitive as it may sound, the result is not surprising. This might be due to the fact that imports, mainly food and fuel, are inelastic in microstates, preventing the expenditure switching effect from taking place as the relative price changes. Moreover, most imports are not produced locally, limiting the ability of substitution. In addition, exports such as tourism and banking are usually conducted in foreign currency, suggesting exports may not be cheaper after devaluation. Imam (2008) documents similar results for microstates.

Robustness Tests

We examined the robustness and sensitivity of our results to different estimation techniques. As in the previous section, we control for GDP per capita, trade openness, NFA, and the volatility of terms of trade. In the first specification, we allow for country fixed effects as well as time effects. The results are very similar to the benchmark model that allows for only country fixed effects. The next specification excludes oil-exporting countries. Here, the coefficients for CAPB

[2]We used a five-year moving standard deviation and changes in terms of trade, but the result remains the same.

weaken to 0.28 and 0.31 for the global sample and microstates, respectively. This is not surprising, given that oil price shocks typically induce large co-movements in public sector balances through oil revenues and in the current account through oil exports in oil-exporting countries. In addition, we estimated the baseline model using a pooled ordinary least squares (OLS) regression and a dynamic panel data model, where the lagged variable of the current account is included as an explanatory variable. The results are similar to those obtained from the benchmark model. We also restricted the sample to a more recent period (1990–2009) and estimated the benchmark model using different estimation methods. Overall, our main results seem to hold (see Appendix Table 10.3).

PANEL VECTOR AUTOREGRESSION

The Model

The next exercise we conduct in this chapter is to examine the impact of fiscal policy on the current account using panel vector autoregresssion (VAR) methodology. The panel VAR technique combines the traditional VAR approach that treats all variables in the system as endogenous with the panel data approach that allows for unobserved individual heterogeneity. In this chapter, the benchmark specification is a second-order panel VAR model of the form:

$$Z_{it} = \propto_0 + \propto_1 Z_{it-1} + f_i + \mathring{a}_i \tag{10.3}$$

where Z_t is a four-variable vector of log of real government consumption, log of real GDP, current-account-to-GDP ratio, and log of real effective exchange rate. We have allowed for individual heterogeneity by adding country fixed effects, f_i. As the fixed effects are correlated with the lags of the dependent variables, instead of the mean-differencing procedure, a forward mean-differencing procedure is used to remove the fixed effects.[3]

Identification of government consumption shocks is achieved through a methodology that is commonly known as the recursive approach. This methodology assumes government spending does not react contemporaneously to shocks to other variables in the system. The argument is that movements in government spending, unlike movements in taxes, are largely unrelated to the business cycle. Therefore, it seems plausible to assume that government spending is not affected contemporaneously by shocks originating in the private sector. To this end, a reduced-form model—with variables ordered as government spending, GDP, current-account-to-GDP ratio, and the real effective exchange rate—is used.

[3]This procedure, also known as the Helmert transformation, is based on Arellano and Bover (1995). The procedure preserves the orthogonality between the transformed variables and the lagged regressors that thus can be used as instruments to estimate the coefficients by system generalized method of moments (GMM).

Results

The results show that a one-standard-deviation shock in government consumption on impact increases government consumption by 12 percent in the global sample and by 11 percent in the microstates. In both cases the effect on government consumption seems to die slowly. The effect on GDP is small in both samples, indicating a very small multiplier. However, while the effect in microstates dies out quickly, it persists in the global sample.

As the current account is used as percent of GDP, we normalize the one-standard-deviation shocks in government consumption to a 1 percentage point increase in the government-consumption-to-GDP ratio, and we assess the result to the recalculated effect on the current-account-to-GDP ratio. To do this, we follow a number of steps. First, we calculate the average government-consumption-to-GDP ratio over the sample period for the global sample and microstates. This gives 18.5 percent and 22.5 percent, respectively. Second, we transform the increase in government consumption to an increase in the government-consumption-to-GDP ratio. For the global sample, an increase in 12 percent of the average 18.5 percent government-consumption-to-GDP ratio translates to a 2.2 percent increase in the average government-consumption-to-GDP ratio. For microstates, a similar calculation gives 2.5 percent. Third, we normalize these changes and the effects on the current-account-to-GDP ratio to a 1 percentage point increase in the government-consumption-to-GDP ratio (Figure 10.2).

A percentage point increase in government-consumption-to-GDP ratio leads to a 0.21 percentage point deterioration in the current-account-to-GDP ratio in the global sample. The equivalent effect for microstates is a worsening of the current account by 0.42 percentage points (Figure 10.3). The result is not surprising, given the fact that the proportion of imports in domestic consumption is high. Although the impact effect of a government consumption shock is larger in microstates, the impact is short-lived and dies out in two years and becomes insignificant. On the other hand, the impact effect of a government consumption shock in the global sample, though smaller, is significant and persistent even after five years.

The effect of an increase in government consumption on the real effective exchange rate is not significant in the global sample, while in microstates there seems to be a significant appreciation of the real effective exchange rate on impact, although it becomes insignificant in the subsequent periods. The appreciation of the real effective exchange rate in microstates might be the result of their limited ability to influence the price of tradable goods as opposed to nontradable goods. However, the real exchange rate is unable to reinforce the deterioration of the current account. Once again, this highlights the weakness of the relative price effect and limits the impact of fiscal policy on the current account in microstates.

Robustness Tests

The robustness of our results is tested by the following measures (see Appendix Tables 10.3 and 10.4, and Appendix Figures 10.1 to 10.4). First, we

Figure 10.2 Panel Vector Autoregression: Global Sample—Impulse Response to One-Standard-Deviation Shocks in Government Consumption

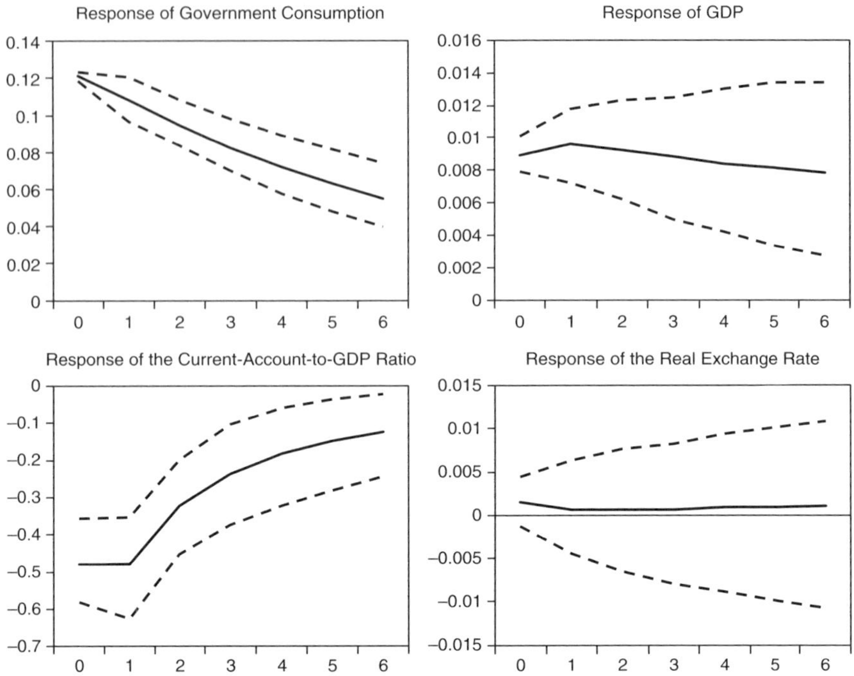

Source: Authors' calculations.

estimated the benchmark model with different specifications, including changing the lag length from 2 to 3 and changing the order of the variables in the model. Second, we reestimated the panel VAR model excluding oil-exporting countries. Third, we restricted the time period to recent years starting from 1990. All in all, the results seem to support our benchmark results for microstates: a short-lived, larger-impact period response of the current account after an increase in government consumption.

SUMMARY AND CONCLUSION

This chapter has examined the empirical link between fiscal policy and the current account in microstates. The results suggest that there is indeed a relationship between fiscal policy and the current account in microstates. Panel regression results suggest that a strengthening of the fiscal balance improves the current account in microstates. However, the real effective exchange rate has no significant impact on the current account in microstates. Panel VAR results show that an increase in government consumption leads to an immediate deterioration of the current

Figure 10.3 Panel Vector Autoregression: Microstates—Impulse Response to One-Standard-Deviation Shocks in Government Consumption

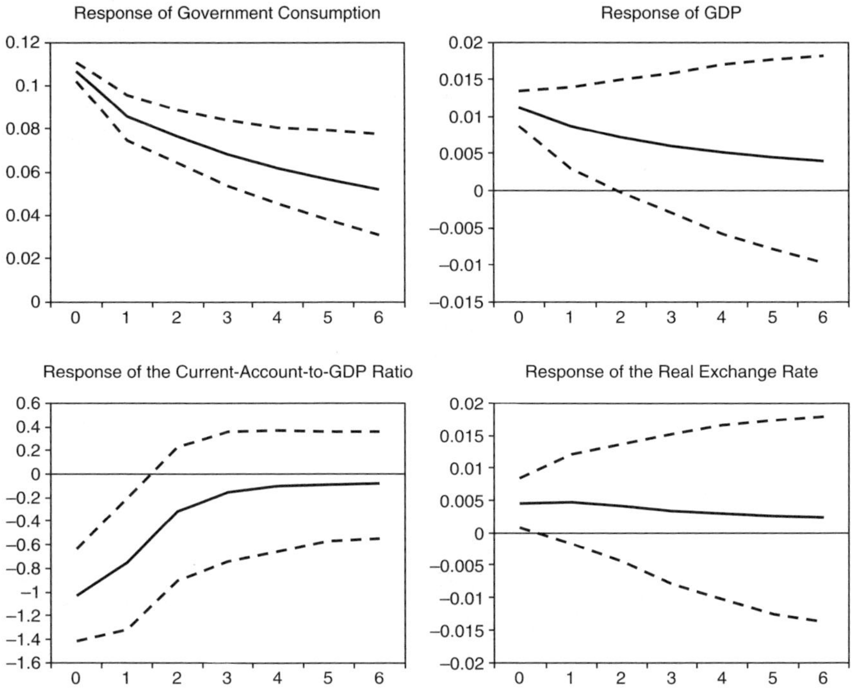

Source: Authors' calculations.

account in microstates. The deterioration effect dies out together with the government consumption, notwithstanding the appreciated exchange rate, which according to theoretical mechanisms should have sustained the deterioration longer. The result implies that fiscal policy has little effect on the current account in microstates beyond its direct impact on imports. Overall, the results suggest that the weak relative price effects make fiscal adjustment much more difficult in microstates.

APPENDIX 10.1

APPENDIX TABLE 10.1

Selected Recent Empirical Works

Selected Works	Sample and Methodology	Results
This chapter	155 countries of which 42 are microstates; annual data, 1970–2009; panel regression and panel VAR	1) 1% of GDP increase in the CAPB improves the current account by 0.35% of GDP in the global sample and 0.4% of GDP in microstates. 2) 1% of GDP increase in government consumption worsens the current account by 0.21% of GDP in the full sample and 0.42% of GDP in microstates on impact.
Ali Abbas and others (2011)	124 countries; annual and quarterly data, 1985–2007; panel regression and panel VAR	1) 1% of GDP increase in the CAPB improves the current account by 0.3% of GDP. 2) 1% of GDP increase in government consumption worsens the current account by 0.3% of GDP on impact.
Abiad, Leigh, and Mody (2009)	135 countries; five-year averages, 1975–2004; panel regression	1% of GDP increase in the budget balance improves the current account by 0.3% of GDP.
Beetsma, Giuliodori, and Klaassen (2008)	14 European Union countries; annual data, 1970–2004; panel VAR	1% GDP increase in government spending worsens the trade balance by 0.5% of GDP on impact and a peak fall of 0.8% of GDP after two years.
Chinn and Prasad (2003)	89 countries; annual data, 1971–95; panel regression	1% of GDP increase in the budget balance improves the current account by 0.25–0.4% of GDP
Corsetti and Müller (2006)	Australia, Canada, the United Kingdom and the United States; quarterly data, 1975–2001; VAR	1% GDP increase in government spending worsens the trade balance by 0.5% of GDP in the United Kingdom, by 0.17% of GDP in Canada and to a non-significant effect of trade balance in the United States and Australia on impact.
Monacelli and Perotti (2006)	Australia, Canada, the United Kingdom and the United States; quarterly data, 1975–2006; VAR	1% GDP increase in government spending worsens the trade balance by 0.4 to 0.9 percentage point of GDP.
Ravn, Schmitt-Grohe, and Uribe (2007)	Australia, Canada, the United Kingdom and the United States; quarterly data, 1975–2005; panel VAR	1% increase in government spending worsens trade balance (to GDP ratio) by around 0.03% at impact and to a peak of 0.05% after one year.

Source: Authors' compilation.
Note: CAPB = cyclically adjusted primary balance; VAR = vector autoregression.

APPENDIX TABLE 10.2

Variables and Sources of Data

Descriptor	Database
Current account balance	WEO
Imports of goods and services	WEO
Exports of goods and services	WEO
Central government balance	WEO
Central government, total expenditure, and net lending	WEO
General government, total revenue, and grants	WEO
General government expenditure, interest	WEO
Public consumption expenditure, current prices	WEO
Gross domestic product, current prices	WEO
Gross domestic product deflator	WEO
Gross domestic product, current prices, U.S. dollars	WEO
Consumer price index	WEO
Terms of trade, goods, and services	WEO
GDP per capita purchasing power parity (constant 2005 international dollars)	WDI
Real effective exchange rate	INSDATA
Net foreign-asset-to-GDP ratio (%)	LM

Source: Authors' compilation.

Note: INSDATA the IMF's Information Notice System database; LM = Lane and Milesi-Ferreti (2007); WDI = the World Bank's World Development Indicators; WEO = the IMF's World Economic Outlook database.

APPENDIX TABLE 10.3

Panel Regressions: Global Sample *(Dependent variable: current-account-balance-to-GDP ratio) (Sample period resticted to 1990–2009)*

	Fixed Effects	Fixed Time Effects	Pooled OLS	Excluding Oil-Exporting Countries	Dynamic Panel GMM
Cyclically adjusted primary balance to potential GDP ratio	0.326***	0.319***	0.358***	0.238***	0.233***
	(8.72)	(8.56)	(9.76)	(6.18)	(5.25)
Lagged log per capita income	−1.920***	−0.494	0.612**	−2.327***	−3.290**
	(−2.94)	(−0.59)	(2.36)	(−3.39)	(−2.30)
Trade openness	−0.0125	−0.0046	−0.0157***	−0.00838	−0.0437***
	(−1.52)	(−0.53)	(−2.83)	(−1.01)	(−3.39)
Lagged net foreign-assets-to-GDP ratio	0.0179***	0.0233***	0.0238***	0.0155***	−0.0309***
	(5.15)	(6.70)	(8.69)	(4.42)	(−5.26)
Volatility of terms of trade	0.00448	0.0131	0.00346	−0.00731	0.00292
	(0.47)	(1.37)	(0.37)	(−0.75)	(0.22)
Lagged log of real effective exchange rate	−1.121*	−0.972	−0.998	−0.841	1.625
	(−1.77)	(−1.54)	(−1.64)	(−1.26)	(1.52)
Lagged current-account-to-GDP					0.266***
					(8.54)
Constant	20.07***	6.213	−1.693	21.55***	19.99
	(3.33)	(0.85)	(−0.45)	(3.45)	(1.55)
Number of observations	1,915	1,915	1,915	1,787	1,641

Source: Authors' calculations.

Note: GMM = generalized method of moments; OLS = ordinary least squares. t-statistics in parentheses. *, **, and *** denote significance at the 10, 5, and 1 percent levels, respectively.

APPENDIX TABLE 10.4

Panel Regressions: Microstates *(Dependent variable: current-account-balance-to-GDP ratio)*

	Fixed Effects	Fixed Time Effects	Pooled OLS	Excluding Oil-Exporting Countries	Dynamic Panel GMM
Cyclically adjusted primary-balance-to-potential-GDP ratio	0.356***	0.417***	0.377***	0.220**	0.431***
	(4.21)	(4.83)	(4.51)	(2.49)	(4.95)
Lagged log per capita income	−0.123	3.002	1.776*	−3.83	−7.76
	(−0.07)	(1.34)	(1.95)	(−1.50)	(−1.61)
Trade openness	−0.0659***	−0.0600***	−0.0659***	−0.0545**	−0.133***
	(−2.95)	(−2.67)	(−3.57)	(−2.33)	(−4.18)
Lagged net foreign-assets-to-GDP ratio	0.0108	0.0171	0.0322***	−0.000521	−0.0171
	(1.04)	(1.56)	(4.86)	(−0.05)	(−1.20)
Volatility of terms of trade	0.00542	0.0286	0.00877	−0.0201	0.0105
	(0.19)	(0.97)	(0.34)	(−0.63)	(0.29)
Lagged log of real effective exchange rate	2.414	0.387	−0.629	4.236	−0.223
	(0.69)	(0.11)	(−0.20)	(1.18)	(−0.05)
Lagged current-account-to-GDP ratio					0.355***
					(7.03)
Constant	−8.589	−24.61	−9.742	12.42	76.76
	(−0.35)	(−0.94)	(−0.54)	(0.43)	(1.58)
Number of observations	415	415	415	382	343

Source: Authors' calculations.

Note: Sample period restricted to 1990–2009. GMM = generalized method of moments; OLS = ordinary least squares. t-statistics in parentheses. *, **, and *** denote significance at the 10, 5, and 1 percent levels, respectively.

Appendix Figure 10.1 Panel Vector Autoregression: Impulse Response to One-Standard-Deviation Shocks in Government Consumption—Length of Lag Set to Three

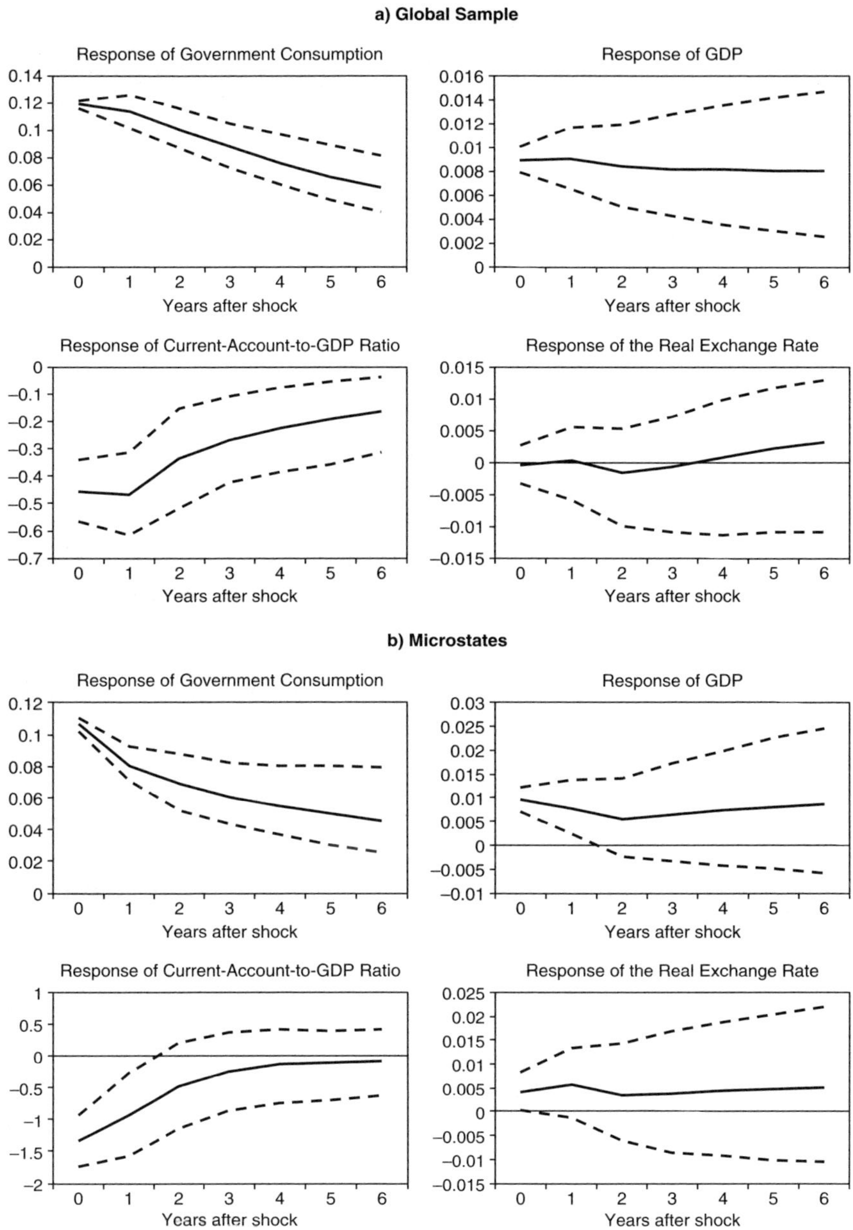

Source: Authors' calculations.

Note: Confidence bands are the 5th and 95th percentiles from Monte Carlo simulations based on 500 replications.

Appendix Figure 10.2 Panel Vector Autoregression: Impulse Response to One-Standard-Deviation Shocks in Government Consumption—Excluding Oil Exporters

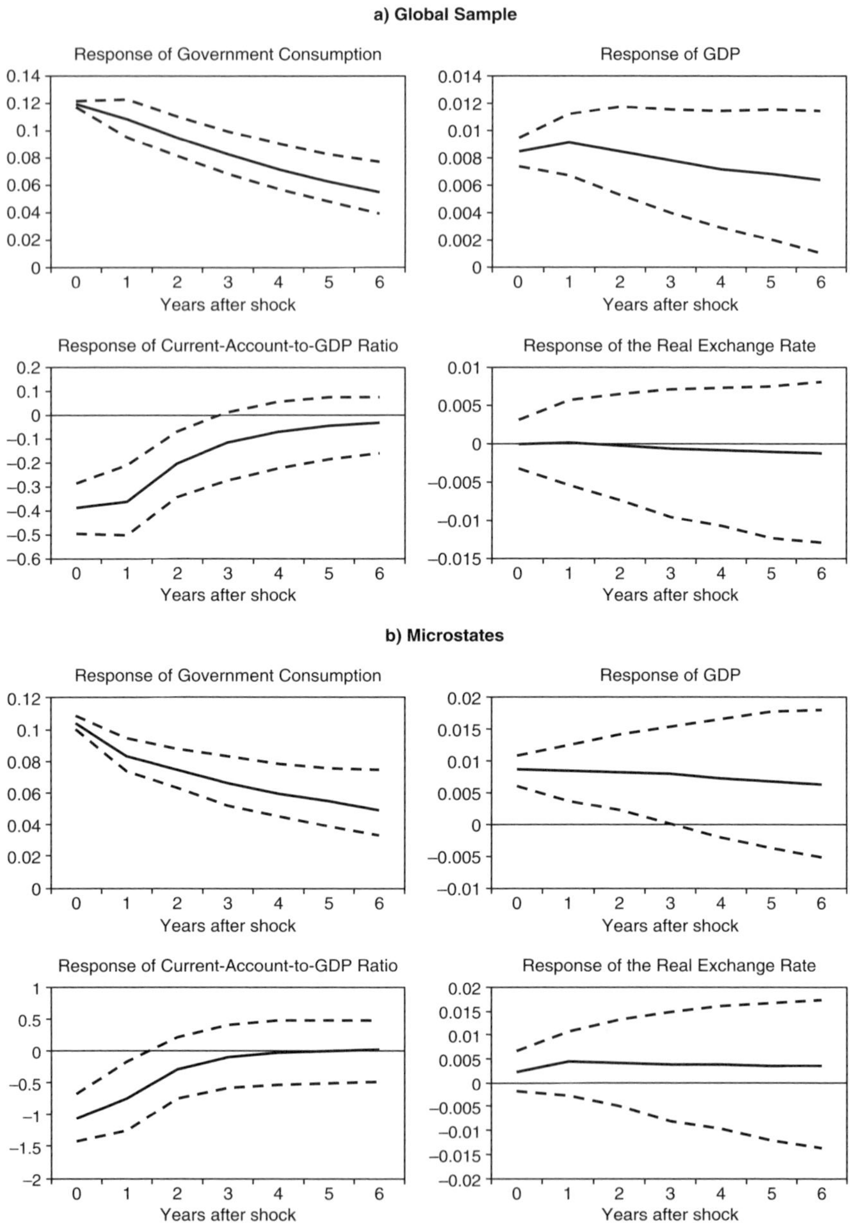

Source: Authors' calculations.
Note: Confidence bands are the 5th and 95th percentiles from Monte Carlo simulations based on 500 replications.

Appendix Figure 10.3 Panel Vector Autoregression: Impulse Response to One-Standard-Deviation Shocks in Government Consumption—Government Consumption Ordered Second

a) Global Sample

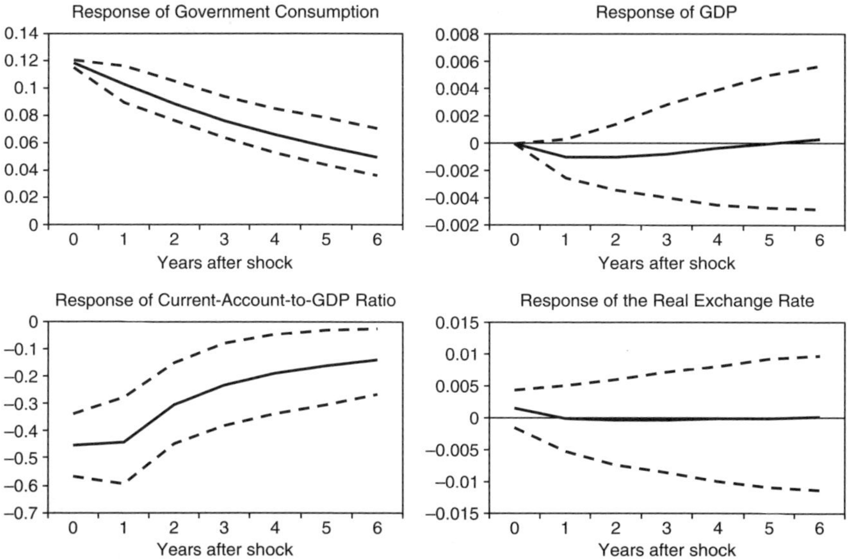

b) Microstates

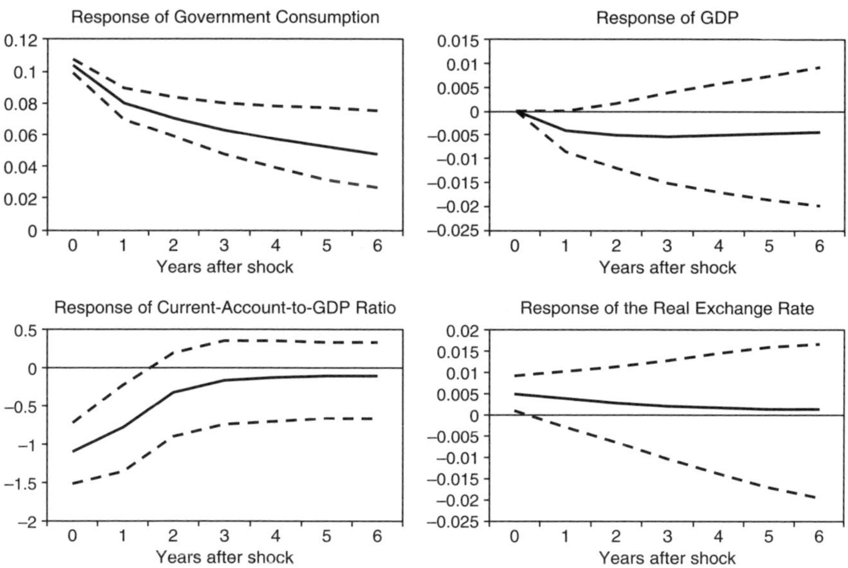

Source: Authors' calculations.
Note: Confidence bands are the 5th and 95th percentiles from Monte Carlo simulations based on 500 replications.

Appendix Figure 10.4 Panel Vector Autoregression: Impulse Response to One-Standard-Deviation Shocks in Government Consumption, 1990–2009

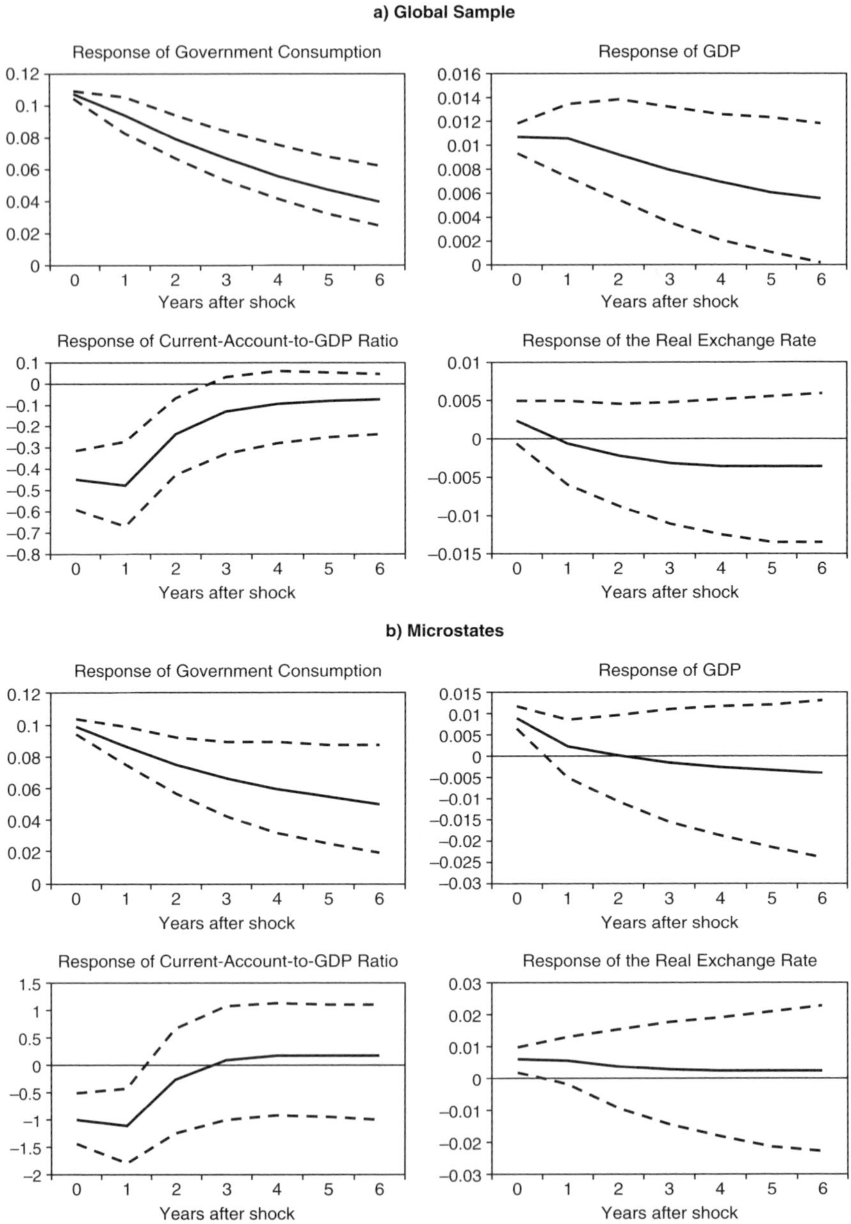

Source: Authors' calculations.
Note: Confidence bands are the 5th and 95th percentiles from Monte Carlo simulations based on 500 replications.

REFERENCES

Abiad, Abdul, Daniel Leigh, and Ashoka Mody, 2009, "Financial Integration, Capital Mobility, and Income Convergence," *Economic Policy,* Vol. 24, pp. 241–305.

Alesina, Alberto, and Allan Drazen, 1991, "Why Are Stabilizations Delayed?" *American Economic Review,* Vol. 81, pp. 1170–80.

Ali Abbas, S. M., Jacques Bouhga-Hagbe, Antonio Fatás, Paolo Mauro, and Ricardo C. Velloso, 2011, "Fiscal Policy and the Current Account," *IMF Economic Review,* Vol. 50, pp. 603–29.

Arellano, Manuel, and Olympia Bover, 1995, "Another Look at the Instrumental Variable Estimation of Error Component Models," *Journal of Econometrics,* Vol. 68, pp. 29–51.

Armstrong, H., R. J. De Kervenoael, X. Li, and R. Read, 1998, "A Comparison of the Economic Performance of Different Micro-States, and between Micro-States and Larger Countries," *World Development,* Vol. 26, pp. 639–56.

Armstrong, H. W., G. Johnes, J. Johnes, and A. I. Macbean, 1993, "The Role of Transport Costs as a Determinant of Price Level Differentials between the Isle of Man and the United Kingdom, 1989," *World Development,* Vol. 21, pp. 311–18.

Baxter, Marianne, 1995, "International Trade and Business Cycles," in *Handbook of International Economics: 1985,* ed. by G. M. Grossmann and K. Rogoff (Amsterdam: North-Holland, Elsevier).

Beetsma, R., Massimo Giuliodori, and Franc Klaassen, 2008, "The Effects of Public Spending Shocks on Trade Balances and Budget Deficits in the European Union," *Journal of the European Economic Association,* Vol. 6, pp. 414–23.

Bhaduri, Amit, Anjan Mukherji, and Ramprasad Sengupta, 1982, "Problems of Long-Term Growth in Small Economies: A Theoretical Analysis," in *Problems and Policies in Small Economies: 1982,* ed. by B. Jalan (London and Canberra: Croom Helm).

Blanchard, Olivier, and Roberto Perotti, 2002, "An Empirical Characterization of the Dynamic Effects of Changes in Government Spending and Taxes on Output," *Quarterly Journal of Economics,* Vol. 117, pp. 1329–68.

Chinn, Menzie D., and Eswar S. Prasad, 2003, "Medium-Term Determinants of Current Accounts in Industrial and Developing Countries: An Empirical Exploration," *Journal of International Economics,* Vol. 59, pp. 47–76.

Commonwealth Consultative Group, 1997, *A Future for Small States: Overcoming Vulnerability* (London: Commonwealth Secretariat).

Corsetti, Giancarlo, and Gernot J. Muller, 2006, "Budget Deficits and Current Accounts: Openness and Fiscal Persistence," *Economic Policy,* Vol. 21, pp. 597–638.

Djankov, Simeon, Caroline Freund, and Cong Pham, 2006, "Trading on Time," Working Paper No. 3909 (Washington: World Bank).

Fleming, J.M., 1962, "Domestic Financial Policies Under Fixed and Under Floating Exchange Rates," *IMF Staff Papers,* Vol. 9, pp. 369–79.

Frenkel, Jacob A., and Assaf Razin, 1996, *Fiscal Policies and Growth in the World Economy* (Cambridge, Massachusetts: MIT Press).

Imam, Patrick, 2008, "Rapid Current Account Adjustments: Are Microstates Different?" IMF Working Paper 08/233 (Washington).

International Monetary Fund, 2010, *World Economic Outlook* (Washington, October).

———, 2011, *World Economic Outlook* (Washington, September).

Kim, Soyoung, and Nouriel Roubini, 2008, "Twin Deficit and Twin Divergence? Fiscal Policy, Current Account, and Real Exchange Rate in the U.S.," *Journal of Economic Literature,* Vol. 74, pp. 362–83.

Lane, Philip R., and Gian Maria Milesi-Ferretti, 2007, "Updated and Extended Version of the External Wealth of Nations Mark II Database Developed by Lane and Milesi-Ferretti, The External Wealth of Nations Mark II," *Journal of International Economics,* Vol. 73, pp. 223–50.

Monacelli, Tommaso, and Roberto Perotti, 2006, "Fiscal Policy, the Trade Balance, and the Real Exchange Rate: Implications for International Risk Sharing," unpublished (Bocconi: Università Bocconi).

Mundell, Robert A., 1960, "The Monetary Dynamics of International Adjustment under Fixed and Flexible Exchange Rates," *Quarterly Journal of Economics* Vol. 74, pp. 227–57.

Ramey, Valerie A., and Matthew D. Shapiro, 1998, "Costly Capital Reallocation and the Effects of Government Spending," in *Carnegie-Rochester Conference Series on Public Policy*, Vol. 48, No. 1, pp. 145–94.

Ravn, Morten O., Stephanie Schmitt-Grohe, and Martin Uribe, 2007, "Explaining the Effects of Government Spending Shocks on Consumption and the Real Exchange Rate," unpublished (Durham, North Carolina: Duke University).

Salter, Wilfred A., 1959, "Internal and External Balance: The Role of Price and Expenditure Effects," *Economic Record,* Vol. 35, pp. 226–38.

Selwyn, Percy, 1975, *Development Policy in Small Countries* (London: Croom Helm).

Streeten, Paul, 1993, "The Special Problems of Small Countries," *World Development,* Vol. 21, pp. 197–202.

CHAPTER 11

Fiscal Policy Rules and Fiscal Performance: Evidence from Microstates

JOEL CHIEDU OKWUOKEI

A number of governments across the world have adopted fiscal policy rules, especially against the backdrop of worsening fiscal performances and rising debt levels. Recently, following the financial crisis, fiscal rules have been advocated to support fiscal consolidation efforts and to ensure long-term sustainability of government finances. This chapter empirically analyzes the impacts of fiscal rules on fiscal performance in microstates with a focus on the Caribbean, where fiscal consolidation has been a major challenge. Broadly, we address three questions. Are there fiscal rules in microstates in general, and in the Caribbean in particular? If the answer is yes, what types of rules exist and what are their characteristics? Is the existence of fiscal rules in microstates associated with improved fiscal performance?

We find ample evidence of the existence of fiscal rules in microstates. In total, 17 countries—equivalent to 40 percent of the microstate sample—have a fiscal rule of some kind (see Table 11.1). These rules are relatively new, about two decades old. Although the institutional coverage slightly favors the central government, the rules in place aim to address fiscal and debt sustainability concerns. Budget balance rules and debt rules constitute 90 percent of all these fiscal rules. The debt rules generally constrain the public-debt-to-GDP ratio to at most 70 percent. Our empirical results show that the presence of these fiscal rules in microstates does significantly influence fiscal performance. It suggests that by increasing discipline and credibility of fiscal policy, fiscal rules tend to bolster fiscal consolidation efforts and lower high debt levels in microstates, including the Caribbean countries.

The remainder of the chapter is organized as follows. First we describe the main types, characteristics, and roles of fiscal rules, followed by an analysis of the main characteristics of the rules in existence in microstates. The chapter then reviews the literature on fiscal policy rules. The last part of the chapter presents our empirical analysis of the rules' impact on fiscal performance and discusses the results.

TABLE 11.1

Fiscal Rules in Microstates

Country	No. of Rules	Coverage	Type[a]	Legal Basis	Start Year
Antigua and Barbuda	2	General government	BBR+DR	International treaty	1998
Botswana	1	Central government	ER	Statutory	2003
Cabo Verde	2	Central government	BBR+DR	Political commitment	1998
Dominica	2	General government	BBR+DR	International treaty	1998
Equatorial Guinea	2	Central government	BBR+DR	International treaty	2002
Gabon	2	Central government	BBR+DR	International treaty	2002
Grenada	2	General government	BBR+DR	International treaty	1998
Guinea Bissau	2	Central government	BBR+DR	International treaty	2000
Iceland[b]	1	Central government	ER	Political commitment	2004–08
Jamaica	2	Central government	BBR+DR	Statutory	2010
Luxembourg[c]	5	General government, Central government, Social security	BBR+DR+ER	Coalition agreement, International treaty	1990, 1993
Malta	2	General government	BBR+DR	International treaty	1993
Mauritius	1	General government	DR	Statutory	2008
Namibia	2	Central government	ER+DR	Coalition agreement	2001, 2010
St. Kitts and Nevis	2	General government	BBR+DR	International treaty	1998
St. Lucia	2	General government	BBR+DR	International treaty	1998
St. Vincent and the Grenadines	2	General government	BBR+DR	International treaty	1998

Sources: Budina and others (2012); European Commission (2006).

[a]BBR = Balance budget rule; DR = debt rule; ER = expenditure rule.

[b]The rule ceased to exist following the global financial crisis.

[c]In addition to the balance and debt rules that apply to the European Union, Luxembourg has national debt, balance, and expenditure rules.

FISCAL RULES: TYPES, CHARACTERISTICS, AND ROLES

In this chapter, we define a fiscal rule along the lines of Kopits and Symansky (1998)—that is, a permanent constraint on fiscal policy through simple numerical limits on indicators of fiscal performance. We focus on rules that impose specific, binding constraints on the government's policy options. The rules under consideration may be fixed by legislation or by political agreement, as is usually the case at the national level. However, at the regional and international level, the rules are backed by a treaty.

Types

In terms of coverage, we are interested in rules that cover at least the central government. Thus, subnational rules are not included. Accordingly, the major fiscal rules include the following (see IMF, 2009; Kopits and Symansky, 1998; Schaechter and others, 2012):

- *Budget balance rules* are usually specified as rules for either overall balance, structural balance or cyclically adjusted balance, or balance "over the cycle."

Set as a percentage of GDP, these rules (with the exception of primary balance and golden rules), aim at ensuring debt sustainability.[1]

- *Debt rules* limit government borrowing and set explicit targets on the public-debt-to-GDP ratio.
- *Reserve rules* limit the stock of total government liability in percent of GDP, or the stock of reserves of an extra-budgetary contingency fund (social security fund) in percent of annual benefits payments.
- *Expenditure rules* set permanent limits on total, primary, or current spending in absolute terms, growth rates, or in percent of GDP. When combined with debt or balanced budget rules, expenditure rules can serve as operational guidance for fiscal consolidation.
- *Revenue rules* are aimed at boosting revenue collection or preventing an excessive tax burden and therefore set ceilings or floors on revenues.

Characteristics

What is an ideal fiscal rule? While recognizing that it is impractically impossible to have a fiscal rule that possesses all desirable characteristics, Box 11.1 summarizes the recommendations of Kopits and Symansky (1998) on the features of an ideal fiscal rule. Some studies have argued that an ideal fiscal rule is one that is transparent, flexible, and implementable (Guichard and others, 2007; and Price, 2010). In addition, Ahrend, Catte and Price, 2006, argue that the adequacy of institutions as well as rules is essential.

Roles and Design

Why are fiscal rules needed? The overarching reason is to address deficit bias—correcting distorted incentives and containing pressures to overspend, especially when times are good, thereby ensuring fiscal responsibility and debt sustainability (Schaechter and others, 2012; IMF, 2009). There are four additional roles, as highlighted by Kopits and Symansky (1998) and Kennedy and Robbins (2003): (1) to ensure macroeconomic stability; (2) to support other financial policies; (3) to minimize negative externalities; and (4) to ensure credibility of fiscal policy.[2]

Policy credibility is important, especially when financial market confidence is in doubt. When such doubt arises, as argued by IMF (2009), a fiscal rule can help raise the credibility in the context of government's medium-term fiscal strategy. However, Chowdhury and Islam (2012) express the concern that rule-based policymaking may pose a risk to both democracy and development. They fear that by

[1]In addition, there are primary balances and golden rules, which do not guarantee debt sustainability (see Schaechter and others, 2012). The latter targets the overall balance net of capital expenditure, and thus permits deficits only to the extent of financing productive investment. An over-the-cycle rule requires the achievement of a nominal budget balance on average over the business cycle.

[2]The credibility issue is mostly relevant for countries that have alternating periods of poor fiscal performance and fiscal adjustment.

BOX 11.1

Desirable Characteristics of a Fiscal Rule

- A fiscal rule should be *well defined* to avoid ambiguity and ineffective implementation. This requires clarity about the indicator being constrained, the institutional coverage, and specific escape clauses, if any.
- It should be *transparent* in relation to government fiscal operations, including accounting, forecasting and institutional arrangement. It should avoid a misrepresentation of the true timing and magnitude of future fiscal obligations, especially contingent liabilities.
- It should be *adequate* with respect to the specified proximate goal. For example, debt sustainability would require a rule expressing debt as a nondecreasing percentage of GDP, or a minimum primary balance in percentage of GDP.
- A fiscal rule should be internally *consistent* with other fiscal rules in place, as well as with other macroeconomic policies. For example, a fixed nominal exchange rate anchor should be accompanied by an explicit restriction on the monetization of budget deficits.
- It should be *simple* to apply. This enhances the understanding of the general public and the parliament, and therefore draws large consensus.
- A fiscal rule should be *flexible* to accommodate exogenous shocks. An example is when the central bank's advances to the government are subject to specified limits and full repayment during the year. In recent times, escape clauses provide some form of flexibility to respond to uncertainties relating to a recession, adverse economic development, banking system bailout, and natural disaster.
- It should be *enforceable* by incorporating penalties for noncompliance and authorities for enforcement. The consequences for noncompliance—judicial, financial, and reputational—should be agreed upon by all parties. Implementation should be within the control of government. A case has been made for an independent fiscal council to monitor compliance.
- A rule should be supported by *efficient* policy actions, including by engaging in more fundamental fiscal reforms to restore public finances to sustainable levels.

Source: Kopits and Symansky (1998).

removing discretion from politicians, fiscal rules could undermine accountability, especially in new democracies, leading them to wonder whether credibility should be a matter for financial markets rather than for the electorate.

A key concern addressed in the literature is whether fiscal rules are in fact effective. There is a general concern that rules might reduce fiscal policy flexibility. For example, they tend to create incentives to artificially achieve targets by adopting dubious accounting practices, thereby reducing the transparency of government budgets (Milesi-Ferretti, 2000; von Hagen and Wolff, 2006; Larch and Turini, 2011; Basdevant, 2012). As Irwin (2012) discusses, governments under pressure to reduce fiscal deficits can be tempted to replace spending cuts or tax increases with accounting devices that give the illusion of change without its substance, or that make a change look larger than the actual situation. However, how much of this creative accounting would occur would depend on the reputation cost to the government and the economic cost of adhering to the rule (von Hagen and Wolff, 2006). Effectiveness is enhanced when rules have regulatory or political support (Wyplosz, 2012).

In view of the above limitations, there is renewed emphasis among policymakers and researchers on the design and monitoring aspects.[3] IMF (2009) notes that fiscal rules are effective only when credible punishment for noncompliance is in place. In the context of the United States, Bernanke (2010) proposes that an effective rule must be sufficiently ambitious to address the underlying problem. It should focus on variables that the legislature can control directly and should have widespread political commitment and public support. In the context of the European Union, Marneffe and others (2011) propose that the effectiveness of rules can be enhanced when they are framed within a medium-term economic management framework. Basdevant (2012) makes a similar point, that the time horizon over which a fiscal target should be met is crucial, especially in providing flexibility.

In designing expenditure rules, Ljungman (2008) suggests that they should exhibit comprehensiveness and have an inflation adjustment, a mechanism to manage expenditure fluctuation, a time horizon, a clear numerical definition, and a legislative requirement. Chowdhury and Islam (2012) insist that since macroeconomic stability is not a sufficient condition for economic growth, the design of fiscal rules should therefore include a growth objective.

Other essential supporting requirements include adequate fiscal institutions, independent fiscal councils and fiscal responsibility laws. This is in recognition that fiscal rules alone are not the solution to ensuring fiscal discipline. Indeed, Wyplosz (2012, 2005); and European Commission, (2006) argue that rules and institutions should not be considered as substitutes but rather as complementary. In particular, Wyplosz (2012) notes that both fiscal rules and institutions can never be adequately contingent—in the face of an unforeseen event, rules are often too rigid while fiscal institutions may be too flexible. The belief is that independent fiscal councils could enhance the credibility of fiscal rules by monitoring their implementation. However, in the absence of formal rules, fiscal frameworks could ensure fiscal discipline, provided that they have transparent and credible strategies backed by proper fiscal institutions.

MAIN CHARACTERISTICS OF FISCAL RULES IN MICROSTATES

To answer the question of whether there exist fiscal rules in microstates, we explore the existence and the main features of fiscal policy rules in a sample of these countries. For this purpose, microstates are defined as countries with populations of less than 2 million.[4] By this definition, we identify 42 microstates, many of which are islands, including eight in the Caribbean. In several respects, microstates are different from other countries, in the sense that they possess unique features that have implications for fiscal policy (See Worrell, 2013; and Chapter 10 of this book).

---

[3]Ljungman (2008) illustrates design issues using the experience of Finland, the Netherlands, and Sweden with expenditure ceilings.

[4]With the exception of Jamaica, added to widen the coverage of the Caribbean countries.

There is ample evidence of the existence of fiscal rules in microstates. In total, 17 countries, equivalent to 40 percent of our sample, have at least a fiscal rule. With the exception of four countries—namely, Cabo Verde, Iceland, Jamaica, and Mauritius—all belong to an economic or monetary union.[5] The rules came into force through international treaties, acts of parliaments, coalition agreements, and political commitments.

Origins and Institutional Coverage

The rules are relatively new, about two decades old. As members of the EU, Luxembourg and Malta, have the earliest rules dating back to 1992. However, before joining the EU, Luxembourg had national debt and expenditure rules. In the ECCU, the rules came into force in 1998. Those in WAEMU and the Central African Economic and Monetary Community (CEMAC) have existed since the early 2000s. Most recently, Jamaica and Namibia adopted fiscal rules.

The institutional coverage of these fiscal rules centers on the general government and the central government (see Figure 11.1). The coverage is important, especially for fiscal consolidation, as the size of fiscal consolidation has tended to be significantly larger when national or supranational rules have been in place (IMF, 2009). In the present study, the coverage is slightly in favor of the central government. Rules in the EU and the ECCU cover the general government, while

Figure 11.1 Coverage of Fiscal Rules in Microstates Sample *(Percent of total rules)*

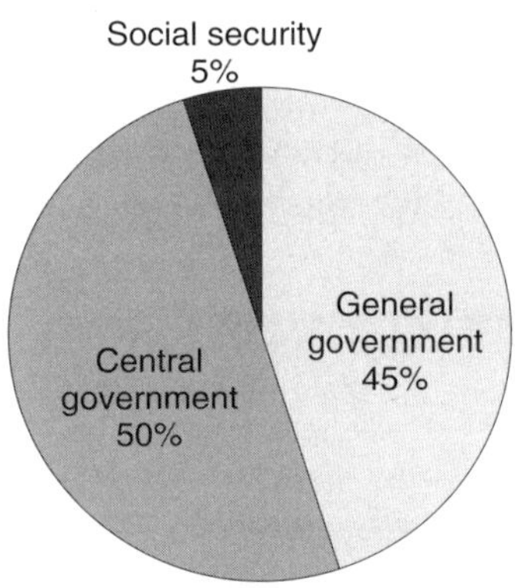

Source: Author's calculations.

[5]They cover four economic and monetary unions: Equatorial Guinea and Gabon in the Central African Economic and Monetary Community (CEMAC); Antigua and Barbuda, Dominica, Grenada, St. Kitts and Nevis, St. Lucia, and St. Vincent and the Grenadines in the Eastern Caribbean Currency Union (ECCU); Luxembourg and Malta in the European Union (EU); Botswana and Namibia in the Southern African Customs Union (SACU); and Guinea Bissau in the West African Economic and Monetary Union (WAEMU).

those in WAEMU and CEMAC relate to the central government. Meanwhile, national rules in Botswana, Cabo Verde, Iceland, Luxembourg, and Namibia mostly cover the central government.

Supranational rules are usually not complemented with national rules. With the exception of Luxembourg, all other members of economic or monetary unions do not have national rules. Under the reformed Stability and Growth Pact, the EU encourages national governments to adopt additional domestic rules to bolster commitment to the rules in place at the EU level (European Commission, 2006). Indeed, Luxembourg has three such rules covering budget balance, expenditure, and debt, framed within a multi-annual context. The budget balance rule is legislated on and covers social security and is monitored by the Ministry of Social Security. Both the expenditure and debt rules cover the central government.

Debt, Expenditure, and Budget Balance Rules

Debt Ceilings

Broadly, the fiscal rules aim to address fiscal and debt sustainability concerns. Currently, the public-debt-to-GDP ratio in more than half of the countries exceeds the generally accepted prudent threshold of 60 percent (Figure 11.2). The need to address fiscal and debt concerns is reflected in the types of rules in place. In the context of a monetary and economic union, another objective is to prevent fiscal policy inconsistency with the needs of the union. In particular, budget

Figure 11.2 Public-Debt-to-GDP Ratios by Country, 2012 *(Percent)*

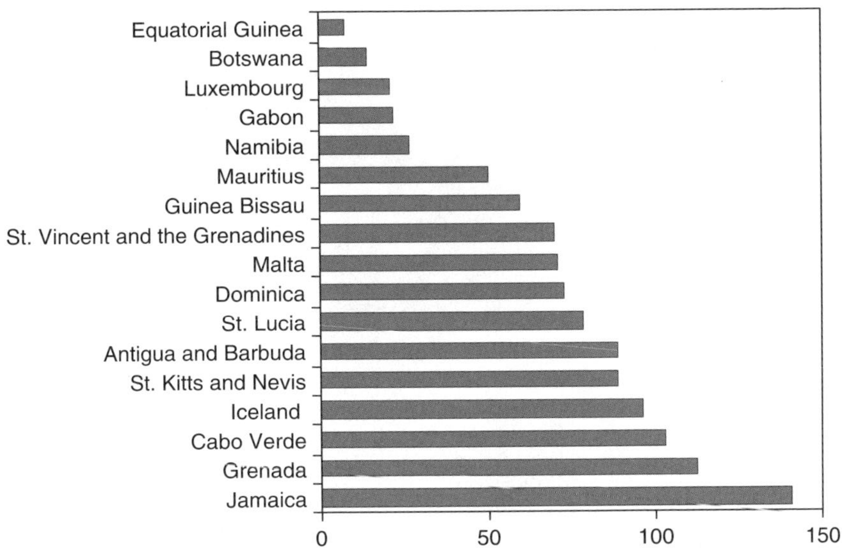

Source: Author's calculations.

balance and debt rules constitute 90 percent of the rules in existence, with expenditure rules accounting for the remaining 10 percent (Figure 11.3), excluding those in Jamaica and the EU that limit an expenditure subcomponent, such as wages and salaries. No country has a revenue rule.

The debt rules mostly constrain the public-debt-to-GDP ratio to at most 70 percent (Table 11.2). The debt ceilings are 70 percent of GDP in WAEMU and CEMAC, and 60 percent of GDP for Cabo Verde, Mauritius, and the EU countries. Of note, Mauritius proposes to lower its public debt further to 50 percent of GDP by 2018 and to hold it under that ceiling subsequently. For the ECCU countries, the target is to reduce the debt-to-GDP ratio to 60 percent by 2020. To achieve this objective, the ECCU member countries are required to set annual debt targets. In Namibia, reflecting the already low debt level, the ceiling is lower at 25–30 percent. Jamaica targets a debt reduction to 100 percent of GDP by March 2016 from its current level of around 140 percent. Botswana does not have a debt rule.

Expenditure

Expenditure rules target the growth rate of public expenditure, or the aggregate relative to GDP. At 40 percent of GDP, the expenditure ceiling in Botswana is the highest among the countries covered, while it is 30 percent of GDP in Namibia. In addition, Botswana has a "golden rule," which requires that 30 percent of total expenditure should be channeled to development activities, including in the health and education sectors. Cabo Verde has a cap on domestic borrowing, equivalent to 3 percent of GDP. Jamaica aims to reduce the wages-to-GDP ratio to 9 percent by 2016. Recently, the EU introduced a new expenditure

Figure 11.3 Number of Fiscal Rules in Microstates Sample

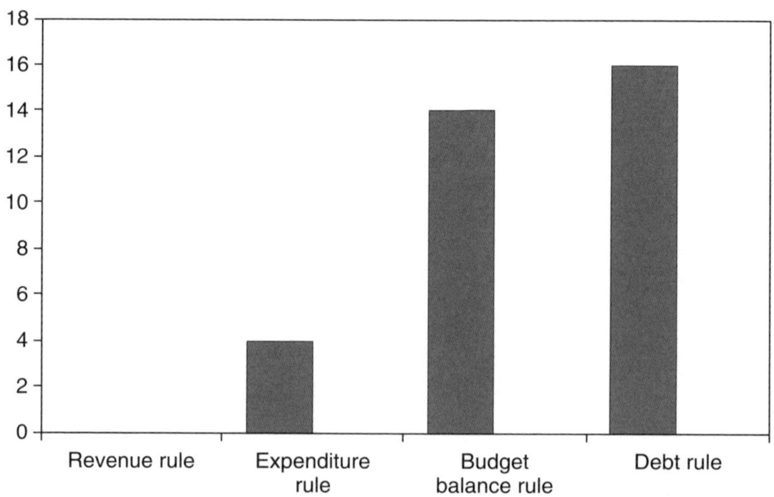

Source: Author's calculations.

TABLE 11.2

Numerical Limits in Fiscal Rules, Selected Microstates and Currency Unions

Country	Budget Balance Rule	Debt Rule	Expenditure Rule
Botswana	None	None	Ceiling on the expenditure-to-GDP ratio of 40 percent
Cabo Verde	None	Debt ceiling of 60 percent of GDP	Ceiling on domestic borrowing of 3 percent of GDP
CEMAC[a]	Basic fiscal balance, basic structural balance, and non-oil structural balance should be in balance or in surplus.	Debt ceiling of 70 percent of GDP	
ECCU	Overall deficit target of 3 percent of GDP up to 2006.	To reduce public-debt-to-GDP ratio to 60 percent by 2020	None
EU[b]	Overall deficit target of 3 percent of GDP	Debt ceiling of 60 percent of GDP	Annual growth of primary expenditure below long-term nominal GDP growth
Iceland	None	None	Real expenditure growth limit of the CG (2 percent for public expenditures and 2.5 percent for transfers)
Jamaica	Reduce the fiscal balance to zero by fiscal year 2015/16.	Reduce total debt to 100 percent of GDP or less by fiscal year 2015/16	Reduce wages-to-GDP ratio to 9 percent by fiscal year 2016
Mauritius[c]	None	Debt ceiling of 60 percent of GDP	None
Namibia	None	Debt ceiling of 25–30 percent of GDP annually	Public expenditure levels below 30 percent of GDP
WAEMU	Overall fiscal balance should be in balance or in surplus	Debt ceiling of 70 percent of GDP	None

Source: Budina and others (2012).

Note: CEMAC = the Central African Economic and Monetary Community; ECCU = the Eastern Caribbean Currency Union; EU = the European Union; WAEMU = the West African Economic and Monetary Union.

[a]The basic fiscal balance is defined as total revenue net of grants less total expenditure net of foreign-financed capital spending. Two new supplementary criteria, the basic structural fiscal balance and the non-oil basic structural fiscal balance were introduced in 2008.

[b]The primary expenditure rule excludes unemployment benefits and discretionary revenue increases, and when the excessive deficit procedure (EDP) is not in force.

[c]A debt ceiling of 50 percent of GDP to start in 2018.

benchmark in the context of the fiscal compact, requiring that annual growth of primary expenditures, excluding unemployment benefits and discretionary revenue increases, should not exceed long-term nominal GDP growth. The benchmark affects countries that are not in an excessive deficit procedure; that is, those whose overall deficits are less than 3 percent of GDP.

Budget Balance

The budget balance rules differ across countries. In the ECCU, the overall deficit of 3 percent of GDP, initially agreed by member countries in 1998, was

TABLE 11.3
Countries with Escape Clauses

Country	Natural Disaster	Economic Recession	Other Exogenous Events
Guinea Bissau	No	Yes	No
Jamaica	Yes	Yes	Yes
Luxembourg[a]	No	Yes	No
Malta	No	Yes	No
Mauritius	Yes	Yes	Yes

Source: Budina and others (2012).
[a] The escape clause is only applicable at the European Union level.

abandoned in 2006, perhaps reflecting an inability to cope with exogenous shocks. In 2009, however, member governments agreed to set annual primary balance targets in the context of the ECCU Eight Point Growth and Stability Agenda. For EU members, the overall deficit target of 3 percent of GDP came into force in 1992, with subsequent reforms in 2011 and 2012.[6] In Jamaica, fiscal balance should be nil by end-march 2016.

Escape Clauses

Few countries have escape clauses (see Table 11.3). Typically, escape clauses provide some form of flexibility to respond to exceptional circumstances, including economic recession and natural disasters. Whereever they exist, it is suggested that escape clauses should be well specified to avoid ambiguity about the potential trigger events. In Botswana, the Public Debt Management Act embeds the cases to which the debt rule will not apply: (1) natural disasters or other emergencies requiring exceptional expenditure; (2) cases where a large investment project in the public sector is considered by the cabinet to be timely and prudent; and (3) general economic slow-downs requiring fiscal stimulus. At the same time, the Act further stipulates that increases in the debt-to-GDP ratio should not exceed one percent relative to the previous year. Similar to Botswana, the applicable act in Jamaica specifies that the fiscal targets may also be exceeded on the grounds of national security, national emergency, or other such exceptional grounds as the Minister of Finance may determine. Escape clauses relating to adverse economic shocks are embedded in the fiscal rules of the EU and the WAEMU and apply to the respective member countries covered in this chapter.

Formal enforcement procedures are generally limited, although the implementation of rules appears adequately monitored, especially by an independent body outside the government. This is the case for the ECCU, EU, and WAEMU

[6] Included in the Maastricht criteria is a limit of 3 percent of GDP for fiscal deficit. If the limit is exceeded, an excessive deficit procedure (EDP) is opened for correction purposes. The reformed Stability and Growth Pact requires that an EDP may be opened subject to two conditions: the deficit exceeds 3 percent of GDP only temporarily and exceptionally and only if the deficit remains close to the 3 percent threshold. See Budina and others (2012) and Schaechter and others (2012) for recent EU governance reforms.

countries, unlike their counterparts. Constitutional rules that are enforced by an independent body appear to be most effective (Kennedy and Robbins, 2003).

THE LITERATURE ON FISCAL POLICY RULES

Several studies have adopted statistical and econometric techniques to investigate the role of fiscal rules in determining fiscal performance or budgetary outcomes. In the simplest cases, a simple correlation of an index of fiscal rules with measures of fiscal performance provides some preliminary guidance on the impact of fiscal rules. Generally, the empirical literature establishes a link between fiscal rules and budgetary outcomes.

In the context of successful fiscal consolidation and debt reduction, empirical evidence associates the presence of fiscal rules with stronger fiscal performance (Schaechter and others, 2012; IMF, 2009; Guichard and others, 2007; Poterba, 1994; Kennedy and Robbins, 2003). In a large sample of member countries of the Organization for Economic Co-operation and Development, the G-20, and the EU, several large fiscal adjustments and debt reduction episodes were found to be supported by fiscal rules (IMF, 2009). Nevertheless, as noted by some studies (IMF, 2009; von Hagen, 2006; Schaechter and others, 2012; Gollwitzer, 2011; Debrun and others, 2008), the interpretation of results regarding impact calls for caution, because the analyses could reflect the effects of omitted variables and other determinants of fiscal behavior, such as political institutions, which, according to Poterba (1994) and Stein, Talvi, and Grisanti (1999), are important. Estimates by Debrun and others (2008) indicate that fiscal rules have a positive and statistically significant impact on budget balances. The relationship between fiscal rules and budgetary outcomes is robust to the possibility of omitted variables and to the definition of the government balance. Reverse causation did not appear as a source of concern.

Lessons from the EU reveal that the coverage, design, and strength of fiscal rules, as well the quality of budgetary procedures, promote fiscal consolidation (Larch and Turrini, 2008; European Commission, 2006). Further results suggest that rules embedded in the law or in a constitution appear to have a larger impact on fiscal outcomes. Tapsoba (2012) supports the introduction of fiscal rules as a remedy for fiscal indiscipline.

A well-designed medium-term expenditure rule could overcome procyclical bias on the expenditure side. Deroose, Moulin, and Weirts (2006) argue that expenditure rules are important in complying with national medium-term expenditure plans. Expenditure rules were very common in cases of large fiscal adjustment and were usually combined with budget balance rules (IMF, 2009). However, expenditure rules could be effective only if the cost of noncompliance were sufficiently large (Wierts, 2008). Two findings that emerge from Holm-Hadulla, Hauptmeier, and Rother (2010) are that (1) government is subject to procyclical bias and (2) expenditure rules reduce government responses to surprises in cyclical conditions.

However, the findings on the impact of expenditure rules differ across expenditure items, with impact being muted for nondiscretionary items. Relative to debt and balance budget rules, the impact of expenditure rules could be insignificant, reflecting limited coverage to central government (Larch and Turrini, 2008). Reviewing the experience of Australia and New Zealand, Campos and Pradhan (1999) demonstrate that certain mechanisms that enhance transparency and accountability could lead to a sufficiently high cost for noncompliance and produce better expenditure outcomes.

Good budgetary institutions are essential. One strand of the literature takes a broader perspective, examining the impact on fiscal outcomes of budget institutions. Usually, the impact is reflected in higher primary balances and lower debt levels, suggesting that good budgetary institutions matter (Marneffe and others, 2011; Dabla-Norris and others, 2010; Stein, Talvi, and Grisanti, 1999; Eichengreen, 1992; Gollowitzer, 2011; von Hagen, 1992, 2006; von Hagen and Harden, 1995; Debrun and others, 2008; Poterba and von Hagen, 1999). Typically under this approach, an index is constructed to measure the quality and adequacy of budget institutions, including fiscal rules. The impact may depend on whether the political environment is appropriate for rule-based policymaking (von Hagen, 2006). With strong budgetary institutions, there is better scope for conducting countercyclical policies (Dabla-Norris and others, 2010).

The experiences of U.S. states overwhelmingly demonstrate that fiscal rules enforce some budget discipline in terms of lower deficits (Eichengreen, 1992; Poterba, 1994; Bohn and Inman, 1996; Auerbach, 2008; Alt and Lowry, 1994; Bayoumi and Eichengreen, 1995). But as argued by Bohn and Inman (1996), rules should be appropriately designed and enforced. In particular, in times of fiscal crisis, Poterba (1994) finds, states with tighter constitutional or statutory fiscal rules experienced more rapid adjustment when revenues fell short of expectations or expenditure exceeded projections. In addition to the impact of budget balance rules in achieving higher fiscal surpluses, Eichengreen (1992) finds that they also significantly affect both bond yields and borrowing. However, there is some evidence that the impact of fiscal rules is not significant, as they have also led to a debt substitution effect—off-budget entities and municipal governments incurring larger debts than otherwise (von Hagen, 1991; Kiewiet and Szakaly, 1996).

Findings are mixed regarding the impact of fiscal rules on governments' ability to engage in countercyclical fiscal policy. While the main motivation in the literature was to analyze the impact of fiscal rules, a related issue is whether the reduced discretion could affect the responsiveness of fiscal policy to output volatility. On the one hand, Fatas and Mihov (2005), Bayoumi and Eichengreen (1995), and Levinson (1998) all find that strict budgetary restrictions lower the responsiveness of fiscal policy to output shocks. In contrast, Alesina and Bayoumi (1996) and Brzozowski and Siwinska-Gorzelak (2010) find limited cost in terms of increased output volatility. As argued by Brzozowski and Siwinska-Gorzelak, the impact of fiscal rules on the extent of fiscal policy volatility may depend on the type of rule and the fiscal measure being constrained.

EMPIRICAL ANALYSIS

Methodology

We estimate a fiscal policy reaction function for a panel of 40 microstates using annual data for 1970–2009. Similar to Debrun and Kumar (2007), and Debrun and others (2008), we characterize fiscal policy as a response of the cyclically adjusted primary balance (CAPB) to fiscal rules, controlling for other determinants of fiscal policy, including measures of institution and temporary events such as natural disasters. Given that we are interested in examining the impact of fiscal rules on fiscal performance, we introduce fiscal rules into the following commonly estimated model:

$$P_{i,t} = \alpha_0 + \rho d_{i,t\text{-}1} + \gamma \text{rules}_{i,t} + x'_{i,t}\beta + \eta_i + \varepsilon_{i,t},\ t=1, \ldots, T,\ i=1, \ldots, N, \quad (11.1)$$

where $P_{i,t}$ is the ratio of the cyclically adjusted primary balance to potential GDP in country i and at time t; $d_{i,t\text{-}1}$ is the government-debt-to-GDP ratio at the end of period $t-1$; $\text{rules}_{i,t}$ is a dummy variable for fiscal rules, which takes the value 1 for the presence of fiscal rules in country i at time t, and 0 otherwise; and $x'_{i,}$ is a vector of other potential determinants of fiscal outcomes, including relevant measures of institution and exogenous events such as natural disasters. The η_i is the unobserved country effects, and $\varepsilon_{i,t}$ is a time- and country-specific error term.

The Data

All fiscal data—CAPB, debt, and output gap—were obtained from the IMF's *World Economic Outlook*. The measure of political risk is taken from the *International Country Risk Guide* compiled by the PRS Group. Data on natural disasters were obtained from EM-DAT.[7]

Cyclically adjusted primary balance

Since we are interested in discretionary policy behavior, we adopt the CAPB as the dependent variable on the ground that it excludes the impact of automatic stabilizers.

Fiscal rules

We assume that a positive value for the estimated γ coefficient in the model would signal a disciplinary effect of fiscal rules on fiscal policy.

Debt

As noted by Bohn (1998), a positive estimated response of primary balance to increases in government debt suggests that fiscal behavior satisfies the

[7]The OFDA/CRED International Disaster Database may be found at www.emdat.be.

inter-temporal budget constraint and hence long-run solvency criterion. Thus, we expect the coefficient of government debt ($\rho > 0$) to be positive.

Output gap

As theory suggests, we expect a positive response of the CAPB to the output gap, indicating that fiscal policy is countercyclical.

Political risk

We use political risk, a composite index from the *International Country Risk Guide*, as a measure of institutional quality. The ICRG Risk Rating System assigns a numerical value to a predetermined range of risk components, according to a preset weighted scale, for each country covered by the system. Each scale is designed to award the highest value to the lowest risk and the lowest value to the highest risk. The components of political risk include law and order, bureaucratic quality, democratic accountability, government stability, and corruption. The composite political risk index is a 100-point scale—the highest overall rating being 100, indicating the lowest risk, and the lowest score being 0, indicating the highest risk. We expect countries with high-quality institutions and therefore low political risk to have a higher CAPB.

Natural disaster

This variable represents the number of natural disasters that occur yearly. The coefficient of natural disaster is expected to be negative.

Model estimation

To estimate the model, we use the fixed-effects and dynamic-panel approaches (system generalized method of moments or GMM). The explanatory variables in the model could either be simultaneously determined with the dependent variable or have a two-way causal relationship with it. There is also potential for the presence of unobserved country-specific effects, which if ignored may produce inconsistent estimates. The GMM approach proposed by Arellano and Bond (1991) and further developed by Blundell and Bond (1998) is appropriate, as it simultaneously addresses the issues of correlation and endogeneity among the variables.

The difference GMM approach of Arellano and Bond begins by specifying a panel model as a system of equations, one per period, and allows the instruments applicable to each equation to differ in subsequent periods (Baum, 2006). The instruments include suitable lags of the levels of the endogenous variables, which enter the equation in differenced form, as well as strictly exogenous regressors. It is assumed that there is no second-order serial correlation in the first differences of the error term to ensure consistency of the GMM estimator.

Blundell and Bond (1998) argue that lagged levels of variables are likely to be weak instruments for current differenced variables when the series are close to random walk. Under these conditions, the differenced GMM estimates are likely to be biased and inefficient. As an alternative, they proposed the more efficient system GMM estimator that combines a difference equation and a levels equation to form a system estimator. For the first differenced equation, the instruments are the lagged levels of the endogenous variables. For the levels equation, the endogenous variables are instrumented with appropriate lags of their own first differences, while the strictly exogenous regressors can directly enter the instrument matrix for use in the levels equation. The system GMM is consistent and more efficient than the difference estimator so long as there is no significant correlation between the differenced regressors and country fixed effects. In this study, we apply the one-step variant of the system GMM estimator.

EMPIRICAL RESULTS

Table 11.4 presents results for four models. The first three models were estimated using the fixed-effects approach, while the fourth model uses the system GMM approach. Model 1 includes lagged debt, output gap, and fiscal rules. The results show that the three variables have the expected positive sign, but only the fiscal rule is significant. In Model 2, we add natural disaster to the variables in Model 1, and find that natural disaster is negatively correlated with fiscal policy, but again only the fiscal rule is significant. Model 3 includes political risk to the variables in Model 2, and reveals that lagged debt, fiscal rules, and political risks are important determinants of fiscal outcomes.

Estimates using the system GMM approach reveal results similar to the estimates in Model 3 using a fixed-effects approach—lagged debt, fiscal rules, and political risk are significant determinants of fiscal policy outcomes in microstates. We also find that fiscal policy responds to its lagged value. In particular, the

TABLE 11.4

Impact of Fiscal Rules on Fiscal Performance *(Dependent variable: cyclically adjusted primary balance)*

	Fixed Effects (1)	Fixed Effects (2)	Fixed Effects (3)	SGMM (4)
Output gap	0.3385	−0.3371	−0.4257	−0.1516
	(0.1762)	(0.1700)	(0.2219)	(0.1134)
Lagged debt	0.0962	0.9977	0.1598**	0.0543**
	(0.0604)	(0.0671)	(0.0528)	(0.0280)
Fiscal rule	5.4322***	5.3445***	8.7559***	4.5622**
	(0.8053)	(0.6892)	(1.7942)	(2.0757)
Natural disaster		−0.4018	0.8916	0.9544
		(0.9921)	(1.6784)	(0.7207)
Political risk			0.1467**	0.1043*
			(0.0499)	(0.0553)
Lagged cyclically adjusted primary balance				0.7649***
				(0.0921)
N	80	52	52	51

Source: Author's calculations.

Note: SGMM = system generalized method of moments. Robust standard errors in parenthesis. ***, **, * denote significance at the 1, 5, and 10 percent levels, respectively.

presence of fiscal rules improves the cyclically adjusted primary balance by 4.5 percentage points, and the result is robust to alternative model specification. The findings suggest that fiscal rules are relevant in microstates, since they would enhance fiscal consolidation and lower high debt levels. The results are consistent with earlier findings in the literature.

SUMMARY AND CONCLUSION

The chapter empirically analyzes the impact of fiscal rules on fiscal performance in microstates with a focus on the Caribbean, where fiscal consolidation has been a major challenge. We estimate a fiscal policy reaction function for a panel of 40 microstates, using annual data for 1970–2009. We find ample evidence of the existence of fiscal rules in microstates. In total, 17 countries, equivalent to 40 percent of the sample, have at least a fiscal rule. The rules are relatively new, about two decades old, mostly take the form of budget balance and debt rules, and aim to address fiscal and debt sustainability concerns. Empirical result shows that the presence of fiscal rules in microstates significantly influences fiscal performance. The findings suggest that by enhancing fiscal discipline and credibility, fiscal rules could bolster fiscal consolidation efforts and lower the high debt levels in microstates generally, including the Caribbean countries.

REFERENCES

Ahrend, Rudiger, Pietro Catte, and Robert Price, 2006, "Interactions Between Monetary and Fiscal Policy: How Monetary Conditions Affect Fiscal Consolidation," Economics Department Working Paper No. 5 (Paris: Organization for Economic Co-operation and Development).

Alesina, Alberto, and Tamim Bayoumi, 1996, "The Costs and Benefits of Fiscal Rules: Evidence from U.S. States," NBER Working Paper No. 5614 (Cambridge, Massachusetts: National Bureau of Economic Research).

Alt, James E., and Robert C. Lowry, 1994, "Divided Governments, Fiscal Institutions, and Budget Deficits: Evidence from the States," *American Political Science Review*, Vol. 88, No. 4, pp. 811–28.

Arellano, Manuel, and Stephen Bond, 1991, "Some Tests of Specification for Panel Data: Monte Carlo Evidence and an Application to Employment Equations," *Review of Economic Studies*, Vol. 58, pp. 277–97.

Auerbach, J. Alan, 2008, "Federal Budget Rules: The U.S. Experience," NBER Working Paper No. 14288 (Cambridge, Massachusetts: National Bureau of Economic Research).

Basdevant, Olivier, 2012, "Fiscal Policies and Rules in the Face of Revenue Volatility Within Southern African Customs Union (SACU)," IMF Working Paper 12/93 (Washington: International Monetary Fund).

Baum, Christopher F., 2006, *An Introduction to Modern Econometrics Using Stata* (College Station, TX: Stata Press).

Bayoumi, Tamim, and Barry Eichengreen, 1995, "Restraining Yourself: The Implications of Fiscal Rules for Economic Stabilization," *IMF Staff Papers*, Vol. 42, No. 1, pp. 32–48.

Bernanke, S. Ben, 2010, "Fiscal Sustainability and Fiscal Rules," Remarks at the Annual Meeting of the Rhode Island Public Expenditure Council, Providence, Rhode Island, October.

Blundell, Richard, and Stephen Bond, 1998, "Initial Conditions and Moment Restrictions in Dynamic Panel Data Models," *Journal of Econometrics,* Vol. 87, pp. 115–43.

Bohn, Henning, 1998, "The Behavior of U.S. Public Debt and Deficits," *Quarterly Journal of Economics*, Vol. 113, No. 3, pp. 949–63.

Bohn, Henning, and P. Robert Inman, 1996, "Balanced Budget Rules and Public Deficits: Evidence from U.S. States," NBER Working Paper No. 5533 (Cambridge, Massachusetts: National Bureau of Economic Research).

Brzozowski, Michal, and Joanna Siwinska-Gorzelak, 2010, "The Impact of Fiscal Rules on Fiscal Policy Volatility," *Journal of Applied Economics*, Vol. 13, No. 2, pp. 205–31.

Budina, Nina, Tidiane Kinda, Andrea Schaechter, and Anke Weber, 2012, "Fiscal Rules at a Glance: Country Details from a New Dataset," IMF Working Paper 12/273 (Washington: International Monetary Fund).

Campos, J. Edgardo, and Sanjay Pradhan, 1999, "Budgetary Institutions and the Level of Expenditure Outcomes in Australia and New Zealand," in *Fiscal Institutions and Fiscal Performance,* ed. by M. James Poterba and Jurgen von Hagen (Chicago: University of Chicago Press).

Chowdhury, Anis, and Iyanatul Islam, 2012, "Fiscal Rules—Help or Hindrance?" A Commentary in the VoxEU debate, "Development and the Crisis, Has Austerity Gone Too Far?" http://www.voxeu.org/debates/commentaries/fiscal-rules-help-or-hindrance.

Dabla-Norris, Era, Richard Allen, Luis-Felipe Zanna, Tej Prakash, Eteri Kvintradze, Victor Lledo, Irene Yackovlev, and Sophia Gollwitzer, 2010, "Budget Institutions and Fiscal Performance in Low-Income Countries," IMF Working Paper 10/80 (Washington: International Monetary Fund).

Debrun, Xavier, and Manmohan Kumar, 2007, "Fiscal Rules, Fiscal Councils and All That: Commitment Devices, Signaling Tools or Smokescreens?" in *Fiscal Policy: Current Issues and Challenges,* ed. by Banca d'Italia, Papers presented at the Banca d'Italia workshop held in Perugia, 29–31 March 2007, pp. 479–512.

Debrun, Xavier, Laurent Moulin, Alessandro Turrini, Joaquim Ayuso-i-Casals, and Manmohan S. Kumar, 2008, "Tied to the Mast? National Fiscal Rules in the European Union," *Economic Policy*, Vol. 23, No. 54, pp. 297–362.

Deroose, Servaas, Laurent Moulin, and Peter Wierts, 2006, "National Expenditure Rules and Expenditure Outcomes: Evidence for EU Member States," *Wirtschaftspolitische Blätter*, No. 1, pp. 27–42.

European Commission, 2006, "National Numerical Rules and Institutions for Sound Public Finances," in *Public Finances in EMU*, No. 3 (Brussels: Directorate-General for Economic and Financial Affairs).

Eichengreen, Barry, 1992, "Should the Maastricht Treaty Be Saved?" *Princeton Studies in International Finance*, No. 74, December.

Fatas, Antonio and Ilian, Mihov, 2005, "The Macroeconomic Effects of Fiscal Rules in the U.S. States," *Journal of Public Economics,* Vol. 90, pp. 101–117.

Gollwitzer, Sophia, 2011, "Budget Institutions and Fiscal Performance in Africa," *Journal of African Economies*, Vol. 20, No. 1, pp. 111–52.

Guichard, Stephanie, Mike Kennedy, Eckhard Wurzel, and Christopher Andre, 2007, "What Promotes Fiscal Consolidation: OECD Country Experiences," OECD Economics Department Working Paper No. 553 (Paris: Organization for Economic Co-operation and Development).

Holm-Hadulla, Federic, Sebastian Hauptmeier, and Philipp Rother, 2010, "The Impact of Numerical Expenditure Rules on Budgetary Discipline over the Cycle," Working Paper No. 1169 (Frankfurt: European Central Bank).

International Monetary Fund (IMF), 2009, "Fiscal Rules—Anchoring Expectations for Sustainable Public Finances," unpublished (Washington).

Irwin, C. Timothy, 2012, "Accounting Devices and Fiscal Illusion," IMF Staff Discussion Note No. 12/02 (Washington: International Monetary Fund).

Kennedy, Suzanne, and Janine Robbins, 2003, "The Role of Fiscal Rules in Determining Fiscal Performance," partially updated version of Department of Finance Working Paper 2001–16 (Ontario: Department of Finance, Canada).

Kiewiet, D. Roderick, and Kristin Szakaly, 1996, "Constitutional Limits on Borrowing: An Analysis of State Bonded Indebtedness," *Journal of Law, Economics and Organization,* Vol. 12, pp. 62–97.

Kopits, George, and Steven Symansky, 1998, *Fiscal Policy Rules,* IMF Occasional Paper No. 162 (Washington: International Monetary Fund).

Larch, Martin, and Alessandro Turrini, 2011, "Received Wisdom and Beyond: Lessons from Fiscal Consolidation in the EU," *National Institute Economic Review,* Vol. 217, R1.

Levinson, Arik, 1998, "Balanced Budgets and Business Cycle: Evidence from the States," *National Tax Journal,* Vol. 51, No. 4, pp. 715–47.

Ljungman, Gosta, 2008, "Expenditure Ceilings: A Survey," IMF Working Paper 08/282 (Washington: International Monetary Fund).

Marneffe, Wim, Bas Van Arle, Wouter Van Der Wielen, and Lode Vereeck, 2011, "The Impact of Fiscal Rules on Public Finances: Theory and Empirical Evidence for the Euro Area," *CESifo DICE Report* No. 9 (3), pp. 18–26.

Milesi-Ferretti, Gian Maria, 2000, "Good, Bad or Ugly? On the Effectiveness of Fiscal Rules with Creative Accounting," IMF Working Paper 00/172 (Washington: International Monetary Fund).

Poterba, M. James, 1994, "State Responses to Fiscal Crisis: The Effects of Budgetary Institutions and Politics," *Journal of Political Economy,* Vol. 102, No. 4, pp. 799–821.

Poterba, M. James, and Jurgen von Hagen, 1999, *Fiscal Institutions and Fiscal Performance* (Chicago: University of Chicago Press).

Price, Robert, 2010, "The Political Economy of Fiscal Consolidation," OECD Economics Department Working Paper No. 776 (Paris: Organization for Economic Co-operation and Development).

Schaechter, Andrea, Tidiane Kinda, Nina Budina, and Anke Weber, 2012, "Fiscal Rules in Response to the Crisis: Toward the 'Next-Generation' Rules. A New Dataset," IMF Working Paper 12/187 (Washington: International Monetary Fund).

Stein, Ernesto, Ernesto Talvi, and Alejandro Grisanti, 1999, "Institutional Arrangments and Fiscal Performance: The Latin American Experience," in *Fiscal Institutions and Fiscal Performance,* ed. by M. James Poterba and Jurgen von Hagen (Chicago: University of Chicago Press).

Tapsoba, Rene, 2012, "Do National Numerical Rules Really Shape Fiscal Behaviours in Developing Countries? A Treatment Effect Evaluation," in *Economic Modeling,* Vol. 29, pp. 1356–69.

Von Hagen, Jurgen, 1991, "A Note on the Empirical Effectiveness of Formal Fiscal Restraints," *Journal of Public Economics,* Vol. 44, pp. 199–210.

———, 1992, "Budgeting Procedures and Fiscal Performance in the European Communities," *Economic Paper No.* 96, II/453/92/-EN/rev (Brussels: Commission of the European Communities, Director General for Economic and Financial Affairs).

———, 2006, "Fiscal Rules and Fiscal Performance in the EU and Japan" (Bonn: Institut für Internationale Wirtschaftspolitik).

Von Hagen, Jürgen, and Ian H. Harden, 1995, "Budgeting Processes and Commitment to Fiscal Discipline." *European Economic Review,* Vol. 39, pp. 771–79.

Von Hagen, Jurgen, and Guntram B. Wolff, 2006, "What Do Deficits Tell Us About Debt? Empirical Evidence on Creative Accounting With Fiscal Rules in the EU," *Journal of Banking and Finance,* Vol. 30, pp. 3259–79.

Wierts, Peter, 2008, "Fiscal Rules and Fiscal Outcomes in EMU: Theory and Evidence," Ph.D. Thesis, University of Reading (Oisterwijk, the Netherlands: Uitgeverij BOX Press).

Worrell, Delisle, 2013, "Small States Are Different: What the Literature Says about Monetary and Exchange Rate Policies," Working Paper, Central Bank of Barbados, May.

Wyplosz, Charles, 2005, "Fiscal Policy: Institutions versus Rules," *National Institute Economic Review,* No. 191, pp. 64–78.

———, 2012, "Fiscal Rules: Theoretical Issues and Historical Experience" NBER Working Paper No. 17884 (Cambridge, Massachusetts: National Bureau of Economic Research).

CHAPTER 12

Fiscal and Debt Sustainability in the Caribbean: A New Agenda

CHARLES AMO-YARTEY AND THERESE TURNER-JONES

This chapter concludes the analysis in this book with an agenda for moving the region forward, drawing on the discussions of preceding chapters and the accompanying empirical analyses. While a survey of current policies through the Caribbean suggests that there is plenty of work yet to do on the fiscal sustainability agenda, the lack of an economic recovery in the presence of high debt for many countries calls for action. While each country will need to tailor its specific strategy, we outline below some key elements that should be part of any medium-term framework that countries in the region may consider adopting. Already, some countries are responding to the need for action by independently selecting some elements of the menu proposed in this book and putting them in place to meet their debt reduction targets. These include some difficult and complex new institutional arrangements, such as Jamaica's proposals for implementing a new fiscal rule.

Highly indebted Caribbean countries should generally aim to lower their debt levels in order to reduce vulnerability and create a better platform for growth. The challenge in a low-growth environment is how to achieve the required debt reduction. The analyses in the previous chapters suggest that by consolidating government finances and improving primary balances, countries could signal their determination to address debt overhang, implying that they intend not to default or inflate their debt away. This achievement would help improve their creditworthiness and reduce borrowing costs in the long run.

This book argues, however, that fiscal consolidation may not be enough to bring down the region's high debt levels, since high primary surpluses need to be run over a long period of time. The region therefore needs a comprehensive and sustained package of reforms to reduce its debt ratios to more manageable levels and to strengthen economic resilience. Reforms should signal a new commitment to credible and sound macroeconomic policies and should include tax policy reforms, public sector rationalization, measures to improve fiscal discipline and credibility, active debt management, the containment of contingent liabilities, active privatization programs or public enterprise reforms, and structural reforms to boost growth and improve competitiveness.

RESTARTING THE FISCAL CONSOLIDATION AGENDA

Fiscal Consolidation Is Inevitable in the Caribbean

Fiscal consolidation is inevitable in the Caribbean region, so the policy question that Caribbean governments must address is this: What is the most appropriate route to follow in the current environment, given that the need to reduce debt comes in a difficult environment of weak growth? These countries can draw lessons from successful fiscal consolidation efforts in other regions to guide their fiscal consolidation efforts.

Based on a survey of country experiences, expenditure-based consolidations with a focus on reducing current spending tend to be more successful than tax-based consolidations (Alesina and Perotti, 1997). However, for countries with large adjustment needs (such as Caribbean countries), fiscal consolidation may need to be a balanced combination of spending cuts and revenue increases (Baldacci, Gupta, Mulas-Granados, 2010). The composition of spending reductions has also been found to be important. Cuts in the wage bill and in transfer spending address budget categories viewed as politically sensitive and enhance the credibility of the adjustment efforts (Alesina and Ardagna, 2009). On the other hand, cuts in capital spending can have a direct negative impact on growth and carry little credibility if markets perceive them as merely postponing needed outlays. Revenue-based consolidations have been found to be associated with less favorable macroeconomic outcomes, and they bring a higher risk of reversal.

International experience and evidence point to the need to address the Caribbean's fiscal consolidation needs mainly from the expenditure side. Given the already sizable public sector, most of the fiscal consolidation would have to be done by restraining spending (Egert, 2011). Better control of the wage bill, increased efficiency in the public sector, and reductions in transfer spending are obvious targets to reduce spending. The ratio of wage spending to GDP is higher in the Caribbean than in Latin America, limiting budget flexibility. Reducing the public sector wage bill could be achieved by a freeze on nominal wages. In addition to reducing the public payroll, improving public sector efficiency could help reduce government spending. The Caribbean has one of the largest public sectors among emerging markets. It is essential to introduce performance management in the budgeting process and to systematically review the efficiencies of public policies.

In particular, we propose a reduction in low-priority spending to facilitate fiscal adjustment, because it lowers the pressure on nondiscretionary spending and limits the momentum of public spending growth. Caribbean countries could achieve the benefits of fiscal consolidation with lower social costs by focusing on expenditure reforms within the context of a medium-term fiscal framework. Implementing ambitious expenditure reforms signals strong government commitment to fiscal sustainability. Social expenditures and subsidies also need to be properly targeted.

The Quality of Past Fiscal Consolidations in the Caribbean Is Questionable

Previous fiscal consolidation episodes were characterized mainly by cuts in capital expenditure, which created infrastructure gaps inimical to growth and hence compromising the achievement of debt sustainability. Country experiences show that reducing public spending in a comprehensive reform program by focusing on nonproductive and nonpriority spending, particularly transfers, subsidies, and general goods and services, is likely to ensure success in the Caribbean. The empirical literature finds that in several successful fiscal consolidation episodes in other regions, spending cuts adopted to reduce deficits were associated with economic expansions rather than recessions (Alesina and Perotti, 1997).

Raising Additional Revenues

To raise revenues, there is significant potential in reducing tax expenditure, eliminating distortions and broadening the tax base. There is scope in many countries to improve the collection of property taxes, which are usually considered the least distorting of major taxes. Broadening the value added tax (VAT) base would also improve the tax structure. In the Caribbean, the average effective rate of VAT, computed as the ratio of VAT revenues to private consumption, is lower than the rate in most advanced economies, indicating the existence of reduced rates and

BOX 12.1

Designing and Implementing a Fiscal Consolidation Plan: A Checklist

The IMF's Fiscal Affairs Department has outlined a number of questions on a checklist to follow when designing and implementing a fiscal adjustment plan:

- Does the proposed adjustment deliver a credible change in debt dynamics?
- Is the size and pace of adjustment appropriate in light of macroeconomic conditions, political considerations, and the need to avoid reform fatigue?
- Are financing constraints taken into consideration?
- Is the operational target for the fiscal consolidation path well defined and well understood? Does it have adequate institutional coverage?
- Does the composition of adjustment take into consideration the size of the public sector?
- Are high-quality measures chosen for the adjustment?
- Are targets met without shifting items off balance sheet?
- Are external factors (if they exist) leveraged to the fullest?
- Are supporting institutional and structural reforms in place?
- Are public enterprises appropriately covered and do subnational levels of government contribute to the adjustment?
- Are distributional effects of the adjustment taken into account?
- Is the adjustment strategy appropriately communicated so as to mobilize broad-based political and public support?

Source: Fiscal Affairs Department, International Monetary Fund exemptions in the tax system. Tax expenditures (currently estimated at between 4–6 percent of GDP in Barbados and Jamaica) also need to be reduced significantly to make room for phased reductions in the statutory rates of the main taxes. In the fiscal adjustment process, raising taxes should be considered only after careful consideration in order to minimize economic distortions and promote economic efficiency, given that taxes in the region are already high.

Protection for the Vulnerable

To be credible, any successful consolidation strategy needs to provide a social safety net. In doing so, social safety nets and well-targeted programs need to be enhanced while reducing or eliminating general subsidies. Targeting subsidies and transfers would also help improve the overall efficiency of non-productive spending. International experiences offer a number of key lessons for protecting the poor during the fiscal consolidation process (Braithwaite, Jyotsna, Subbarao, 1995), including these three:

- Social safety nets needs to be designed as an integral part of the overall package of economic reforms rather than as add-ons during the adjustment process;
- The instrument for protecting the poor should build on and complement existing programs; and
- The range of programs and benefits needs to be controlled and the targeting must be effective in order to avoid adverse effects on work incentives and the crowding-out of private transfers.

Credibility Is Key to a Successful Fiscal Consolidation Strategy

Country experiences suggests that support for growth is essential to cope with the contractionary effects of fiscal consolidation, so policies need to stress the removal of underlying structural problems within the economy. Since debt reduction takes time, fiscal consolidation should focus on enduring structural changes. In this regard, strengthening fiscal institutions is essential (IMF, 2012).

Fiscal consolidation in the Caribbean needs to be credible in order to anchor market expectations about fiscal sustainability (Baldacci, Gupta, and Mulas-Granados, 2010). Governments in the region need to demonstrate that the debt burden is manageable and that strong fiscal policies are likely to continue under most situations. Developing this credibility requires not only the implementation of fiscal reforms but also a record of strong implementation of effective reforms in both good and bad times (IMF, 2003). It is essential to strengthen the fiscal framework by adopting fiscal rules and independent fiscal agencies to guide the budget process and improve fiscal transparency.

Fiscal Rules Could Enhance the Credibility of Fiscal Policy in the Caribbean

Mechanisms such as fiscal rules can increase the discipline and credibility of fiscal policy while helping to reduce debt, if appropriately designed and implemented. They are also useful in securing the gains of fiscal consolidation. Empirical evidence (as discussed in Chapter 11) shows that fiscal rules, in particular those that have an expenditure focus, have affected several dimensions of fiscal consolidation. The size of fiscal consolidation has been significantly larger and the consolidation efforts have been sustained longer when such rules were present (Kumar, Leigh, and Plekhanov, 2007).

Multiple Rules Are Helpful in Stabilizing Debt

The adoption of a spending rule on top of a budget balance rule helps in the achievement and maintenance of a primary balance that is sufficient to stabilize the debt-to-GDP ratio. Caribbean countries could create a stable general fiscal rule to strengthen current fiscal frameworks by defining the rule in terms of primary deficit for the general government, which could take the form of expenditure ceilings and revenue floors. It is also essential to support the fiscal rule by creating an independent fiscal council to assess macroeconomic projections underlying the budgeting process and assess the compatibility of the fiscal framework with fiscal rules and general government policies.

It is important to stress that fiscal rules do not solve fiscal problems such as determining the appropriate level of expenditure or taxes. A comprehensive fiscal strategy needs to focus on the short- and medium-term evolution of fiscal policy as well as the longer-term development strategies (Carenas and Tessada, 2011). Policies and initiatives aimed at reducing tax evasion and improving the efficiency of the public sector should remain essential components of a comprehensive strategy to improve fiscal capacity and performance.

Fiscal Consolidation Is Necessary But Not Sufficient for Debt Reduction

Fiscal consolidation is necessary, but it may not be sufficient to bring down debt levels, since high primary surpluses would have to be maintained over a relatively long period to have a lasting impact on debt. The very highly indebted Caribbean countries would also need to reduce the net present value of their outstanding debt stock to levels that provide fiscal space and room for countries to resume their growth. Past episodes of large debt reductions in Caribbean countries were largely associated with debt relief (Box 12.2). Further initiatives to secure additional debt relief would need to take into account the size and structure of public debt. Accordingly, a menu approach is proposed, one in which different options to reduce

BOX 12.2

Debt Relief Received by Caribbean Economies Since 2000

Since 2000, a number of Caribbean countries have received debt relief. These have involved a combination of debt write-offs, debt restructuring, debt swaps, and debt buy-backs. These operations have taken place at different times and have benefited different countries.

Debt write-offs. Three countries have benefitted from debt write-offs during the 2000s. In particular, in the early 2000s, Guyana received additional debt relief under the enhanced Heavily Indebted Poor Countries Initiative and the Multilateral Debt Relief Initiative, including from the IMF. In 2004, Jamaica received some debt relief from the United Kingdom under the Commonwealth Debt Initiative. In 2007, both Antigua and Barbuda and St. Vincent and the Grenadines (US$56 million) benefited from an Italian debt write-off initiative.

Debt restructuring. Debt restructuring has been the most frequently used form of debt relief in the Caribbean. Five countries restructured their debts in the 2000s. In the early 2000s, Suriname successfully restructured a number of its external loans. In 2004, Dominica restructured its public debt, in the context of an IMF program, reducing its interest rates to 3.5 percent from 8 percent. Grenada also restructured its debts in 2004–05, amid extensive infrastructure destruction caused by hurricane Ivan. In 2007, Belize restructured its external debts, which provided front-loaded interest payment relief, and postponed amortization payments until 2019. In 2010, Antigua and Barbuda also received debt relief from its Paris Club creditors, which agreed (under the baseline accord) to suspend accumulating penalties and interest charges and postponed amortization until 2017. Also in 2010, Jamaica launched a comprehensive debt exchange to address its looming debt problem. The objective of the debt exchange was to enable the government to reduce its interest bill and expand the maturity profile of the debt stock. Jamaica repeated its domestic debt restructuring in 2013, achieving a reduction in its public-debt-to GDP ratio by about 8½ by 2020.

Debt swaps and buy-backs. Debt swaps and debt buy-backs have been used by Belize and Antigua and Barbuda. Belize benefitted from a debt swap arrangement (US$8 million) with the U.S. government. In 2005, Antigua and Barbuda engaged in a debt buy-back operation with private creditors, which lowered its external debt by approximately US$500 million.

the existing debt stock or debt service payments can be chosen by individual countries depending on their circumstances. Among the options to be considered should be debt conversion for climate adaptation and debt restructuring.

OTHER ELEMENTS OF A COMPREHENSIVE DEBT REDUCTION STRATEGY

Reforms should signal a new commitment to credible and sound macroeconomic policies and should include tax policy reforms, public sector rationalization, measures to improve fiscal discipline and credibility, active debt management, containing contingent liabilities, active privatization programs, and structural reforms to boost growth and improve competitiveness.

Tax Policy Reform

There is some scope for raising revenues and retiring debt through tax policy reforms. Tax policy reforms need to focus on broadening the tax base while reducing rates, ensuring sufficiency of revenues, and supporting growth and competitiveness. Simplifying the tax system (including introduction and/or strengthening of VAT) by reducing excessive tax rates, broadening the tax base, and reducing discretionary waivers and differential rates could help improve revenue collection while shifting the burden of taxes away from the productive sectors.

Debt Management

Active debt management could help lengthen the maturity structure of debt and reduce debt servicing costs. A number of countries are already involved in active debt management. Where possible, countries should continue to lengthen maturities and reduce the average interest costs by substituting high-interest, short-term debt with lower-interest, long-term debt. In parallel, many countries must significantly improve institutional debt management capabilities.

Public Sector Rationalization

There is scope in the region to further reduce spending through the rationalization of the public sector. The Fiscal Affairs Department of the IMF estimates that expenditure rationalization could reduce public spending on a cumulative basis by 3 to 5 percent of GDP over the medium term in the Eastern Caribbean Currency Union. Savings could be gained from consolidating administrative services and personnel through mergers or the closing of agencies. This should be accompanied by implementing a broad-based public expenditure reform to rationalize the public sector wage structure and employment. Some countries are already moving in this direction. Similarly, it would be important to review the functions and rationale of existing public enterprises with the objective of rationalizing them. The oversight of public enterprises could be strengthened by enforcing existing legislation on governance and reporting requirements.

Active Privatization Programs

An active privatization program, which reduces debt and develops the private sector, should also form part of a debt reduction strategy. There is scope in some Caribbean countries to raise revenues and reduce public debt through privatization and debt swaps. The problem with privatization is that it does not change the net worth of the government and it cannot be relied upon to bring durable improvement in the net worth of the government. The scope for privatization varies across countries, but this method cannot be relied upon to produce large reductions in public debt.

A number of lessons could be learned from previous privatization experiences in the region (Sahay, 2006). Privatization receipts have generally been low in the region, ranging from between 4 and 6 percent of GDP in a year. Privatization schemes need to be carefully planned, and distress sales should be avoided to maximize revenues.

The privatization process needs to be transparent to ensure that deals are conducted in a fair manner. In cases where full privatization is not feasible, corporatization of public enterprises could be useful in improving financial viability and limiting the risk to the budget.

Containing Contingency Liabilities

Measures to contain fiscal risks posed by contingent liabilities should remain an integral part of any debt reduction strategy. Contingent liabilities present significant fiscal risks in many Caribbean countries. The experience of many countries in the Caribbean in recent times has shown that the recognition of contingent liabilities can significantly increase public debt and raise issues of debt sustainability. As a result, Caribbean policymakers need to be fully aware of these risks and the alternative fiscal strategies that may be needed to contain them. Budgets in the region need to provide a detailed discussion of the risks of explicit contingent liabilities and their implications for fiscal and debt sustainability. A better understanding of fiscal risks and greater public awareness would encourage governments to adopt prudent fiscal policies, including stronger fiscal positions in the short to medium term (IMF, 2003). Containing contingent liabilities will require improving the regulation and supervision of the financial system, implementing pension reforms, and clarifying rules for issuing public guarantees.

Growth-Enhancing Structural Reforms

The analyses in Chapter 4 of this book suggest that it is very difficult to reduce public debt without improving growth prospects. In this direction, implementing growth-enhancing structural reforms will complement the region's fiscal consolidation efforts and help improve the debt outlook in the region. Improved growth prospects would require greater emphasis on competitiveness and private sector development. Measures to make labor and product markets more competitive would help boost productivity with direct feedback on the speed and credibility of fiscal consolidation (IMF, 2003).

Key areas for reforms include increasing labor market flexibility, achieving greater regional cooperation, creating an enabling environment for private sector development, and reducing the size of the public sector, including the high levels of public employment. Addressing weaknesses in the private sector (both financial and the nonfinancial corporate sector) will also be crucial, while further steps to promote foreign investments will bring lasting growth benefits (IMF, 2003).

BOX 12.3

Reducing Public Debt in the Caribbean

Credible fiscal consolidation

- Focus fiscal consolidation on expenditure reforms within the context of a medium-term fiscal framework to signal government commitment to fiscal sustainability.
- Begin fiscal consolidation with a large up-front adjustment to restore market confidence and deliver a credible change in debt dynamics.
- Some front-loading of fiscal consolidation can help avoid reform fatigue and present political economy benefits, especially if the adjustment is initiated by a new government.

Fiscal rules and a medium-term fiscal framework

- Create a stable general fiscal rule to strengthen the current fiscal framework. Define the rule in terms of the primary deficit for general government, which could take the form of expenditure ceilings and revenue floors.
- Support the fiscal rule by creating an independent fiscal council to assess macroeconomic projections underlying the budgeting process and assess the compatibility of the fiscal framework with fiscal rules and general government policies.
- Implement multiyear or medium-term budgeting, supported by political institutions and consistent with the fiscal rule.

Public sector efficiency and rationalization

- Introduce an incentive element into central government grants by setting efficiency targets and rewarding ministries that outperform the targets.
- Review the role of government and identify government agencies that could be streamlined, closed, or divested.
- Enhance the oversight of public enterprises by strengthening and enforcing existing regulations on governance and reporting requirements.

Tax policy reforms

- Focus tax policy reform needs on broadening the tax base while reducing excessive tax rates and ensuring sufficiency of revenues. Simplify the tax system through a reduction in discretionary waivers and differential rates.
- Assess the effectiveness of new or existing tax expenditures on a systematic and regular basis. Handle higher taxes carefully to minimize economic distortions and promote economic efficiency.

Expenditure reforms

- Reduce public spending, with a focus on nonproductive and nonpriority spending, particularly transfers, subsidies, and general goods and services in a comprehensive reform program.
- Safeguard social safety nets by targeting and enhancing social programs while reducing or eliminating general subsidies.
- Improve the efficiency of nonproductive spending by improving the targeting of transfers and subsidies.

Debt management

- Lengthen maturities and reduce the average interest cost by substituting high-interest, short-term debt with lower-interest, long-term debt. Improve debt management capabilities.

Growth-enhancing reforms

- Continue with key reforms to increase labor market flexibility, achieve greater regional cooperation, and create an enabling environment for private sector development.

SUMMARY AND CONCLUSION

This chapter has discussed policy options for reducing the high debt levels in the Caribbean. It has argued that significant fiscal consolidation is inevitable in the region and that by consolidating government finances and improving primary balances, countries could signal their determination to implement prudent fiscal policies. Country experiences suggest that support for growth is essential to cope with the contractionary effects of fiscal consolidation, and therefore policies need to stress the removal of underlying structural problems within the economy. Since debt reduction takes time, fiscal consolidation should focus on enduring structural change. In this direction, strengthening fiscal institutions would be very helpful. It is essential to strengthen the fiscal framework by adopting fiscal rules and independent fiscal agencies to guide the budget process and improve fiscal transparency.

Fiscal consolidation may not enough to bring down the high debt levels, since high primary surpluses need to be run over a long period of time. The region therefore needs a comprehensive and sustained package of reforms to reduce debt ratios to more manageable levels and strengthen economic resilience. Reforms should signal a new commitment to credible and sound macroeconomic policies and should include tax policy reforms, public sector rationalization, measures to improve fiscal discipline and credibility, active debt management, the containment of contingent liabilities, active privatization programs, and structural reforms to boost growth and improve competitiveness.

To conclude, this book is intended to be a useful tool for policymakers and policy advisors in addressing the complex challenges that face the Caribbean in the years ahead. The Caribbean can benefit by learning from successful fiscal strategies around the world, including those distilled here. A new agenda is waiting to be adopted and implemented.

REFERENCES

Alesina, Alberto, and Silvia Ardagna, 2009, "Large Changes in Fiscal Policy: Taxes versus Spending," NBER Working Paper No. 15438 (Cambridge, Massachusetts: National Bureau of Economic Research).

Alesina, Alberto, and Roberto Perotti, 1997, "Fiscal Adjustments in OECD: Composition and Macroeconomic Effects," *IMF Staff Papers*, Vol. 44, No. 2, pp. 210–48.

Baldacci, Emanuele, Sanjeev Gupta, and Carlos Mulas-Granados, 2010, "Getting Debt under Control," *Finance and Development,* Vol. 47, No. 4, December (Washington: International Monetary Fund).

Braithwaite, Jeanine, Jyotsna Jalan, and K. Subbarao, 1995 "Strategies for Protecting the Poor During Adjustment and Transitions," Human Capital Development and Operations Policy Working Paper No. 58 (Washington: World Bank).

Carenas, Mauricio, and Tessada, Jose, 2011, "Fiscal Policy Rules and Latin America: Lessons from the Crisis," Available at: http://www.brookings.edu/opinions/2009/1123_fiscal_policy_latin_america_cardenas.aspx.

Egert, Balazs, 2011, "Bring French Public Debt Down: The Options for Fiscal Consolidation," OECD Economics Department Working Paper No. 858 (Paris: Organization for Economic Co-operation and Development).

International Monetary Fund (IMF), 2003, "Public Debt in Emerging Markets: Is It Too High?" Chapter 3 in *World Economic Outlook*, May (Washington).

———, 2012, "The Good, the Bad, and the Ugly: 100 Years of Dealing with Public Debt Overhangs," Chapter 3 in *World Economic Outlook,* October (Washington).

Kumar, Manmohan, S., Daniel Leigh, and Alexander Plekhanov, 2007, "Fiscal Adjustments: Determinants and Macroeconomic Consequences," IMF Working Paper 07/178 (Washington: International Monetary Fund).

Sahay, Ratna, 2006, "Stabilization, Debt, and Fiscal Policy in the Caribbean," in *The Caribbean: From Vulnerability to Sustained Growth,* ed. by Ratna Sahay, David Robinson, and Paul Cashin (Washington: International Monetary Fund).

Index

Page numbers followed by *b, f, n,* or *t* refer to boxed text, figures, footnotes, or tables, respectively.

A

B

G

H

I

K

L

M

N

O

T